GEORG BRANDES

CW01636701

MAIN CURRENTS IN NINETEENTH CENTURY LITERATURE

VOLUME IV

NATURALISM IN ENGLAND

(1875)

Elibron Classics
www.elibron.com

Elibron Classics series.

ISBN 0-543-83238-4 (paperback)
ISBN 0-543-83237-6 (hardcover)

This Elibron Classics Replica Edition is an unabridged facsimile of the edition published in 1905 by William Heinemann, London.

MAIN CURRENTS IN NINETEENTH CENTURY LITERATURE

VOL. IV.

MAIN CURRENTS IN
NINETEENTH CENTURY
LITERATURE

By GEORGE BRANDES

I. THE EMIGRANT LITERATURE
II. THE ROMANTIC SCHOOL IN GERMANY
III. THE REACTION IN FRANCE
IV. NATURALISM IN ENGLAND
V. THE ROMANTIC SCHOOL IN FRANCE
VI. YOUNG GERMANY

By the same Author

WILLIAM SHAKESPEARE. A Critical Study. Demy 8vo, buckram uncut, 10s. net.

HENRIK IBSEN. BJÖRNSTJERNE BJÖRNSON. Critical Studies. With Introduction by WILLIAM ARCHER. Demy 8vo, Roxburgh, gilt top, or buckram, uncut. 10s. net.

LONDON: WILLIAM HEINEMANN
21 BEDFORD STREET, W.C.

MAIN CURRENTS IN NINETEENTH CENTURY LITERATURE

BY

GEORGE BRANDES

AUTHOR OF

"WILLIAM SHAKESPEARE," ETC.

IN SIX VOLUMES

VOL. IV.

NATURALISM IN ENGLAND

(1875)

LONDON

WILLIAM HEINEMANN

1905

CONTENTS

"I am as a spirit who has dwelt
Within his heart of hearts; and I have felt
His feelings, and have thought his thoughts, and known
The inmost converse of his soul, the tone
Unheard but in the silence of his blood,
When all the pulses in their multitude
Image the trembling calm of summer seas.
I have unlocked the golden melodies
Of his deep soul as with a master-key,
And loosened them, and bathed myself therein—
Even as an eagle in a thunder-mist
Clothing his wings with lightning."

—Shelley (Fragment).

INTRODUCTION

It is my intention to trace in the poetry of England of the first decades of this century, the course of the strong, deep, pregnant current in the intellectual life of the country, which, sweeping away the classic forms and conventions, produces a Naturalism dominating the whole of literature, which from Naturalism leads to Radicalism, from revolt against traditional convention in literature to vigorous rebellion against religious and political reaction, and which bears in its bosom the germs of all the liberal ideas and emancipatory achievements of the later periods of European civilisation.

The literary period which I now proceed to describe is a vigorous, highly productive one. It has authors and schools of the most dissimilar types, sometimes not merely unlike, but antagonistic to, each other. Though the connection between these authors and schools is not self-evident, but only discernible to the understanding, critical eye, yet the period has its unity, and the picture it presents, though a many-coloured, restless one, is a coherent composition, the work of the great artist, history.

NATURALISM IN ENGLAND

I

UNIVERSAL CHARACTERISTICS OF THE PERIOD

ONE of the first and chief things observable in this English literary group, is that it has certain characteristics in common with the whole European intellectual tendency of the period. These characteristics are universal because of the universal existence of their cause. Napoleon was threatening Europe with a world-wide Empire. To escape annihilation, all the threatened nationalities either instinctively or deliberately re-invigorated themselves from the sources of their national life. The national spirit is awakened and spreads and grows in Germany during the War of Liberation; in Russia it bursts into flames along with the ancient capital of the country; in England it inspires enthusiasm for Wellington and Nelson, and vindicates in bloody battles, from the Nile to Waterloo, the ancient English claim to the sovereignty of the sea; in Denmark the cannonade of the battle of Copenhagen awakens a new national spirit and produces a new literature. It is this patriotic spirit which leads all the different nations to the eager study of their own history and their own customs, their own legends and folk-lore. The devotion to everything national incites to the study and the literary representation of the "people"—that is to say, the lower classes of society, with whom the literature of the eighteenth century had not concerned itself. The reaction against French as a universal language brings even dialect into high repute.

In *Germany*, as we have already seen, patriotism led to

enthusiasm for the country's past, for the Middle Ages—their faith, their superstitions, and their social order. In *Italy* we have, in Manzoni's religious verse, an apparent return to Catholicism. The faith which had petrified into dogma, and meant renunciation of the flesh, is upheld as synonymous with poetry and morality; it is transformed from a religion into an art *motif*. Manzoni's religious enthusiasm is the same enthusiasm as that which accompanied the Pope back to Rome and inspired Alexander with the idea of the Holy Alliance. Even *France*, the country which had produced Napoleon, was driven by the spirit of the age into a path leading in much the same direction as that taken by Germany; the new French literary movement was directed against the Academy, against the so-called classical, *i.e.*, universal, cosmopolitan literature; the age of Louis XIV. was neglected, and the poets of the sixteenth century, Du Bellay, Ronsard, nay, even the poor grotesque poets whom Boileau had scoffed at and rejected, came into vogue again. (Victor Hugo's attack on the literary opinions of the period previous to his own; Sainte-Beuve's earliest literary criticism; Théophile Gautier's *Les Grotesques.*) In *Denmark* at the beginning of the century it was mainly in the wake of the German current that men's minds moved. They assumed an antagonistic attitude to French culture. But in the second and equally important stage of the literary movement, the antagonism becomes an antagonism to everything foreign, and more especially to Germany, which had for so long played the part of the oppressor in Denmark.

In *England* we find the same essential features which distinguish the movement in all the other countries. The influence of France, which in the eighteenth century had been paramount in the upper classes of society, was shaken off. Pope, the last poet of the classical school, did not long remain a master in the eyes of the younger generation. They began to pluck at the little man's elaborate wig and trample over the trim beds of his garden. And now it became apparent what a powerful intellectual reserve force the British nation possessed in those countries which lay remote from the centre of political life, fresh, unexhausted by civilisation. Ireland, which in the eighteenth century had produced such a thinker as Swift and such a writer as Goldsmith, owned a treasury of lovely melodies which, as soon as a great lyric poet lent them words, were poured forth by all the singing throats of Europe. The Welsh collected and published their old songs and poems. And in Scotland, to which country the mean, depressing conditions prevailing among the English industrial classes had not as yet spread, but where a people, proud of its past and its land, preserved its national songs, its superstitions, and its political peculiarities, there appeared in the second half of the eighteenth century, as a protest against cold reason and artificiality in poetry, Macpherson's *Ossian*. The influence of *Ossian* was alike great upon Alfieri and Foscolo in Italy, upon Herder and Goethe in Germany, and upon Chateaubriand in France. On it follow in England Percy's collection of old English, and in Scotland Walter Scott's collection of Scotch, ballads.

But in the interval between these two publications our attention is demanded by one of those literary currents flowing from one country to another and back again, which it is our chief aim to trace, and which in this case is remarkably plain. Not long after Percy's *Reliques* appeared, a luckless young German lawyer in Government employ, Bürger by name, was appointed to a small post in Göttingen, where he lived in straitened circumstances and in unhappy and demoralising marital relations with two sisters. Into this man's house Percy's book finds its way. It makes a powerful impression on him, and fires him with the desire to write something which had long been proscribed by the rules of poetical art, but which he himself calls (to Baggesen, see *The Labyrinth*) poetry proper, namely, a ballad. He begins the famous *Lenore*, and works at it slowly, week after week, with such a conviction of the importance of the step he is taking that his letters to his friends are full of nothing else. The ballad appears, and is soon read in every country in Europe. In the year 1795 an Edinburgh young lady introduces it to the notice of another lawyer in Crown employ; and this young man, Walter Scott by name, who was also to be an author, and a very much greater one, makes his literary *début* with a translation of *Lenore* and another ballad of Bürger's, *The Wild Huntsman*. His translations meeting with a favourable reception, Scott began to regard himself as a poet. And it was upon the basis of these translations and that of *Götz von Berlichingen*, which he published in 1799, that the national Scottish Romanticism of his poetry was founded.

There is, then, originally in this literature a distinct trace of the general European reaction against the eighteenth century. The strong national feeling which superseded the feeling of cosmopolitanism is to be found in England in Wordsworth in the form of patriotic poetical description, in Southey in the form of eulogy (at times partly, at times purely, official) of the Royal Family and the national exploits, in the Scottish-born Campbell in the form of passionately British songs of liberty and war; whilst Scott and Moore are positive literary personifications of Scotland and Ireland. The universal return to the popular has its chief representative and spokesman in Wordsworth, whose special theme is the life of the lower and lowest classes. The predilection for the Middle Ages is strongest in Scott, who combines the antiquarian's delight in memories and survivals of the past with the Tory politician's desire to represent the traditional in the most attractive light. The Romanticism of superstition finds its poet in Coleridge, whose studied childishness and simplicity are near of kin to Tieck's; and it is Coleridge, too, who, thoroughly imbued with the doctrines of the German philosophy of the day, enters a general scientific protest against those of the age of enlightenment. His philosophy is quite un-English; it is, in contradiction to the experimental nature of English science, purely transcendental; it is conservative, pious, and historical, because the philosophy preceding it had been radical, infidel, and metaphysical; it is a "Schellingism," which at first endeavours to preserve as many of the philosophic conclusions of the preceding century as possible, but which, ever more obstinate and ever more narrow-minded, hastens towards the opposite extreme from that which had proved fatal to the preceding period. The confusedly fantastic side of Romanticism is represented by Southey with his Oriental narrative poems; and as for the passionate, despairing heroes of Chateaubriand and Romanticism generally, we find them, more passionate and more manly, in the works of Byron; whilst Shelley's spiritualism and dissolution of all solid form into ethereal music recalls the ardour and vagueness of Novalis.

II

NATIONAL CHARACTERISTICS

BUT these general and most marked characteristics of the period are modified in a very perceptible manner by certain peculiarly English characteristics, which, observable nowhere else, are to be found in all the English authors of the day, however little resemblance there may be between them in other respects.

These English characteristics can all be traced back to one original distinctive quality, namely vigorous *Naturalism*. As we have observed, the first advance in the new literary movement is the inspiration of the authors of every country by a national spirit. Now in England this meant becoming a Naturalist, just as in Germany it meant becoming a Romanticist, and in Denmark a devotee of the Old-Scandinavian. The English poets, one and all, are observers, lovers, worshippers of nature. Wordsworth, who loves to parade his propensities as ideas, inscribes the word *nature* on his banner, and paints pictures, grand in spite of their minute detail, of the hills, the lakes, the rivers, and the rustic population of the North of England. Scott's descriptions of nature, based upon close observation, are so accurate that a botanist might acquire a correct idea of the vegetation of the district from them. Keats, with all his devotion to the antique and to Greek mythology, is a sensualist, who, gifted with the keenest, widest, most delicate perceptions, sees, hears, feels, tastes, and inhales all the varieties of glorious colour, of song, of silky texture, of fruit flavour, of flower fragrance, which nature offers. Moore is the personification of spiritualised sensuality; the pampered, pampering poet, he seems to live surrounded by all that is rarest and most beautiful in nature; he dazzles our minds with sunshine, deafens them with the song of the nightingale, drowns them in sweetness; we live with him in endless dreams of wings, flowers, rainbows, smiles, blushes, tears, kisses—always kisses. The strongest tendency even of works like Byron's *Don Juan* and Shelley's *Cenci* is in reality Naturalism. In other words, Naturalism is so powerful in England that it permeates Coleridge's Romantic supernaturalism, Wordsworth's Anglican orthodoxy, Shelley's atheistic spiritualism, Byron's revolutionary liberalism, and Scott's interest in the past. It influences the personal beliefs and the literary tendencies of every author.

This realism, so full of sap and vigour, is a result of various strongly-marked and almost universal English characteristics. There is, in the first place, the English love of the country and of the sea. Almost all the English poets of this period are either countrymen or seamen. The English Muse of poetry has from time immemorial frequented the country seat and the farm. Wordsworth's genuinely English poetry is in exact keeping with the well-known paintings and engravings representing English country life, which produce an impression of health and tranquillity, and, when such subjects as family worship or the country clergyman's fatherly ministrations are portrayed, also of piety. Burns, the ploughman poet, Scotland's greatest poetic genius, early dedicated Scottish poetry to the country; and there is truth in Emerson's caustic remark that Scott, in his narrative poems, simply wrote a rhymed guide-book to Scotland. That the same idea had occurred to the poet's own contemporaries is evident from the satirical manner in which Moore writes of Scott's "doing" the one country-seat after the other.[1]

[1] Should you feel any touch of poetical glow
We've a Scheme to suggest—Mr. Scott, you must know,
Having quitted the Borders, to seek new renown
Is coming, by long Quarto stages, to Town.
And beginning with Rokeby (the job's sure to pay)
Means to *do* all the Gentlemen's Seats on the way.
Now the Scheme is (though none of our hackneys can beat him)
To start a fresh Poet through Highgate to meet him;
Who, by means of quick proofs—no revises—long coaches,
May do a few Villas, before Scott approaches.
Moore: *Intercepted Letters*, No. 7.

And what an important part country seats play in the lives of two such antipodal literary characters as Byron and Scott! Newstead Abbey is as inseparably connected with Byron's name as Abbotsford is with Sir Walter Scott's. The old abbey, with its medieval and fantastic architecture, is to Byron the indispensable accompaniment of his peerage and the pledge of his English citizenship. He does not dispose of it until he has turned his back on his native land for ever. Scott's proprietorship is not so ancient and venerable; but he buys Abbotsford when the desire to own land, which has always been strong in him, becomes irresistible, and, during the happy period of his life passed there, lives as if he had grown up with no other prospect before him than that of exercising the regal hospitality of an old Scottish landed proprietor and living his hardy out-of-door life. His greatest delight is in such perilous amusements as wading through a raging stream—with a bridge not fifty yards off, riding a horse unmanageable by any one else, spearing salmon by torch-light, soaked with rain or shivering in the cold night air. And is not every reader of Byron's life here reminded of that poet's love of wild rides and daring swimming exploits?

Nevertheless there is in the attitude of the two authors to their estates a difference, characteristic of their different natures. Byron's love for Newstead Abbey had its origin in his aristocratic proclivities, Scott's for Abbotsford in his historic instincts. Just as Sir Walter's estate had Ettrick Forest for its background, Newstead had Sherwood Forest, with its memories of Robin Hood and his merry men. But these memories exercised no perceptible influence on Byron's poetry, though we have an admirable description of the Abbey itself in the Thirteenth Canto of *Don Juan*. The whole of Scott's poetry, on the contrary, is pervaded, as by a refrain, by the memories of Ettrick Forest; and it is Scott, instead of Byron, who (in *Ivanhoe*) brings the poetry of Sherwood Forest to life again.

Another English qualification for Naturalism is the love of the poets for the nobler animals, and their intimacy with the animal world in general. They have that affection for all domestic animals which is a result of their English love of home. When they travel they carry home and their domestic animals with them. Almost all the authors of our period are devoted to manly exercises, and in particular to riding. And in observing this we must not fall into the common error of mistaking a thoroughly national characteristic for a personal and rare one. It is not without its significance that the English race traces its descent from two mystic heroes bearing the names of horses (Hengist and Horsa). The love of horses, dogs, and all kinds of wild animals, which is so often mentioned as a peculiar characteristic of Byron, the misanthropical exile, is quite as marked a characteristic of Scott, living at home in the happiest domestic circumstances. Matthew's well-known letter describing the life at Newstead Abbey shows us Byron, the youth, surrounded by a whole menagerie, including a bear and a wolf; in Medwin's account of the poet's life in Italy we read that he took with him when he left Ravenna in 1821, "seven servants, five carriages, nine horses, a monkey, a retriever, a bull-dog, two cats, three Guinea fowls, and other birds." One is apt to think this an exhibition of purely personal singularity, until one reads, in Lockhart's Life, Scott's own description of the removal to Abbotsford. "The neighbours have been much delighted with the procession of my furniture, in which old swords, bows, targets, and lances made a very conspicuous show. A family of turkeys was accommodated within the helmet of some *preux* chevalier of ancient Border fame; and the very cows, for aught I know, were bearing banners and muskets. I assure your ladyship that this caravan, attended by a dozen of ragged rosy peasant children, carrying fishing-rods and spears, and leading poneys, greyhounds, and spaniels, would, as it crossed the Tweed, have furnished no bad subject for the pencil." The only difference is that the old curiosity shop of the collector is added to the menagerie. Byron's love for his dog, Boatswain, and the solemn inscription engraved on the stone marking the favourite's grave, are apt to be instanced as signs of the poet's rooted melancholy. But it helps us to a more correct appreciation of such feelings to remember that the cheerful-minded Scott had his favourite dog, Camp, solemnly buried in the garden at Abbotsford, the whole family standing weeping round the grave.

But even more characteristically English than the attachment to horses and dogs and land, and the witness in literature to the same, is the love of the sea. The Englishman is an amphibious animal. A considerable part of the description of nature in the literature of this period is marine painting. It was an ancient tradition, gloriously maintained at this particular time, that England was the mistress of the sea; and English writers have always been the best delineators and interpreters of the sea. There is a breath of its freshness and freedom in all the best poetry of the country. To the Englishman the sea has always been the great symbol of liberty, as the Alps have been to the freedom-loving Swiss. Wordsworth exclaims with truth in one of his *Sonnets Dedicated to Liberty*:—

> "Two Voices are there; one is of the Sea,
> One of the Mountains; each a mighty voice:
> In both from age to age thou didst rejoice,
> They were thy chosen music, Liberty!"

We understand, therefore, how it was that the long-dormant Viking spirit re-awoke in the best poets of the country during this remarkable period of English literature. In Coleridge's *Ancient Mariner* we have all the terror and horror of the sea; Campbell's *Mariners of England* is an entrancingly melodious and manly glorification of the heroism and might of the English seamen; Byron's Viking-like expeditions are mirrored in the exploits of Childe Harold and Don Juan; Shelley's passion for the sea and sailing lives and breathes in the billowy rhythm of his verse and in all the poems which extol wind and wave—above all others that masterpiece, the *Ode to the West Wind*.

Transferred to the domain of society, Naturalism becomes, as it did in Rousseau's case, revolutionary; and beneath that attachment to the soil, and that delight in encountering and mastering the fitful humours of the sea, which are the deep-seated causes of Naturalism, there is in the Englishman the still deeper-seated national feeling, which, under the peculiar historical conditions of this period, naturally led the cleverest men of the day in the direction of Radicalism. No nation is so thoroughly penetrated by the feeling of personal independence as England. This is best seen in the Englishman abroad; it is with a flourish of trumpets that he proclaims himself to be an Englishman. It is the transmission of this independence and self-sufficiency to English literature which has at decisive moments made its art a "character-art"; and at the period under consideration it is this peculiar quality which, asserting itself, actually produces the new movement in the literature of Europe. It took an Englishman to do what Byron did, stem alone the stream which flowed from the fountain of the Holy Alliance—in the first place, because only an English author would have had the audacity to do it, in the second, because at that time only English literary men had the strong political tendency and the keen political intelligence which have always distinguished the first, possibly the only, parliamentary nation. And an Englishman, too, was needed to fling the gauntlet boldly and defiantly in the face of his own people. Only in the haughtiest of nations were there to be found great men haughty enough to defy the nation.

This personal independence which distinguishes the country's most eminent authors is the outcome of a genuinely English peculiarity. These men are the followers of no particular doctrines; they rarely profess any artistic principles, and certainly never any philosophical creed. The great German authors, Lessing, Goethe, Schiller, all do most important services to science; but amongst the Englishmen there is not a single scientist. And a still more remarkable fact is that they never even consult one another. Goethe and Schiller carry on an interminable correspondence on the subject of the nature and proper treatment of the different varieties of poetic themes; they even sometimes discuss at great length the propriety of the addition or suppression of a single stanza. Heiberg, the Dane, and his school follow certain definite artistic principles which they have agreed to observe, and are almost as critical as they are productive. But Scott and Byron and Moore, in spite of the cordial friendship subsisting between them, are perfectly isolated as regards authorship ; each produces his works without receiving or desiring any suggestion or advice whatever from his brother authors. Even in the very exceptional case when one is influenced by another—as Byron, for instance, occasionally is by Wordsworth, and still more perceptibly by Shelley—the thing happens, as it were, secretly, quite insensibly, so that it is not alluded to, or at any rate not acknowledged as influence by the recipient. An American author has aptly described this characteristic of the race in the words : "Each of these islanders is himself an island."

We have already spoken of intelligent interest in politics. Just as there is not one among these authors who is a scientist, so there is hardly one among them who is not a politician. This interest in politics is a direct product of the national practicality. The opinions held by the different authors may be very dissimilar, but they are all party men ; Scott is a Tory, Wordsworth a Monarchist, Southey and Coleridge are first supporters, then antagonists, of the democratic ideas of the day ; Moore is on the side of the Irishmen ; Landor, Campbell, Byron, and Shelley, as Radicals, side with all the oppressed nations. In excepting such an author as Keats, who may almost be said to have been devoted to art for art's sake, we must not forget that he died at the age of twenty-five.

The intense interest taken in practical matters explains why purely literary questions (such as that of the respective merits of Classicism and Romanticism), in their utter disconnectedness with life, never became of such exaggerated importance in English as they did at this period in German, Danish, and even French literature. It is, however, amusing to observe how our authors combine the Englishman's impulse towards practical action with the fantastic proclivities of the poet. Scott carried his antagonism to the Revolution to a perfectly Quixotic length. He arranged with one of his friends, a duke, that, if the French landed in England, they two would take to the woods and live the life of Robin Hood and his followers. And it was about the same time that

Southey and Coleridge, in the first Jacobinical ardour of their youth, informed their acquaintances that it was their intention to emigrate to a scantily populated part of America; the banks of the Susquehanna were chosen because the name of this river struck the young men as being peculiarly *beautiful and melodious;* they proposed to found a community there, a pantisocrasy, with community of goods and equality of all the members under natural conditions. Landor, who, as a soldier in Spain, proved that he was prepared to risk his life for his opinions, as a youth cherished the idea of reviving, at home in Warwickshire, the Arcadian idyllic age; he is the literary counterpart of Owen, the Socialist. Shelley, as politician, showed such keenness of perception that, studying him as such, we are constantly reminded of the characterisation in *Julian and Maddalo:*

> "*Me*, who am as a nerve o'er which do creep
> The else unfelt oppressions of this earth."

He foresaw many a political revolution that actually came to pass. But the same Shelley who, half a century before the passing of the Reform Bill of 1867, published an accurate draft of it in a political pamphlet, and who in his drama, *Hellas*, prophesied the success of the revolt of the Greeks at a time when their cause seemed hopeless, is an utter fantast as soon as he begins to enlarge on the coming Golden Age of humanity. Read his description of it in a youthful work, *Queen Mab*. The Polar icebergs melt, the deserts are cultivated, the basilisk licks the infant's feet, the hurricane blasts become melodious, the fruits of the earth are always ripe and its flowers always in bloom, no animal is killed and eaten by man, the birds no longer fly from him, fear no longer exists. We cannot but be reminded of some of the wildest dreams of the French Socialists of the same period. The spread of the Phalansteries devised by Fourier was expected to bring about such a change in the whole economy of the world that at last even natural conditions would be entirely altered; an immense aurora borealis, perpetually suspended above the North Pole, would make Siberia as warm as Andalusia; man would deprive the sea of its salt and give it in return a flavour of lemonade; and the monsters of the deep would allow themselves to be harnessed, like sea-horses, to our ships. The invention of the steam-engine fortunately rendered this species of traction superfluous. Even Byron, who is decidedly the most practical of these poets, is often the poet in his politics. It hardly admits of doubt that he had the crown of Greece before his eyes as the recompense of his exertions in the cause of that country.

There was plenty of fantasticalness in practical matters in the English poets, too; but there undoubtedly is more practicality in their morality and their view of life than in those of the poets of other nations. There are a few more grains of sound sense in their works. They are, one and all, distinguished by a strong *desire for justice.* Wordsworth inherits it from Milton; Campbell, Byron, and Shelley feel it intuitively, and are ready in the strength of the feeling to defy the world. It plays no part, this feeling, in the life of Byron's great German predecessor, Goethe, or of his richly gifted French successor, De Musset. Neither of these ever summoned monarchs and governments before the tribunal of justice. But what is peculiarly English is, that this justice of which the Englishmen dream is not, like that which Schiller, for instance, worships, a cherished, preconceived idea, but a child of utility. To prove this let us take a poet as ethereally idealistic as Shelley, and we shall see that even his morality is as distinctly utilitarian as Bentham's and John Stuart Mill's. Here is a striking passage taken from the second chapter of his *Speculations on Morals*:—
"If a man persists to inquire *why* he ought to promote the happiness of mankind, he demands a mathematical or metaphysical reason for a moral action. The absurdity of this scepticism is less apparent, but not less real than the exacting a moral reason for a mathematical or physical fact." In the maxim, "the greatest happiness of the greatest number," and in the profound, practical desire for justice, which is its psychological basis, we have the real point of departure of the Radicalism of English poetry during the period of the great European reaction.

III

THE POLITICAL BACKGROUND

THE English being at once the most persevering and the most enterprising people, the nation which is most attached to home and fondest of travel, the slowest to make changes and yet, in matters political, the most broad-minded, the thinking men of the country naturally fall into two great political groups, the one representing the jealously conservative, the other the daringly liberal tendency. The English parties have no resemblance to the French. It may be exaggeration to say, with Taine, that France has only two parties—the party of the men of twenty and the party of the men of forty; yet this division is perhaps the essential one, which the other acknowledged party names merely modify. The English division is determined by the national character; and in the stirring literary period under consideration, Wordsworth is the representative of the one set of qualities, Byron the type of the other.

In the first years of the century there was another source of political division in the dual nature of the chief event of the period. This great event was the war with France. Of the German War of Liberation I have already remarked that it was certainly revolt against a terrible despotism, but a despotism which was an expression of the ideas of the Revolution; that it was a fight for hearth and home, but undertaken at the command of the old reactionary reigning houses. And if such a remark is applicable to Germany's struggle, how much more applicable is it to the war waged by England. The independence of England was not assailed, but its interests were seriously threatened; and during the lengthy war, and for long afterwards, there were not, as in Germany, liberty-loving men at the head of affairs, but all power was given into the hands of the most determinedly reactionary Tory government that the country had ever known.

Hence it is that the background of this whole period of literature is so dark. The clouds which form it are heavy and black, "sunbeam-proof" Shelley would have called them. England itself, as the background of the panorama which I am about to unroll, is like a night landscape. The *great* qualities of the nation were misguided; its extraordinary resoluteness was applied to the suppression of another nation's desires for liberty; its own noble love of liberty was first utilised to overthrow the despotism of Napoleon and then misapplied in re-erecting all the old mouldering thrones which, under cover of the gunpowder smoke of Waterloo, were run up in as great haste as scaffolds are. The *neutral* qualities of the nation were educated into bad ones. Self-esteem and firmness were nursed into that hard-heartedness of the aristocratic, and that selfishness of the commercial classes which always distinguish a period of reaction; loyalty was excited into servility, and patriotism into the hatred of other nations which is apt to develop during long wars. And the national *bad* qualities were over-developed. The desire for outward decorum at any price, which is the shady side of the moral impulse, was developed into hypocrisy in the domain of morality; and that determined adherence to the established religion which is the least attractive outcome of a practical and not profoundly reasoning turn of mind, was fanned either into hypocrisy or active intolerance. No period was ever more favourable to the development of hypocrisy and fanaticism than this, during which the nation was actually encouraged by its leaders to boast of its religious superiority to free-thinking France.

Those who suffered most were the country's greatest authors. It is out of fashion now to talk of the cant which drove Byron from his home; and many scrupulous critics are disposed to give the name of honest, if narrow-minded, conviction to what used to be frankly called hypocrisy. But this view of the matter is untenable. A piety which behaves as English piety did to Byron and Shelley is not mere stupidity, but narrow-minded, repulsive hypocrisy.

The dicta upon this subject of the keen American observer, Ralph Waldo Emerson, are of value; for as America's most eminent critic, as England's greatest admirer, and as judge of his own race, he has every claim to credence. He says:—"The torpidity on the side of religion of the vigorous English understanding shows how much wit and folly can agree in one brain. Their religion is a quotation, their church is a doll, and any examination is interdicted with screams of terror. In good company, you expect them to laugh at the fanaticism of the vulgar; but they do not; they are the vulgar. . . . The English, abhorring change in all things, abhorring it most in matters of religion, cling to the last rag of form, and are dreadfully given to cant. The English (and I wish it were confined to them, but 'tis a taint in the Anglo-Saxon blood in both hemispheres), the English and the Americans cant beyond all other nations. The French relinquish all that industry to them. What is so odious as the polite bows to God in our books and newspapers? The popular press is flagitious in the exact measure of its sanctimony, and the religion of the day is a theatrical Sinai, where the thunders are supplied by the property-man. . . . The Church at this moment is much to be pitied. She has nothing left but possession. If a bishop meets an intelligent gentleman and reads fatal interrogations in his eyes, he has no resource but to take wine with him."[1] This description is of the England of 1830, so we can imagine what the condition of matters must have been twenty years earlier.

The most lamentable national failing, the inclination to oppression, was positively reduced to a system, and was more conspicuous during this period of the country's history than any other. England, Scotland, and Ireland combine to oppress the distant colonies; England and Scotland, making common cause, oppress Ireland—keep down the Irish Church and repress Irish industry and commerce; England does what she can to repress Scotland; and in England itself the rich man oppresses the poor man, and the ruling class all the others. Of the

[1] Emerson: *English Traits*, chap. xiii.

thirty million inhabitants of the country only one million possessed the franchise. And any one who cares to read the attack on the English landed proprietors in Byron's *Age of Bronze* will see how shamelessly the landowners enriched themselves at the expense of the other classes during the war, and how their whole political aim was to insure the continuance of their power to do so.

Such are the conditions which exercise a partly pernicious, partly inspiring and stimulating influence on the country's authors. In those of them in whose breasts the sacred fire burns feebly it is soon extinguished, and they become reactionary supporters of the existing conditions. But those of them whose lightning-charged spirits were fitted to defy the direction of the wind, develop under the oppression of these conditions an emancipatory literary force which communicates a shock to the political atmosphere. To these latter England seems a very "Gibraltar of custom," and they leave their native land that they may attack and bombard their home with all the artillery of satire and indignation.

In order to arrive at a proper understanding of the soil from which the Naturalistic literature springs, and to understand the principles (not artistic, but political, social, and religious principles) which divide the authors into antagonistic groups, we must enter a little more into detail with regard to the political conditions prevailing in this home. At the beginning of the century there sat on the throne of England the king who had reigned since 1760, George the Third. From his earliest childhood George's mother had endeavoured to inoculate him with the exaggerated and un-English notions of sovereignty which prevailed on the Continent, and she had succeeded so well that one after another of the eminent noblemen who were chosen to be governors to the Prince resigned the office because their influence was counteracted. One of these, Lord Waldegrave, who was not merely a shrewd observer, but also a devoted adherent of the House of Hanover, has drawn a portrait of his royal pupil which is anything but attractive. He is described as not altogether deficient in ability, but wholly without power of application; as honest, but without the frank and open behaviour which makes honesty amiable; as sincerely pious, but rather too attentive to the sins of his neighbours; resolute, but obstinate and strong in prejudices. The tutor tells how, when his pupil is displeased, his anger does not break out with heat and violence, but produces a fit of sullenness and silence. And, "when the fit is ended, unfavourable symptoms very frequently return, which indicate on certain occasions that his Royal Highness has too correct a memory." And this same King, who had such a lively recollection of injuries, had a more than royal forgetfulness of services. But perhaps his greatest fault as a public personage and a ruler was his absolute petrifaction in prejudices. In private life he was honest, respectable, and reliable, and inspired his subjects with great esteem, though the defects in his education were never supplied. When he began to reign he had little or no knowledge of either books or men, and to the end of his life he remained perfectly ignorant as regarded literature and art. But in his selfish court he was not long in acquiring a considerable knowledge of human nature; the man to whom all, great and small, held out their hands whenever they saw him, soon learned to ascertain every man's price and to calculate his value. His naturally sound understanding was enlarged neither by study, nor travel, nor conversation; but on matters the discussion of which does not require much cultivation of mind he generally went to the point, and acquitted himself with as much ability as was necessary in a ruler who was very unwilling to be a king only in name.[1]

George III. was England's Frederick VI. He was a true patriarchal ruler, who felt himself to be the father of his people. During his reign England lost the North American colonies, as Denmark under Frederick VI. lost Norway, without this loss, or the foolish policy which had led to it, damaging the personal popularity of the sovereign. King George's household was a model of an English gentleman's household. Early rising was its first rule. Simplicity, order, frugality, a real bourgeois spirit, reigned. It was

[1] Massey: *History of England*, i. 59, &c.

stupid to a degree which its historian Thackeray "shuddered to contemplate."

Often, we are told, the King rose before any one else was up, ran upstairs and awoke all the equerries, and then went for an early walk, and had a talk with every one he met. He was in the habit of poking his nose into every cottage; now he would give a child a silver coin, now present an old woman with a hen. One day, when the King and Queen were walking together, they met a little boy and talked to him. At last the King said, "This is the Queen; kneel down, and kiss her hand." But this the little fellow obstinately declined to do, out of consideration for his new breeches; and the thrifty King was so delighted with such a sign of youthful prudence that he pressed the child to his heart.

The days passed at this court with a dreary monotony which drove the young princes from home, and was in part responsible for their turning out so badly. In the evening the King either played his game of backgammon or had his evening concert, during which he always nodded, while the gentlemen-in-waiting almost yawned themselves to death in the ante-room.

The family took their daily walk in Windsor Park; the people crowded round quite familiarly, and the Eton boys thrust their chubby cheeks under the crowd's elbows. The open-air music over, the King never failed to take his cocked hat off and salute his band, and say, "Thank you, gentlemen."

What Dane can fail to be reminded by these scenes of Frederick VI.'s walks and sails as Chief Admiral in the grounds of Frederiksberg! Like our Danish monarch, George III. won the affections of the people by the simplicity of his habits and his shabby coat. Equally applicable to King George is Orla Lehmann's remark about Frederick VI., "that his simplicity, both of mind and behaviour, and his kindly interest in the well-being of individuals were regarded as compensations for his failings as a statesman and ruler." But indeed there were not many who detected these last. To the great majority of his subjects old George seemed a very wise statesman and very powerful sovereign.

There is a famous print of him (by Gillray) which represents him—in the old wig, in the stout old hideous Windsor uniform—as the King of Brobdingnag, peering at a little Gulliver, whom he holds up in one hand, whilst in the other he has an opera-glass, through which he surveys the pigmy. And who, think you, is the little Gulliver? He wears a cocked-hat and the little grey Marengo coat.

Danish readers will remember an old picture, a photographic reproduction of which was very popular some years ago. It was called "The Well-beloved Family," and represented Frederick VI. taking a walk with his whole family, from eldest to youngest. Is not the following picture (from the pages of Miss Burney) of one of the afternoon walks at Windsor its exact counterpart? "It was really a mighty pretty procession. The little Princess Amelia, just turned of three years old, in a robe-coat covered with fine muslin, a dressed close cap, white gloves, and fan, walked on alone and first, highly delighted with the parade, and turning from side to side to see everybody as she passed; for all the terracers stand up against the walls, to make a clear passage for the royal family the moment they come in sight. Then followed the King and Queen, no less delighted with the joy of their little darling. The Princess Royal leaning on Lady Elizabeth Waldegrave, the Princess Augusta holding by the Duchess of Ancaster, the Princess Elizabeth led by Lady Charlotte Bertie, followed. General Bude and the Duke of Montague, and Major Price as equerry, brought up the rear of the procession." What a charming picture! exclaims Thackeray. Whilst the procession passes, the band plays its old music, the sun lights up the ancient battlements, the rich elms, the royal standard drooping from the great tower, and the loyal crowd, whom the charming infant caresses with her innocent smiles.

This is the domestic idyll which in public life has its counterpart in the King's passionate determination to oppress North America, oppose the French Revolution, annihilate the Irish Church, and maintain negro slavery with all its horrors. But the idyllic family life was at an end before the century was out. In 1788 the King had his first attack of insanity, and even then the question of the Regency of the Prince of Wales, which was not finally determined until 1810, was discussed with an extraordinary display of passion. The Opposition believed that if they could procure the appointment of the Prince of Wales as Regent, they would be able to keep the Tories out of power for a lengthy period. But the character and morals of the Prince were so repugnant to the great majority of the nation that his accession to power was regarded with dread. However, before the Regency Bill was actually proceeded with, Pitt was in a position to lay before Parliament a medical bulletin informing his subjects of the probable speedy and complete restoration of their King's health. The Prince's disappointment was great, and his having displayed anything but proper filial feeling during the King's illness made it difficult for him to disguise it. He had a talent for mimicry, and had amused the witty and profligate men and women who were his constant companions by *taking off*, as the saying was, the gestures and actions of his insane father. This alone is sufficient to show his character—the character of the man who, on account of a certain outward polish, went by the name of "the first gentleman in Europe."

Even though he retained it only for a short time, one cannot but admire the cleverness with which this Prince managed to win the friendship of many of the most gifted men of the day. Burke and Fox and Sheridan were his associates. Certainly, as Thackeray says, it was not his opinions about the constitution, or about the condition of Ireland, which they cared to hear—*that* man's opinions, indeed! But he talked with Sheridan of dice, and with Fox of wine; those were interests which the fool and the geniuses had in common; and Beau Brummell's friend and rival was an authority among the fashionable men of the day on such questions as the suitable button for a waistcoat and the best sauce for a partridge. He even attached Moore to himself for a short time. From the tone of a letter which Moore writes to his mother in June 1811 (*Memoirs*, i. 225), we understand plainly that he feels flattered by the Prince Regent's "cordial familiarity." And the same is true for a moment of Byron ; his letter of reconciliation to Sir Walter Scott shows how susceptible he was to the Regent's flatteries on the subject of *Childe Harold.* And Scott himself! Good, honourable gentleman though he was, in his capacity of obstinate Tory he was always the Regent's faithful liegeman. And when the latter, as King George the Fourth, came to Scotland (where he figured in the dress of a Highland chief, with his fat legs bared and a kilt round his enormous body, as satirically described by Byron at the end of *The Age of Bronze*), Scott went on board the royal yacht to welcome him, seized a glass from which his Majesty had just drunk, begged to be allowed to keep it, vowed that it should remain for ever as an heirloom in his family, clapped it in his pocket, and, finding an unexpected guest when he went home, sat down upon it, and was quickly and painfully reminded of the royal keepsake. Scott continued faithful to George IV. long after Moore had riddled him with the darts of his wit, and Byron lashed him with his savage epigrams, and after even Brummell, walking in Hyde Park, had looked at him through his eye-glass and asked the Prince's companion, "Who is *your fat friend?*"

For the insinuating heir-apparent in time became extremely corpulent. The life he led, the perpetual feasting and drinking bouts, produced such a habit of body that at last he could not walk. When he was to drive out, a board was put out at the window, and down it he was slid into his carriage. While the starving weavers in Glasgow and Lancashire were crying aloud to Heaven, he was arranging magnificent festivities, and receiving the exiled Bourbon as Louis XVIII. "The child is father of the man," says Wordsworth. George IV. signalised his entrance into society by a feat worthy of his future life. He invented a new shoe-buckle. It was an inch long and five inches broad. "It covered the whole instep, reaching down to the ground on either side of the foot." At his first appearance at a court ball his coat was, we read, of pink silk, with white cuffs ; his waistcoat, white silk, embroidered with various-coloured foil, and adorned with a profusion of French paste. His hat was ornamented with a profusion of steel beads, five thousand in number, with a button and loop of the same metal, and cocked in a new military style.

A military style, indeed! It exactly suited the head that wore it. This head was full, at the time its owner began housekeeping in his splendid new palace of Carlton House, of vague projects of encouraging literature, science, and the arts; and for a moment it seemed as if they were really to be carried out—when at the Prince Regent's table Sir Walter Scott, the best *raconteur* of his time, with loyal devotion and real generosity poured forth humorous, whimsical stories from his inexhaustible store, or Moore sang some of his sweet Anacreontic songs, or Grattan, Ireland's proud leader, contributed to the entertainment his wondrous eloquence, fancy, and feeling. But how soon did these men make way for a company much better suited to the Prince—French cooks, French ballet-dancers, horse-jockeys, buffoons, procurers, tailors, boxers, jewellers, and fencing-masters! With such people he spent the time left him by his mistresses and his bacchanalian orgies. He showed his love for art and his taste by purchasing at extravagant prices whole cart-loads of Chinese monstrosities. It was but natural that this royal *bel esprit*, when he came into power, should quarrel with the clever Whigs whose society he had sought. He suddenly wheeled round and became a Tory.

Four of the European monarchs of the first half of this century—Ludwig I. of Bavaria, Frederick William IV. of Prussia, Christian VIII. of Denmark, and this English Prince Regent—bear a strong resemblance to each other. They are the four reigning reactionary dilettanti. In England, as in Denmark, literary dilettantism succeeds patriarchal simplicity. In the case we are at present considering, it was combined with shocking morals and an almost incredible indolence. In March 1816, fifty-eight prisoners under sentence of death were lying in Newgate prison waiting until the Prince Regent's amusements and distractions should allow him time to sign their death-warrants or their pardons, and many of them had lain there since December. In vain did Brougham make his terrible attack in Parliament upon those "who, when the gaols were filled with wretches, could not suspend for a moment their thoughtless amusements to end the sad suspense between life and death." In connection with this subject, Moore's satires in *The Twopenny Post-Bag* are well worth reading. They show plainly that the sweet Irish song-bird had beak and claws. In *The Life of Sir Walter Scott* we read with what a good-humoured smile the Regent, in 1815, could refer to and quote the verses by Moore which describe his table as loaded with fashion-journals on the one side and unsigned death-warrants on the other. The satire of the verses was only too well deserved, but was of little avail. As early as 1812 Castlereagh had said, in a speech in Parliament: "It would be impossible for his Royal Highness to disengage his person from the accumulating pile of papers that encompass it." In "The Insurrection of the Papers," Moore puts it thus:—

"On one side lay unread Petitions,
On t'other hints from five Physicians;
Here tradesmen's bills,—official papers,
Notes from my Lady, drams for vapours—
There plans of saddles, tea and toast,
Death-warrants, and the *Morning Post*."

Four years later, the Regent had actually allowed fifty-eight death-warrants to accumulate.

As already mentioned, he was hardly invested with the signs of power before he quarrelled with his Whig friends and became a Tory. The great, long-lasting Tory Government was formed. At its head was the Earl of Liverpool, an obstinate, but lazy and good-natured reactionary; the displeasure of the public never fell upon him, but always on his colleagues; he was, as Prime Minister, a kind of monarch with limited power, honest intentions, and modest abilities. He and his colleague, Lord Sidmouth, the Home Secretary, enjoyed the privilege of not being envied and feared for the force of their characters or the splendour of their talents. The most notable and most fiercely criticised member of the ministry was Lord Castlereagh, a moderately gifted man of energetic character, whom Wilberforce once declared to be as cold-blooded as a fish. He had a handsome face and a commanding voice, and to these added the outward show of honours which had not been bestowed on a commoner since the days of Sir Robert Walpole. He was "the noble lord in the blue ribbon." He had a natural leaning towards arbitrary principles, and his intercourse with the irresponsible rulers of the continent tended to strengthen him in ideas which were extremely dangerous for a constitutional minister. No consciousness of the narrowness of his intellect and the defects of his education prevented him from pouring out torrents of unformed sentences and disjointed arguments. These often aroused the laughter of the House; but he withstood all attacks with unflinching determination; none of the hostility or suspicions expressed moved him a hair's-breadth from his path; in his intercourse with Parliament, he again and again adopted the standpoint of absolutism: "We alone know." Byron, Shelley, and Moore all flagellate him in their poetry. There remains to be named Lord Chancellor Eldon, the personification of Toryism, whose thought by day and dream by night was the maintenance of what he called the constitution. In his opinion the man who attempted to do away with any ancient privilege, any antiquated restriction of the liberty of the subject, and still more the man who attempted to repeal any cruel penal law, was laying his hand on the constitution. Yet no one was more ready than he himself to suspend the laws of the country whenever they stood in his way. The suspension of the Habeas Corpus Act, the gagging of the press, &c.—such amputations as these were life to the constitution; to infuse new blood was death.

This was the ministry which, in 1814, astonished Alexander of Russia by its ardour in re-asserting and re-establishing the principles which had been shaken by the Revolution. He slighted it by expressing pity for its reactionary tendencies and cultivating the acquaintance of the leaders of the Opposition in London. The first tidings of the French Revolution had been received with approval by the English Government and nation. The antagonists Pitt and Fox united in hailing it as one of the greatest and most beneficent events in the history of humanity. But hardly had blood been shed on the other side of the Channel, before the mass of the people, including even the majority of the Opposition, saw their whole national inheritance—monarchy, religion, the rights of property—endangered, and formed an enormous party of order. Amongst the Whigs, Burke was the first to condemn the Revolution violently, and as violently to condemn his friend and political ally, Fox, for defending its spirit. The old Whigs sided with Burke. Pitt, who had planned a whole series of necessary reforms, took alarm, dared not even make any alterations in the disgraceful election system, and, on being challenged, confessed that, though fully persuaded of the necessity of Parliamentary reform, the time was not a favourable one for such a daring attempt. Jacobinism was scented in every liberal movement, however innocent and justifiable. When Wilberforce began his agitation against the negro slave-trade, he was supported both by the Government and the Opposition. He had against him only the King, the shipowners, and the House of Peers. But when, in 1791, he tried the temper of the nation for the second time, the revulsion had been so great that the champions of the abolition of the slave-trade were almost regarded as Jacobins, and Wilberforce's bill was rejected by a majority of 163 to 88.

The impression produced in Ireland by the Revolution was another cause of affright in England. The Irish hailed the tidings of the Revolution as slaves and serfs hail the news of emancipation. Although the Irish nation, under the leadership of the noble Henry Grattan (so enthusiastically eulogised by Byron), had succeeded in 1782 in obtaining the absolute independence and supremacy of its own Parliament, both the commerce and the religion of the country were still oppressed. Thomas Moore, a very moderate man, writes that, as the child of Catholic parents, he came into the world with the yoke of the slave round his neck. He tells how, when a boy, he was taken, in 1792, by his father to a public dinner in Dublin, at which one of the toasts was: "May the breezes of France blow our Irish oak into verdure!" In his *Memoirs* we have a description of the movement amongst the youth of the country. He knew and admired its leader, Robert Emmet. When, in the Dublin Debating Society, of which he was the moving spirit and chief ornament, Emmet gave an eloquent description of the doings of the French Republic—when, with an allusion to the story of Cæsar swimming across the river with his sword in one hand and his *Commentaries* in the other, he said: "Thus France at this time swims through a sea of blood, but, while in one hand she wields the sword against her aggressors, with the other she upholds the interests of literature uncontaminated by the bloody tide through which she struggles"—his young countryman listened not only to the literal meaning of the speech, but for every little allusion or remark which he might apply to Ireland. And such allusions were forthcoming. "When a people," cried Emmet one day, "advancing rapidly in civilisation and the knowledge of their rights, look back after a long lapse of time, and perceive how far the spirit of their Government has lagged behind them, what then, I ask, is to be done by them in such a case? What, but to pull the Government up to the people."

The day was not far off when Robert Emmet was to pay dearly for all his bold words. In 1798 the long-prepared-for explosion took place; and, as Byron puts it, Castlereagh "dabbled his sleek young hands in Erin's gore." The fury with which the Government set to work to crush the rebellion and the rebels was so animal and ferocious, that the horrors accompanying the proceeding are almost unequalled in the history of rebellion-suppressing in modern times.

The hatred of the Revolution prolonged itself into hatred of Napoleon. This last went beyond all reasonable bounds. Thackeray tells an anecdote which gives an idea of its character. "I came," he writes, "from India as a child, and our ship touched at an island on the way home, where my black servant took me a long walk over rocks and hills until we reached a garden, where we saw a man walking. 'That is he,' said the black man: 'That is Bonaparte! He eats three sheep every day, and all the little children he can lay hands on.'" And Thackeray adds: "There were people in the British dominions, besides that poor Calcutta serving-man, with an equal horror of the Corsican ogre." We have it strong in Wordsworth's sonnets, Southey's poems, and in Scott's notorious "Life of Napoleon." The wars with France inaugurated the great British reaction—repeated suspension of the Habeas Corpus Act, extension of the definitions of treason contained in the old statutes of Edward III., encroachments on the right of public discussion and petition, and also on the virtual liberty of the press. In Scotland, more particularly, barbarous old statutes were revived, and highly cultured men were banished as common convicts to the Australian penal settlements. Those in power were not afraid, in addressing the English republicans and advocates of equality, to talk of the absolute power of the sovereign, and of the comparative insignificance of Parliament and the representatives of the people. An all-powerful party was formed, with the watchword: The King and the Church!

The King himself was insane, the Prince Regent worse than insane, and the Church hypocritical. In 1812 came floods, a failure of the harvest, and famine. Starvation drove crowds of the poor classes from their homes, to wander aimlessly about the country. Expression is given to their mood in Shelley's *Masque of Anarchy*. The workmen of Nottingham, in their despair, broke into the lace-factories and destroyed the frames. It was in defence of these men that Byron made his well-turned maiden speech in Parliament.

We see from Romilly's Journal how impossible it was for the few liberally inclined politicians to pass even the smallest measure of a reformatory nature. Romilly was universally revered as the reformer of the barbarous English penal code, but is best known nowadays as the legal adviser of the Princess of Wales and of Lady Byron. In 1808 he writes: "If any person be desirous of having an adequate idea of the mischievous effects which have been produced in this country by the French Revolution and all its attendant horrors, he should attempt some legislative reform on humane and liberal principles. He will then find, not only what a stupid dread of innovation, but what a savage spirit it has infused into the minds of many of his countrymen." When Romilly brought in a bill to repeal the Act of William III. which made death the punishment for shop-lifting, Lord Ellenborough, actively supported by Lord Eldon, opposed the bill, along with two others of a similar nature, declaring that "they went to alter those laws which a century had proved to be necessary, and which were now to be overturned by speculation and modern philosophy." And it was not the Government alone which appeared to be, as it were, possessed by the lust of hanging; it was widely spread among the members of Parliament. Romilly tells how one of the young members answered all his arguments and objections with the one monotonous retort: "I am for hanging all." And yet one would have imagined that in the nineteenth century the time had come to put an end to that partiality for hanging which in England still bore lamentable witness to the amount of savagery existing in the national character. In the reign of Henry VIII., 72,000 thieves were hanged, and under George III. they were still hanged by the dozen. In 1817, a regular system of suppression of free-thought and liberty of publication was evolved during the different prosecutions of the old bookseller, William Hone, who, with a rare combination of honesty and shrewdness, time after time defeated every attempt to convict him of blasphemy. In 1819 occurred the Manchester riots, when a cavalry charge was ordered, and the poor unarmed rioters were maltreated by the soldiers. The impression produced by the events of the immediately preceding years is preserved in Shelley's poems of the year 1819.

The political background of the intellectual life of this period is, thus, undoubtedly a dark one—dark with the terror produced in the middle classes by the excesses of the liberty movement in France, dark with the tyrannic lusts of proud Tories and the Church's oppressions, dark with the spilt blood of Irish Catholics and English artisans. And on the pinnacle of society the crown is set on the insanity in George the Third's head, and the sceptre is placed in the hands of the careless lewdness which, in the person of the Prince Regent, occupies the throne as proxy for the narrow-mindedness which had occupied it in the person of his father. And it is this throne which Lord Eldon supports with the six "gagging bills" into which he has transformed England's ancient constitution—this throne which is lauded and glorified in Castlereagh's ungrammatical, anti-liberal speeches, and in Southey's unmelodious, highly-paid adulatory verse—until the horrible, incredible scandals of George IV.'s divorce suit, spreading like a great sewer from the tribunal of the Upper House, drown the glory of the throne and the dignity of the court in a flood of mire, and the revolutions of Spain, Greece, and South America, following on each other without intermission, clear the air, and Castlereagh cuts his throat ("slits a goose-quill," as Byron says), and England, under Canning, recognises the South American republics, and paves the way for the battle of Navarino.

The writings of Shelley, Landor, Byron, and Campbell, have political equivalents in Canning's actions as minister. Indeed, Canning's speeches complement these authors' works. Castlereagh's invertebrate speeches and his dull, meagre official letters (the more meagre because, as a good business man of the school of Metternich, he preferred verbal communications) were at once succeeded by Canning's frank and glowing eloquence. Castlereagh, like his surviving colleagues of the ignominious Congress of Vienna, endeavoured, under the guise of evangelic peace, to maintain silence and darkness in Europe; Canning's speeches shone through the dark night of the Holy Alliance like a forest conflagration. The great idea that inspired him was the belief in the right of a people to free action. He died on the 8th of August 1827; but on the 10th of October of the same year was fought the battle of Navarino, which was, as it were, the last will of the dead man, and which to our generation is the political symbol of the awakening of the new spirit in Europe.[1]

[1] Miss Martineau: *The History of England during the Thirty Years' Peace*, I., II. Massey: *History of England during the Reign of George III.*, I–IV. Thackeray: *The Four Georges*. Reinhold Pauli: *Geschichte Englands seit den Friedensschlüssen* 1814 *and* 1815. Emerson: *English Traits*.

IV

THE BEGINNINGS OF NATURALISM

DURING the summer of 1797, the talk of the inhabitants of a village on the coast of Somersetshire ran much on the subject of two young men who had lately taken up their residence there, and were daily to be seen walking together, absorbed in eager, endless discussions, in which foreign words and foreign names, unintelligible to the natives, were of frequent occurrence. The elder of the two was twenty-seven. The expression of his face was profoundly serious, his manner dignified, almost solemn; he was not unlike a young Methodist parson, and had a monotonous and fatiguing voice. His companion, who was a year or two younger, and whose words, accompanied by much violent gesture, flowed in an unceasing stream, had a large round head (the shape of which indicated remarkable gifts), flattish features, and deep hazel eyes, as full of confused depression as of inspiration. The whole figure and air might be called flabby and irresolute, expressive of weakness with a curious possibility of strength. The youth's voice was musical, and his eloquence seemed to entrance even his reserved auditor and friend. Who and what were these two young men, who desired acquaintance with no one in the place or neighbourhood? This was the question the inhabitants put to themselves. What could they be discussing so eagerly but politics? and if so, what could they be but conspirators, possibly Jacobins hatching treasonous plots?

The rumour soon spread that the elder of the two friends, Mr. Wordsworth, had been in France at the beginning of the Revolution, and had amply shared the enthusiasm of the day for social reform; and that the younger, Mr. Coleridge, had distinguished himself as a keen democrat and Unitarian, had written a drama called *The Fall of Robespierre*, and two political pamphlets entitled *Conciones ad populum*, and had even formed the plan of founding, with others holding the same opinions, a socialistic community in the backwoods of America. No further confirmation of the suspicions entertained was required. A kind neighbour communicated with the authorities in London, and a detective with a Bardolph nose promptly appeared on the scenes, and, himself unobserved, followed the two gentlemen closely. Seeing them with papers in their hands, he made no doubt that they were drawing maps of the neighbourhood. He occasionally addressed them, and he hid himself for hours at a time behind a sandbank at the seaside, which was their favourite seat. According to Coleridge's account of the affair, which is, however, not entirely to be relied on, he at first thought that the two conspirators were aware of their danger, for he often heard them talk of one Spy-nosy, which he was inclined to interpret as a reference to himself; but he was speedily convinced that it was the name of a man who had made a book and lived long ago. Their talk ran most upon books, and they were perpetually desiring each other to look at *this* and to listen to *that;* but he could not catch a word about politics, and ere long gave up the attempt and took himself off.

There was, as a matter of fact, nothing alarming to discover. The two friends had long ago slept off their revolutionary intoxication, and even with the Spinoza about whom they talked so much they had only a second-hand acquaintance; they discussed him without understanding him, much less assimilating him. Coleridge had made acquaintance with Spinozism in the course of his study of Schelling's early works, and he now initiated his friend, who was unlearned in philosophy, into his newly-acquired wisdom. But the name of Spinoza was in these conversations merely the symbol of a mystic worship of nature; Jacob Bõhme's was to be heard in peaceful conjunction with it. The matter under consideration was not science, but poetry; and if, during these long discussions, there was any mention of a revolution, it was a purely literary and artistic revolution, with respect to which the two friends, from very different starting-points, had arrived at remarkably similar conclusions.

What was really accomplished in the course of these conversations was nothing less than that *conscious* literary rupture with the spirit of the eighteenth century, which, assuming different forms in different countries, took place at this time all over Europe.

Coleridge was of an inquiring nature. His antipathy to French Classical powder and paint dated from his school-days, when a teacher of independent opinions had warned his intelligent pupil against harps, lutes, and lyres in his compositions, demanding pen and ink instead; had bid him beware of Muses, Pegasus, Parnassus, and Hippocrene in poetry, affirming everything of the sort to be nothing but rococo style and convention. Coleridge, therefore, refused the title of poet to Pope and his successors, and swore by Bowles' sonnets. He decried Pope in the same manner as Oehlenschläger's young friends in Denmark soon afterwards decried Baggesen. His Germanic temperament made him the born enemy of *esprit*, epigram, and points. It appeared to him that the excellence of the school which had its origin in France had nothing to do with poetry. "The excellence consisted in just and acute observations on men and manners in an artificial state of society, as its matter and substance; and in the logic of wit, conveyed in smooth and strong epigrammatic couplets, as its form. Even when the subject was purely fanciful the poet appealed to the intellect; nay, even in the case of a consecutive narration, a *point* was looked for at the end of each second line, and the whole was, as it were, a chain of epigrams." In other words, the compositions of this school consisted, according to Coleridge, not of poetic thoughts, but of unpoetic thoughts translated into a language which was, by convention, called poetic. In the conception of the poem there was nothing fanciful; nay, so little imagination did the author possess, that "it depended on the compositor's putting or not putting *a small capital*, whether the words should be personifications or mere abstracts." England's great poets, Spenser for example, had been able to express the most fanciful ideas in the purest, simplest of English; but these newer writers could not express common, everyday thoughts except in such an extraordinarily bad and fantastic style that it seemed as if Echo and Sphinx had laid their heads together to produce it. Coleridge turned with aversion from these attempts to conceal want of imagination under affectation of style. He detested Odes to Jealousy, Hope, Forgetfulness, and all such abstractions. They reminded him of an Oxford poem on the subject of vaccination, which began: "Inoculation! heavenly maid, descend!" Even in the best English poetry of a later day the bad habit of personifying abstractions was too long adhered to. (Shelley, for example, presents us with "the twins Error and Truth.") All these affectations appeared to Coleridge to arise from the custom of writing Latin verses in the public schools. The model style, according to him, was that which expressed natural thoughts in natural language, "neither bookish nor vulgar, neither redolent of the lamp nor of the kennel." The old English ballads in Percy's collection, with their unadulterated natural, popular tone, seemed to him excellent guides. He, too, would fain write in such a tone.

It was at this stage that Coleridge was initiated into all Wordsworth's ideas and projects. Wordsworth's was one of those natures which find satisfaction and a sense of security in dogmatic and strongly condemnatory verdicts. His idea of the whole of English poetry after Milton was, that the nation, after producing that great man, had lost the poetic power it, formerly possessed and had preserved only a form of composition, so that poetry had come to mean the art of diction—the poet being judged by the degree of mastery he had attained in that art. Hence there had been an ever more marked departure in metrical composition from the rules of prose. The poet's aim now must be to retrace the path that had been taken, and produce verse which should be distinguished only by its metrical form from the language of daily life. Whilst Coleridge was all for natural melody, Wordsworth went the length of demanding that poetry should be simply rhymed conversation.

And with this naturalistic conception of form was combined a similar naturalistic conception of the subject matter of poetry. One of Wordsworth's favourite assertions and one of the most bitter reproaches he levelled at the prevailing literary taste was, that hardly one original image or new description of nature had been introduced into English verse in the age between Milton and Thomson. Himself endowed with an extraordinary receptivity for all the phenomena of external nature, he took the cry: "Nature! nature!" for his watchword—and by nature he meant the country as opposed to the town. In town life men forgot the earth on which they lived. They no longer really knew it; they remembered the general appearance of fields and woods, but not the details of the life of nature, not its varying play of smiling, sober, glorious, and terrible scenes. Who nowadays could tell the names of the various forest trees and meadow flowers? who knew the signs of the weather—what the clouds say when they hurry so, what those motions of the cattle mean, and why the mists roll down the hill? Wordsworth had known all these signs from the time when he played as a child among the Cumberland hills. He had a familiar acquaintance with all the varieties of English nature, at all seasons of the year; he was constituted to reproduce what he saw and felt, and to meditate profoundly over it before he reproduced it—was fitted to carry out, with full consciousness of what he was undertaking, the reformation of poetry which had been begun by poor Chatterton, "the sleepless soul," and by the peasant Burns, a much more gifted poet than himself. Though he was but one of the numerous exponents of that love of nature which at the beginning of the century spread like a wave over Europe, he had a stronger, more profound consciousness than any man in the United Kingdom of the fact that a new poetic spirit was abroad in England.

The friends agreed that there were three distinct periods of English poetry—the period of poetic youth and strength, from Chaucer to Dryden; the period of poetic barrenness, from (and including) Dryden to the end of the eighteenth century; and the period of regeneration, which was now beginning with themselves, after being heralded by their predecessors. Like the men of the new era in Germany and Denmark, these young Englishmen sought for imposing terms to express the difference between themselves and those whom they attacked ; and the terms they found were exactly the same as those adopted by their Continental contemporaries. They credited themselves with *imagination*—in other words, with the true creative gift, and wrote page upon page of vague eulogy of it as opposed to *fancy;* exactly as Oehlenschläger and his school eulogised imagination and allowed Baggesen at best only humour. They themselves were distinguished by *reason,* their predecessors had only had *understanding;* they had genius, their predecessors had only had talent; they were creators, their predecessors had only been critics. Even an Aristotle, not being a poet, could lay claim to no more than talent. In England, too, Noureddin[1] was belittled ; the new men were conscious of the infinite superiority of their methods to his "un-natural" procedure.

[1] A character in the Danish poet Oehlenschläger's play, *Aladdin*, who represents talent as opposed to genius, which is embodied in Aladdin.

V

STRENGTH AND SINCERITY OF THE LOVE OF NATURE

WORDSWORTH'S real point of departure, then, was the conviction that in town life and its distractions men had forgotten nature, and that they had been punished for it; constant social intercourse had dissipated their energy and talents and impaired the susceptibility of their hearts to simple and pure impressions. Amongst his hundreds of sonnets there is one which is peculiarly eloquent of this fundamental idea. It is the well-known:—

"The World is too much with us; late and soon,
Getting and spending, we lay waste our powers;
Little we see in Nature that is ours;
We have given our hearts away, a sordid boon!
This Sea that bares her bosom to the moon,
The winds that will be howling at all hours
And are up-gather'd now like sleeping flowers,
For this, for everything we are out of tune;
It moves us not.—Great God! I'd rather be
A Pagan suckled in a creed outworn,—
So might I, standing on this pleasant lea,
Have glimpses that would make me less forlorn;
Have sight of Proteus rising from the sea;
Or hear old Triton blow his wreathèd horn."

These are remarkable words to have come from Wordsworth's pen—remarkable, because they show what all sincere naturalism really is, let it be decked with as many theistic trappings as it will. In its inmost essence it is akin to the old Greek conception of nature, and antagonistic to all the official creeds of modern days; it is vitally impregnated with the pantheism which reappears in this century as the dominating element in the feeling for nature in every literature.

In the preceding volume of this work (*The Romantic School in Germany*) we made acquaintance with the pantheism which lay concealed under Tieck's Romantic view of nature. Now we come upon it in the form of the human being's self-forgetful and half unconscious amalgamation with nature, as a single tone in the great harmony of the universe. This idea has found expression in a curious little poem :—

> "A slumber did my spirit seal ;
> I had no human fears :
> She seem'd a thing that could not feel
> The touch of earthly years.
>
> No motion has she now, no force ;
> She neither hears nor sees ;
> Roll'd round in earth's diurnal course
> With rocks, and stones, and trees."

If we transport ourselves into the mood which gave birth to such a poem as this, we are conscious that it is the outcome of purely pantheistic ideas ; unconscious life is regarded as the basis and source of conscious life, and every earthly being is conceived of as having lain in nature's womb, an inseparable part of her until the moment when consciousness began. One of the germs of the poetry of the new century lies in this little poem ; for here, in place of the cultivated human being as developed and extolled by the eighteenth century, we have the human being as seen by the new era in the circle of his kin—birds and wild beasts, plants and stones. Christianity commanded men to love their fellow-men ; pantheism bade them love the meanest animal. *Hart-Leap Well*, undoubtedly one of Wordsworth's finest poems, a simple little romance in two parts, is a movingly eloquent plea for a poor, ill-used animal, a hunted stag—that is to say, a creature in whom the classical poets would have been interested only in the shape of venison, and belonging to the species which the admirers of the age of chivalry, including Scott himself, would have allowed their heroes to kill by the hundred. Deeply affecting, in spite of the comparative insignificance of its subject, grandly simple in its style, the little poem is a noble evidence of the heartfelt *piety* towards nature which is Wordsworth's patent of nobility.

This piety in his case consists mainly in reverence for the childlike, and for the child. And this same reverence for the human being who in his unconsciousness is nearest to nature, is another of the characteristic features of the new century. In a little poem with which Wordsworth himself introduces all the rest, he writes :—

"My heart leaps up when I behold
A rainbow in the sky :
So was it when my life began,
So is it now I am a man,
So be it when I shall grow old,
Or let me die !
The Child is father of the Man :
And I could wish my days to be
Bound each to each by natural piety."

Here we have reverence for the child developed to such an extent that it supplants reverence for age. But this conferring of his natural poetic rights on the child is, as the history of every country shows us, only one of the many signs of the reaction against the eighteenth century's worship of the enlightened, social human being, and its banishment of the child to the nursery. Wordsworth carries the reaction inaugurated by the nineteenth century to its logical conclusion. In one of his sonnets he describes a walk which he takes on a beautiful evening with a little girl. After describing the tranquil evening mood—

"The holy time is quiet as a nun
Breathless with adoration ;"

he turns to the child beside him, and says:

"Dear child ! dear girl ! that walkest with me here,
If thou appear untouch'd by solemn thought
Thy nature is not therefore less *divine :*
Thou liest in Abraham's bosom all the year,
And worship'st at the Temple's *inner shrine,*
God being with thee when we know it not."

The pious ending is inevitable with Wordsworth ; but, as any intelligent reader may see for himself, it is only tacked on to the main idea, that of the child's own divine nature. In his famous *Ode on Intimations of Immortality* Wordsworth develops this idea with a fervour of enthusiasm which carried him too great a length for even such a devotee of naïveté as Coleridge. A child of six he apostrophises thus:—

> "Thou, whose exterior semblance doth belie
> Thy soul's immensity;
> Thou best philosopher, who yet dost keep
> Thy heritage; thou eye among the blind,
> That, deaf and silent, read'st the eternal deep,
> Haunted for ever by the eternal Mind,—
> Mighty Prophet! Seer blest!
> On whom those truths do rest
> Which we are toiling all our lives to find."

These assertions are, doubtless, explained away in a poetico-philosophical manner by the subsequent attribution of the child's greatness to the fact that it stands nearer than we do to the life before birth, and, consequently, to the "intimations of immortality"; but even this is not to be taken as Wordsworth's literal meaning, if we are to believe an assertion of Coleridge's which remained uncontradicted by the author. The child is revered as earth's "foster-child," and

> "The Youth, who daily farther from the east
> Must travel, still is Nature's priest."

In numerous poems Wordsworth refers to the strong impression made upon him as a youth by the pageantry of nature. In one of them, to which, according to his frequent custom, he gave a prolix title, *Influence of Natural Objects in Calling Forth and Strengthening the Imagination in Boyhood and Early Youth,* he thanks the Spirit of the Universe for having from the first dawn of his childhood intertwined for him

> "The passions that build up our human soul;
> Not with the mean and vulgar works of man,—
> But with high objects, with enduring things,
> With life and nature, purifying thus
> The elements of feeling and of thought
> . . . . . . until we recognise
> A grandeur in the beatings of the heart."

Observe the vivid, delicate perception of nature in the following description:—

"Nor was this fellowship vouchsafed to me
With stinted kindness. In November days,
When vapours rolling down the valleys made
A lonely scene more lonesome; among woods
At noon; and 'mid the calm of summer nights,
When, by the margin of the trembling lake,
Beneath the gloomy hills, I homeward went
In solitude, such intercourse was mine:
Mine was it in the fields both day and night,
And by the waters, all the summer long;
And in the frosty season, when the sun
Was set, and visible for many a mile,
The cottage windows through the twilight blazed,
I heeded not the summons:—happy time
It was indeed for all of us; for me
It was a time of rapture!—Clear and loud
The village clock tolled six—I wheeled about,
Proud and exulting like an untired horse
That cares not for his home.—All shod with steel
We hissed along the polished ice, in games
Confederate, imitative of the chase
And woodland pleasures,—the resounding horn,
The pack loud-chiming, and the hunted hare.
So through the darkness and the cold we flew,
And not a voice was idle: with the din
Smitten, the precipices rang aloud;
The leafless trees and every icy crag
Tinkled like iron; while the distant hills
Into the tumult sent an alien sound
Of melancholy, not unnoticed, while the stars,
Eastward, were sparkling clear, and in the west
The orange sky of evening died away.

Not seldom from the uproar I retired
Into a silent bay,—or sportively
Glanced sideway, leaving the tumultuous throng,
To cut across the reflex of a star,
Image, that, flying still before me, gleamed
Upon the glassy plain: and oftentimes,
When we had given our bodies to the wind,
And all the shadowy banks on either side
Came sweeping through the darkness, spinning still
The rapid line of motion, then at once
Have I, reclining back upon my heels,

Stopped short; yet still the solitary cliffs
Wheeled by me—even as if the earth had rolled
With visible motion her diurnal round!
Behind me did they stretch in solemn train,
Feebler and feebler, and I stood and watched
Till all was tranquil as a summer sea."

This is a picture of nature which it would be difficult to match in later English poetry.

In one of his most beautiful and profound poems, *Lines Composed a few Miles above Tintern Abbey*, Wordsworth has described his own feeling for nature in expressions which he declared that he recognised again in the most famous and most poetical passages of Byron's *Childe Harold*, and which, in any case, were indisputably epoch-making in English poetical art. He writes:—

"For nature then
(The coarser pleasures of my boyish days,
And their glad animal movements all gone by)
To me was all in all.—I cannot paint
What then I was. The sounding cataract
Haunted me like a passion: the tall rock,
The mountain, and the deep and gloomy wood,
Their colours and their forms, were then to me
An appetite: a feeling and a love,
That had no need of a remoter charm,
By thought supplied, nor any interest
Unborrowed from the eye."

Granted that it was very absurd of Wordsworth to talk (to Moore in 1820) of Byron's plagiarisms from him, and to declare that the whole Third Canto of *Childe Harold* was founded on his style and sentiments—and granted that Lord John Russell is right when he remarks drily in this connection that if Wordsworth wrote the Third Canto of *Childe Harold*, it is his best work—it is, nevertheless, easy to understand that Wordsworth could not but feel as if, in the chief passages in that canto, and the celebrated passages about solitude in the earlier cantos, what was naturally expressed by him had been worked by Byron into a laboured and antithetical sort of declamation.[1] It is not difficult to

[1] See Thomas Moore: *Memoirs*, iii. 161.

discern, in these outbursts, the wounded vanity of a narrow mind which felt itself eclipsed; but it cannot be denied that it really was Wordsworth who first struck the chord which Byron varied with such skill, nor that single striking and vivid lines of Wordsworth's had impressed themselves on Byron's memory. Who can read, for example, the following lines of *Childe Harold* (Canto iii. 72):—

> "I live not in myself, but I become
> Portion of that around me; and to me
> High mountains are a feeling,"

without thinking of Wordsworth's verses just quoted? And who can deny that Byron, as it were, adopted Wordsworth's idea, and added thoughts of his own to it when he wrote (*Childe Harold*, iii. 75):—

> "Are not the mountains, waves, and skies, a part
> Of me and of my soul, as I of them?
> Is not the love of these deep in my heart
> With a pure passion? should I not contemn
> All objects, if compared with these?"

Wordsworth, in *Tintern Abbey*, describes his passion for nature as something past, as something which only lasted for a moment during an age of transition, and very soon turned into reflection and questioning; but Byron's passion is a permanent feeling, the expression of his nature. In his case the Ego in its relations with nature is not forced into the strait-jacket of orthodox piety; no obstruction of dogma is set up between nature and him; in his mystical worship of it he feels himself one with it, and this without the help of any *deus ex machina*.

Passion is not the special characteristic of Wordsworth's attitude to nature. The distinguishing quality in his perception and reproduction of natural impressions is of a more delicate and complex kind. The impression, although it is received by healthy, vigorously perceptive senses, is modified and subdued by pondering over it. It does not directly attune the poet to song. If Wordsworth can say, with

Goethe: "I sing like the bird that sits on the bough," it is, at any rate, not like the nightingale that he sings; his is not the love-song which streams forth, rich and full, telling of the intoxication of the soul and breaking and mocking at the silence of the night. He himself, after describing the song of the nightingale in similar terms to these, adds (*Poems of Imagination*, x.):—

"I heard a stock-dove sing or say
His homely tale this very day;
His voice was buried among trees,
Yet to be come at by the breeze;
He did not cease; but cooed—and cooed;
And somewhat pensively he wooed:
He sang of love with quiet blending,
Slow to begin, and never ending;
Of serious faith and inward glee;
That was the song—the song for me!"

It was himself that Wordsworth tried to paint in describing the pensive, serious wooer. According to the custom of so many poets, he attempted to formulate his methods into a theory and to prove that all good poetry must possess the qualities of his own. All good poetry is, he says, "the spontaneous overflow of powerful feelings. But poems to which any value can be attached were never produced on any variety of subjects but by a man who, being possessed of more than usual organic sensibility, had also *thought long and deeply*." This theory he supports by the argument that "our continued influxes of feeling are directed and modified by our thoughts, which are indeed the representatives of all our past feelings"—a profound and striking, if not scientifically satisfactory utterance, as well as an excellent characterisation of his own poetic thought and deliberation.

His method consists, exactly defined, in storing up natural impressions, in order to dwell on and thoroughly assimilate them. Later they are brought forth from the soul's store-house and gazed on and enjoyed again. To understand this peculiarity of Wordsworth's is to have the key to his originality. In *Tintern Abbey* he tells how the direct, passionate joy in the beauties of nature which he felt in his youth turned, in his riper years, into this quiet assimilation of the human-like moods of nature :—

> "That time is past,
> And all its aching joys are now no more,
> And all its dizzy raptures. Not for this
> Faint I, nor mourn, nor murmur ; other gifts
> Have followed ; for such loss, I would believe,
> Abundant recompense. For I have learned
> To look on nature, not as in the hour
> Of thoughtless youth ; but hearing oftentimes
> The still, sad music of humanity,
> Nor harsh nor grating, though of ample power
> To chasten and subdue. And I have felt
> A presence that disturbs me with the joy
> Of elevated thoughts ; a sense sublime
> Of something far more deeply interfused,
> Whose dwelling is the light of setting suns,
> And the round ocean, and the living air,
> And the blue sky, and in the mind of man :
> A motion and a spirit, that impels
> All thinking things, all objects of all thought,
> And rolls through all things."

In this passage Wordsworth has delimited his territory, has poetically yet plainly indicated his special province. What a contrast to Byron, who seldom or never heard the human voice in nature, and certainly never except in harsh and grating tones—the man who in *Childe Harold* actually calls human life "a false nature—not in the harmony of things!"

But we have not yet come to the most remarkable lines in *Tintern Abbey,* namely those in which Wordsworth describes the silent influence on the mind of the hoarded, carefully preserved impressions of nature. He writes :—

> "These beauteous forms,
> Through a long absence, have not been to me
> As is a landscape to a blind man's eye :
> But oft, in lonely rooms, and 'mid the din
> Of towns and cities, I have owed to them,
> In hours of weariness, sensations sweet,
> Felt in the blood, and felt along the heart,
> And passing even into my purer mind,
> With tranquil restoration :—feelings, too,
> Of unremembered pleasure : such, perhaps,

As have no slight or trivial influence
On that best portion of a good man's life,
His little, nameless, unremembered acts
Of kindness and of love."

And he asserts that he is indebted to the influence of nature for yet another gift,

"Of aspect more sublime; that blessed mood
In which the burthen of the mystery,
In which the heavy and the weary weight
Of all this unintelligible world
Is lightened";

and his train of thought reaches its conclusion in the feeling of assurance that this happiness produced in him by the sight of the familiar places is not mere momentary pleasure, but *life and food for future years.*

Again and again this last idea recurs in Wordsworth's poetry. We have it very marked, for instance, in No. XV. of the *Poems of Imagination,* in which he tells of the impression produced on him, during a lonely walk, by the sudden sight of "a host of golden daffodils,"

"Beside the lake, beneath the trees,
Fluttering and dancing in the breeze.
. . . .
I gazed—and gazed—but little thought
What wealth the show to me had brought.

For oft when on my couch I lie
In vacant or in pensive mood,
They flash upon that inward eye
Which is the bliss of solitude,
And then my heart with pleasure fills,
And dances with the daffodils."

Nothing could be more unlike the lyric poet's usual habit of living in the present, than this lyric poet's conscious saving of the present for future use. He himself tells us that he is of a saving disposition; he collects a winter store of bright summer moments; and there is in this something genuinely human, which is too often overlooked. But there is, above all, something national in it; it is not surprising that *English* Naturalism should begin by carefully and economically providing itself with a store, a capital, of impressions of nature.

We are all familiar with the feelings that might lead to the attempt. Many of us, gazing on the boundless blue ocean, sparkling in the sunlight, have felt that to have this sight before our eyes every day would widen the soul and cleanse it of all its little meannesses; and we have turned away unwillingly and with the conscious desire to preserve the impression so as to be able to renew its effect. Or with beautiful landscapes before our eyes, especially those which we have seen in the course of travel, with the certainty of not being able to enjoy their beauty soon again, we have tried to be as passive as possible, so as to allow the picture to impress itself firmly on our memory. And we have often instinctively recalled the beautiful scene to mind; for the soul involuntarily calls up bright memories to draw strength and courage from them. But in us such impressions have been almost effaced by stronger ones. We have not been able to preserve them efficaciously for the future, or to ruminate over them again and again. The preoccupations of society and of our own passions have made it impossible for us to find our deepest and most inspiring joy in memories of sunlight falling upon flowers, or of entwisted giant trees. But the soul of the English poet, whose mission it was to re-awaken the feeling for all these elementary moods and impressions, was of a different stamp; unagitated by any practical activity, it vegetated in these day-dreams of natural beauty. And it is undeniable that this constant occupation of himself with the simplest natural impressions, kept his soul pure and free to perceive and to feel beauty in its simple, earthly manifestations, without fancifulness and without excitement.

How rare is this capacity! how often wanting in the very greatest and best minds! And how quickly was it lost again in English poetry! It displays itself most exquisitely and completely in the few lightly-sketched female figures of the short poems. The heroes and heroines of the narrative poems, some of them portrayed with the design of arousing sympathy with the rural population and the lowest classes, others with the intention of edifying, are of distinctly inferior quality. But these few delicately-drawn figures, seen with the same tranquil and yet loving eyes with which Wordsworth looked at trees and birds, are nature itself. They are the English feminine nature ; and never have the essential qualities of this nature been more exactly expressed. Take as an example of what I mean, the following little poem :—

"She was a phantom of delight
When first she gleamed upon my sight ;
A lovely apparition, sent
To be a moment's ornament;
Her eyes as stars of twilight fair ;
Like twilight's too, her dusky hair :
But all things else about her drawn
From May-time and the cheerful dawn ;
A dancing shape, an image gay,
To haunt, to startle, and waylay.

I saw her upon nearer view,
A spirit, yet a woman too !
Her household motions light and free,
And steps of virgin liberty ;
A countenance in which did meet
Sweet records, promises as sweet ;
A creature not too bright or good
For human nature's daily food ;
For transient sorrows, simple wiles,
Praise, blame, love, kisses, tears, and smiles.

And now I see with eye serene
The very pulse of the machine ;
A being breathing thoughtful breath,
A traveller between life and death;
The reason firm, the temperate will,
Endurance, foresight, strength, and skill ;
A perfect woman, nobly planned,
To warn, to comfort, and command ;
And yet a spirit still, and bright
With something of angelic light."

This is a genuine, faithful portrait of the pattern English woman ; and to compare this sober, truthful description with the ideal women whom the greatest English poets a few years later found satisfaction in depicting, is to prepare an easy victory for Wordsworth. Take Shelley's description, in *The Sensitive Plant,* of the ethereal protectress of flowers and insects. The picture of the fairy-like beauty is charming, as everything is that comes from Shelley's pen ; her tenderness for the plants and her touching compassion for all the small, ugly, despised animals, "the poor banished insects, whose intent, although they did ill, was innocent," are genuine human traits ; and yet she is not a real human being, any more than the Witch of Atlas is, or the dim heroine of *Epipsychidion.* Shelley, like the lark he sang of, was a "scorner of the ground." Or take the passionate Oriental heroines of Byron's earliest poetic narratives—Medora, Gulnare, Kaled. They never attain to the beautiful simplicity of this woman described by Wordsworth. Their passionateness is the principal quality impressed upon us; their love, their devotion, their determination know no bounds. They are heroines invented for readers in whom the numbing life of crowded London and the constant occupation with contemporary great historical events, have induced a kind of nervous craving for the strongest intellectual stimulants. But from the very beginning Wordsworth regarded it as a pleasant and profitable task to show how profoundly men's minds may be moved without the employment of coarse or violent stimulants. He knew that those who were accustomed to striking effects would be unlikely at first to appreciate works the distinguishing feature of which was their soft and natural colouring ; but he resolved that he would turn the reader's expectations in the matter of the agencies of a poem back into the natural track.

VI

RURAL LIFE AND ITS POETRY

It is impossible thoroughly to understand Wordsworth's poetic strength and limitations without a glance at his life. We discover it to have been an unusually idyllic and comfortable one. Belonging to the well-to-do middle class (his father was an attorney), he studied at Cambridge and then travelled. In 1795, not long after his return from abroad, he received a legacy of £900 from an admirer of his genius, which, added to his share of a debt of £8500 due to his father by an English nobleman, and paid to the family about this time, placed him in a position to live without taking up any profession. In 1802 he married; in 1813 he settled at Rydal Mount in the Lake district. He held the appointment of Distributor of Stamps, which was practically a sinecure, from 1813 to 1842, when he resigned in favour of one of his sons. The salary of this appointment was £500. In 1843 he succeeded Southey as Poet Laureate, and as such enjoyed a pension of £300 a year till his death, which occurred in 1850, when he had just completed his eightieth year. Sheltered on every side from the outward vicissitudes of life, he regarded them from a Protestant-philosophical point of view.

A career such as this was not calculated to stir the passions; nor is passion discoverable either in Wordsworth's life or his poetry. In the lives of most eminent authors we find some preponderant circumstance, one or more turning-points, one or other ostensible source of melancholy, or of strength of character, or of productivity; in Wordsworth's nothing of the kind is to be found. No congenital misfortune crippled him, no implacably violent animosity goaded him and set its mark on his spirit. The critics did not spare him with mockery and contempt, and they continued their attacks for a long time. From 1800 to 1820 his poetry was trodden under foot; from 1820 to 1830 it struggled; after 1830 it received universal recognition. But the animosity was not stupid and violent enough, the struggle was not hot enough, the victory not brilliant enough, to give colour and lustre to his career, or to make it a subject of song. His inmost, personal life was never so intense that it could absorb his poetry or provide it with subjects. On the contrary, it led him to look outwards. The wars on the Continent, the natural surroundings of his home, and the little, insignificant set of human beings amongst whom he lived, engrossed his thoughts. He was not, like Byron, too much absorbed in his own affairs to have tranquillity of mind to dwell upon the small things and the small people whom he exhibits and describes with tender sympathy.

He undoubtedly felt himself the centre of his world. From his retired, idyllic home there issued from time to time collections of short poems or single long ones, provided with explanatory prefaces which, piling example on example, demonstrated to the reader that all great poets have been misunderstood or despised by their contemporaries; that every author, in so far as he is great and at the same time original, is obliged to create the taste by means of which his works can be enjoyed. His predecesors have, no doubt, smoothed the way for all that he has in common with them; but for what is peculiarly his own he is in the condition of Hannibal among the Alps. (Preface of 1815.)

Wordsworth was well aware that no intellectual pioneer can expect complete recognition from any but his younger contemporaries. But the criticism meted out to him, which was not aggressive enough to rouse in him a recklessly bellicose spirit like Byron's, made him self-absorbed and arrogant. The one variety in his daily life was provided by occasional visits from admirers who were making a tour in the neighbourhood and had letters of introduction to him. These strangers he received surrounded by his admiring family; he conversed with them in a cold and dignified manner, and not unfrequently repelled them by the egotism with which he quoted and praised his own works, the indifference he manifested to everything else, the rigour with which he insisted on every outward sign of respect being shown him, and the solemnity with which he repeated even the most insignificant things that had been said in his praise.

A number of anecdotes illustrating his egotism have been preserved. Thomas Moore (*Memoirs*, iii. 163) tells how one day, in a large party, Wordsworth, without anything having been previously said to introduce the subject, called out suddenly from the top of the table to the bottom: "Davy, do you know the reason why I published the 'White Doe' in quarto?" "No, what was it?" "To show the world my opinion of it." He never read any works aloud but his own. At the time when *Rob Roy*, which has a motto taken from one of his poems, was published, he happened to be visiting a family who received the book the day it came out. They were all looking forward with eagerness to the new tale. Wordsworth seized the book, and every one expected him to read the first chapters aloud; but instead of doing this, he went to the bookcase, took out a volume of his own poetry, and read his poem aloud to the company.

We have Emerson's notes written immediately after two different visits to Wordsworth, paid with a year's interval. After the second, he writes: "He was nationally bitter on the French: bitter on Scotchmen too. No Scotchman, he said, can write English. . . . His opinions of French, English, Irish, and Scotch seemed rashly formalised from little anecdotes of what had befallen himself and members of his family, in a diligence or stage-coach." After his first visit (in 1833) Emerson writes: "He had much to say of America, the more that it gave occasion for his favourite topic—that society is being enlightened by a superficial tuition, out of all proportion to its being restrained by moral culture. Schools do no good. Tuition is not education. . . . He wished to impress on me and all good Americans to cultivate the moral, the conservative, &c. . . . He proceeded to abuse Goethe's *Wilhelm Meister* heartily. It was full of all manner of fornication. It was like the crossing of flies in the air. He had never gone farther than the first part; so disgusted was he that he threw the book across the room. . . . He cited his sonnet 'On the Feelings of a High-minded Spaniard,' which he preferred to any other (I so understood him), and 'The Two Voices'; and quoted, with evident pleasure, the verses addressed to the Skylark." These jottings give us an excellent idea of what Wordsworth was in ordinary intercourse: the contemptuous verdicts passed on all foreign races, the objection to modern civilisation (the same which the Mohammedans in Asia and Africa prefer against it to this day) that it is compatible with great immorality; the eulogy on conventional morality as the society-preserving element (true morality being the most radical element in existence), the displeasure with Goethe (which reminds us of Novalis), and the recital of his own verses as finale!

Emerson sums up his impressions in the following words: "His face sometimes lighted up, but his conversation was not marked by special force or elevation. . . . He honoured himself by his simple adherence to truth, and was very willing not to shine; but he surprised by the hard limits of his thought. To judge from a single conversation, he made the impression of a narrow and very English mind; of one who paid for his rare elevation by general tameness and conformity."

In 1843 Wordsworth and Dickens met for the first time. Wordsworth had a great contempt for all young men, and the mutual friend at whose house the meeting took place was, consequently, curious to learn his impression of the great humorist. "After pursing up his lips in a fashion peculiar to him, and swinging one leg over the other, the bare flesh of his ankles appearing over his socks, Wordsworth slowly answered, 'Why, I am not much given to turn critic on people I meet; but, as you ask me, I will candidly avow that I thought him a very talkative, vulgar young person—but I dare say he may be very clever. Mind, I don't want to say a word against him, for I have never read a line he has written.' Some time after this the same querist guardedly asked Dickens how he had liked the Poet Laureate? 'Like him? Not at all. He is a dreadful old ass.'"[1]

The reader will naturally refuse to subscribe to so sweeping a judgment. But so much is certain, that in private intercourse there must have been something extremely irritating about Wordsworth. A contemporary declares that when he spoke he blew like a whale, and uttered truisms in an oracular tone. The word "truism" is applicable to more than his verbal utterances; it applies to the whole reflective and didactic side of his poetry. In it there is no remarkable force or passion, but a Hamlet-like dwelling upon the great questions of "to be or not to be." "Birth, death, the future, the sufferings and misdeeds of man in this life, and his hopes of a life to come; the littleness of us and our whole sphere of knowledge, and the awful relations in which we stand to a world of the supernatural—these, if any," says Masson, "are the permanent and inevitable objects of all human, as they were peculiarly of Wordsworth's, contemplation and solicitude."[2] But these ideas, lying, as they do, rather at the circumference of the sphere of our knowledge than within it, unfortunately tempt us into certain ancient and well-worn tracks of thought that lead nowhere; they go round in a ring, and we can follow them with a tranquil and dignified melancholy, but without much benefit either to ourselves or others. The fact that Wordsworth is perpetually finding his way to this said circumference of the sphere of our knowledge, which adherents of the so-called revealed religions regard as the natural centre of our thoughts, has contributed more than anything else to prevent his fame, great as it is in England, from spreading to any considerable extent in other countries.

When Coleridge made Wordsworth's personal acquaintance, the latter had already written enough to show plainly what was the nature of his originality. What struck Coleridge in Wordsworth's poetry "was the union of deep

[1] R. S. Mackenzie: *Life of Dickens*, p. 243.
[2] Masson: *Wordsworth, Shelley, Keats, and other Essays.*

feeling with profound thought ; the fine balance of truth in observing, with the imaginative faculty in modifying the objects observed ; and, above all, the original gift of spreading the tone, the atmosphere of the ideal world around forms, incidents, and situations of which, for the common view, custom had bedimmed all the lustre."

Wordsworth and Coleridge's first conversations turned upon what to them appeared the two cardinal points of poetry, the power of exciting the sympathy of the reader by a faithful adherence to the truth of nature, and the power of giving the interest of novelty by the modifying colours of imagination. The sudden charm which accidents of light and shade, which moonlight or sunset, diffuse over a known and familiar landscape, appeared to represent the practicability of combining both. These are the poetry of nature, and these were to be reproduced. It was not simply nature that was to be imitated, but the poetry of nature.

The thought suggested itself that a series of poems might be composed of two sorts. In the one the incidents and agents were to be, in part at least, supernatural, and the excellence aimed at was to consist in the interesting of the affections by the dramatic truth of such emotions as would naturally accompany such situations, supposing them real. And real in this sense they have been to every human being who, from whatever source of delusion, has at any time believed himself to be under supernatural agency. The execution of this part of the undertaking fell to Coleridge's share, and there can be no doubt whatever that the successful accomplishment of it was due to him. Any one at all well acquainted with European literature sees at once how closely related this task is to those which German Romanticism set itself and accomplished. The only thing peculiarly English is, that the emphasis is not laid upon the supernatural and fantastic, but upon the realistic element, so that Romanticism in this case becomes simply one of the forms of Naturalism.

In the poems of the other sort the themes were to be chosen from real life. But Wordsworth, to whose share this division fell, resolved to communicate to the commonest and most natural events an unusual, new, almost supernatural colour by awakening the mind from the slumber of custom, and forcing it to direct its attention to the beauty and the marvels which the natural world is constantly offering to heedless man. He made the attempt for the first time in the *Lyrical Ballads*, which in the preface are designated an "Experiment"—an experiment intended to prove the possibility of making themes unsuited to ornate representation attractive, even when presented to the reader in the language of real life—and he repeated it in hundreds of poems of extremely varied quality, whose heroes and heroines all belong to the lower and lowest classes, have followed rural avocations from their youth, and are represented on a background of rural life.

In Danish literature there is no series of poems of this description; but the careful student of Wordsworth will every now and then be reminded, by the form given to a poetic anecdote or by the tone of the narrator, of Runeberg's *Fänrik Stål.* There is occasionally even a resemblance of rhythm and metre. It would be interesting to know if Runeberg had any acquaintance with the works of the English poet. Possibly the whole faint resemblance is due to the fact that the incidents in the poems of both writers all occur in one small district—the neighbourhood of the English, and the neighbourhood of the Finnish Lakes. The difference is far more striking than the resemblance. In Runeberg we have a warlike background and mood, a fiery lyric style, patriotic ardour; in Wordsworth, stagnant, rurally peaceful life, an epic attitude, and a purely local patriotism—attachment to the life and history of a couple of parishes. Runeberg's is a soldier's feeling for the army; Wordsworth's, a parish priest's for his flock.

Resolution and Independence, one of Wordsworth's most characteristic, though certainly not one of his best poems, is a good example of his capacity and manner of casting over the most everyday incidents and phenomena a tinge of almost supernatural colour. The poet describes his walk on a summer morning—the glistening of the dew, the song of the birds, the fleet racing of the hare across the moor. Then it occurs to him that he himself has lived as thoughtlessly as the beasts of the field and the birds of the air, and that such a life is only too likely one day to bring its own punishment. He calls to mind how many great poets have ended in misery, and the most prosaic fears for the future depress him. Then suddenly, in that lonely place, he comes upon an old man :—

> "The oldest man he seemed that ever wore grey hairs.
>
> As a huge stone is sometimes seen to lie
> Couched on the bald top of an eminence ;
> Wonder to all who do the same espy,
> By what means it could thither come and whence ;
> So that it seems a thing endued with sense :
> Like a sea-beast crawled forth, that on a shelf
> Of rock or sand reposeth, there to sun itself;
>
> Such seemed this man, not all alive nor dead,
> Nor all asleep—in his extreme old age :
> His body was bent double, feet and head
> Coming together in life's pilgrimage ;
> As if some dire constraint of pain, or rage
> Of sickness felt by him in times long past,
> A more than human weight upon his frame had cast.
>
> . . . .
>
> Motionless as a cloud the old man stood,
> That heareth not the loud winds when they call ;
> And moveth all together, if it move at all."

How clever the double simile is, and what a feeling of mystery it produces! The old man is like the gigantic stone on the top of the hill ; and the stone in its turn resembles some sea-beast which must have crawled up there. The impression of great age is most forcibly produced. This old man seems the oldest man that has ever lived. If we were in Germany or any other territory of Romanticism, we should not be surprised to learn that we had the shoemaker of Jerusalem before us. But we are in England, and our guide is Wordsworth ; and the old man turns out to be a most ordinary human being, by trade a leech-gatherer, an occupation suited to the capacity of the frail old inhabitants of a marshy district. The old man's confident, piously resigned words, his tranquillity of mind even in extreme loneliness and poverty, allay the young man's fears for the future; and he resolves, whenever such fears beset him, to think of the leech-gatherer on the lonely moor. "This is not ode-flight," as Ewald remarks somewhere or other; but it is a good specimen of Wordsworth's power of giving a certain imprint of fantasy and grandeur to the most everyday, most realistic material by his manner of treating it.

The attempt to exercise this capacity has, in not a few of Wordsworth's poems, resulted in caricature. It has always done so when he has tried to produce a mystically religious or terrifying effect by endowing some simply painful or odd incident with the so-called supernatural quality. We can call it nothing but childish when, in the poem entitled *The Thorn*, the narrator (whose position in life is not indicated, but whom Wordsworth himself told Coleridge he had imagined as an old ship captain, almost in his dotage) tells in the strain of horror with which one relates a ghost story, the tale of the poor mad woman who sits at night in a scarlet cloak, weeping and wailing, under the thorn tree. And *Peter Bell*, the poem which Wordsworth presented to the public with such a flourish of trumpets, but which, had it not been for Shelley's satire of the same name, would have been forgotten by this time, produces the effect of a parody. It tells of the terror induced in a coarse, cruel man by the supernatural fortitude with which a poor ass bears the most terrible blows rather than move—a terror which, in combination with the excited imaginings due to the darkness, brings about a complete change in the man. Time showed the reason of the ass's fortitude to have been its desire to draw attention to the fact that its master had fallen into the river at the spot where it was standing. We have here a striking contrast—the moral greatness of the brute and the brutish stupidity of the man—and Wordsworth, who had no sense of the comic, did not fail to enlarge on the subject.

And that he does so is not a mere accident, but a characteristic trait. The new school, with its dislike of the brilliant and its love of the simple and plain, felt a real attraction towards asses, these obstinate, patient, and peculiarly misunderstood children of nature, which are always outshone by less contented animals. Coleridge, in his poem, *To a Young Ass—its mother being tethered near it*, allowed himself to be carried away by his enthusiasm to the extent of exclaiming: "I hail thee Brother!" and declaring that if it were granted him in a better and more equitably ordered state of society to provide peaceful pasture for this ass, its joyful bray would sound more melodious in his ears than the sweetest music. It is not surprising that the scoffer Byron promptly made merry over this fraternal greeting in his first satire, *English Bards and Scotch Reviewers*. But in Coleridge this extreme Naturalism did not go deep; he himself was the first to denounce his own excesses. Wordsworth, on the contrary, who was by nature consistent, not to say obstinate, carried purely literary Naturalism to its final and extreme conclusions.

He almost always chose his themes from humble and rustic life; and this he did, not for the same reason as the French writers of the previous century, who, themselves elegant and cultivated, enjoyed inelegance and uncultivatedness with a feeling of superiority, but because he believed that in that condition of life the essential passions of the heart find a better soil in which they can attain their maturity, are less under restraint, and speak a plainer language. He was of opinion that in that condition our elementary feelings co-exist in a state of greater simplicity, and consequently may be more accurately contemplated than in town life; and he was also persuaded that constant association with the beautiful and permanent forms of nature, in combination with the necessary and unchanging character of rural occupations, must make all feelings more durable and strong.

Here, at the moment of the century's birth, we find the germs of the æsthetic movement, which, spreading from country to country, continued for more than fifty years to produce, in Germany, France, and Scandinavia, peasant poetry and peasant tales, and in several countries a cult of the peasant dialect. By dissecting these germs in the manner of the botanist, we shall learn the complete natural history of the plant.

Wordsworth's point of departure is purely *topographical.* There is more topography, taking the word in its widest sense, in his works than even in Scott's. His life-task was to describe English nature and English natures as he saw them, face to face. He would never describe anything with which he was not perfectly familiar, and he finally evolved the theory that it was necessary for every poet to associate himself closely with some one particular spot. He associated himself with the English Lake district, which provided him with backgrounds for most of his poems. He went so far as to assert that the birthplace of the individual is the place best suited to be the scene of the activity of his whole life.

Thus it was that he became the painter specially of English nature, and that his descriptions have an essentially local interest. Ruskin was right when he called Wordsworth the great poetical landscape painter of the period. Whilst Byron time after time escaped from his own country to paint the nature of Greece and the East in glowing foreign colours ; whilst Shelley shrank from the climate of England as death to a man of his delicate constitution, and never wearied of extolling the coast and rivers of Italy ; whilst Scott sang the praises of Scotland, and Moore tirelessly proclaimed the beauty of green Erin, Wordsworth stood alone as the pure-bred Englishman, deep-rooted in his native soil as some old spreading oak. His ambition was to be a true English descriptive poet. He had the most intimate, circumstantial acquaintance with the life of the lower classes, and the rural life generally, of the district in which he had his home, walked, sailed, went to church, and received visits from his admirers. He has the same eye for it as a worthy and benevolent parish priest of the type he describes in *The Excursion.* To his special province belong all the events and calamities of common occurrence in an English country parish—the return of a totally forgotten son of the place, to find his home gone and the names of those dear to him carved on gravestones (*The Brothers*) ; the fate of a deceived and deserted girl (*Ruth*) ; an idiot boy's night ride for the doctor, with its mischances (*The Idiot Boy*) ; the strange adventure of a blind Highland boy, with its fortunate ending (*The Blind Highland Boy*); the sorrow caused to an excellent father by the degeneracy of his son (*Michael*); the unfortunate carouse of a carrier beloved by the whole district, and his consequent dismissal from his post (described in four cantos under the title *The Waggoner*).

The only thing un-English about the manner in which these events, even the more cheerful and amusing ones, are communicated to us, is the complete absence of humour. In the place of humour Wordsworth has, as Masson aptly puts it, "a hard, benevolent smile." But the pathos with which he relates the tragic or serious among these simple local stories is pure and heartfelt. It has neither the Pythian tremor nor modern fervour, but its effect is all the more powerful in the case of the great majority of readers, who prefer that the poet should not rise too high above their level, and are conscious of the helpful, healing quality in the compassion which is the source of the pathos—a compassion which resembles that of the clergyman or the doctor, and which, though less spontaneous than professional, moves us by the perfection of its expression.

Nowhere more beautiful is this expression than in such poems as *Simon Lee* and *The Old Cumberland Beggar*. The former tells of an old huntsman who in his youth had surpassed all others in his skill with hounds and horn, his fleetness on foot and on horseback, but who has become so feeble that when the poet meets him one day he is struggling in vain to unearth the rotten root of an old tree.

> "You're overtasked, good Simon Lee,
> Give me your tool," to him I said;
> And at the word right gladly he
> Received my proffered aid.
> I struck, and with a single blow
> The tangled root I severed,
> At which the poor old man so long
> And vainly had endeavoured.
>
> The tears into his eyes were brought,
> And thanks and praises seemed to run
> So fast out of his heart, I thought
> They never would have done.

I've heard of hearts unkind, kind deeds
With coldness still returning;
Alas! the gratitude of men
Hath oftener left me mourning."

Few poets have shown such beautiful reverence as Wordsworth for those humble ancients of the human race who, from no fault of their own, are helpless and useless. Of this *The Old Cumberland Beggar* is the best example. The poet tells how this man, whom every one knows, goes round the neighbourhood calling at every house.

" Him from my childhood have I known; and then
He was so old, he seems not older now:
He travels on, a solitary man,
So helpless in appearance, that for him
The sauntering horseman-traveller does not throw
With careless hand his alms upon the ground,
But stops,—that he may safely lodge the coin
Within the old man's hat; nor quits him so,
But still, when he has given his horse the rein,
Watches the aged beggar with a look
Sidelong—and half-reverted. She who tends
The toll-gate, when in summer at her door
She turns her wheel, if on the road she sees
The aged beggar coming, quits her work,
And lifts the latch for him that he may pass.
The post-boy, when his rattling wheels o'ertake
The aged beggar in the woody lane,
Shouts to him from behind; and, if thus warned
The old man does not change his course, the boy
Turns with less noisy wheels to the road-side,
And passes gently by—without a curse
Upon his lips or anger in his heart.

. . . .

But deem not this man useless.—Statesmen! ye
Who are so restless in your wisdom, ye
Who have a broom still ready in your hands
To rid the world of nuisances; ye proud,
Heart-swoln, while in your pride ye contemplate
Your talents, power, and wisdom, deem him not
A burthen of the earth! 'Tis nature's law
That none, the meanest of created things,
Of forms created the most vile and brute,

The dullest or most noxious, should exist
Divorced from good—a spirit and pulse of good,
A life and soul; to every mode of being
Inseparably linked.

. . . .

Where'er the aged beggar takes his rounds,
The mild necessity of use compels
To acts of love; and habit does the work
Of reason; yet prepares that after-joy
Which reason cherishes. And thus the soul,
By that sweet taste of pleasure unpursued,
Doth find itself insensibly disposed
To virtue and true goodness. . . .
. . . . The easy man
Who sits at his own door,—and, like the pear
That overhangs his head from the green wall,
Feeds in the sunshine; the robust and young,
The prosperous and unthinking, they who live
Sheltered, and flourish in a little grove
Of their own kindred;—all behold in him
A silent monitor, which on their minds
Must needs impress a transitory thought
Of self-congratulation."

Though it must be confessed that this is a sermon, it is a sermon in the very best style. In that same Naturalism which in due time consistently developed into pure humanism and revolt against convention, there was at first an inclination to admonition and to evangelic piety. It sought out the simple-hearted, the poor, the mean in the eyes of the world—for this was Gospel morality. It rejected the highly cultured, and chose as its heroes fishermen and peasants—in this also following Gospel example. Hence it is that we have in Wordsworth perfectly consistent worship of nature along with the exhortatory and evangelically homiletic element which finds such favour in England. And even his purely didactic poems are not to be indiscriminately rejected. There is often a peculiar grandeur in the manner in which the simple lesson is enforced. There is, for instance, real sublimity in the passage in *Laodamia* in which it is impressed upon the sorrowing wife that, instead of craving for the return of her husband, she ought to renounce her desire, and purify herself through her love to enjoy another, nobler, more spiritual life:—

> "Learn by a mortal yearning to ascend
> Towards a higher object.—Love was given,
> Encouraged, sanctioned, chiefly for that end:
> For this the passion to excess was driven—
> That self might be annulled."

Even the abstract *Ode to Duty*, which is inspired by an enthusiasm of the nature of Kant's, contains a couple of magnificent lines which are as contrary to reason as one of the sublime paradoxes of the Fathers of the Church. It is to Duty that the poet cries:

> "Thou dost preserve the Stars from wrong;
> And the most ancient Heavens, through thee, are fresh and strong."

From all the poems of this species, however, the reader will quickly turn again to Wordsworth's specialty, his idylls.

Let us cast another glance at these, and at the theory which their author intended them to illustrate. It is quite certain that Wordsworth attributed more poetical importance to the representation of rural life than is really its due. His surroundings were calculated to produce this theoretical overvaluation. The possibility of making heroes of the shepherd-farmers of Cumberland and Westmoreland was due to the fact that these men (who, though they were independent enough not to be compelled to work for others, were nevertheless obliged to lead an industrious, frugally simple life) possessed real poetical qualifications. The theory that rural life in itself improves and ennobles, is a superstition; it is quite as apt to dull and blunt. Coleridge has, for example, pointed out that when the manner in which the poor-laws were administered in Liverpool, Manchester, and Bristol, was compared with the manner in which relief was distributed in the country, the result was distinctly in favour of the towns.

Wordsworth has, further, over-estimated the importance of the part which the representation of rural occupations plays in his own poetry. Not only do we observe that many of the principal personages in his best poems (such as *Ruth*, *Michael*, *The Brothers*) are not expressly peasants or dwellers in the country ; but we are also conscious that his passion for Naturalism and, in close connection with this, his inclination to try to edify by glorification of the lower classes, have often led him to attribute to a man or woman of low position, qualities and powers which there is little probability of his or her possessing. A paradox which he enounces with evident satisfaction in *The Excursion* is, that many a gifted poet exists, unsuspected, among the lower classes.[1] It is satisfactory to a man with Wordsworth's religious tendencies to believe that talent is independent of wealth and outward position. But even allowing this to be true, would it not still be absurd to make the poet-hero of a poem a chimney-sweep by profession, and then explain in a carefully invented biography how it came to pass that he was, at one and the same time, poet, philosopher, and sweep? Only in real biography are such phenomena permissible; in fiction, Naturalism carried to such an extreme repels by its unlikeliness. And what difference is there between this and the many cases in which Wordsworth puts into the mouth of a pedlar, a leech-gatherer, a labourer, words which we cannot but be astonished to hear from such lips? Hence, to justify and explain his characters, he is obliged to introduce numbers of accidental, subordinate details of the kind required to prove the possibility of a fact in real life, but of the kind which we willingly forgo in poetry. The excessive attention paid to probability, the petty anxiety to explain the reason of everything, have a fatiguing effect—especially in the long introductions and descriptions in *The Excursion*, which Byron wittily calls Wordsworth's "eternal: Here we go up, up, and up, and here we go down, down, and here round about, round about!"

Wordsworth's choice of themes leads him, moreover, to

[1] Oh! many are the poets that are sown
By nature! men endowed with highest gifts,
The vision and the faculty divine,
Yet wanting the accomplishment of verse.
—*Excursion:* Book I.

a singularity in the matter of language which may be termed the extreme literary issue of this Naturalism. It was his theory that the language spoken by the class which he described was, when purified from its defects, the best of all, "because such men hourly communicate with the best objects from which the best part of language is originally derived; and because, from their rank in society and the sameness and narrow circle of their intercourse, being less under the influence of social vanity, they convey their feelings and emotions in simple and unelaborated expressions." It is, consequently, his opinion, that it is impossible for any author to find a better manner of expression, no matter whether he is writing in prose or in verse. And this leads him to the enunciation of his famous and interesting paradox: *that there neither is nor can be any essential difference between the language of prose and metrical composition.* If this only meant disapprobation of all the tiresome and foolish distortions of language, to which the scarcity of rhymes and the lack of the gift of rhythm have driven so many of even the most eminent poets, we should heartily agree with him. Théodore de Banville has, with reason on his side—though it is the severe reason which demands the impossible—given as contents to the chapter in his *Petit Traité de Poésie française* entitled *Licentia poetica,* simply the words: "Il n'y en a pas." But it is an entirely different meaning which Wordsworth intends his maxim to convey. He maintains not only that the language of a large portion of every good poem must necessarily, except with reference to the metre, in no respect differ from that of good prose, but likewise that some of the most interesting parts of the very best poems will be found to be strictly the language of prose. For, however lively and truthful the poet's language may be, there cannot be a doubt, says Wordsworth, that it must, in liveliness and truth, fall far short of that which is uttered by men in real life; in other words—it can never surpass, and only at its best approach, the prose of reality. This theory he defended with genuine English obstinacy against the attacks made upon it from every direction. He quotes, as a specimen of the parodies of poetry in which the language closely resembles that of life and nature, Dr. Johnson's stanza:

"I put my hat upon my head
And walked into the Strand,
And there I met another man,
Whose hat was in his hand."

This is not poetry, says the public. Granted! says Wordsworth. But the proper thing to be said is not: This is not poetry; but: This is wanting in meaning; it is neither interesting in itself, nor can it lead to anything interesting; consequently it cannot excite thought or feeling in the reader. "Why take pains to prove that an ape is not a Newton, when it is self-evident that he is not a man?" The accepted idea is, according to Wordsworth, that an author, by the act of writing in verse, makes a formal engagement that he will gratify certain known habits of association, that certain classes of idea and expression will be found in his book, but that others will be carefully excluded. This doctrine Wordsworth opposes with the declaration of his conviction of the similarity of good poetry and good prose, a conviction which was founded on dislike of poetic affectation, but which led him in his own poetry, now to the narrowest limitation, now to the utmost possible flattening out of his own in many respects masterly and model style.

There is more than one argument against the extremely high estimation of the language of the rural population which forms Wordsworth's starting-point, and which is not without its resemblance to the cult of the peasant language initiated in Denmark by Grundtvig and in Norway by the "Maalstræverе" (agitators for the universal employment of the peasant language). The principal one is, that the language of the peasant, purified, as Wordsworth demands, from provincial expressions and subjected to the rules of grammar, is not different from that of any other sensible man, except in this, that the peasant's ideas are fewer and vaguer. By reason of its inferior degree of development, his mind dwells only upon single, isolated facts, drawn from his own narrow experience, or from the records of traditional belief, whereas the educated man sees the connection between things, and seeks for universal laws. Wordsworth is of opinion that the *best* part of language is derived from the objects which surround and occupy the peasant. But the ideas connected with food, shelter, safety, comfort, are surely not those which provide the best part of language. Nor can we agree with him when he asserts that nothing but the infusion of a certain degree of passion into this language is required to entitle it to be called poetic; for passion neither creates new thoughts nor new provision of words; it only increases the force of those already in existence; it cannot be expected to make the language of daily intercourse poetry, when it is hardly capable of making it prose.

What strikes us from the very first in Wordsworth's vindication of Naturalism is his confounding of two things—prose, and what he calls "ordinary language," terms which he applies indiscriminately. Good prose is language which has been purified from the vain and meaningless repetitions and the uncertain, halting phraseology which are the inevitable outcome of the confusion due to insufficient education. Wordsworth has too frequently neglected this purifying process, when introducing dramatic dialogue into his own poems. It is this unfortunate passion for the most grovellingly exact imitation, which produces the sudden and disagreeable transitions from passages in a noble, elevated style, to passages with no style at all. See, for example, *The Blind Highland Boy*.

"Poetry," says Wordsworth, "takes its origin from emotion recollected in tranquillity." The aim of the poet is the truthful imitation of nature, with the one restriction, that of the necessity of giving pleasure—not merely the straightforward, direct truth; therefore he employs the metrical form of composition, which provides the reader with small, but continual and regular impulses of pleasurable surprise. Metre produces its effect by continually arousing and satisfying curiosity, but in such a simple manner that it does not draw any separate attention to itself. It acts powerfully but unobservedly upon the mind, like artificially altered air, or the wine drunk during an eager discussion. By its steady recurrence it tempers and modifies the excitement or pain produced by the intelligence communicated; and by its tendency to divest language of its reality, it throws a sort of half consciousness of unsubstantial existence over the whole composition. Except for this, declares Wordsworth, even the best poetry can in no respect differ from prose. He forgets to ask himself if there are not numbers of common phrases and expressions which, though they are perfectly allowable in prose, would produce a most unpleasant effect in poetry; and forgets, too, to ask if it is not possible that in every serious poem there may occur, without any artificiality, sentences of a construction, and imagery of a kind, which would be impossible in prose.

The only way in which the best poetry corresponds with "the very language of men," is in its expressions resembling those which some few of the most highly cultivated would use on the rarest occasions. In daily converse language wanders unrestrainedly; in public speech it is restrained by imperative connection and continuity of thought; in the prose work, the carefully elaborated sentence progresses naturally through all its twists and turnings; in verse, the form cannot be too exquisite or too compact. Here the doctrine applies which Théophile Gautier preached in his splendid poem, *L'Art*:—

"Oui, l'œuvre sort plus belle
D'une forme au travail
Rebelle,
Vers, marbre, onyx, émail!

Point de contraintes fausses!
Mais que pour marcher droit
Tu chausses,
Muse, un cothurne étroit!"

But, however much there is to be said against Wordsworth's poetics, or "prosaics," as they might more correctly be called—against theories which were at first accepted as synonymous with the "Fair is foul, and foul is fair" of the witches in Macbeth—they are in the highest degree interesting to the student of literature to-day as an accurate and unambiguous expression of the first literary extreme to which English Naturalism went.

VII

NATURALISTIC ROMANTICISM

We have for a moment lost sight of Coleridge. When Wordsworth and he divided the new kinds of poetry between them, there fell to his share, as the reader will remember, a task which was the exact opposite of Wordsworth's, namely, the treating of supernatural subjects in a natural manner. He fulfilled it in his contributions to the volume published under the title of *Lyrical Ballads*, and indeed in the greater proportion of the little collection of poems which entitles him to rank high among English poets.

Samuel Taylor Coleridge was a country boy, the son of a Devonshire clergyman. He was born in October 1772. From 1782 to 1790 he was at school in London. It was during those school-days, spent at Christ's Hospital, that his friendship with another English Romanticist, his warm admirer, Charles Lamb, was formed. From 1791 to 1793 he studied at Cambridge. He had neither means nor prospects, and in a fit of despair, occasioned either by his debts or by an unhappy love affair, he suddenly enlisted in the 15th Regiment of Light Dragoons, under the name of Silas Titus Cumberback.[1] It certainly does not seem to have been ambition (as in the case of Johannes Ewald a few years earlier) which prompted him to try his fortune as a soldier, but simply want of any other means of subsistence. He was only four months a dragoon. On the stable wall underneath his saddle, he one day scribbled the Latin lament :—

"Eheu quam infortuni miserrimum est fuisse felicem !"

---

1 "Being at a loss, when suddenly asked my name, I answered Cumberback ; and verily my habits were so little equestrian, that my horse, I doubt not, was of that opinion."

This was discovered by his captain, who inquired into the position of affairs, and arranged with Coleridge's family for his return to Cambridge. On this followed the short period during which the young poet was an anti-orthodox democrat. As such he could expect no advancement in the University. His and Southey's glorification of Robespierre (the first act of *The Fall of Robespierre* was written by Coleridge, the second and third are Southey's) and their wild project of a communistic settlement have been already mentioned. The little emigrant society they founded consisted only of themselves and two other members, a young Quaker named Lovell, and George Burnet, a school friend of Southey's. But the God Hymen had decided that the year 1795 should witness the wreck of the plans which boded so ill for society. In 1795 Coleridge went to lecture at Bristol, where he displayed the eloquence which (as in the case of the similarly eloquent and persuasive Welhaven) seems to have sapped his power of poetic production. A young lady in the town of Bristol won his heart; and before the year was over, Sara Fricker was married to Coleridge, her sisters, Edith and Mary, to Lovell and Southey—and the emigration plan was abandoned. Coleridge, who was without will-power all his life, could never have carried out a plan laid so long beforehand. He never succeeded in doing anything except what he had not determined to do, or what, from its nature, could not be determined beforehand.

In 1796 the young man, who was still an enthusiastic Unitarian, allowed himself to be persuaded by some other philanthropists—he is always "persuaded"—to publish a weekly magazine called *The Watchman*, which was to consist of thirty-two pages, large octavo, and to cost the reasonable price of fourpence. Its flaming prospectus bore the motto, "Knowledge is power." With the object of enlisting subscribers, the young and ardent propagandist undertook a tour of the country between Bristol and Sheffield, preaching in most of the great towns, "as an hireless volunteer, in a blue coat and white waistcoat, that not a rag of the woman of Babylon might be seen on me." The description he has given of this, his Odyssey, shows us the young English Romanticist as he was then and as he continued to be—imprudent in worldly matters, enthusiastic in behalf now of this, now of that religious or political half-truth, yet with a humorous appreciation of his own and others' ridiculousness.

"My campaign commenced at Birmingham; and my first attack was on a rigid Calvinist, a tallow-chandler by trade. He was a tall, dingy man, in whom length was so predominant over breadth that he might almost have been borrowed for a foundry poker. O that face! I have it before me at this moment. The lank, black, twine-like hair, *pinguinitescent*, cut in a straight line along the black stubble of his thin gunpowder eyebrows, that looked like a scorched after-math from a last week's shaving. His coat collar behind in perfect unison, both of colour and lustre, with the coarse yet glib cordage that I suppose he called his hair, and which with a bend inward at the nape of the neck (the only approach to flexure in his whole figure) slunk in behind his waistcoat; while the countenance, lank, dark, very hard, and with strong perpendicular furrows, gave me a dim notion of some one looking at me through a used gridiron, all soot, grease, and iron! But he was one of the thorough-bred, a true lover of liberty, and (I was informed) had proved to the satisfaction of many, that Mr. Pitt was one of the horns of the second beast in the Revelation, *that spoke like a dragon*." For half-an-hour Coleridge employed all the resources of his eloquence—argued, described, promised, prophesied, beginning with the captivity of nations and ending with the millennium. "My taper man of lights listened with perseverance and praiseworthy patience, though (as I was afterwards told on complaining of certain odours that were not altogether ambrosial) it was a melting-day with him. 'And what, sir,' he said, after a short pause, 'might the cost be?' 'Only fourpence, only fourpence, sir, each number, to be published on every eighth day.' 'That comes to a good deal of money at the end of the year. And how much did you say there was to be for the money?' 'Thirty-two pages, sir! large octavo, closely printed.' 'Thirty and two pages? Bless me, why, except what I does in a family way on the Sabbath, that's more than I ever reads, sir! all the year round. I am as great a one as any man in Brummagem, sir! for liberty and truth and all them sort of things, but as to this, no offence, sir, I must beg to be excused.'"

Thus ended Coleridge's first attempt at recruiting for the war against the Holy Trinity. His second he made in Manchester, where he tried to enlist a stately and opulent wholesale dealer in cottons. This man measured him from top to toe, and asked if he had any bill or invoice of the thing. Coleridge presented him with the prospectus. He rapidly skimmed and hummed over the first side, and still more rapidly the second and concluding page, then most deliberately and significantly rubbed and smoothed one part against the other, put it in his pocket, turned his back with an "Overrun with these articles!" and retired into his counting-house.

After these unsuccessful attempts, the young man gave up the plan of canvassing from house to house, but nevertheless returned from this memorable tour with almost a thousand names on his list of subscribers. But, alas! the publication of the very first number was, as any one knowing Coleridge might have expected, delayed beyond the day announced for its appearance; the second, which contained an essay against fast-days, lost him nearly five hundred subscribers at a blow; and the two following numbers, which were full of attacks on French philosophy and morals, and directed against those "who pleaded to the poor and ignorant instead of pleading for them," made enemies of all his Jacobin and democratic patrons. Coleridge, who communicates all these details himself, does not seem to have any suspicion that he was only receiving a natural punishment for his indecision—an indecision which consisted in never being prepared to accept the consequences of his own theories. He was undecided in politics, undecided in religion. Writing, as an old man, of this time, he himself says: "My head was with Spinoza, though my whole heart remained with Paul and John;" and he hastens to provide his readers with those convincing proofs of the existence of God and the Holy Trinity which he had not been capable of perceiving in his youth.[1] After the appear-

[1] See *Biographia Literaria.*

ance of about a dozen numbers, *The Watchman* had to be given up, and Coleridge took to writing for the newspapers. He began by attacking Pitt's Government, but in course of time, his opinions tending ever more in a conservative direction, he became its ardent supporter, and also, after the occupation of Switzerland by the French, an enemy of France. So hostile to that country were his articles in the *Morning Post*, that they even attracted the attention of Napoleon, and Coleridge became the object of the First Consul's special enmity. He would probably have been arrested during his residence in Italy, if he had not received timely warning from the Prussian ambassador, Wilhelm von Humboldt, and, through an inferior official, from Napoleon's own uncle, Cardinal Fesch.

The year 1797, in the course of which Coleridge became acquainted with Wordsworth, was, as regards his poetry, the most important in his life; for it was in this year that he wrote his famous ballad, *The Ancient Mariner*, and *Christabel*, the fragment which marks a new era in English poetry.

Christabel was planned as the first of a series of poetical romances, the remainder of which never came into being. It is, without doubt, the first English poem which is permeated by the genuine Romantic spirit; and the new cadences, the new theme, the new style of versification, the novelty generally, made a powerful impression on contemporary poets. The irregular and yet melodious metre appealed so strongly to Scott that he employed it in his first Romantic poem, *The Lay of the Last Minstrel.* He frankly confesses how much he owed to the beautiful and tantalising fragment, *Christabel*, which he, like the other poets of the period, made acquaintance with in manuscript; for Coleridge read it aloud in social gatherings for twenty years before it saw the light as public property. Byron, too, heard it first on one of these occasions. Before hearing it he had, in one of his longer poems (*The Siege of Corinth*, xix.), written some lines which were not unlike some in *Christabel.* To these lines he, on a future occasion, appended a note in which he praises Coleridge's "wild and singularly original and beautiful poem." But we see from Moore's *Life and Letters* that there were critics who refused the meed of admiration accorded to *Christabel* by Scott and Byron, and still more freely by Wordsworth. Jeffrey and Moore himself consider it affected (*Memoirs*, ii. 101; iv. 48). Danish critics, thoroughly initiated into the mysteries of this style by Tieck and the brothers Schlegel, and by their own poet Ingemann, cannot possibly attach so much importance to this fragment. Its excessive naïveté and simplicity, the intentional childishness in style and tone, are to us what buns are to bakers' children. The chief merit of the poem, apart from its full-toned, sweet melody, lies in the peculiar power with which the nature of the wicked fairy is presented to us, the *dæmonic* element, which had never been present in such force in English literature before. We must, however, remember that, though the first part of the poem was written in 1797, the second was written and the first revised in 1800—that is to say, *after* Coleridge had travelled with Wordsworth in Germany, and there made acquaintance with contemporary German poetry, its medieval ground-work, and its latest tendency.

Coleridge's one other poem of any length, *The Ancient Mariner*, which is even more artificially naïve in style than *Christabel*, and is provided, in the manner of the medieval ballads retailed in the little shops in back streets, with a prose index of contents on the margin of the pages, is now the most popular of all his poems, although it was fiercely attacked on its first appearance. On a very unnatural introduction (three guests on their way to a wedding are stopped, and one of them is led to forget his destination, so eloquent is the ancient mariner—"and on the street, too," as Falstaff says) follows a story of all the horrors, ghostly and material, which ensue, because one of the sailors on a ship has been thoughtless enough to kill an albatross which had alighted on the rigging. The whole crew, with the exception of this one man, die, as a punishment for the act of inhospitality. Swinburne tells that, when the poem was new, the English critics were greatly occupied with the question whether its moral (that one should not shoot albatrosses) was not so preponderant that it destroyed the fantastic effect of the poem ; whilst others maintained that the defect of the poem was its want of a practical moral. Long afterwards the same matter formed the subject of a dispute between Freiligrath and Julian Schmidt. Modern criticism would willingly excuse the absence of any moral in the ballad if it could find a poetic central idea in it.

A comparison may serve to show its chief shortcoming. In a collection of poems by the Austrian lyric poet, Moritz Hartmann, entitled *Zeitlosen*, there is to be found one which, although it does not profess to owe its origin to *The Ancient Mariner*, at first sight strikes the reader as being a direct imitation of it. The metrical form is the same, and in the theme there is a close resemblance. *Der Camao* is the title of the poem. The Camao, which answers to Coleridge's albatross, is a bird which, in the Middle Ages, was kept in every house in the Pyrenean Peninsula, and treated with a reverence which had its source in a widespread superstition. It was believed, namely, that this bird could not thrive in a house on which rested the stain of a wife's infidelity ; it died if there was even the slightest spot on the honour of its master. Its beautiful cage generally hung in the entrance chamber. In Hartmann's poem the old, deranged man who answers to Coleridge's demented mariner, tells how he, as a page, was seized with a violent passion for his master's wife, and how, every time he rushed from her presence, in despair at her coldness and displeasure, he was tortured as he left her apartments by the bird's song in honour of the chastity of the lady to whom it owed its life. The master of the house returns from the war bringing with him his friend, a handsome young minstrel and hero, whom the lady honours with her friendship, and who is, in consequence, soon hated by the jealous page. Quite beside himself, the young man denounces the lady and her friend to his master ; but the latter calmly answers that Camao is still alive, and at that moment singing in his mistress's honour. In his jealous, vindictive rage the page kills the bird ; Vasco kills his wife ; and thenceforward the criminal wanders, demented and restless, from country to country, seeking rest, but finding it nowhere.

As regards virtuosity and originality in the matter of diction, *Der Camao* is not for a moment to be compared with *The Ancient Mariner;* but as regards the poetic central idea, the German poem is not only much superior to its English model, but is in itself a complete, satisfactory criticism of Coleridge's ballad and all the artificial English theories which it represents. In *Der Camao* the slaughter of the bird is a real human action performed with a real human motive; the punishment is not a caprice, but a just and natural consequence of the misdeed. The misfortune which the killing of the bird brings to Vasco and his wife has a natural cause and effect connection with that deed, whilst the death of the whole ship's crew, as the result of the cruelty shown to the albatross, is folly. The comparison assists us to a clear understanding of the difference between a true poetical conception of the superstitious idea and a Romantic treatment of it. The story in both poems is founded on a superstition. Hartmann has no desire to submit the superstition to the criticism of reason; but he forces it upon no one; the beauty of his poem is quite independent of the belief or disbelief of his reader in the miraculous susceptibility of the Camao. Romantic extravagance, on the other hand, proclaims reverence for the marvellous and inexplicable to be the sum and substance of all wisdom and of all poetry.

But though *The Ancient Mariner* may not take a high place when compared with poetry which has extricated itself from Romantic swaddling-bands, it stands high above most of the kindred productions of German Romanticism. In spite of all its Romantic fictitiousness, it breathes of the sea, the real, natural sea, whose changing moods and whose terrifying, menacing immensity it describes. The fresh breeze, the seething foam, the horrible fog, and the hot, copper-coloured evening sky with its blood-red sun—all these elements are nature's own; and the misery of the men tossing helplessly on the ocean, the starvation, the burning thirst that drives them to suck the blood from their own arms, the pallid countenances, the terrible death-rattle, the horrible putrefaction—all these elements are realities, represented with English realistic force.

And it is a very English trait that Coleridge himself should have been thoroughly capable of seeing the weak points of such a poem as his own famous ballad. The national quality of humour assisted him to this independence of judgment. We have the following anecdote from his own pen. "An amateur performer in verse expressed a strong desire to be introduced to me, but hesitated in accepting my friend's immediate offer, on the score that he was, he must acknowledge, the author of a confounded severe epigram on my *Ancient Mariner*, which had given me great pain. I assured my friend that if the epigram was a good one, it would only increase my desire to become acquainted with the author, and begged to hear it recited, when, to my no less surprise than amusement, it proved to be one which I had myself inserted in the *Morning Post.*" When Coleridge tells us, too, that he himself wrote three sonnets expressly for the purpose of exciting a good-natured laugh at the artificial simplicity and doleful egotism of the new poetical tendency, and that he took the elaborate and swelling language and imagery of these sonnets from his own poems, we cannot deny that his endeavours to keep free from the entanglement in theories which was the weak point in German Romanticism, bespeak rare intellectual superiority.

It was, nevertheless, from Germany that Coleridge's intellect received its most invigorating and essential nourishment. He was the first Englishman who penetrated into the forest of German literature, which was as yet unexplored by foreigners; he made his way into it about the same time as Madame de Staël, the pioneer of the Latin races. Whilst he was producing the famous poems just described, he began the study of German. Schiller and Kant attracted him first. In 1798 he and Wordsworth went to Germany on a literary voyage of discovery. In Hamburg they visited the patriarch Klopstock, who praised Bürger to them, but spoke coldly and disparagingly of the rest of the younger literary men, and especially of Coleridge's idols, Kant and Schiller. The latter's *Die Räuber* he professed himself unable to read. But he had plenty to say on the subject of *The*

Messiah and his extreme satisfaction with the English translations of it. While in Germany, Coleridge studied the Gothic language, and read the Meistersingers and Hans Sachs; and on his return he published a translation of Schiller's *Wallenstein*, the play which Benjamin Constant was soon afterwards to adapt for the French stage.

It was about this time that Coleridge settled in the *Lake* district, where Wordsworth and Southey had already taken up their abode—the district which gave its name to the literary school constituted, as their contemporaries chose to consider, by these three poets. The name, as a matter of fact, does not mean much more than if, in Denmark in 1830, Hauch, Ingemann, Wilster, and Peder Hjort, had been dubbed Sorists. The English poets of the Lake School were quite as unlike each other in their gifts as were these Sorö professors. But the criticism of the day always coupled Coleridge's name with Wordsworth's and Southey's because it was known that he was on intimate and friendly terms with them, because he never missed an opportunity of praising them, nor they of praising him, and because he and the other Lakists were crowned every three months with fresh laurels in the *Quarterly Review*, whilst the sinner Byron was chastised with fresh scorpions. Though Coleridge published almost nothing, Wordsworth and Southey were hardly ever under the cascade of criticism without some drops of it falling upon him. The circumstance that the Lake poets aimed (in much the same manner as the Pre-Raphaelite and the Nazarene painters) at poetic intensity, a childlike disposition and a childlike faith, pious blandness and priestly unction, exposed the man who could not but be regarded as the teacher of the school to much satire and derision. As a youth, in his poem *Fire, Famine, and Slaughter*, Coleridge had made all the horrors, one by one, reply to the question: Who bid you rage? with the following refrain, applying to Pitt:—

"Who bade you do't?
        The same! the same!
Letters four do form his name.
He let me loose, and cried Halloo!
To him alone the praise is due."

Now he was Mr. Pitt's journalistic henchman, and, like all the other members of the Lake School, a strict Tory, the enemy of liberal opinions in everything relating to church and state. What wonder that he was classed along with the others in the constant party attacks made by the Liberals! And yet it would have been so easy and so natural to distinguish him as a poet from all the others, and to pay him the honour which was due to his originality. The few poems which he wrote in the course of a comparatively long life are distinguished by the exquisite melodiousness of their language; their harmonies are not only delicate and insinuating like Shelley's, but contrapuntally constructed and rich; they have a peculiar, ponderous sweetness; each line has the taste and weight of a drop of honey. In poems such as *Love* and *Lewti*, which are the two sweetest, and in an Oriental fantasy like *Kubla Khan*, which was inspired by a dream, we hear Coleridge flute and pipe and sing with all the changing cadences of the most exquisite nightingale voice. It is Swinburne who makes the apt remark that, in the matter of harmonies, Shelley is, compared with Coleridge, what a lark is compared with a nightingale.

But Coleridge's poetry is as unplastic as it is melodious, and as unimpassioned as it is mellifluous. It is of the fantastic Romantic order; that is to say, it neither expresses strong, personally experienced emotions, nor reproduces what the author has observed in the surrounding world. In this last connection it is interesting to know that Coleridge's long tour in the south was altogether without results as far as his poetry was concerned. The only poem he brought home with him, the *Hymn Before Sunrise in the Vale of Chamouni*, a valley in which he never set foot, was composed with the assistance of the description of the locality given by the well-known Danish authoress, Friederike Brun. His historic sense was as defective as his sense of locality. He says himself: "Dear Sir Walter Scott and myself are exact, but harmonious opposites in this—that every old ruin, hill, river, or tree called up in his mind a host of historical or biographical associations . . . whereas for myself, I believe I should walk on the plain of Marathon without taking more interest in it than in any other plain of similar features. . . . Charles Lamb wrote an essay on a man who lived in past time:—I thought of adding another to it on one who lived not *in time* at all, past, present, or future—but beside or collaterally."[1] His poetry is, thence, in the literal sense of the word, visionary; the poem which the best critics consider the finest, he composed in a dream.

In his own life there was as little of will and plan as in a dream. Somewhat indolent by nature, he became more and more procrastinating as years went on; and the result of his procrastination was an accumulation of difficulties which he had not energy and application enough to overcome. To relieve physical suffering he had recourse to opium, and soon became a confirmed opium-eater, thereby increasing his incapacity to carry out any plan. After a period of wandering, living first in one, then in another friend's house, and either writing for magazines or giving lectures on the history of literature, he decided that he was unfit to manage himself and his affairs, and from 1816 onwards he lived at Highgate in the house and under the control of a doctor named Gillman—separated from his own family, whom he left to the care of his friend and brother-in-law, Southey.

On the indulgence in opium followed remorse and self-reproach and increasingly orthodox piety. Most of what Coleridge now wrote was written with the object of refuting the heresies of his youth and defending the doctrine of the Trinity and the Church of England against all attacks.[2] Emerson, who paid him a visit, describes him as "old and preoccupied"; enraged by the effrontery with which a handful of Priestleians dared to attack the doctrine of the Trinity propounded by Paul and accepted unchallenged for centuries; and falling in his talk into all manner of commonplaces. Eighteen years passed, spent in dreaming, talking, and composing edifying essays. His influence during this

[1] *Specimens of the Table Talk of the Late Samuel T. Coleridge*, ii. 225.

[2] "On the Constitution of Church and State according to the Ideal of Each": *Lay Sermons*.

period was due much less to his productive power than to the manner in which he incited to production. He stimulated and goaded others to the pitch of expressing themselves publicly. Residing close to London, and constantly visited, because of his conversational powers, by the best writers of the day—Charles Lamb, Wordsworth, Southey, Leigh Hunt, Hazlitt, Carlyle—he was a looker-on on life during the years when the great representatives of the opposite intellectual tendency to his, Shelley and Byron, were pouring forth their fiery denunciations of the order of society and state which he considered so excellent. Without will of his own, under control, and himself protected like a child, Coleridge became ever more and more the would-be protector of society, whilst the two great poets of liberty, banished from their homes and thrown entirely on their own resources, developed an independence unexampled in the history of literature, and, protected neither by themselves nor any one else, were shattered long before their time by the ardour of conflict. The right of personal investigation and personal liberty were as precious treasures to them as the Church of England was to Coleridge.

VIII

THE LAKE SCHOOL'S CONCEPTION OF LIBERTY

COLERIDGE and the other members of the Lake School would never have dreamt of calling themselves anything but warm friends of liberty; the days were past when the reactionaries called themselves by another name. Coleridge wrote one of his most beautiful poems, the *Ode to France,* in the form of a hymn to liberty, to his constant love for which he calls clouds, waves, and forests to testify; and Wordsworth, who dedicated two long series of his poems to liberty, regarded himself as her acknowledged champion. A cursory glance at the works of these poets might well leave us with the impression that they were as true lovers of liberty as Moore, or Shelley, or Byron. But the word liberty in their mouths meant something different from what it did in Moore's, or Shelley's, or Byron's. To understand this we must dissect the word by means of two simple questions: freedom, from what?—liberty, to do what?

To these conservative poets freedom is a perfectly definite thing, a right which England has and the other countries of Europe have not—the right of a country to govern itself, untyrannised over by an autocratic ruler of foreign extraction. The country which has this privilege is free. By liberty, then, the men in question understood freedom from foreign political tyranny; there is no thought of liberty of action in their conception at all. Look through Wordsworth's *Sonnets Dedicated to Liberty*, and see what it is they celebrate. It is the struggle of the different nations against Napoleon, who is described as a species of Antichrist. (Scott calls him "the Devil on his burning throne.")

The poet mourns the conquest of Spain, Switzerland, Venice, the Tyrol, by the French; he chants the praises of Hofer, the undaunted, of brave Schill, and daring Toussaint L'Ouverture, the men who ventured to face the fierce conquerors; and he sings with quite as great admiration of the King of Sweden, who with romantically chivalrous folly threw down the gauntlet to Napoleon, and proclaimed his longing for the restoration of the Bourbons. (Ere long Victor Hugo and Lamartine, in their character of supporters of the Legitimist monarchy, followed suit in singing the praises of the Swedish king and his son, Prince Gustavus Vasa.) Hatred of Napoleon becomes aversion for France. In one of the sonnets ("Inland, within a hollow vale, I stood") Wordsworth tells how the "barrier flood" between England and France for a moment seemed to him to have dwindled to the dimensions of a river, and how he shrank from the thought of "the frightful neighbourhood"; in another he rejoices in the remembrance of the great men and great books England has produced, and remarks that France has brought forth "no single volume paramount . . . no master spirit," that with her there is "equally a want of books and men."

He always comes back to England. His sonnets are one long declaration of love to the country for which he feels "as a lover or a child," the country of which he writes: "Earth's best hopes are all with thee." He follows her through her long war, celebrating, like Southey, each of her victories; and it is significant of his attitude that, appended to the *Sonnets Dedicated to Liberty*, we find the great, pompous thanksgiving ode for the battle of Waterloo. We of to-day ask what kind of liberty it was that Waterloo gained; but we know full well that the group of poets whose heroes were the national heroes—Pitt, Nelson, and Wellington, and who sang the praises of the English constitution as being in itself liberty, and lauded England as the model nation, won a degree of favour with the majority of their countrymen to which their great poetic antagonists have not even yet attained. Wordsworth and his school considered the nation ideal as it was, whereas the others tried to compel it to turn its eyes towards an ideal, not only unattained, but as yet unrecognised; the former flattered it, and were rewarded with laurels; the latter educated and castigated it, and were spurned by it. Scott was offered the post of Poet Laureate, and Southey and Wordsworth in turn occupied it; but to this day the English nation has shown no public recognition of what it owes to Shelley and Byron.[1] And the reason is, that these men's conception of liberty was utterly different from that of the Lake School. To them it was not realised in a nation or a constitution—for it was no accomplished, finished thing; neither was their idea of the struggle for liberty realised in a highly egoistic war against a revolutionary conqueror. They felt strongly what an absence of liberty, political as well as intellectual, religious as well as social, there might be under a so-called *free* constitution. They had no inclination to write poems in honour of the glorious attainments of the human race, and more especially of their own countrymen; for in the so-called land of freedom they felt a terrible, oppressive want of freedom—of liberty to think without consideration of recognised dogmas, to write without paying homage to public opinion, to act as it was natural to men of their character to act, without injury from the verdict of those who, because they had no particular character of their own, were the most clamorous and unmerciful condemners of the faults which accompanied independence, originality, and genius. They saw that in this "free" country the ruling caste canted and lied, extorted and plundered, curbed and constrained quite as much as did the one great autocrat with his absolute power—and without his excuse, the authority of intellect and of genius.

To the poets of the Lake School, coercion was not coercion when it was *English*, tyranny was not tyranny when it was practised under a *constitutional monarchy*, hostility to enlightenment was not hostility to enlightenment when it was displayed by a *Protestant* church. The Radical poets called coercion coercion, even when it proceeded to action with the English flag flying and the arms of England as its policemen's badge; they cherished towards monarchs generally, the objection of the Lake School poets to absolute monarchs; they desired

[1] This year (1875) Disraeli, as Chairman of the Byron Memorial Committee, has started a subscription for the erection of a statue to Byron on some prominent site in London.

to free the world not only from the dominion of the Roman Catholic priesthood, but from priestly tutelage of every description. When they heard poets of the other school, who in the ardour of youth had been as progressive as themselves, extolling the Tory Government of England with the fervour which distinguishes renegades, they could not but regard them as enemies of liberty. Therefore it is that Shelley, in his sonnet to Wordsworth, writes:—

> "In honoured poverty thy voice did weave
> Songs consecrate to truth and liberty.
> Deserting these, thou leavest me to grieve,
> Thus having been, that thou shouldst cease to be."

Therefore it is that Byron is tempted again and again "to cut up Southey like a gourd." And therefore it is that the love of liberty of the Radical poets is a divine frenzy, a sacred fire, of which not a spark is to be found in the Platonic love of the Lake School. When Shelley sings to liberty:—

> "But keener thy gaze than the lightning's glare,
> And swifter thy step than the earthquake's tramp;
> Thou deafenest the rage of the ocean; thy stare
> Makes blind the volcanoes; the sun's bright lamp
> To thine is a fen-fire damp;"

we feel that this liberty is not a thing which we can grasp with our hands, or confer as a gift in a constitution, or inscribe among the articles of a state-church. It is the eternal cry of the human spirit, its never-ending requirement of itself; it is the spark of heavenly fire which Prometheus placed in the human heart when he formed it, and which it has been the work of the greatest among men to fan into the flame that is the source of all light and all warmth in those who feel that life would be dark as the grave and cold as stone without it. This liberty makes its appearance in each new century with a new name. In the Middle Ages it was persecuted and stamped out under the name of heresy; in the sixteenth century it was championed and opposed under the name of the Reformation; in the seventeenth it was sentenced to the stake as witchcraft and atheism; in the eighteenth it became first a philosophical gospel, and then, through the Revolution, a political power; in the nineteenth it receives from the champions of the past the new nickname of Radicalism.

What the poets of the Lake School extolled was a definite, actually existing *sum of liberties*—not liberty. What the revolutionary poets extolled was undoubtedly true liberty; but their conception was so extremely ideal, that in practical matters they too often shot beyond the mark. In the weakening of all established government they saw only the weakening of bad government; in the half-barbaric revolts of oppressed races they saw the dawn of perfect liberty. Shelley had so little knowledge of his fellow-men that he thought the great victory would be won if he could exterminate kings and priests at a blow; and Byron's life was almost over before he learned by experience how few republican virtues the European revolutionists leagued together in the name of liberty possessed. The poets of the Lake School were safeguarded against the generous delusions and overhastiness of the Radical poets; but posterity has derived more pleasure and profit from the aberrations due to the love of liberty in the latter than from the carefully hedged in and limited Liberalism of the former.

IX

THE LAKE SCHOOL'S ORIENTAL ROMANTICISM

THIS is the time to notice the man who was Byron's and Shelley's worst enemy and Coleridge's best friend, and who, inferior as his productions are to those of his friend, deserves also to have his name coupled with Coleridge's as a famous English Romanticist.

Robert Southey, born in Bristol in 1774, was the son of a linen-draper there, and to the end of his life a man who produced the impression that he had been born in narrow circumstances, in a corner of the world with a narrow spiritual horizon. After studying a short time at Oxford, he, like the other poets of the Lake School, became infected by the spirit of the Revolution. In 1794 he wrote an extremely Jacobinical poem, *Wat Tyler.* About the same time he composed the following inscription for the room in which Martin, the regicide, had been confined:—

> "For thirty years secluded from mankind
> Here Martin linger'd. Often have these walls
> Echo'd his footsteps, as with even tread
> He paced around his prison. Not to him
> Did Nature's fair varieties exist;
> He never saw the sun's delightful beams,
> Save when through yon high bars he pour'd a sad
> And broken splendour. Dost thou ask his crime?
> *He had rebell'd against the King, and sat*
> *In judgment on him;* for his ardent mind
> Shaped goodliest plans of happiness on earth,
> And peace and liberty. Wild dreams! but such
> As Plato lov'd. . . ."

The following rather clever parody was inserted by Mr. Canning in the *Anti-Jacobin*:—

"INSCRIPTION FOR THE DOOR OF THE CELL IN NEWGATE, WHERE MRS. BROWNRIGG, THE 'PRENTICE-CIDE, WAS CONFINED, PREVIOUS TO HER EXECUTION.

" For one long term, or ere her trial came,
Here Brownrigg linger'd. Often have these cells
Echo'd her blasphemies, as with shrill voice
She scream'd for fresh geneva. Not to her
Did the blithe fields of Tothill, or thy street,
St. Giles, its fair varieties expand;
Till at the last in slow-drawn cart she went
To execution. Dost thou ask her crime?
She whipp'd two female 'prentices to death,
And hid them in the coal-hole. For her mind
Shaped strictest plans of discipline. Sage schemes!
Such as Lycurgus taught. . . ."

After Southey, too, had given up his project of emigration and won the hand of *his* Miss Fricker, he settled in London, in 1797. From 1807 onwards the Government granted him an annual allowance of £150, and after Pye's death he became Poet Laureate, with a salary of £300. This post, which entailed the obligation to compose a poem on the occasion of every special event in the royal family, had first been offered by the Prince Regent to Scott, who asked his friend and patron, the Duke of Buccleuch, for advice in the matter. The Duke wrote: "Only think of being chanted and recitatived by a parcel of hoarse and squeaking choristers on a birthday, for the edification of the bishops, pages, maids of honour, and gentlemen-pensioners! Oh horrible! thrice horrible!" &c., &c. Scott declined the proffered honour, and suggested Southey, a loyal and needy poet, as a fit recipient. For the greater part of his life Southey was obliged to live by his pen, and consequently often wrote under compulsion. Industrious, economical, a model of all the domestic virtues, he amassed a capital of £12,000. With him, as with the Germans, Romanticism, instead of precluding the bourgeois virtues, throve along with them. It had, after all, so little connection with real life. His respectable Philistinism did not forbid of his allowing his imagination to take the wildest Oriental flights.

During the first, the liberal-minded, stage of Southey's

career, we are conscious of a sympathetic ardour in his writing. He possessed both enthusiasm and courage. His epic, *Joan of Arc,* published in 1797, is a poem inspired by as fervent an admiration for the heroine of France as that displayed by Schiller five years later in his *Jungfrau von Orleans.* Southey's work is, like Schiller's, of an exactly opposite character to Voltaire's *Pucelle,* which, the English poet in his preface informs his readers, is a book he has "never been guilty of looking into." In *Joan of Arc* Southey is not yet the Romanticist. Once or twice he projects his vision as far as his own day. In the Third Book he extols Madame Roland as "the martyred patriot," in the Tenth he refers to Lafayette's as "the name that Freedom still shall love." And in his representation of Jeanne's exploits we have not, as in Schiller, any reference to witchcraft. At a decisive moment, when the Maid is being questioned as to her beliefs, she (and through her, her poet) makes such a frank confession of her faith in nature that we feel satisfied that in Southey's case too, the Naturalism which dominates the English poetry of the day is the foundation upon which everything rests.

"Woman," says a priest to Joan of Arc,—

> "Woman, thou seem'st to scorn
> The ordinances of our holy Church;
> And, if I rightly understand thy words,
> Nature, thou say'st, taught thee in solitude
> Thy feelings of religion, and that now
> Masses and absolution and the use
> Of the holy wafer, are to thee unknown.
> But how could Nature teach thee true religion,
> Deprived of these? Nature doth lead to sin,
> But 'tis the priest alone can teach remorse,
> Can bid St. Peter ope the gates of Heaven,
> And from the penal fires of purgatory
> Set the soul free."

The Maid replies :—

> "Fathers of the holy Church,
> If on these points abstruse a simple maid
> Like me should err, impute not you the crime
> To self-will'd reason, vaunting its own strength

Above eternal wisdom. True it is
That for long time I have not heard the sound
Of mass high-chaunted, nor with trembling lips
Partook the holy wafer: yet the birds
Who to the matin ray prelusive pour'd
Their joyous song, methought did warble forth
Sweeter thanksgiving to Religion's ear
In their wild melody of happiness,
Than ever rung along the high-arch'd roofs
Of man: . . . yet never from the bending vine
Pluck'd I its ripen'd clusters thanklessly,
Or of that God unmindful, who bestow'd
The bloodless banquet. Ye have told me, Sirs,
That Nature only teaches man to sin!
If it be sin to seek the wounded lamb,
To bind its wounds, and bathe them with my tears,
This is what Nature taught! No, Fathers, no!
It is not Nature that doth lead to sin:
Nature is all benevolence, all love,
All beauty! In the greenwood's quiet shade
There is no vice that to the indignant cheek
Bids the red current rush; no misery there;
No wretched mother, who with pallid face
And famine-fallen hangs o'er her hungry babes,
With such a look, so wan, so woe-begone,
As shall one day, with damning eloquence
Against the oppressor plead! . . ."[1]

In this little harangue the attentive reader is conscious, not only of the echo of the revolutionary cries on the other side of the Channel, repeated in the language of English nature-worship, but also of the young poet's want of ability to give his subject the proper local colouring or to impart to it the spirit of the age. France and the Middle Ages are to him here what the East and the world of legend were to become—a costume in which his English and Protestant ideas figure. Of one thing, however, there is no doubt, namely, that it required courage to sing the praises of the French national heroine at a moment when the animosity to France was so strong; and the poem, in spite of its aridity both as regards feeling and colour, is a work which does honour to a young poet. But the brave spirit which elevated his talent was soon to disappear from his writings.

[1] *Joan of Arc*, Book iii.

The lower the flood of unselfish enthusiasm for the great tasks and dreams of humanity ebbed in Southey's soul, the stronger became the impulse to remedy the aridity by pouring in a stream of purely external Romanticism. He had by degrees attained to a certain mastery over the resources of language, had acquired the art of writing loosely constructed but melodious verse, expressive in spite of its vagueness and monotony. Employing this melodious, flexible metre in the representation of the superstitions of Arabia and the most fantastic dreams of the Oriental races, he now produced his two principal works, *The Curse of Kehama* and *Thalaba the Destroyer*. The Oriental tendency is common to Romanticism in every country. Oehlenschläger, the Dane, displays it simultaneously with Southey; it reaches France a little later, when Victor Hugo writes *Aly et Gulhyndi* and *Les Orientales*. But in the case of the English poets, the colourless, Protestant life of their own country, with its severe, cold propriety, must have invested the East with a peculiarly attractive charm. It required an Irishman, however—Thomas Moore, a colourist with Celtic blood in his veins—to arrive at anything resembling an understanding of a race like the ancient Persians and of their legends, and to reproduce the nature of the East in a style loaded with jewels and barbaric ornaments. *Lalla Rookh* is no masterpiece; its personages and ideas are far too European and tame; but *Thalaba*, a work which enjoyed a certain amount of celebrity in its day, is tame in comparison with *Lalla Rookh*, and as moral as an English sermon. It suffers from the sharp contrast between the gaudy tinsel of the scenery and the sober modesty of the feelings represented. We are transplanted into a world which is not less marvellous than that of the *Thousand and One Nights*, but a world in which, nevertheless, love of our fellow-men and faith in one God are perpetually inculcated. The hero's life is presided over by the most special providence. When the fit time has arrived for him to leave his foster-father's house, the flight of a swarm of Syrian grasshoppers, pursued by a flock of birds, is directed so as to pass above the house. A grasshopper which one of the birds drops from its bill bears on its forehead in minute letters the inscription :—

> "When the sun shall be darkened at noon,
> Son of Hodeirah, depart!"

But even though the poet employs such miraculous machinery as this, he can no more refrain here than he did in *Joan of Arc* from safeguarding his reader against the erroneous religious ideas of the period and the country. All his chief characters are rationalists in so far as their Oriental religion is concerned, and do not fall far short of being good Protestants. When the swarm of grasshoppers comes, Thalaba's foster-father, Moath, says :—

> "Deemest thou
> The scent of water on some Syrian mosque
> Placed with priest mummery and fantastic rites
> Which fool the multitude, hath led them here
> From far Khorassan? Allah who appoints
> Yon swarms to be a punishment of man,
> These also hath he doom'd to meet their way."

A pure-bred Arabian could not well view things in a more rationalistic light than this. And we have the same sort of thing throughout. Southey piles up fantastic edifices, only to topple them over with the help of some Gospel text when he is tired of them, or thinks that his reader requires an admonition.

Upon his finger Thalaba wears a ring which is a talisman against evil spirits. One day the evil spirit, Lobaba, who is determined to rob him of it, tries to draw it off his finger while he is asleep. But one of the good genii sends a wasp which stings Thalaba's finger close to the edge of the ring, making it impossible for the evil one to slip the ring over the swollen part. All Lobaba's plans are defeated in some such manner. At last the dread sorcerer, Mohareb, succeeds in ensnaring the youth. After Thalaba has defeated Mohareb repeatedly, the latter jeers at him because he defeats his enemies, not in open conflict, but with the aid of a talisman. He barbs his jeers so successfully that at last Thalaba casts the ring into an abyss. Then the struggle begins anew.

We expect that Thalaba, now defenceless against the supernatural power of his foes, will be overcome. Not at all! He conquers. How, and why? A voice from heaven informs us. The ring was not the true talisman: "The Talisman is Faith!" Why, then, all the machinery?

The poet conducts us into subterranean caves, where human heads have to be thrown to the serpents who guard the entrances, where the taper can only be carried in the hewn-off hand of a hanged murderer, &c., &c.—in short, into a world which has no points of resemblance with Great Britain. But the whole is nothing but a ballet; the scene suddenly changes; the Oriental garments and trappings vanish, and the prompter reads aloud one of the Thirty-nine Articles. After this the ballet begins again. The scene represents a banquet, with costly dishes, with delicious wines in golden goblets—"ruby and amber, rosy as rising morn, or softer gleam of saffron like the sunny evening mist." But all these temptations are of no avail. Thalaba is far too good a Mussulman to allow himself to be led astray:—

"But Thalaba took not the draught;
For rightly he knew had the Prophet forbidden
That beverage, the mother of sins.
Nor did the urgent hosts
Proffer a second time the liquid fire,
When in the youth's strong eye they saw
No movable resolve."

He might be a member of an English Total Abstinence society, this "Destroyer"—he will drink nothing but spring water; and along with it he eats water melons.

"Anon a troop of females form'd a dance,
Their ancles bound with bracelet bells
That made the modulating harmony.
Transparent garments to the greedy eye
Exposed their harlot limbs,
Which moved, in every wanton gesture skill'd."

But there is no cause for alarm. Thalaba is a determined adversary of the polygamy of his native country. Like a young Englishman travelling abroad, he fortifies himself with the thought of the girl at home to whom he is engaged:—

> "And Thalaba, he gazed,
> But in his heart he bore a talisman,
> Whose blessed alchemy
> To virtuous thoughts refined
> The loose suggestions of the scene impure.
> Oneiza's image swam before his sight,
> His own Arabian maid."

Thalaba was born in England about the time when Aladdin saw the light in Denmark. (*The Curse of Kehama* was published in 1810, *Aladdin* in 1804, *Thalaba* in 1801.) What a cold-blooded animal he is compared with his Danish brother!

He attains the object of his desire; he is married to his "own Arabian maid." That everything may be thoroughly edifying and pious, the bride is made to die on the wedding night. To restore the Oriental character to the proceedings, Thalaba is compelled by his fate to kill an innocent young girl, named Laila. But that things may end in a satisfactorily Christian manner, his last recorded act is to forgive the sorcerer who has caused all his misfortunes—who proves to be the man he has been in search of all his life for the purpose of avenging the death of his father—and who is now unable to escape from him. In the course of a pompous funeral oration—

> "'Old Man, I strike thee not!' said Thalaba;
> 'The evil thou hast done to me and mine
> Brought its own bitter punishment.'"

Thalaba! you speak like a book—but like one of the books we open only to close again.

Let us close *Thalaba*, then, and give a parting glance at its author. Even Thackeray, who cannot say enough in praise of Southey as a man, is obliged, in writing of his chief works, to allow the possibility that, in the struggle between Thalaba the Destroyer and the destroyer Time, the latter will remain master of the field. It would be interesting to know how many living Englishmen have read the poem. To our own generation Southey's name is chiefly known, as it will be to posterity, by his hysteric assaults on Byron, and Byron's inimitable retorts. We have Southey's *Vision of Judgment* to thank for Byron's—and for this service we are ready to forgive him both the *Curse of Kehama* and *Thalaba.* We observe, however, in these poems, what is not to be observed in the works of the German Romanticists, namely, that the empty fantasticalness gives place to something better, when it is nature that is described. In the midst of all the Romantic confusion the Englishman's quiet realism asserts itself. Undeniably beautiful is the very first stanza of *Thalaba*, with its description of night in the desert, the sweet cadences of which the youthful Shelley imitated in his *Queen Mab.*

"How beautiful is night!
A dewy freshness fills the silent air;
No mist obscures, nor cloud, nor speck, nor stain
Breaks the serene of heaven.
In full-orb'd glory yonder Moon divine
Rolls through the dark blue depths.
Beneath her steady ray
The desert-circle spreads,
Like the round ocean, girdled with the sky.
How beautiful is night!"

This rivals the description of moonlight falling on the desert sands given in The Caravan Song in the fifth act of *Aladdin.* And many such pictures are to be found in Southey's poems. When he describes the timid antelope, hearing the wanderers' steps, and standing, doubtful where to turn in the dim light; and the ostrich which, blindly hastening, meets them full; and the deep, moveless mist which mantles all (Book IV., Canto 19), we are aware that this is not scenery in the German Romantic style, but a picture of the East which is faithful to nature, a picture which we owe to the English habit of observation.

It would be difficult to find another man of the same doubtful political and literary reputation whose friends and contemporaries have borne such high testimony to his personal character as did Southey's. He was Wordsworth's trusted friend; he was Coleridge's chief and most unwearied benefactor; and, a fact which carries as much weight as any, Walter Savage Landor honoured him, in spite of their diametrically opposite political opinions, with a friendship which was only put an end to by death, and of which there are many reminiscences in Landor's *Imaginary Conversations*. On the 15th of May 1833, Emerson wrote: "I dined with Landor. He pestered me with Southey; but who is Southey?" So we see that Landor tried to make friends for his friend. And Thackeray, when in search of a typical English gentleman, did not hesitate to take as his model the poor, industrious, generously helpful Robert Southey.

But no testimony in favour of Southey's personal character can clear his literary reputation. It is stained by his eulogies of the English royal family and his denunciation of Byron. That he, like the other members of the Lake School, should assume a cold and hostile attitude to this new and alarming literary phenomenon was natural. But that he, himself a poet, should inflame the educated mob against another poet, an infinitely greater one than himself, by a mean accusation of immorality and irreligion, is a crime which history cannot forgive, and which it punishes by recording Southey's name only in an appendix to Byron's life.

At the time of the publication of *Don Juan*, Southey wrote:—"I am well aware that the public are peculiarly intolerant of literary innovations. Would that this literary intolerance were under the influence of a saner judgment, and regarded the morals more than the manners of a composition! Would that it were directed against these monstrous combinations of horrors and mockery, lewdness and impiety, with which English poetry has, in our days, first been polluted! For more than half a century English literature had been distinguished by its moral purity, the effect, and, in its turn, the cause of an improvement in national manners. A father might, without apprehension of evil, have put into the hands of his children any book which issued from the press, if it did not bear, either in its title-page or frontispiece, manifest signs that it was intended as furniture for the brothel. There was no danger in any work which bore the name of a respectable publisher, or was to be procured at any respectable bookseller's. This was particularly the case with regard to our poetry. It is now no longer so; and woe to those by whom the offence cometh! The greater the talents of the offender, the greater is his guilt, and the more enduring will be his shame. Whether it be that the laws are in themselves unable to abate an evil of this magnitude, or whether it be that they are remissly administered, and with such injustice that the celebrity of an offender serves as a privilege whereby he obtains impunity, individuals are bound to consider that such pernicious works would neither be published nor written if they were discouraged as they might, and ought to be, by public feeling; every person, therefore, who purchases such books or admits them into his house promotes the mischief, and thereby, as far as in him lies, becomes an aider and abettor of the crime.

"The publication of a lascivious book is one of the worst offences which can be committed against the well-being of society. It is a sin, to the consequences of which no limits can be assigned, and those consequences no after-repentance in the writer can counteract. Whatever remorse of conscience he may feel when his hour comes (and come it must!) will be of no avail. The poignancy of a death-bed repentance cannot cancel one copy of the thousands which are sent abroad. . . . Men of diseased hearts and depraved imaginations, who, forming a system of opinions to suit their own unhappy course of conduct, have rebelled against the holiest ordinances of human society, and hate that revealed religion which, with all their efforts and bravadoes, they are unable entirely to disbelieve, labour to make others as miserable as themselves by infecting them with a moral virus that eats into the soul! The school which they have set up may properly be called the Satanic school; for though their productions breathe the spirit of Belial in their lascivious parts, and the spirit of Moloch in those loathsome images of atrocities and horror which they delight to represent, they are more especially characterised by a Satanic spirit of pride and audacious impiety, which still betrays the wretched feeling of hopelessness wherewith it is allied."

It was necessary to give this long specimen of Southey's Biblical eloquence, because it is so typical of him and of men of his description; besides, every passionate outbreak of a strong party-spirit possesses historical interest. But Nemesis was not asleep. In 1821, the same year in which Southey discharged this volley of abuse, an unauthorised edition of his own old revolutionary work, *Wat Tyler*, was brought out by a bookseller who thought it might be a profitable speculation. Southey went to law, hoping to have the edition suppressed and the publisher punished. But Nemesis struck again, harder than before. Lord Eldon discharged the appeal, on the ground that it was illegal to grant any author right of property in works calculated to do injury to public morality! It was in this same year that Southey, on the occasion of the death of the old, deranged King, George III., wrote his long, dull *Vision of Judgment*, a poem in hexameters, which it is interesting (not only because of the resemblance in subject, but also because of the employment of the supernatural element in both) to compare with Victor Hugo's loyal poem, *La Vision*. Southey characteristically apotheosised poor old George III. on the ground of his possessing the virtues which were the only ones the poet himself understood—and, indeed, the only ones George did possess—the domestic and bourgeois virtues; he was a faithful husband, a kind father, &c., qualities which no more make a man a good king than they make him a good poet. Byron could stand no more. The insulted Apollo rose in his wrath, seized the wretched Marsyas by the ear, and flayed him alive with merciless satire in *his Vision of Judgment*.

X

HISTORICAL NATURALISM

LET us turn from Southey to a better man, to the author who, building on the groundwork of national character and history, originated the distinctively British type of Romanticism. This man did not, like his contemporaries of the Lake School, require to play the renegade in order to become conservative in religion and politics; he was conservative from his earliest youth, but without animosity to men of the opposite tendency. Pure-minded and gentle by nature, of a noble, resolute character, richly endowed with the creative gift, he for twenty years provided all the countries of Europe with wholesome, entertaining literature; and so original was his conception of race-character and history, that his influence in every civilised country upon the writing of history was not less great than his influence on fiction.

Walter Scott, the ninth child of a family "of gentle blood," was born in Edinburgh on the 15th of August 1771. His father, a lawyer by profession, resembled Goethe's father in his severe sense of order; the old merchant in *Rob Roy* is said to be a portrait of him. Ardent loyalty, displaying itself in devotion, first to the Stuarts, then to the house of Hanover, was one hereditary quality in the family; and orthodox piety was another. In his earliest infancy Walter was healthy and strong, but in his second year he suddenly became lame in the right leg. The sweet temper with which throughout life he bore this physical infirmity, presents a remarkable contrast to the resentful impatience which his great English rival displayed with regard to a similar affliction. The boy grew up an ardent Jacobite and a lover of the old songs and ballads which tell of the Scottish wars and raids, Highland and Lowland. When he was little more than an infant, he could repeat most of that ballad of Hardicanute with which in 1815 he drew tears from Byron's eyes. Anything of the nature of a story, especially if it was in rhyme, he learned with ease, but—a fact significant of the character of his future productions—dates and *general principles* were things which he assimilated with difficulty. The little lame boy, who rode about on a pony not much bigger than a Newfoundland dog, was an admirer of Percy's collection of old poems and fragments; and, what is more remarkable, himself collected old ballads and songs, as other children collect coins or seals. At the age of ten he had several volumes of them; and he continued to be a ballad-hunter all his life. Keen observation of his surroundings was another thing that developed early in Scott; he had an eye for every ruin, every monument of antiquity, every curious old stone; but he had not Wordsworth's intensity of regard for nature as simply nature; it was its historical and poetic interest that attracted him. A group of old trees which had grown together was not in itself capable of arousing in him the devotional spirit which it did in Wordsworth; but if he was told: Under this tree Charles II. rested; or: That tree was planted by Mary Queen of Scots—he broke a twig to keep in memory of his visit to the place, and never forgot these trees.

At the age of fifteen he made acquaintance with the picturesque Scottish Highlands, which were ere long to be of such importance to him, as providing his fictitious characters with a background of scenery as yet totally unknown to Europe. From the moment when he became conscious of his poetic calling, he studied nature in the manner of the painter who takes sketches. Before describing any district he took a special journey there, made a minute record of the appearance of the hills, of the lie and shape of the woods, even of the nature and outlines of the clouds at a given moment. He actually noted single flowers and bushes by the road-side or at the entrance to a cave. Though he had, in common with the Romanticists of Germany and Denmark, the poetic eye for nature, this did not stand in the way of vigorous, exact realism in description.

Whilst Oehlenschläger long contented himself with "speedwell" and roses, Scott, as he himself said, knew hill, brook, dell, rock, and stone, and the whole flora of his country.

Before the young man's true vocation was revealed to him, he had made of himself a reliable, industrious lawyer, who engrossed his legal documents in the typical law hand in which he was afterwards to write so many famous books. In spite of his lameness he was healthy, active, and strong, and so well-trained in manly exercises that he was able to defend himself with his stick for a whole hour against three men who attacked him one day on a lonely road. It is of interest, in the case of such a man, to note the fact that this perfect health was not accompanied by any corresponding perfection of the sensual organs. Scott had hardly any sense of smell, and his Homeric appetite was the opposite of dainty; he never learned to distinguish good wine from bad, or well-cooked from badly-cooked food—in both of these points forming the antipodes of his younger contemporary, Keats. His feelings towards the other sex were so cold that his companions were always teasing him on the subject. Nevertheless he had, in his youth, a romantic attachment to a lady who chose another mate. Scott controlled his feelings so perfectly that no one suspected this attachment. He soon recovered from his disappointment, and, at the age of twenty-six, with a chaste, tranquil youth behind him, married Miss Carpenter, a lady of French Protestant family, whose father had died at the time of the Revolution. Most of the winter of 1796–97, during which an invasion of Scotland by the French was expected, he spent in assisting to raise regiments of volunteers. In his enthusiasm he himself undertook the duties of quartermaster, paymaster, and secretary of one of these regiments.

His first translations from the German have already been noticed. He had long been a living repertory of songs, ballads, and tales; in 1803 he published, under the title of *Minstrelsy of the Scottish Border*, a collection of ballads, which he dedicated to his native land, the "dearest half of Albion." Part Third of this book, *Modern Imitations*, contains poems by Scott himself.[1] In one of the criticisms of the day occurred the prophetic remark, that the book "contained the elements of a hundred historical romances."

With all his loyalty to the English royal family, Scott never felt himself anything but the thoroughbred Scotchman; indeed, there can be no doubt that what lies at the very root of his originality is his Scottish character. His strong interest in the poetry of history is a Scottish interest. One of the most pronounced characteristics of Scotchmen in every age has been an intense spirit of nationality. The phrase *Perfervidum ingenium Scotorum*, used centuries ago on the Continent to express the idea of the Scottish character then universally current, had originally no other meaning than this. If we for a moment overlook the many internal dissensions, which do not really undermine the feeling of community, we feel how difficult it would be to match in any other country the solidarity of this small nation placed on the frontier of one so much larger and more powerful, which speaks the same language. The Englishman, too, has an intense spirit of nationality, but it is much less salient and active; it is purely of a corroborative nature—corroboration of the claim advanced by his country to the possession of many and various attributes. The Scotchman's spirit of nationality is continuously active, constantly on the alert, because it is essentially of a negative character. When the Englishman says: I am an Englishman—he means exactly what he says; but when the Scotchman says or thinks: I am a Scotchman—it is tantamount to: I am not an Englishman.[2]

To understand this feeling properly, we must remember the smallness of the nation in comparison with its great neighbour. When we learn that in the year 1707 the entire population of Scotland did not exceed a million, we understand what concord, what determination, what defensive pugnacity, were imperative in the less numerous race if its individuality was not to be flooded out or stamped out by

[1] In the same year the Danish poet Oehlenschläger made his first appearance before the public, also with a collection of remodelled ballads. (*Digte*, 1803).

[2] Masson: *Scottish Influence in British Literature.*

the other. Thus it came about that bleak and rugged Scotland, as compared with verdant, fertile England, was the object of a very special love and admiration; its hills, its moors, its mists, inspired an almost martial patriotism. And it is therefore not surprising that, at the period when the spirit of nationality was breaking forth into poetry all over Europe, this country should produce a great descriptive, great narrative, poet—that it should be Scotland which brings forth the first and the most vigorous fruits of historical, ethnological Romanticism. What more natural than that an author in such a country as Scotland should be deeply interested in the peculiar customs of the Highlanders, and take pleasure in describing them in their picturesque garb! What more natural than that the man whose very name seemed to stamp him as a personification of his country, should endeavour, by recalling its great historical achievements in the past, to efface, as it were, the impression of its smallness and present insignificance!

Scottish national feeling was, then, in the first instance, distinguished by its solidarity; the subordinate nation felt itself more one than the greater nation; there were fewer conflicting interests at work within it. Scott frequently describes this strong feeling of kinship among his countrymen —nowhere more beautifully than in the *Heart of Midlothian*, the poor peasant heroine of which is encouraged by it to apply for help to the Duke of Argyle almost as if he were a relative. But Scottish national feeling possessed another distinguishing feature; being, in its character of attachment to an ancient, once entirely independent, state, itself a tradition, it was related to every other old tradition. This explains Scott's exaggerated reverence for royalty, its emblems and appurtenances. When he was a member of the Commission entrusted to institute a search after the ancient regalia of Scotland, the discovery of it filled him with such reverential emotion that, when one of the other Commissioners proposed to try the crown on a young lady's head, he could not help shouting: "By God, no!"

The first great feeling of separate nationalism brought in its train a whole host of new separative feelings. If there were not many nations that rivalled the Scotch in the way they held together as a people, there were still fewer that could show such inward division into parties and camps. The individual's feeling of his public duty did not begin with the nation, but with the tribe, the clan, nay, the family.

Hence we find Scott, the true Scotchman, showing preference, as a ballad-writer, for the legends which treat of the exploits of his own ancestors or kin, and in his private life exhibiting strong family feeling. He was a model son and husband; he was, as his letters to his eldest son show, a devoted father; in the education of his children he neglected neither body nor soul—though his chief requirements of them seem to have been the ancient Persian ones, that they should ride well and speak the truth; but his conception even of these relations was not modern. In his private life as in his poetry, the family was more to him than the individual. He had a brother, Daniel by name, who fell into bad habits, and, though he never did anything actually dishonourable, was a disgrace to the family. Scott procured a small appointment in the West Indies for this brother, but in his correspondence about him never called him anything but "relation," and also required of him that he should never divulge the nearness of the relationship. He refused to see Daniel when the latter returned to Scotland, never mentioned his name, and would neither attend his funeral nor wear mourning for him. Such behaviour as this shows the bad side of the society-preserving virtues. It is not surprising that the man who, with all his tender-heartedness, could sacrifice so much on the altar of "family," was unable to become the poet of personality, and was stamped as of the past the moment Byron appeared.

In 1802 the *Edinburgh Review* was founded. Scott was a contributor to it from the beginning. Its editor was his fellow-countryman, Jeffrey, a man whose critical pronouncements were regarded as of the utmost importance by the authors of the day, though his only gift as a critic was a kind of untrained, straightforward common-sense. Scott's contributions ceased in 1809, when, dissatisfied with the liberal-minded attitude assumed by the *Edinburgh Review* in the

Catholic question, and annoyed by Jeffrey's disparaging notice of *Marmion,* he founded the *Quarterly Review.*

Scott's first narrative poem, *The Lay of the Last Minstrel,* appeared in 1805. It was a remarkable success. The reading public rejoiced at this return to nature and to national poetry. Pitt expressed the opinion that in several passages Scott had succeeded in producing the effect of a fine painting, and his opponent Fox was for once of the same opinion with him. Scott's personal amiability as Sheriff of Selkirkshire had, ere this, made him such a favourite that, as Wordsworth wrote in 1803, his name acted as *an open sesame* throughout the Border country; now he became equally beloved as a poet. In a very short time 30,000 copies of his work were sold. In it he introduced his readers, with something approaching historical accuracy, to the Scotland of the sixteenth century. The acceptance with which his descriptions of the Border customs were received, suggested the idea of writing something of the same kind in prose, an idea which in its embodiment received the name of *Waverley.* In the meantime interest had been aroused in the Middle Ages, chivalry, feudal conditions, and Scottish national characteristics generally. English tourists began to make romantic pilgrimages to the ruins of the old castles, and to the battle-field of Killiecrankie, where their countrymen had been defeated by the bare-legged, tartan-clad monsters.

Until this time Scott had been in the habit of writing in the evening, and far on into the night; but after he devoted himself entirely to authorship, the early morning became his working time. He rose before five, went first to the stables to visit his horses and favourite dogs and other domestic animals, then seated himself at his desk and wrote so easily and fast that by the time the family assembled for breakfast, between nine and ten, he had, to use his own words, "broken the neck of the day's work." He left his study at twelve, and spent the rest of the day with his family and his guests. Scott's works were, thus, written in the fresh morning hours, whilst Byron, characteristically enough, wrote his at night. And we seem, even when the two poets are likest each other, to feel the influence of the bright, and the influence of the dark, hour of conception.

It is in the poem which he began in November 1806, *Marmion, a Tale of Flodden Field,* that Scott is most like Byron. As far as the plot is concerned, this work is quite in Scott's usual style; the scene is laid in sixteenth-century Scotland, and it is the life of the castle and the court that is described. But the hero's character makes him an unmistakable forerunner of the Byronic heroes, and the whole poem is written in the easy-flowing, but somewhat monotonous, four-footed iambics which Byron employed in most of his poetical narratives. Marmion is a proud and brave, but also wicked knight. A young, beautiful nun, Constance of Beverley, whom he has abducted, follows him everywhere, disguised as a page; but he grows tired of her, and is determined to compel a young girl of high birth to marry him, though he knows that she loves another. In her jealous despair, Constance makes an attempt on Marmion's life; and he, indifferent and cruel, gives her up to the convent to suffer punishment as a runaway nun. The abbess pronounces sentence; and, in a Romantic scene of horror of the kind which Byron painted frequently, and with much less consideration for his readers' nerves, we see Constance immured alive in an underground vault.

There is not much psychology in Scott's poem. The gorgeousness of the knight's armour, the gloom of the convent crypt, the architecture of the old castle, are of more importance to him than complicated emotions. Nevertheless he has given us in *Marmion* something very like a first sketch of *The Giaour* and of *Lara*. The Giaour's mistress suffers a terrible death; Lara's follows him everywhere, in the disguise of a page; and the scene in *Marmion,* in which the hero is publicly put to shame, has a certain resemblance to the scene in which Lara's past is brought to mind. Is there not something almost Byronic in the lines?—

"Marmion, whose steady heart and eye
Ne'er changed in worst extremity;
Marmion, whose soul could scantly brook,
Even from his king, a haughty look;

Whose accent of command controlled,
In camps, the boldest of the bold—
Thought, look, and utterance failed him now,
Fallen was his glance, and flushed his brow;
For either in the tone,
Or something in the Palmer's look,
So full upon his conscience strook
That answer he found none."

And the lines which describe his pangs of conscience:—

"High minds, of native pride and force,
Most deeply feel thy pangs, Remorse!
Fear for their scourge mean villains have,
Thou art the torturer of the brave!"

do they not seem to foreshadow the famous passage in *The Giaour?*—

"The mind that broods o'er guilty woes,
Is like the scorpion girt by fire;
. . . . . .
The sting she nourished for her foes,
Whose venom never yet was vain,
Gives but one pang and cures all pain,
And darts into her desperate brain."

There is not merely a certain similarity between Marmion's and Lara's position and character; they also die in the same manner—fall on the battle-field, unyielding and ungodly to the last moment of their lives.

But this is all the resemblance between them; and it is just sufficient to throw Byron's distinguishing characteristics into relief. To Scott, Marmion's personality is not the principal matter; he makes use of it for the purpose of grouping round it figures and incidents illustrative of his country's past; he requires the vices of his hero to set his simple tale going, but he is not the least absorbed in them, and describes them quite *impersonally*. When Byron, on the other hand, describes his earliest criminal heroes, his main object is to arouse interest in them. Their countenances attract the attention and interest of every one that sees them, and suggest pride, guilt, hatred, and defiance; never once in their lives are they, like Marmion, unable to look their accusers in the face; they live the life of the fabulous scorpion, "around it flame, within it death." Without hope in heaven, without solace upon earth, their hearts writhe in haughty agony until they cease to beat. Marmion was a stony-hearted, selfish knight, but his last thought and his last words were given to England; he is part of a greater whole than his own egoistic life. It is quite different with Byron's earliest heroes. They live entirely in their own inner life, which forms, as it were, a complete and separate world in itself; and the poet has been careful to allow the reader to catch sight of a similar dark, complete, and separate world in his, Byron's, soul. We catch a glimpse of his own *Ego* behind the fictitious one; we are conscious of a heart that has suffered, and that seeks relief in veiled confessions and mysterious outbursts: the manner of presentation is, in short, personal in the highest degree; and this means a revolution in English poetical art.

The success of Scott's genuinely epic poem was not due to its hero, but to its events, and especially to the battle scenes in the last canto, which enthusiastic critics declared to be the finest out of Homer. And if the poem was well adapted to excite the admiration of Scott's sedate countrymen, it was not less adapted to please the court. Byron was right when he said to the Prince Regent that Scott struck him as being "more particularly the poet of *Princes*, as *they* never appeared more fascinating than in *Marmion* and *The Lady of the Lake*." It is even probable that there are in *Marmion* direct allusions to the Prince Regent and his wife. The former can hardly have read unmoved the description of King James in his gorgeous court dress:—

> "For royal was his garb and mien,
> His cloak of crimson velvet piled,
> Trimmed with the fur of marten wild;
> His vest of changeful satin sheen,
> The dazzled eye beguiled."
>
> —*Marmion*, v. 8.

And the unfortunate, disgraced Princess of Wales, whose personal acquaintance Scott made when he was lionised in London for the first time, in 1806, and to whose party he, as a Tory, belonged, may well have applied to her own case the poem's description of the forsaken Queen Margaret, who led such a lonely life whilst the chivalrous, dissolute monarch spent his time with his mistresses.

Begun in 1806, *Marmion* was published in 1808, and when, in the following year, Scott for the second time visited London, he met with a reception that would have turned any other man's head. He played his part of lion with a good-nature and humour rare in a man who is the hero of the moment in a great metropolis. We read that once, after he had been entertaining a large company with his stories and quaint humour, when most of the guests had gone, leaving him with only a few intimate friends, he laughed at himself and quoted: "I know that I one Snug the joiner am—no lion fell." And so modest was he that, when the conversation one day turned on himself in connection with Burns, he emphatically declared himself unworthy to be named on the same day as that great poet.

But if Scott was a tame, gentle lion, he was a remarkably fierce Tory. The special purpose of his journey to London was the enlistment of contributors to the *Quarterly Review*. He desired that this periodical should be conducted on strictly Conservative principles, and he was especially firm on the subject of Catholic Emancipation. His theory was that if a particular sect of religionists are *ipse facto* connected with foreign politics and placed under the spiritual direction of a class of priests of unrivalled dexterity and activity, the state ought to be excused from entrusting them with confidential posts. "If a gentleman chooses to walk about with a couple of pounds of gunpowder in his pocket, if I give him the shelter of my roof, I may at least be permitted to exclude him from the seat next the fire." Scott continued all his life to be of this opinion. Only a few years before his death, he said to his son-in-law: "I hold Popery to be such a mean and depraving superstition, that I am not sure I could have found myself liberal enough for voting the repeal of the penal laws as they existed before 1780. But now that you have taken the plaster off the old lady of Babylon's mouth, and given her free respiration, I cannot see the sense of keeping up the irritation about the claim to sit in Parliament." We understand in what need the English public stood of poets like Moore, like Byron and Shelley, when we hear a man of Scott's noble nature and culture express himself with such shameful and cruel narrow-mindedness.

In 1810 appeared the *The Lady of the Lake*, a work which still further increased its author's popularity. The fresh breezes from the woods and hills which blow through this beautiful poem, its gentle ardour, its genuine feeling, which never becomes wild passion, its story, the effect of which is not, as so often with Wordsworth, destroyed by the introduction of charitable sentiments and religious exhortations—all this captivated the reading public. As a proof of the interest taken in the book, it may be mentioned that the receipts of the post-houses nearest the district where its scene is laid were doubled. To find a parallel incident we must again turn to the pages which tell the story of Scott's life. When *Guy Mannering*, of which 6000 copies were sold in two days, came out, it was reported that Scott had called Dandie Dinmont's two dogs, Pepper and Mustard, after two actually existing terriers, to which a Liddesdale farmer had given these odd names. This man, whose name was Davidson, and who was not really portrayed in the novel at all, became so famous that people took long journeys to see him; a lady of rank, who desired to possess a couple of dogs of the famous breed, but who did not know the farmer's name, addressed her letter to "Dandie Dinmont," and it reached its proper destination.

The Lady of the Lake met with an almost equally cordial reception. We read that on the day when it reached Sir Adam Fergusson, a Scottish captain serving in Portugal, he was posted with his company on a point of ground exposed to the enemy's artillery. The men were ordered to lie prostrate on the ground, and while they kept that attitude, the captain, kneeling at their head, read aloud the description of the battle in Canto VI., and the listening soldiers only interrupted him by a joyous huzza whenever the French shot struck the bank close above them.

What the modern and foreign reader of this poem finds

in it now is, in the first place, strong national feeling; the memories of ancient days, of feudal customs, of Scottish royalty, of the clan's fidelity to its chief, are chanted in lucid, vivid, simple verse. Along with this, he finds descriptions of nature with the dew as fresh on them as on Christian Winther's. What he does not find is any attempt at psychological character portrayal. There is an old bard, Allan by name, and another Romantic old character, half Druid, half prophet, Brian by name; there are Romantic dreams which come true, and prophecies which are fulfilled. But these personages and incidents have their place in the poem because they belong to the period and the people, not because they are mysterious. There is not a trace to be found of the Romantic belief in horrors. For, much as Scott enjoyed hearing or writing anything of the nature of a ghost story, he was, unlike the German Romanticists, totally unimpressionable as regarded the mysteriously horrible. He tells somewhere that, having arrived one evening at a country inn, he was informed that there was no bed for him. "No place to lie down at all?" said he. "No," said the people of the house, "none, except a room in which there is a corpse lying." "Well," said he, "did the person die of any contagious disorder?" "Oh no; not at all," said they. "Well, then," continued he, "let me have the other bed." "So," said Sir Walter, "I laid me down, and never had a better night's sleep in my life."

There is no want of freshness in the Romantic flavour of *The Lady of the Lake;* what really takes away from its attractiveness for us, nowadays, is the theatricalness of its representation of manners and customs. Scott has not succeeded in steering quite clear of this most perilous of reefs for the Romantic epic, the reef on which Southey suffered shipwreck. Take, for example, the description of the call of the clan to arms by the youth bearing the blood-stained cross. Everything is pushed to an extreme to produce the theatrical effect. The young man comes first to a house where funeral rites are being held, and forces the son to leave his father's corpse and his weeping mother; then he meets a wedding procession, and takes the bridegroom away from the bride. We seem to see the procession crossing the stage, and to feel the impressive effect produced by the sudden appearance of the cross-bearer from behind the scenes. Things happen just as they do in the theatre: a loud whistle, and empty valleys are filled and bare heights covered with armed men—a wave of the hand, and they disappear again. They are *general effects* that we are conscious of; we feel that the poet is interested in the people, not in the individual. His first and chief aim was to represent in strong relief the beautiful traditional customs of his country: the stranger is welcomed in the hut without a question being asked—the combatant chivalrously shares his plaid with his exhausted antagonist. His second aim was to excite his reader pleasurably by means of surprises: Fitzjames's Highland guide suddenly makes himself known as the redoubted chief, Roderick Dhu—Fitzjames himself proves to be the King of Scotland. But how light and joyous and healthfully pure is the flow of this hymn of praise of Scotland and the Scotch! The King, high-spirited and honourable as one of Calderon's kings, masters his own passion; and the Highlanders and the Lowlanders, men and women, have their hearts in the right place. We enjoy the glimpse into the harmonious world, and do not miss Wordsworth's castigatory and admonitory psychology.

We have a really interesting counterpart to *The Lady of the Lake* in Wordsworth's *White Doe of Rylstone*, a narrative poem founded on one of the ballads in Percy's collection, and also begun in 1809. It is in this work that the poet of Rydal Mount, who probably felt the spirit of rivalry stir within him, approaches nearest to Scott's peculiar domain. No one would dream of denying that the feeling in Wordsworth's poem is much deeper. His dislike of dazzling virtues and brilliant vices has led him to choose a hero who, although an obedient son and a valiant knight, refuses, from a sense of duty, to follow his father and his brother when they raise the standard of revolt against Queen Elizabeth of England, and who, misunderstood and repudiated, is obliged, without taking his share of the danger, to witness his kinsmen's defeat and ignominious punishment. Wordsworth has endowed this hero with self-abnegation, fortitude, generosity, and Christian piety ; but there is too much affectation of profundity in the poem, too much dragging in of the half-supernatural, too much sentimentality and unction. Scott viewed nature and the old customs with the eye of a lover of the chase, Wordsworth with the eye of the moralist. Wordsworth's ponderous cargo-boat ploughs its way heavily through the water ; Scott's poet's skiff flies along with all sails set, leaving only light bubbles of fancy behind in the reader's memory ; it is like the boat in the Third Canto of his poem, which flies so fast that

> "The bubbles where they launched the boat
> Were all unbroken and afloat,
> Dancing in foam and ripple still,
> When it had neared the mainland hill."

It is easy to understand that Scott's writings, with their glorification of the chivalrous virtues, of daring and courage, even when displayed by rebel chiefs, pirates, gipsies, smugglers, &c. ; in short, with its tendency in the direction of Byronic partiality for the bold and wild, were, from one point of view, highly objectionable in the eyes of the moral and Christian poets of the Lake School. Coleridge charged his novels with "ministering to the depraved appetite for excitement, and creating sympathy for the vicious and infamous, solely because the fiend is daring" ; and he concluded his ill-natured attack with the incorrect prophecy: "Not twenty lines of Scott's poetry will ever reach posterity ; it has relation to nothing."

In 1812 the first two cantos of *Childe Harold* saw the light. Not long after their publication, Byron wrote a most friendly letter to Scott, containing a hearty apology for the foolish attack in *English Bards and Scotch Reviewers*. The younger poet had hastily taunted and reproached the elder, not only with choosing as his favourite hero a mixture of felon and knight ("not quite a felon, yet but half a knight"), but with accepting payment for his works ("racking his brains for lucre, not for fame")—a thing which, in his youth, Byron's aristocratic pride prevented his doing, much as he stood in need of money. After he left England for the second time, he, too, learned to make his art a lucrative profession. He repented his rash condemnation of Scott as heartily as he repented all his other hasty judgments of the same nature, and the strained relationship between the two great and noble-hearted men gave way to the most friendly feeling.

The influence of *Childe Harold* on Scott's literary career was decisive. He was unbiassed enough to see plainly that he could not compete with Byron in narrative poetry, and he therefore determined to turn his attention to another branch of literature, that in which he was soon to stand unrivalled.

The various utterances on this subject, and all the utterances regarding Byron, which are to be found in Scott's Life and Letters testify to the kindly disposition and attractive frankness of the great Scottish author. In 1821 he said to a friend: "In truth, I have long given up poetry. I have had my day with the public; and being no great believer in poetical immortality, I was very well pleased to rise a winner, without continuing the game till I was beggared of any credit I had acquired. Besides, I felt the prudence of giving way before the more forcible and powerful genius of Byron. If I were either greedy, or jealous of poetical fame, I might comfort myself with the thought, that I would hesitate to strip myself for the contest so fearlessly as Byron does; or to command the wonder and terror of the public by exhibiting, in my own person, the sublime attitude of the dying gladiator. But with the old frankness of twenty years since, I will fairly own, that this same delicacy of mine may arise more from conscious want of vigour and inferiority, than from a delicate dislike to the nature of the conflict." And when, the year before his death, he was asked why he had relinquished poetry, he said quite simply: "Because Byron beat me." The gentleman with whom he was talking rejoined that he, for his part, remembered as many passages of his friend's poetry as of Byron's. Scott replied: "That may be, but he beat me out of the field in the description of the strong passions, and in deep-seated knowledge of the human heart." The recognition of this fact must have been a blow to Scott, but he could seek solace in the thought which he himself expressed thus: "If I had occasion to be mortified by the display of genius which threw into the shade such pretensions as I was then supposed to possess, I might console myself that, in my own case, the materials of mental happiness had been mingled in a greater proportion."

Waverley, published anonymously in February 1814, was the first of the long series of novels which made Scott and his country famous throughout the whole civilised world. These works appeared at the time when the conclusion of peace with France and the hopeful prospects of the country generally, had occasioned a special access of national pride. They are not works which, like those of the greatest writers, Goethe and Shelley, for instance, indicate different stages of their author's development and culture; nor are they works inspired by profoundly moving personal experiences; they are the mature productions of an inexhaustible gift of story-telling and an extraordinary talent for description both of men and things. They mark a distinct advance in two matters—the understanding of history, and the representation of the life of the middle and lower classes.

The historians of the eighteenth century, who saw, or expected, the realisation of the ideal in their own day, took up the position rather of orators than of authors; they occupied themselves with theoretical questions of government and civilisation, without consideration of the influence of climatic and geographical conditions, or of the past history of a nation—the conception of a nation as a race seldom suggesting itself to them. Sir Walter Scott, on the other hand, made it his endeavour as a writer of historical fiction to give a vivid impression of the peculiarities of certain periods and countries; and he felt the less temptation to endow his heroes with the characteristics of his own day, as he in his inmost heart preferred the bright, stirring life of the past to the colourless reasonableness of that of his own century.

A few years previously, Chateaubriand had, in *Les Martyrs*, made the first attempt to measure each age by its own standard, and to present the past to us in living pictures. But Scott was the real discoverer and first employer of that *local colouring* in literature which became the basis of the whole production of French Romanticism. Hugo, Mérimée, and Gautier took to it at once. And Scott's historic sense not only made him the pioneer of a whole school of poetry ; it gave his unassuming novels an immense influence over the whole historical literature of the new century. It was, for example, his *Ivanhoe*, with its description of the strained relations between the Normans and the Saxons, which first suggested to Augustin Thierry the idea that the original force which produced such results as the exploits of Clovis, Charlemagne, and Hugo Capet, was the racial antagonism between the Gauls and the Franks. The man whose gift of insight into the inner life of the modern individual human being was so slight, and who in an age of peculiarly independent individual development, was hampered and biassed by the prejudices of patriotism, loyalty, and orthodox piety—this man, thanks to his vigorous Naturalism, had, when he observed these same individuals as a clan, as a nation, or as a race, a perfect understanding of their character as such. Accustomed as he was to reflect on the difference between Scotchmen and Englishmen, it was not unnatural that the idea of the racial antipathy between the Anglo-Saxons and the Normans should, as by an inspiration, occur to him ; and his understanding in such matters makes his descriptions of the same value to the student of racial, as Byron's are to the student of individual, psychology.

And to this merit has to be added the great merit of his tales as descriptions of typical representatives of all classes of society. In the novels of the eighteenth century—Fielding's, for example—we pass from one tavern scene to another ; in Scott's we are introduced into private life, with all its domestic details. The descriptions owe their peculiar excellence to the vigorous realism with which each separate personage is depicted. Englishmen have always specially prized in their authors the gift of describing with such distinct, tangible detail that the object described stands out in relief before the reader's eye ; their sturdy, healthy intellects enjoy the graphic vigour. They like the poetical picture executed in such strong colours that we see it before us as if it were a coat of arms painted on a shield. Scott, as a novelist, gratified this taste. His readers gladly forgave him the terrible prolixity of his descriptions and his conversations, because the result was a graphic representation, attained either by enumerating a long list of attributes or by perpetual insistence upon some one characteristic trait. And there is no doubt, that, tiresome as his procedure may sometimes be, he is one of the greatest character portrayers in all literature. Romanticism has produced nothing finer than such female characters as Diana Vernon in *Rob Roy* and Jeanie Deans in *The Heart of Midlothian*, or such a historic portrait as Louis XI. in *Quentin Durward*.

But in his production of fiction, Scott was from the beginning guilty of one great malpractice, a malpractice which descended to a whole group of talented novelists of a younger generation, namely, the inartistic hurry with which, tempted by the prospect of an enormously high price, he produced book after book as if they had been so many articles of manufacture. In 1809, he had entered into business relations with a firm of printers and publishers of the name of Ballantyne, who printed and published the *Quarterly Review* for him; after he began to write novels he actually became a partner in this firm, which was, unfortunately, a more enterprising than safe one. *Guy Mannering* was written and printed in twenty-five days; and Scott was soon producing at the average rate of twelve volumes in a year; it was quite an ordinary thing for him to write forty printed pages in a morning. The sale corresponded to the enormous production; 10,000 copies of *Rob Roy* were sold in one week; and the later novels were disposed of even faster. In the year 1822, 145,000 volumes of the novels, old and new, were issued. The prices Scott received increased with the circulation of his books. For the two first editions of the Life of Napoleon he was paid £18,000, and his yearly receipts until 1826 were never less than £12,000. He spent his money in improving and enlarging his estate of Abbotsford, and in the erecting thereon of a castle-like mansion, where, with princely hospitality, he entertained hosts of visitors, many of whom settled down and made a lengthy stay. His fame and popularity increased steadily.

On the occasion of a visit to London in 1815, during which he was *fêted*, not only as the author, but as the patriot—the distinguished citizen of Edinburgh who had made himself conspicuous by his ardent hatred of Napoleon—he was presented to the Prince Regent, who showed him many marks of favour. An anecdote has been preserved which gives an idea of the kind of wit with which the heir-apparent succeeded in ingratiating himself for a short time with those whose friendship he desired. There was a supper-party at the Prince Regent's, and Scott, as the guest of the evening, had been kept talking and telling stories almost without intermission, the Prince all the time trying, jestingly, to inveigle him into owning himself to be the author of the Waverley Novels. Scott skilfully extricated himself from one dilemma after another. To prevent further questioning he entertained the company with a true story of an old acquaintance, the Scottish judge, Lord Braxfield. When on circuit, Braxfield was in the habit of spending a night at the house of a wealthy landed proprietor, who, like himself, was a keen chess-player. They often left a game to be finished the following year. The said landed proprietor committed a forgery, and it fell to Braxfield's lot to pronounce the sentence of death on his friend, and opponent in the game. He put on the black cap and read the sentence, which ends with the words, "to be hanged by the neck until you be dead." Having concluded the awful formula with due solemnity, he took off the cap, and with a satisfied smile and nod to his old partner, added: "And now, Donald, my man, I think I've checkmated ye for ance!" The words were hardly out of Scott's mouth when the Prince Regent shouted: "A bumper with all the honours to the author of *Waverley!* and another of the same to the author of *Marmion!*" adding, with a laugh at Scott's conscious expression and gestures of denial: "And now, Walter, my man, I have checkmated you for *ance!*"

The Heart of Midlothian, one of the best of Scott's works, appeared in 1818, and raised him to the height of his fame. It was followed, in December 1819, by *Ivanhoe*, which was also received with the most enthusiastic approbation. We learn, in connection with this masterly novel, how few and how insignificant were the elements of reality which Scott required as a foundation for his imaginary world. A certain Mr. Skene, who had been travelling in Germany, told him a good deal about the condition of the Jews there, their peculiar dress and customs, and the severity with which they were treated. This was enough foundation for a story of such quality as that of Isaac and Rebecca. Scott in private life held, as we have seen, extremely narrow-minded opinions on the question of the political rights of dissenters from the established religion of the country; it is, consequently, all the greater honour to him that, as an author, he was unprejudiced enough to make a Jewess the heroine of his novel, and to endow her with such a matchlessly ideal and yet natural character.

In 1823 appeared *Quentin Durward*, a work in which Sir Walter for the first time chose a foreign theme, and which made his fame as great in France, Germany, and Italy as it already was in England and America. A perusal of the journal of Mr. Skene's tour in France was all that was necessary to enable the author to give his tale its admirable local colouring.

Scott's name was now in every one's mouth, and was familiar even to the most uneducated of his countrymen. In London, at the time of the coronation of George IV., he got into a crowd on the line of the royal procession, and was in actual danger because of his lameness. He addressed a sergeant, begging to be allowed to pass by him into the open ground in the middle of the street. The man answered shortly that his orders were strict, that the thing was impossible. Some new wave of turbulence approaching from behind, Sir Walter's companion cried in a loud voice: "Take care, Sir Walter Scott, take care!" The stalwart dragoon, on hearing the name, said: "What! Sir Walter Scott! He shall get through anyhow!" He then addressed the soldiers near him—"Make room, men, for Sir Walter Scott, our great countryman!" The men answered: "Sir Walter Scott!—God bless him!"—and he was in a moment within the guarded line of safety. We are reminded of the story of the French army in Africa receiving Horace Vernet with flourish of trumpet and beat of drum, and all the military honours due to a general. One can hardly imagine a greater triumph for an artist than this homage of the people.

In 1826 came a turn in the great man's fortunes. The firm of Ballantyne, in which he was a partner, failed; and to the horror of Sir Walter, who in all private money matters was scrupulously exact, the deficit proved to amount to the enormous sum of £117,000. He bore his ruin like a man. The Royal Bank sent a deputation to him with the message that it placed itself at his disposal; he received an anonymous offer of a gift of £30,000; but these and all other offers of assistance he refused. He heroically resolved on the desperate course of endeavouring to pay off the enormous debt with his pen, determining to work without respite until he had discharged the liabilities with which the recklessness and carelessness of others had burdened him. It is not surprising that from this time onwards the quality of his works degenerated steadily. The unfortunate author signed contracts for books—bound himself to produce so and so many volumes per year, of the contents of which, nay, of the very titles of which he had not even thought.

At this unhappy time, only a few months after the failure, he lost his beloved wife. The pressure of business was such that he was unable to sit by her deathbed. He wrote ceaselessly—half a volume of *Woodstock* in four days—harassed all the time by the claims of unfortunate creditors. The man who was accustomed to have his house full of visitors, now lived the life of a hermit. Captain Basil Hall has described the painful impression it made on him to see Sir Walter Scott, who had been in the habit of taking his meals with his wife opposite him and friends and strangers round his table, sitting down alone, to a table laid for one.

He undertook several journeys—one to Paris, for the purpose of collecting authentic anecdotes concerning Napoleon. On this occasion a deputation of the *dames de la halle* presented him with a monster bouquet. He issued a complete edition of his works; of the first nine volumes

35,000 copies were sold. He paid many of his debts. The political reforms in England were a subject of great grief to him; in 1830 he declared: "England is no longer a place for an honest man." Exhausted, ill, with part of his face disfigured by a stroke of paralysis, he went abroad for the last time. In Naples he actually still busied himself in collecting the greatest possible number of old Italian ballads and songs. He became so ill that he hastened home to die in his own country, and breathed his last at Abbotsford in September 1832, exactly six months after Goethe.

All his life Scott was a sincere, mildly rationalistic believer, entirely unaffected by the questioning, daring science of his century. In 1825 he said: "There are few, I trust, who disbelieve the existence of a God; nay, I doubt if at all times, and in all moods, any single individual ever adopted that hideous creed." In the course of the same conversation, however, he allowed that "penal fires and heavenly melody" were possibly only metaphorical expressions. And we know that Lord Byron's dedication of *Cain* to him, instead of offending him, gave him pleasure. In religion, as in politics and literature, he never attained to personal emancipation from the traditions by which the individual is fettered from his birth. Here, too, he left a task which the position of affairs plainly imposed, to be accomplished by the next generation of authors.

When we look back from the vantage-ground of our own day on the second, the prose, period of Scott's authorship, we find it impossible to see the long series of the Waverley Novels in the same light in which they appeared to his contemporaries. We understand the satisfaction which lay in the certainty that they would never give offence, that they might always be welcomed gladly, not only as gifted, but as perfectly moral works. This particular qualification is, however, exactly what makes them less attractive to us. There is no exaggeration in declaring it to be a law in the modern literature of every country, that an author *must* cause offence to at least one generation of his contemporaries, and be considered immoral by it, if he is not to seem tiresome and narrow-minded to readers of the period immediately succeeding his own. To us the defects of Scott's novels are very plain. They give pleasure by their excellent character-drawing and the liveliness of their dialogue, but they do not satisfy the reason, do not appeal very strongly to the feelings, do not even arouse any great degree of curiosity. They are soulful, but idealess. We feel that Scott, as a patriotic author, was determined to keep up the interest in Scotland which Macpherson and Burns had awakened in the reading public; therefore he writes in such a manner as to estrange not even the most narrow-minded reader. Himself denied the sensual organisation of the artist, he is so discreet in his treatment of the relations between the sexes that there is next to no description of erotic situations. And, the moral to be conveyed seeming of greater importance to him than art, he represents past ages with such a toning down of all the coarse elements that historic truth suffers terribly. The species of fiction which Scott introduced, and which indicated a distinct step in advance of the older novel, is now in its turn antiquated; the literary critics of every country lean to the opinion that the historical novel, with all its merits, is a bastard species—now it is so hampered with historical material that the poetic development of the story is rendered impossible, again it is so free in its paraphase of history that the real and the fictitious elements produce a very discordant whole. In the third volume of *The Heart of Midlothian* (Chap. x.), for example, the manner in which imaginary speeches are mixed up with the historical utterances of the Duke of Argyle, distinctly offends the critical taste. It becomes, moreover, increasingly evident how different the general impression conveyed by Scott's pictures of past times is from the essential character of these far-off days, an unvarnished representation of which, supposing it to be understood at all, would certainly fail to awaken sympathy. His *Tales of the Crusaders* are circulating-library novels, which describe the wonder-lands and the romantic, adventurous deeds of the Crusades with almost as little regard to reality as Tasso's *Gerusalemme Liberata;* but which do not display anything like the Italian's poetic talent, or his artistically conscientious attention to style.

How could it be otherwise in the case of an author like Scott, who wrote without ever re-reading, much less correcting, a page, who had not the gift of conciseness, and who made no serious demands on himself in the matter of composition? He demands still less of his readers, as far as attention and quick apprehension are concerned. He repeats himself and allows his characters to repeat themselves, puts in his word in the middle of the story, points out and explains. Not satisfied with showing the temperament and character of his personages by their mode of action, he makes them, when necessary, give account of themselves in such phrases as: "I am speaking with calmness, though it is contrary to my character"; or in speeches in which the speaker draws the moral lesson from his own wicked actions, in case the reader should by any chance miss it and be tempted to imitation. (Read, for example, George Staunton's whole confession to Jeanie Deans, a model of bad style and false psychology.) With such serious faults as these in the details, it is of little avail that the plots of the best novels are excellent, leading up naturally to dramatic crises, one or more as the case may be. A book which is to retain its fame for centuries must not only be poetically planned, but artistically elaborated in every detail—a task for which Scott, from the moment he began to write in prose, never left himself time. Even the most dramatic scene he ever wrote—the splendid and powerfully affecting trial-scene in *The Heart of Midlothian*, in which Jeanie, with a bleeding heart, but with noble devotion to the truth, gives witness against her own sister—loses half of its effect from the careless prolixity of the style. We learn from Moore's *Memoirs* that the main theme of the book—the story of the young girl who refuses to give witness in court in favour of her sister, and afterwards undertakes the long journey to beg a pardon for her—is a true story, which was communicated to Scott in an anonymous letter. He has evidently had the keenest perception of the moral beauty of the incident, but very little of its essentially dramatic character. If he had possessed only half the amount of talent that he had, along with double the amount of culture and instinct of self-criticism, he would doubtless have made less stir in the world, but he would have produced works of greater and more enduring value.[1] He himself felt that what prevented him from attaining to the highest in the domain of literature was his defective education. In his *Journal* (i. 56, 57) there is a curious little survey of his life: "What a life mine has been!—*half educated, almost wholly neglected or left to myself,* stuffing my head with most nonsensical trash, undervalued in society for a time by most of my companions, getting forward, and held a bold, clever fellow, contrary to the opinion of all who thought me a mere dreamer. . . . Now taken in my pitch of pride, and nearly winged, because London chooses to be in an uproar, and in the tumult of bulls and bears, a poor inoffensive lion like myself is pushed to the wall."

It is a dangerous thing for a modern author to be entirely unaffected by the progress of science. If he has not, like Byron, the gift of divining by a kind of clairvoyance what science is seeking and ascertaining, his works fall from the hands of the cultivated reader, to be seized by readers who are only seeking entertainment; or they are preserved and bound by the cultivated readers, to be given away as birthday and Christmas gifts to their sons and daughters, nephews and nieces. Such has been Scott's fate. The author who in the second and third decades of the nineteenth century ruled the book-market, whose influence was felt in every country of Europe, who in France had imitators like Alfred de Vigny, Hugo, Mérimée, Balzac, and the elder Dumas (*The Three Musketeers*), in Italy a disciple like Manzoni, in Germany an intellectual kinsman like Fouqué, in Denmark admirers and pupils like Poul Möller, Ingemann, and Hauch, has become, by the silent, instructive verdict of time, the favourite author of boys and girls of fourteen or thereabouts, an author whom all grown-up people have read, and no grown-up people read.

[1] He does not seem to have had any understanding of plastic art. Desiring to give an impression of the old Puritan in *The Heart of Midlothian*, he evolves the following artistically impossible fabulous creature: "The whole formed a picture, of which the lights might have been given by Rembrandt, but the outline would have required the force and vigour of Michael Angelo."

XI

ALL-EMBRACING SENSUOUSNESS

IN Keats's magnificent fragment, *Hyperion*, there is a scene in which the whole overthrown race of Titanic gods hold counsel in a dark, underground cavern. Their chief, old Saturn, concludes his despondent speech with the words:

> "Yet ye are here,
> O'erwhelm'd and spurn'd, and batter'd, ye are here!
> O Titans, shall I say, 'Arise!'—Ye groan:
> Shall I say 'Crouch!'—Ye groan. What can I then?
> O Heaven wide! O unseen parent dear!
> What can I? Tell me, all ye brethren Gods,
> How we can war, how engine our great wrath!"

Then Oceanus, the thoughtful, meditative sea god, rises, shakes his locks, no longer watery, and, in the murmuring voice which his tongue has caught from the break of the waves on the shore, bids the passion-stung deities take comfort from the thought that they have fallen by the course of Nature's law, and not by the force of thunder or of Jove:—

> "Great Saturn, thou
> Hast sifted well the atom-universe;
> But for this reason, that thou art the King,
> And only blind from sheer supremacy,
> One avenue was shaded from thine eyes,
> Through which I wandered to eternal truth.
> And first, as thou wast not the first of powers,
> So art thou not the last; it cannot be:
> Thou art not the beginning nor the end.
> From Chaos and parental Darkness came
> Light, the first fruits of that intestine broil,
> That sullen ferment, which for wondrous ends
> Was ripening in itself. The ripe hour came,
> And with it light, and light engendering
> Upon its own producer, forthwith touch'd

The whole enormous matter into life.
Upon that very hour, our parentage,
The Heavens and the Earth, were manifest:
Then thou first-born, and we the giant race,
Found ourselves ruling new and beauteous realms.
Now comes the pain of truth, to whom 'tis pain;
O folly! for to bear all naked truths,
And to envisage circumstance, all calm,
That is the top of sovereignty. Mark well!
As Heaven and Earth are fairer, fairer far
Than Chaos and blank Darkness, though once chiefs;
And as we show beyond that Heaven and Earth
In form and shape compact and beautiful,
In will, in action free, companionship,
And thousand other signs of purer life;
So on our heels a fresh perfection treads,
A power more strong in beauty, born of us
And fated to excel us, as we pass
In glory that old Darkness: nor are we
Thereby more conquer'd, than by us the rule
Of shapeless Chaos. Say, doth the dull soil
Quarrel with the proud forests it hath fed,
And feedeth still, more comely than itself?
Can it deny the chiefdom of green groves?
Or shall the tree be envious of the dove
Because it cooeth, and hath snowy wings
To wander wherewithal and find its joys?
We are such forest-trees, and our fair boughs
Have bred forth, not pale solitary doves,
But eagles golden-feather'd, who do tower
Above us in their beauty, and must reign
In right thereof; for 'tis the eternal law
That first in beauty should be first in might:
Ye by that law, another race may drive
Our conquerors to mourn as we do now.
Have ye beheld the young God of the Seas,
My dispossessor? Have ye seen his face?
Have ye beheld his chariot, foam'd along
By noble wingèd creatures he hath made?
I saw him on the calmèd waters scud,
With such a glow of beauty in his eyes,
That it enforc'd me to bid sad farewell
To all my empire."

Thus speaks Oceanus. And the fallen deities, either convinced or in sullen anger, keep silence. At last one, of whom no one has thought, the goddess Clymene, breaks the long silence, speaking timidly among the fierce, with hectic lips and gentle glances :—

"O Father, I am here the simplest voice,
And all my knowledge is that joy is gone,
And this thing woe crept in among our hearts,
There to remain for ever, as I fear :
I would not bode of evil, if I thought
So weak a creature could turn off the help
Which by just right should come of mighty Gods ;
Yet let me tell my sorrow, let me tell
Of what I heard, and how it made me weep,
And know that we had parted from all hope.—
I stood upon a shore, a pleasant shore,
Where a sweet clime was breathèd from a land
Of fragrance, quietness, and trees, and flowers.
Full of calm joy it was, as I of grief ;
Too full of joy and soft delicious warmth ;
So that I felt a movement in my heart
To chide, and to reproach that solitude
With songs of misery, music of our woes ;
And sat me down, and took a mouthèd shell
And murmured into it, and made melody—
O melody no more ! for while I sang,
And with poor skill let pass into the breeze
The dull shell's echo, from a bowery strand
Just opposite, an island of the sea,
There came enchantment with the shifting wind,
That did both drown and keep alive my ears.
I threw my shell away upon the sand,
And a wave fill'd it, as my sense was fill'd
With that new blissful golden melody.
A living death was in each gush of sounds,
Each family of rapturous hurried notes,
That fell, one after one, yet all at once,
Like pearl beads dropping sudden from their string :
And then another, then another strain,
Each like a dove leaving its olive perch,
With music wing'd instead of silent plumes,
To hover round my head, and make me sick
Of joy and grief at once. Grief overcame,
And I was stopping up my frantic ears,
When, past all hindrance of my trembling hands,
A voice came sweeter, sweeter than all tune,
And still it cried, 'Apollo ! young Apollo !
The morning-bright Apollo ! young Apollo !'
I fled, it followed me, and cried 'Apollo !'"

Keats has surpassed himself in this passage, which is as profound in thought as it is beautiful. It is not only a proof of the quality of his poetic gift, but the announcement of the appearance of a younger generation of poets in the field held by the poets of the Lake School and Scott. In the name of the reigning deities, the human intellect is too often condemned to inactivity and stagnation. If there is to be progress, a change of rulers is frequently called for. Wordsworth and Scott were mighty Titans whose glory paled when the younger generation appeared. Keats himself was the golden-feathered bird that rose high into the air above Wordsworth's leafy old oak. And Byron—was not he the new ocean god, who "troubled the waters" of passion with such power that the greatest literary genius of the day abdicated in his favour, assured that it was in vain to compete with him? And Shelley's melodies, intoxicatingly sweet, unprecedentedly daring—were they not borne on all the winds, and are they not still penetrating everywhere, though many, like Clymene, stop their ears and refrain as long as possible from listening to the new tones? The struggle is a vain one, for now on every side resounds the cry: "Apollo! morning-bright Apollo!"

The old gods, as in the poem, assumed different attitudes at this crisis in their fates. Scott, the noblest of them all, acknowledged his defeat by Byron with an amiable dignity which still further enhanced his reputation. Wordsworth retired to his Lakes, muttering an accusation of plagiarism. Southey poured forth volleys of abuse. Meanwhile the new, young gods mounted the thrones of the old, and round their heads shone the bright halo of the light that they gave forth.

Keats was the youngest of the young race of giants, and he had peculiar qualities and a peculiar domain of his own, into which none of the others intruded. He is one of the many examples of singularly delicate and refined organisms appearing in the most unlikely outward surroundings and developing almost unaided by circumstances. This youth who, dying at the age of twenty-six, has left behind him master-works which none who read them can forget, and whose name is immortalised in Shelley's *Adonais,* was the son of a London livery-stable keeper, and was bred an apothecary. Few of the elder literary celebrities knew him. Wordsworth, the only one among them on whom his eyes were steadily turned, and with more reverence than was felt by any of the other young men—even Wordsworth showed himself cold. At Haydon the painter's, one evening, when Wordsworth was present, Keats was induced to repeat to him the famous Hymn to Pan from the First Book of *Endymion.* The "iron-grey poet" heard it to the end, and then only remarked that it was "a pretty piece of paganism." And so, praise be to Keats, it is! Wordsworth, however, meant nothing flattering by the remark. Such was the verdict of the most influential member of the elder school of poetry. The elder school of criticism was distinctly adverse. Its verdict was harsh and scathing. Both the *Quarterly Review* and *Blackwood's Magazine* jeered foolishly at *Endymion.* The author was told that "it is a better and a wiser thing to be a starved apothecary than a starved poet," and was bidden "back to his gallipots." Calmly as the young poet writes of the ignominious treatment he received, there can be no doubt that the sting rankled deeply. It is most improbable that the report spread among Keats's acquaintances of the ruinous effect of these criticisms on his health, was, as is now maintained, entirely without foundation. He certainly was not, as Byron in *Don Juan* declares him to have been, killed by a savage article in the *Quarterly;* and his own utterances give ample proof of his profound contempt for these disparagements of his art and his personality; but his ambition was excessive, his susceptibility equally so, and his body contained the germs of a fatal disease; and it would be surprising if rancorous attacks from without had not affected an organism which was preyed upon from within by consuming passion and consuming disease.

John Keats was born in October 1795. At the age of nine he lost his father. His mother sent him to a good school; but she, too, to his inexpressible grief, died while he was still a boy. His appearance corresponded to the impression which his poetry makes on us. Whilst the feminine and ethereal Shelley had a slender, slightly-built, narrow-chested figure and a shrill voice, the heavier footed, more earth-bound Keats was deep-chested and broad-shouldered ; his lower limbs were small in comparison with the upper ; and he had a deep, grave voice. His small head was covered with thick brown curls ; the eyes were large and of a dark, on occasion glowing, blue ; the handsome mouth had a projecting lower lip, which gave the face a defiant and pugnacious expression. And as a matter of fact he was, as a boy, a perfect little terrier for resoluteness and pugnacity, and seemed much more likely to distinguish himself in war than in literature. He early displayed great personal courage, and was an adept in all athletic exercises ; just before he was attacked by consumption he thrashed an insolent butcher in a regular stand-up fight.

At the age of fifteen he left school, and was apprenticed by his relations to a clever surgeon-apothecary at Edmonton, with whom he remained till he was twenty, when he began, as a medical student, to walk the London hospitals. He soon, however, gave up medicine for literature, and lived for several years in close companionship with some of the rising young literary men and artists of the day. Then he was attacked by the disease which had carried off his mother and his younger brother. The absence of any prospect of earning a living, and the ever-increasing pressure of poverty, favoured its development, which was farther hastened by a violent and hopeless passion for a young Anglo-Indian lady —a passion only rendered hopeless by Keats's poverty and ill-health—his love being returned. His health obliged him to quit the neighbourhood of his beloved and take a journey to Italy, where he died.

Glancing over the non-literary part of Keats's life, we distinguish three facts of leading importance—his want of any real prospect of gaining a livelihood (he had thoughts of emigrating to South America, or applying for a post as surgeon on an Indiaman) ; the ardent and hopeless passion for the woman without whom life was worthless to him ; and the wasting disease.

Miss Fanny Brawne was eighteen, five years younger than Keats, when he made her acquaintance in 1818. He and his friend, Brown, had settled at Hampstead, in a semi-detached house, the other half of which was occupied by Miss Brawne and her mother. The first six months after he fell in love were to Keats months of real happiness. In December 1818 he began *Hyperion*. In February 1819, the most fruitful month in his life, he wrote the *Ode to Psyche*, *The Eve of St. Agnes*, and great part of *Hyperion*. And early in the spring, sitting under a plum-tree in the Brawnes' garden, he wrote his *Ode to the Nightingale*. In other words —his most beautiful poetry was written in the half year during which he took long walks with Fanny, and was still a healthy man. Unfortunately, it being possible for him to see his beloved every day, we have not a single love-letter dating from this, his short period of happiness. In July 1819 he wrote to her for the first time; and all the letters which he sent her from that date until the time of his death were published in 1878.

They are not melancholy to begin with. In one of the earliest he writes: "I want a brighter word than bright, a fairer word than fair;" and to some objection made by her he answers: "Why may I not speak of your Beauty, since without that I could never have lov'd you?—I cannot conceive any beginning of such love as I have for you but Beauty. There may be a sort of love for which, without the least sneer at it, I have the highest respect and can admire it in others; but it has not the richness, the bloom, the full form, the enchantment of love after my own heart."

Very soon, however, the jealousy which was to have such a wearing effect upon the lover appears in his letters. Again and again he exacts promises of eternal devotion. Though not yet ill, he has a vague presentiment that his end is not far off. "I have two luxuries to brood over in my walks," he writes; "your Loveliness and the hour of my death. O that I could have possession of them both in the same minute!"

Her letters had really only a depressing effect on him. He read them so often that each sentence assumed a distorted proportion ; and they seemed to him now cold, now full of reproaches. He tortured first himself and then her with his suspicious irritableness and perversity ; he would, for example, pass her door without going in, though he was longing to see her, and knew that his not appearing was a disappointment to her. There are a few perfectly happy, tender letters, dated October 1819. But in February 1820 commences a period of miserable excitement. He begins to spit blood, and "reads his death-warrant in its colour." After this the letters are short, some of them still playful and hopeful, others suspicious and violent in their jealousy—all brimming over with passion. Here is a fragment: "You know our situation—what hope is there if I should be recovered ever so soon—my very health will not suffer me to make any great exertion. I am recommended not even to read poetry, much less write it. I cannot say forget me—but I would mention that there are impossibilities in the world. No more of this. I am not strong enough to be weaned—take no notice of it in your good-night."

During his apparent convalescence he is constantly begging her to come and show herself only for half a minute outside of the window through which he can see her, or to walk a little in the garden. Then he asks her not to come every day, because he cannot always bear to see her. But when, according to his wish, she does not come, he is restless and jealous.

As the end approaches, the letters become ever sadder and more distressing to read. The last of them are positively harrowing. He is as wild and helpless in his passionate despair as a child who believes himself forgotten. It is the mental death-struggle preceding the physical.

Fanny Brawne's tenderness for her lover never wavered. It is now evident that, as was only natural, this young girl with the touch of coquetry in her nature had no suspicion whatever of the gifts and powers of the poor consumptive youth who worshipped and tortured her. But she loved him for his own sake, and when, from the last letter, she learned in what a sad condition he really was, she and her mother would no longer leave him to the care of his friend, but took him into their own house in Wentworth Place, where he lived for the last month before he left for Italy. A stay in that country had been prescribed, as giving him a last chance of recovery.

The man to whom, in other circumstances, the prospect of seeing the country for which he had always longed, and whose gods he had awakened from the dead, would have given supreme happiness, now writes: "This journey to Italy wakes me at daylight every morning, and haunts me horribly. I shall endeavour to go, though it be with the sensation of marching up against a Battery." On board ship he writes, referring to his attachment to Miss Brawne: "Even if my body would recover of itself, this would prevent it. The very thing which I want to live most for will be a great occasion of my death. I cannot help it. . . . I wish for death every day and night to deliver me from these pains, and then I wish death away, for death would destroy even those pains which are better than nothing. Land and sea, weakness and decline, are great separators, but death is the great divorcer for ever. . . . I seldom think of my brother and sister in America. The thought of leaving Miss Brawne is beyond everything horrible—the sense of darkness coming over me—I eternally see her figure eternally vanishing." And in another letter he writes: "The persuasion that I shall see her no more will kill me. My dear Brown, I should have had her when I was in health, and I should have remained well. I can bear to die—I cannot bear to leave her. O God! God! God! Everything I have in my trunks that reminds me of her goes through me like a spear. The silk lining she put in my travelling cap scalds my head. My imagination is horribly vivid about her—I see her—I hear her. There is nothing in the world of sufficient interest to divert me from her for a moment. . . . I cannot say a word about Naples; I do not feel at all concerned in the thousand novelties around me. I am afraid to write to her—I should like her to know that I do not forget her. Oh, Brown, I have coals of fire in my breast. It surprises me that the human heart is capable of containing and bearing so much misery. Was I born for this end?"

On the last day of November 1820, Keats wrote his last letter. His intimate old friend, Dr. Clark, a skilful physician, preserved his life till the end of the winter. While in Naples, Keats received a letter from his brother poet, Shelley, inviting him to come to Pisa, where he would be nursed and cared for in every way. But this invitation he did not accept. After several weeks of great suffering came rest and sleep, resignation and tranquillity. He desired that a letter from his beloved, which he had not dared to read, along with a purse and a letter which he had received from his sister, should be placed in his coffin; and that on his gravestone should be inscribed:

"Here lies one whose name was writ in water."

The touch of Shelley's magic wand stiffened the water into crystal, and the name stands inscribed for all time.[1]

Keats's poetry is the most fragrant flower of English Naturalism. Before he appeared, this Naturalism had had a long period of vigorous growth. Its active principle had been evolved by Wordsworth, who developed it so methodically that he divided his poems into groups, corresponding to the different periods of human life and the different faculties of the soul. Coleridge provided it with the support of a philosophy of nature which had a strong resemblance to Schelling's. In Scott it assumes the highly successful form of a study of men, manners, and scenery, inspired by patriotism, by interest in history, and by a wonderful apprehension of the significance of race. Both in Moore and Keats it takes the form of gorgeous sensuousness, is the literary expression of the perceptions of beings whose sensitiveness to impressions of the beauty of the external world makes that of the average human being seem blunt and dull. But the sensuousness of Moore's poetry, which reveals itself

[1] "Death, the immortalising winter, flew
Athwart the stream—and time's printless torrent grew
A scroll of crystal, blazoning the name
Of Adonais."—*Fragment on Keats:* Shelley.

artistically in his warm, bright colouring, is confined to the erotic domain, and is of a light and playful character. Keats's is full-blooded, serious sensuousness, by no means specially erotic, but all-embracing, and, in this its comprehensiveness, one of the most admirable developments of English Naturalism. This Naturalism led Wordsworth into one extreme, which has already been referred to; Keats it led into a different and more poetical one.

Keats was more of the artist than any of his English brother poets. He troubled himself less about principles than any of them. There is no groundwork of patriotism in his poetry as there is in Scott's and Moore's; no message of liberty, as in Shelley's and Byron's; it is pure art, owing its origin to nothing but the power of imagination. It was one of his favourite sayings, that the poet should have no principles, no morality, *no self*. Why? Because the true poet enjoys both light and shade—has as much delight in conceiving an Iago as an Imogen. All poets who have forgotten themselves in the theme of their flights of fancy, have, when engaged in production, to the best of their ability banished their private peculiarities and preferences. Few have managed to make such a clean sweep as Keats of their personal hopes, enthusiasms, and principles. His study was, as one of his admirers has said, "a painter's studio with very little in it besides the easel."

Keats's poetical indifference to theories and principles was, however, in itself a theory and a principle—was the philosophy which has its foundation in poetic worship of nature. To the consistent pantheistic poet all forms, all shapes, all expressions of life on earth which engage the imagination, are precious, and all equally precious. Keats, as poet, recognises no truth of the kind that means improvement or exclusion; but he has an almost religious faith in imagination as the source of truth. In one of his letters he expresses himself thus:—"I am certain of nothing but of the holiness of the heart's affections, and the truth of Imagination. What the Imagination seizes as Beauty must be Truth, whether it existed before or not;—for I have the same idea of all our passions as of Love: they are all, in their sublime, creative of essential Beauty. . . . The Imagination may be compared to Adam's dream ; he awoke and found it truth." He enlarges on the difference between this kind of truth and the truth arrived at by consecutive reasoning, and concludes with an exclamation which is a key to the whole of his poetry :—" However it may be, O for a life of sensations rather than of thoughts!"

He led in great part a life of passive sensation, of pleasure and pain through the senses. "Take," says Masson, "a book of physiology and go over the so-called classes of sensations one by one—the sensations of the mere muscular states ; the sensations connected with such vital processes as circulation, alimentation, respiration, and electrical intercommunication with surrounding bodies ; the sensations of taste ; those of odour ; those of hearing; and those of sight —and Keats will be found to have been unusually endowed in them all."

He had, for example, an extreme sensitiveness to the pleasures of the palate, and tried to heighten them by extraordinary stimulants. A friend tells us that he once saw Keats covering his tongue with cayenne pepper, that he might enjoy the delicious sensation of a draught of cold claret after it. "Talking of pleasure," he says himself in one of his letters, "this moment I was writing with one hand and with the other holding to my mouth a nectarine." It is therefore not surprising that imagery drawn from the domain of the sense of taste is of frequent occurrence in Keats's poetry. In his deservedly famous *Ode to Melancholy* we are told that this goddess has her sovran shrine in the very temple of Delight—

> "Though seen of none save him *whose strenuous tongue*
> *Can burst Joy's grape against his palate fine.*"

And in one of his last sonnets he characteristically mentions "the palate of my mind losing its gust" as an indication of approaching death.

Naturally the senses of hearing and sight provided him with a much greater proportion of his imagery than the inferior, less noble senses. He had a musician's love of music and a painter's eye for variations of light and colour. And for all the different kinds of sound and smell and taste and sensations of touch, he possessed a store of words which any of the greatest poets might have envied. In short, he was by nature endowed with qualities which in combination, and in their full development, constituted supreme capacity to perceive and to reproduce all the beauty of nature.

To be able to reproduce it was from the very beginning his dream; and the man who affirmed that, except in the matter of art, he had no "opinions," expressed enthusiastic approval of the revolution of opinion in regard to the artificial, so-called classical, poetry of the eighteenth century, which had been brought about by Wordsworth and Coleridge. Spenser was Keats's idol, the classic poets were his aversion. In his poem, *Sleep and Poetry*, he has embodied an artistic confession of faith in language which could not well be more violent. After describing the old poetic triumphs of England, he exclaims:

> "Could all this be forgotten? Yes, a schism
> Nurtured by foppery and barbarism
> Made great Apollo blush for this his land.
> Men were thought wise who could not understand
> His glories: with a puling infant's force
> They sway'd about upon a rocking-horse
> And thought it Pegasus. Ah! dismal-soul'd!
> The winds of heaven blew, the ocean roll'd
> Its gathering waves; ye felt it not. The blue
> Bared its eternal bosom, and the dew
> Of summer night collected still to make
> The morning precious; Beauty was awake!
> Why were *ye* not awake? . . . .
> . . . . No, they went about,
> Holding a poor decrepit standard out,
> Mark'd with most flimsy mottoes, and, in large,
> The name of one Boileau!"

Long before the French assault upon this ancient, honoured name, Keats blows the war-trumpet! Théophile Gautier himself does not treat it with greater contempt.

It was probably the above passage, the energetic style of which reminds one of that picture of Kaulbach's in Munich, in which the artist of the rococo period is painted asleep with the lay-figure in his arms, which gave occasion to Byron's repeated thrusts at Keats as the traducer of Pope. For Keats never published a line against Pope; and when Countess Guiccioli, in her naïve work on Byron, refers to attacks which infuriated her lover, she is only repeating vague remarks she has heard. It is, however, highly probable that Keats included Pope among those whom he reproached with being deaf to the music of the waves and the winds, and with sleeping whilst the morning unfolded its beauties.

He himself was not of that company. If we examine the distinctive individuality of Keats's genius, we find its determining element to be the all-embracing sensuousness already alluded to. Read this stanza of the *Ode to a Nightingale*:—

> "O, for a draught of vintage! that hath been
> Cool'd a long age in the deep-delvèd earth,
> Tasting of Flora and the country green,
> Dance, and Provençal song, and sun-burnt mirth!
> O for a beaker full of the warm South,
> Full of the true, the blushful Hippocrene,
> With beaded bubbles winking at the brim,
> And purple-stainèd mouth;
> That I might drink, and leave the world unseen,
> And with thee fade away into the forest dim."

And compare with it the following lines of *Endymion*:—

> "Taste these juicy pears,
> Sent me by sad Vertumnus; . . . . . .
> . . . . here is cream,
> Deepening to richness from a snowy gleam;
> Sweeter than that nurse Amalthea skimmed
> For the boy Jupiter: and here, undimmed
> By any touch, a bunch of blooming plums
> Ready to melt between an infant's gums."

The delicate, highly developed sense of taste is accompanied by an equally delicate and highly developed sense of touch and sense of smell. Read the passage in *Isabella*—a poem which, following Boccaccio, treats of the same theme as Hans Andersen's tale of the "Rose Fairy"—the passage which tells how the young girl took the head of her murdered lover from the grave:—

> "Then in a silken scarf,—sweet with the dews
> Of precious flowers pluck'd in Araby,
> And divine liquids come with odorous ooze
> Through the cold serpent pipe refreshfully,
> She wrapp'd it up." . . . .

and the lines in *Lamia*, describing the reception of the guests who come to take part in the wedding festivities:—

> "When in an antechamber every guest
> Had felt the cold full sponge to pleasure press'd,
> By minist'ring slaves, upon his hands and feet,
> And fragrant oils with ceremony meet
> Pour'd on his hair, they all mov'd to the feast
> In white robes, and themselves in order placed
> Around the silken couches."

In one of the *Epistles* occurs a line, about a swan, into which is compressed an incredible amount of sensuous imagery. It is: "Kissing thy daily food from Naiads' pearly hands."

It is unnecessary to draw the reader's attention in detail to all the delicate charms of these fragments. Proceeding to the domain of the sense of sight, we find that it pre-eminently is Keats's territory, although it is never his eye alone which is impressed by his surroundings. Words-worth's poetry of nature leads us out into the open air; following Keats, we enter a hot-house: a soft, moist warmth meets us; our eyes are attracted by brightly coloured flowers and juicy fruits; slender palms, amidst whose branches no rough wind ever blows, beckon gently with their huge fans. His *Ode to Autumn* is a characteristic specimen of his descriptions of nature. After telling of autumn's conspiracy with the sun

> "to load and bless
> With fruit the vines that round the thatch-eaves run;
> To bend with apples the moss'd cottage trees,
> And fill all fruit with ripeness to the core;
> To swell the gourd, and plump the hazel shells
> With a sweet kernel,"

he with a masterly hand portrays autumn as a person:

> "Who hath not seen thee oft amid thy store?
> Sometimes whoever seeks abroad may find
> Thee sitting careless on a granary floor,
> Thy hair soft-lifted by the winnowing wind:
> Or on a half-reap'd furrow sound asleep,
> Drowsed with the fume of poppies, while thy hook
> Spares the next swath and all its twinèd flowers."

It is impossible for Keats to name any conception or any thought without at once proceeding to represent it in a corporeal, plastic form. His numerous allegories have the same life and fire as if they were executed in stone by the best Italian artists of the sixteenth century. He says of Melancholy:

> "She dwells with Beauty—Beauty that must die;
> And Joy, *whose hand is ever at his lips*
> *Bidding adieu.*"

He says of Poetry:

> "A drainless shower
> Of light is poesy; 'tis the supreme power;
> 'Tis *might half-slumb'ring on its own right arm.*"

We see the scope of Keats's poetic powers steadily increasing. His point of departure, especially in some of the most beautiful of his smaller poems (for example, the *Ode to the Nightingale*), is the description of a purely physical condition, such as weariness, nervousness, thirst, languor, the drowsiness produced by opium. Upon this background of sensitiveness the sensuous pictures rise, distinct and round, like the reliefs upon a shield. The word "welded" comes involuntarily to one's lips when one thinks of Keats's pictures. There is something firm and finished about them, as if they were welded on a metal plate.

Observe how the figures rise gradually into relief in the following stanzas, the first and third of the beautiful *Ode to Indolence*:—

> "One morn before me were three figures seen
> With bowèd necks and joinèd hands, side-faced;
> And one behind the other stepped serene,
> In placid sandals, and in white robes graced;

They passed like figures on a marble urn,
When shifted round to see the other side ;
They came again ; as when the urn once more
Is shifted round, the first green shades return,
And they were strange to me, as may betide
With vases, to one deep in Phidian lore.
. . . .
A third time passed they by, and, passing, turned
Each one the face a moment whiles to me ;
Then faded, and to follow them I burned
And ached for wings, because I knew the three ;
The first was a fair maid, and Love her name ;
The second was Ambition, pale of cheek,
And ever watchful, with fatiguèd eye ;
The last, whom I love more, the more of blame
Is heaped upon her, maiden most unmeek,—
I knew to be my demon, Poesy."

But not until he wrote the two completed books of *Hyperion* did Keats attain to absolute mastery over his artistic material, and realise the ideal of sensuous plasticity which was ever before his eyes. In this work the relief has been superseded by the statue ; and they are statues, these, which impress us with the feeling that Michael Angelo's chisel must have played a part in their production. Granted that the influence of Milton is clearly perceptible—there is more than Milton here. The nature of the subject demanded the colossal.

We are told of the goddess Thea:

"By her in stature the tall Amazon
Had stood a pigmy's height ; she would have ta'en
Achilles by the hair and bent his neck ;
Or with a finger stay'd Ixion's wheel."

And read this description of the cavern where the Titans are assembled after their fall :—

"It was a den where no insulting light
Could glimmer on their tears ; where their own groans
They felt, but heard not, for the solid roar
Of thunderous waterfalls and torrents hoarse,
Pouring a constant bulk, uncertain where.
Crag jutting forth to crag, and rocks that seem'd
Ever as if just rising from a sleep,

Forehead to forehead held their monstrous horns;
And thus in thousand hugest phantasies
Made a fit roofing to this nest of woe.
Instead of thrones, hard flint they sat upon,
Couches of rugged stone, and slaty ridge
Stubborn'd with iron. All were not assembled:
Some chain'd in torture, and some wandering.
Cœus, and Gyges, and Briareüs,
Typhon, and Dolor, and Porphyrion,
With many more, the brawniest in assault,
Were pent in regions of laborious breath;
Dungeon'd in opaque element, to keep
Their clenchèd teeth still clench'd, and all their limbs
Lock'd up like veins of metal, crampt and screw'd;
Without a motion, save of their big hearts
Heaving in pain, and horribly convuls'd
With sanguine feverous boiling gurge of pulse."

Byron, who had been very severe in his criticism of Keats's previous works, said, and said truly, of *Hyperion*: "It seems actually inspired by the Titans, and is as sublime as Æschylus."

The specimens of his poetry here quoted afford sufficient proof of Keats's imaginative power. It is to it, and not to his melodies, sweet as they are, that he owes his rank among English poets.[1] The purely artistic character of his verse makes of him the connecting link between the conservative and the progressive poets. He has a distinct bias in the direction of progress. Of this his enthusiastic friendship for the Radical editor of the *Examiner*, Leigh Hunt, is a striking proof. He felt what he wrote when, in his indignation at the proceedings of the Liverpool-Castlereagh ministry, he exclaimed (in his poem *To Hope*):

"O, let me see our land retain her soul,
Her pride, her freedom; and not freedom's shade!"

And William Tell, Wallace, and, chief of all, Kosciuszko, are named again and again in his verse with the profoundest

[1] Note the melodiousness of the Fairy Song:

"Shed no tear! O shed no tear!
The flower will bloom another year.
Weep no more! O weep no more!
Young buds sleep in the root's white core," &c.

admiration. What he might have developed into if he had reached maturity, it is impossible to tell. When he wrote his last poems he was still but a child, ignorant of the world.

And it must not be forgotten that while he wrote them he was enduring great physical suffering, and mental anxiety amounting to torture. Perhaps it is for this very reason they are so beautiful. Let the artist keep his private life long enough out of his work—let him, like Keats, hardly make any allusion in his poetry to his most absorbing passion—and no work will have such life, such colour, such divine fire as that executed whilst he not only wrought, but lived and suffered. Neither the precariousness of Keats's circumstances, nor his hopeless state of health, nor his passion for Fanny Brawne, set any distinct mark on his poetry; but from all this poison for himself he drew nourishment for it.

He sank into his early grave, but hardly had the earth closed over him before he rose again from the dead in Shelley's great elegy. He ceased to exist as Keats; he was transformed into a myth, into Adonais, into the beloved of all the Muses and the elements; and henceforward he had, as it were, a double existence in the consciousness of the age.

> "He lives, he wakes—'tis Death is dead, not he;
> Mourn not for Adonais. . . .
>
> He is made one with Nature. There is heard
> His voice in all her music, from the moan
> Of thunder to the song of night's sweet bird. . . .
>
> He is a portion of the loveliness
> Which once he made more lovely. He doth bear
> His part, while the One Spirit's plastic stress
> Sweeps through the dull dense world, compelling there
> All new successions to the forms they wear. . . .
>
> The inheritors of unfulfilled renown
> Rose from their thrones, built beyond mortal thought,
> Far in the unapparent. Chatterton
> Rose pale, his solemn agony had not
> Yet faded from him; Sidney, as he fought,
> And as he fell, and as he lived and loved,
> Sublimely mild, a spirit without spot,
> Arose . . . . . .

And many more, whose names on earth are dark,
But whose transmitted effluence cannot die
So long as fire outlives the parent spark,
Rose, robed in dazzling immortality.
'Thou art become as one of us,' they cry ;
'It was for thee yon kingless sphere has long
Swung blind in unascended majesty,
Silent alone amid an heaven of song.
Assume thy wingèd throne, thou Vesper of our throng!'"[1]

We search the history of literature in vain for a parallel to this elegy. It is instant transfiguration after death—a poetic transfiguration of a purely naturalistic and purely human kind. To Shelley, Keats's true apotheosis was what he expresses in the words: "He is made one with Nature."

[1] Shelley: *Adonais.*

XII

THE POETRY OF IRISH OPPOSITION AND REVOLT

In November 1825 Sir Walter Scott writes in his diary: "I saw Moore . . . There is a manly frankness and perfect ease and good breeding about him which is delightful. Not the least touch of the poet or the pedant . . . His countenance is decidedly plain, but the expression is so very animated, especially in speaking or singing, that it is far more interesting than the finest features could have rendered it. I was aware that Byron had often spoken, both in private society and his Journal, of Moore and myself in the same breath, and with the same sort of regard; so I was curious to see what there could be in common betwixt us, Moore having lived so much in the gay world, I in the country and with people of business, and sometimes with politicians; Moore a scholar, I none; he a musician and artist, I without knowledge of a note; he a democrat, I an aristocrat—with many other points of difference; besides his being an Irishman, I a Scotchman, and both tolerably national. Yet there is a point of resemblance, and a strong one. We are both good-humoured fellows, who rather seek to enjoy what is going forward than to maintain our dignity as lions; and we have both seen the world too widely and too well not to contemn in our souls the imaginary consequence of literary people, who walk with their noses in the air, and remind me always of the fellow whom Johnson met in an alehouse, and who called himself 'the *great* Twalmley—inventor of the floodgate iron for smoothing linen.' . . . It would be a delightful addition to life if T. M. had a cottage within two miles of one.—We went to the theatre together, and the house, being luckily a good one, received T. M. with rapture. I could have hugged them, for it paid back the debt of the kind reception I met with in Ireland."

In these cordial words the great Scottish author compares himself with the Irish national poet. The resemblance between their position, as recognised and highly esteemed organs of the two dependent countries united to England, makes the difference between them the more clearly perceptible. There is, first of all, the dissimilarity produced by the dissimilar relations of Scotland and Ireland to the dominant race. Scotland's position was a subordinate one, but it was legally established, and the country sent representatives to Parliament. The Irish, on the other hand, divided by a much more marked difference of race, and, as regarded the majority, of religion, from their English masters, had been for six centuries under the rule of a Government in which they had no more share than have the Hindoos or the Cingalese in theirs. The Protestant Irish Parliament existed in its day in Ireland like a hostile garrison in a conquered country. It was a body of absolute rulers, governing and oppressing in the name of a foreign power; any attempt at opposition on the part of its members was at once put a stop to either by bribery or force. The Irish Protestant was not in reality in a better position than his Catholic fellow-countryman; he could purchase the favour of his masters only by sacrificing the interests of his country, and enjoyed only the one pitiful privilege of being at the same time vassal and master.

It has been a fortunate thing for the English people that their faults as well as their virtues have ensured them success in the struggle for political independence and power; their egoism and their pride have been of almost as much service to them as their sober sagacity and their energy. The Irish, on the other hand, seem, like the Poles, to be condemned both by their virtues and their vices to political subordination. Even making allowance for the fact that the character of the conquered race is invariably maligned in the descriptions of it given by the conqueror, it must be granted that the sprightliness, ardour, and charm of the Irish, their turbulent bravery, their fitful chivalry, their independent and, under certain conditions, rebellious tendencies, co-existing with a love of the pomp and splendour of royalty, form a bad foundation for a tranquil and independent existence as a state. The virtues of the Irish are not the modern, civic virtues, but those of an earlier age—their piety verges on the blindest superstition; their fidelity consists, like that of their Breton brothers, in a kind of vassal-fealty to the old nobility of the country, and their splendid bravery is of an undisciplined, impetuous nature. Long-continued oppression has, moreover, set its imprint on their souls. They lack self-confidence, and have a tendency to dissimulation and to indolence; they are too reckless of danger and too easily intimidated when brought face to face with it; they cannot, when liberty is granted them for a short time, make a good use of it, this being an art which can only be learned by long practice.

There are inexperienced races just as there are inexperienced individuals. One side of the Irish character has a strong resemblance to the French (and the Irish have always had a warm sympathy for the French), another reminds us of the Polish character, and there is a third which is almost Oriental. In a poem entitled "The Parallel" (one of the *Irish Melodies*), which Moore composed in answer to an anti-Irish pamphlet written to prove that the Irish were originally Jews, he compares the fate of the two nations:—

> "Like thee doth our nation lie conquer'd and broken,
> And fall'n from her head is the once royal crown;
> In her streets, in her halls, desolation hath spoken,
> And 'while it is day yet, her sun hath gone down.'"

And there undoubtedly is an Oriental quality in the race. Byron, writing of Moore, says that the wildness, tenderness, and originality of the Irish—the magnificent and fiery spirit of the men, the beauty and feeling of the women, are the best proofs of the Oriental descent which they claim. A race with such a character necessarily fell an easy prey to a determined, cruel English despotism.

A hasty glance at the history of Ireland during Thomas Moore's youth will help us to understand how this man with the gentle nature and the sweet lyric gift was the first to rouse English poetry from its engrossed preoccupation with nature, to impress it into the service of liberty, and to give the start to political poetry.

Moore was born in May 1779. The years of his early youth were the period of the revolting events now to be related. From the time when the English Government showed, by the appointment of Lord Camden as Lord Lieutenant of Ireland (1795), that it had abandoned the humaner policy of 1782, the Society of United Irishmen, a powerful political organisation, which had hitherto aimed at the emancipation of the country by lawful means, completely changed its character. The separation of Ireland from England became its aim; it had dreams of the establishment of an Irish Republic. But there were two powerful elements of dissension in the country itself, namely, the existence of two races, hostile to each other, and the strong animosity in the lower classes between Protestants and Catholics. To put an end to the disturbances and riots which were constantly resulting from these internal dissensions, the Government formed a force of Protestant constabulary, 37,000 strong. These troops were permitted, under the pretence of searching for concealed weapons, to capture, torture, and put to death any unfortunate person whom an enemy, or any ruffian whatever, chose to accuse of suspicious behaviour. Hundreds of unoffending people, who were guilty of no other offence than professing the creed of their fathers, were flogged until they were insensible, or made to stand upon one foot on a pointed stake, or were half hanged, or had the scalp torn from their heads by a pitched cap. Militia and yeomanry, as well as the regular troops, were billeted in private houses; and this billet appears to have been construed as an unlimited license for robbery, devastation, ravishment, and, in case of resistance, murder. It was boasted by officers of rank that within certain large districts no home had been left undefiled; and upon its being remarked that the sex must have been very complying, the reply was that "the bayonet removed all squeamishness."[1]

It was not surprising that the despair induced by such proceedings drove numbers of the most peaceable and sensible Irishmen into the arms of a secret society, which sent Lord Edward Fitzgerald (whose biography Moore wrote with such warm admiration) as its deputy to France, to arrange with General Hoche for the landing of a French army in Ireland at the time appointed for a general rising of the Irish rebels. Grattan, the old, passionless leader of the national party, refused to countenance foreign interference, and retired from public life in despair over the latest plans both of the rulers and the oppressed. The Irish patriots elected a governing body, a species of Directoire, which was negotiating with France for the loan of money and troops, when all its plans were discomfited by the treason of a single Catholic Irishman. His name, which deserves to be remembered, was Reynolds. Moore undoubtedly had this man in his mind when he wrote the description, in *The Fire-worshippers*, of the base betrayal of the rebel chief to the Mohammedans.[2]

Lord Edward Fitzgerald was in bed when the soldiers forced their way into the house where he lay hidden. A reward of £1000 had been offered for his head. Although undressed, and with no weapon but a sword, he defended himself for a long time against three fully armed English officers, of whom one received three and another fourteen wounds; the third disarmed him with a pistol-shot, and he was taken to prison. Fitzgerald was acquainted with the most distinguished of the French revolutionists; he was a friend of Thomas Paine; and his wife was a charming daughter of Philippe Egalité. He carried on a steady correspondence with France; and had he not died in prison, he would have been executed. It speaks well for Moore's courage and independent judgment, that, though he belonged to a circle in which Fitzgerald was regarded as

[1] Massey: *History of England*, iv. 302. The whole account is founded upon descriptions given by *English* patriots.

[2] *Lalla Rookh: The Fire-worshippers.*

a traitorous madman, he paid him all the honour due to his heroism.

The rebels having thus lost their leader, the prospect of a general rising was at an end ; but the Government took the opportunity to treat persons suspected of sedition with a cruelty bordering on frenzy. Martial law was proclaimed, and those employed to administer it are described by English historians as "a set of ignorant, bloodthirsty ruffians, who first, by torture and promises of pardon, converted Catholic prisoners into witnesses against the accused, and then treated them in the most shameful manner." The first notable man who fell a victim to this species of justice was a peaceable member of the party which desired reform by lawful means, Sir Edward Crosbie. He was hanged, and his body mutilated afterwards. It was not the difference of religion which excited the cruel passions of these torturers, for all the best leaders of the United Irishmen (Fitzgerald, O'Connor, Harvey, Thomas Emmet) were Protestants, who unselfishly embraced the cause of their Catholic countrymen ; it was the Anglo-Saxons' old race-hatred of the Celts.

The Government chose as its chief tool a man who was known to be such an ignorant, ferocious partisan that any degree of violence might be expected of him. This was Thomas Judkin Fitzgerald, a small proprietor, who in 1799 was appointed High Sheriff. His plan of ingratiating himself with his employers was to seize persons whom he chose to suspect, and, by dint of the lash and threats of instant death, to extort confessions of guilt and accusations of other persons. So abject was the terror of the peasantry who were abandoned to the mercy of this miscreant, that they fell on their knees before him. I give two examples of his manner of proceeding, chosen from the many which were made public during the lawsuit brought against him for having abused his authority—the result of which was, of course, his acquittal with honour.

He received a poor teacher of languages (Wright by name), who, hearing that he was "suspected," had come to the court-house of his own accord, with the order to fall upon his knees and receive his sentence. "You are a rebel," said the Sheriff, "and a principal in this rebellion. You are to receive five hundred lashes, and then to be shot." The poor man begged for time, and was so rash as to ask for a trial. This aroused Fitzgerald to fury, and Wright was hurried to the flogging-ladders. Fitzgerald himself dragged his fainting victim by the hair, kicked him, and slashed him with a sword. Fifty lashes had been inflicted, when an English Major came up and asked what Wright had done. The Sheriff answered by flinging him a note, taken from Wright's pocket. It was in French, a language of which Fitzgerald was wholly ignorant, and proved to be an excuse for inability to fulfil a professional engagement. Major Riall assured Fitzgerald that the note was perfectly harmless; nevertheless the lash continued to descend until the victim's entrails were visible through the flayed flesh. The hangman was then ordered to apply his thongs to a part of the body which had not yet been torn.

This case of Wright's was one of those which created the greatest sensation during the proceedings against the Irish High Sheriff. But "the trial," says Massey, "would not have been complete had not an Orange parson been called on the part of the defendant to swear that this notorious bloodshedder, who throughout Ireland was called 'flogging Fitzgerald,' was a mild and humane man." The fact that the Government, contrary to the principles of the constitution, had given a special permission at the time of his appointment for the employment of torture, made it easy for him to triumph over all his denouncers. Addressing the jury as defendant, he actually boasted of having flogged several persons under circumstances more aggravated than those before the court. He mentioned one man who had cut his throat to escape the horrors and ignominy of torture. It remains to be told that Judkin Fitzgerald received a special pension as reward of his services, and was, after the Union, made a baron of the United Kingdom.

One more specimen of the proceedings during the suppression of the rebellion must be given; it furnishes an idea of the impressions received by Moore during the years when he was ripening into manhood.—"A part of the Mount

Kennedy corps of yeomanry were, on an autumn night in the year 1798, patrolling the village of Delbarg, in the county of Wicklow. Two or three of the party, led by Whollaghan, one of their number, entered the cottage of a labouring man named Dogherty, and demanded if there were any bloody rebels there. The only inmates of the cabin were Dogherty's wife, and a sick lad, her son, who was eating his supper. Whollaghan asked if the boy was Dogherty's son, and, being told that he was—'Then, you dog,' said Whollaghan, 'you are to die here.' 'I hope not,' answered the poor lad; and begged, if there were any charge against him, that he might be tried. Whollaghan, with a volley of abuse, raised his gun and pulled the trigger twice, but the piece missed fire. A comrade then handed him another gun; and the mother rushed at the muzzle to shield her son. In the struggle the piece went off, and the ball broke young Dogherty's arm. When the boy fell, the assassins left the cabin; but Whollaghan returned, and seeing the lad supported by his mother, he cried out: 'Is not the dog dead yet?' O yes, sir,' cried the poor woman, 'he is dead enough.' 'For fear he is not,' said Whollaghan, 'let him take this.' And with deliberate aim he fired a fourth time, and Dogherty dropped dead out of his mother's arms. Whollaghan was tried for murder. The real defence was that the prisoner and his companions had been sent out with general orders from their officer to shoot any one they pleased. The court seem to have been of opinion that such orders were neither unusual nor unreasonable. They found 'that the prisoner did shoot and kill one Thomas Dogherty, a rebel'; but acquitted him 'of any malicious or wilful intention of murder.'"

It was by means such as these that tranquillity was restored in Ireland, and that its people were ripened for the great administrative change in which Castlereagh's cold, diplomatic keen-sightedness saw the one chance of escape from the Irish deadlock, namely, the discontinuance of the independent Irish Parliament which held its sessions in Dublin, and its incorporation with the Parliament meeting in London. The only opposition which required to be overcome was that of the Irish Parliament itself, which, corrupt as it was, was not yet pliable enough. Castlereagh, who was Secretary of State for Ireland, and who does not seem in his capacity of Protestant Irishman to have had a particularly high opinion of his Protestant countrymen, had recourse to the simple expedient of purchasing one by one a sufficient number of the votes of the Opposition. In every official letter which he wrote to the Government at home between the beginning of 1799 and the accomplishment of the Union in 1800, he insisted on the necessity of bribery; and he received the Government's answer in the shape of one million five hundred thousand pounds, of which he made the best possible use. In their despair, the few patriots in the Parliament resolved to try the only expedient which they thought likely to be of any avail; they arranged that Grattan, who was still idolised by the nation, but who had long kept silence and was now dangerously ill, should suddenly appear in Parliament in the middle of the debate on the Union. The scene was arranged with the Irish love of dramatic effect. A vacancy having occurred a few days before the meeting of Parliament in the representation of Wicklow, an arrangement was made with Mr. Tighe, the patron of the borough, to return Grattan. Tighe himself took the return, and, riding all night, arrived in Dublin at five o'clock in the morning. Grattan, wasted by sickness, was taken out of bed, dressed, wrapped in a blanket, and conveyed in a sedan chair to the Parliament House. At seven in the morning, when the jaded House was half asleep, the speech of an orator named Egan was interrupted by the voice of the Speaker summoning a new member to the table to take the oaths. The House started from its slumber as the spectral figure of Grattan paced slowly up the floor. The man of 1782, the champion of the revolution which had made Ireland a nation, had come back as from the grave to rescue the independence of his country. He concluded his speech with the words: "Against such a proposition, were I expiring on the floor, I should beg to utter my last breath and record my dying testimony." When Corry, the Chancellor of the Exchequer, dared to reply to these words with an accusation of treason, Grattan answered with a challenge.

A few days afterwards they fought a duel with pistols ; Corry, fortunately for himself, was wounded in the arm ; had he been the victor, he would undoubtedly have been torn in pieces by the mob.

But even Grattan was powerless against the weapons employed by the Government. The eloquence, the brilliancy and solidity of which were compared by Moore to those of a precious gem, and which Byron declared to be superior to that of Demosthenes, found no echo.[1] The day the Union was decided on, the galleries were crowded with an anxious, excited audience. But Castlereagh, who felt assured of success, awaited the result with a smile on his lips. When the time for voting came, the Speaker, dwelling on the words, said: "All who desire the Union hold up their hands!" Member after member slowly and shamefacedly raised his hand. For a moment the Speaker stood as still as a statue; then crying: "The Union is carried!" he threw himself on his chair with a gesture of disgust and anger. During this stormy debate, in the course of which the most notable Irishmen of the day proclaimed opposition and rebellion at the present juncture to be a duty—none of them, however, with any intention of carrying their principles into action—there sat in one of the galleries a youth with a pale face and sparkling eyes, who meant all that the others only said, and swore in his heart that he would be the liberator of his country. This young man was Ireland's best and noblest son, Robert Emmet, the friend who, in all probability, inspired Thomas Moore with most of the force and fire to be found in the enchanting *Irish Melodies*.

1 "An eloquence rich, wheresoever its wave
Wander'd free and triumphant, with thoughts that shone through,
As clear as the brook's 'stone of lustre,' and gave,
With the flash of the gem, its solidity too."
—Moore: *Shall the Harp be silent.*

"Ever glorious Grattan! the best of the good!
So simple in heart, so sublime in the rest!
With all which Demosthenes wanted endued,
And his rival or victor in all he possess'd."
—Byron: *The Irish Avatar.*

The notable Irish poet who came into the world in the same year as our Danish poet, Oehlenschläger, was the son of a Dublin wine-merchant. He had a good father and an affectionate, capable mother, and spent a happy childhood in the bosom of his family. He very early showed himself to be an unusually clever and talented boy ; he acted, wrote and recited poetry, and sang with a peculiarly sweet voice, which he retained all his life. In reading his own account of his boyhood, we observe how early his peculiar poetic gift, which was that of the improvisatore and singer, the lyrist proper, reveals itself. He possessed the same talent which distinguished Bellmann, the Swede, that of fusing words and music together into a whole ; and along with this, he had the actor's and singer's power of moving by his interpretation. He was short, considerably under middle height; his brown hair curled close to his head, and in his childhood he resembled a little Cupid. His forehead was large and radiant, so interesting that it must have been the delight of phrenologists. He had beautiful, dark eyes—the kind of eyes, says Leigh Hunt, which we think of surmounted by a wreath of vine leaves—a refined, merry mouth, a dimpled chin, a sensual nose, slightly turned up, as if it were inhaling the fragrance of a feast or an orchard. The little man as a whole produced an impression of vitality and energy; he was of the stuff to have made a fiery raider of the old Irish type ; he was always high-spirited, and in his younger days so quick-tempered that he challenged Jeffrey on account of the latter's first review of his poetry, and afterwards Byron for jeering (in *English Bards and Scotch Reviewers*) at the bloodless endeavour at a duel which was the result of the first challenge.

In spite, however, of this martial element in his disposition, it is highly probable that Moore, if he had lived at a less critical, distressing period, and had not come into personal contact with tyranny and oppression, would never have risen to a higher rank as poet than that of the sweet Anacreontic singer. His temperament inclined him in this direction. But it was vouchsafed to him to do more for his country than ever man had done for it before, more even than Burns had done for Scotland, namely, to knit its name, its memories, its sufferings, the shameful injustice done it, and the most admirable qualities of its sons and daughters, to imperishable poetry and music.

At the early age of fifteen Moore was entered as a student at the University of Dublin. The political leaven which was beginning to leaven the whole of Ireland had penetrated the walls of the University. A young man, destined to a great and tragic fate, was attracting the attention both of his fellow-students and the professors. This was the Robert Emmet already alluded to, a youth of singular purity of character, who at the age of sixteen was already a distinguished student of mathematics and physics, and a political orator of the first rank. His speeches at the meetings of the "Historical Society," and the deep impression made by them on Moore, a lad of his own age, but of a much weaker and less developed character, have already been mentioned. Although he had been warned against allowing himself to be seen in the streets with Emmet, Moore was soon connected with him by the ties of warm admiration and close friendship. And little wonder! It was the Irish national hero whom the Irish poet had met, in the springtide of their youth. Neither of them had any prevision of the other's future greatness, but the instinct which unites harmonious minds kept them together long enough for the poet to receive his consecration from the hero. "Were I to number," says Moore, "the men among all I have ever known, who appeared to me to combine in the greatest degree pure moral worth with intellectual power, I should, among the highest of the few, place Robert Emmet."[1]

Robert Emmet was born in 1780. His elder brother, Thomas, was one of the leaders of the rebellion of 1798, and, after its failure, was first imprisoned and then banished. Robert's earliest emotions were hatred of English tyranny and love of the Irish martyrs. Even as a boy he displayed a strength of character which foreshadowed the greatness of soul that he displayed as a man. At the age of twelve he was already

[1] Thomas Moore: *Memoirs of Lord Edward Fitzgerald.*

absorbed in the study of mathematics and chemistry.[1] One day, immediately after making a chemical experiment, he sat down to solve a difficult mathematical problem, and, absently putting his hand to his mouth, poisoned himself with a corrosive sublimate which he had been handling a few moments before. The violent pains which he immediately felt, informed him of his danger. The fear of being forbidden to make such dangerous experiments in future led him to suppress anything of the nature of a cry. He went downstairs to his father's library, looked up the article on "Poison" in an encyclopædia, and found that chalk was recommended as an antidote in such cases as his. Remembering that he had seen a piece of chalk in the coach-house, he went there, broke open the door, which was locked, found the chalk, prepared and drank a solution of it, and returned to his mathematical problem. He appeared at breakfast next morning with a face so altered that it was hardly recognisable, and then confessed to his tutor that he had suffered excruciating tortures during the night, but added that one good result of his sleeplessness was that he had solved his problem.

A boy with courage and composure of this quality was sure to grow into a man with a powerful influence over others.

One of those whom Emmet influenced most strongly was Thomas Moore. The simplicity of appearance and manner which, in combination with the most delicate consideration for others, distinguished the young politician, changed, when the spring was touched that set his feelings, and through them, his intellect in motion, into an air of intellectual nobility and superiority which enchained the sympathy of the poet to be. "No two individuals," writes Moore, "could be much more unlike to each other, than was the same youth to himself, before rising to speak, and after; —the brow that had appeared inanimate, and almost drooping, at once elevating itself to all the consciousness of power, and the whole countenance and figure of the speaker assuming a change as of one suddenly inspired. Of his

[1] Madden: *The United Irishmen, Their Lives and Times.*

oratory, it must be recollected, I speak after youthful impressions; but I have heard little, since, that appeared to me of a loftier or purer character." Moore further asserts that Emmet's influence over his surroundings was due quite as much to the blamelessness of his life and the grave suavity of his manners as to his scientific attainments and his eloquence.

In 1797 a newspaper named *The Press* was started by the brothers Emmet, O'Connor, and other Irish popular leaders; and Moore was not a little eager to see something of his own in its patriotic and widely-read columns. But his mother's constant anxiety about him made him fearful of hazarding anything that might agitate her, so he resolved to write anonymously, at any rate to begin with. He sent in an imitation of Ossian, which was printed, but excited no attention. Then, with trembling hand, he entrusted to the post a *Letter to the Students of Trinity College*, which, as he himself observes, was richly seasoned with treason; it was a witty satire on Castlereagh, who, as long as he lived, was the butt of Moore's wit.

"I hardly expected," writes Moore, "that it would make its appearance; but, lo and behold, on the next evening of publication, when seated, as usual, in my little corner by the fire, I unfolded the paper for the purpose of reading it to my father and mother, there was my own letter staring me full in the face, occupying a conspicuous station in the paper, and, of course, one of the first and principal things that my auditors wished to hear." Overcoming his emotion, he read the letter aloud, and had the gratification of hearing it much praised by his parents, who, however, pronounced both language and sentiments to be "very bold." On the following day, Edward Hudson, the only friend entrusted with the secret, paid a morning call, and had not been long in the room conversing with Mrs. Moore, when he looked significantly at Tom and remarked: "Well, you saw——." "That letter was yours, then, Tom?" cried the mother; and new entreaties to be cautious followed on Tom's confession.

"A few days after," writes Moore, "in the course of one of those strolls into the country which Emmet and I used often to take together, our conversation turned upon this letter, and I gave him to understand that it was mine; when with that almost feminine gentleness of manner which he possessed, and which is so often found in such determined spirits, he owned to me that on reading the letter, though pleased with its contents, he could not help regretting that the public attention had thus been called to the politics of the University, as it might have the effect of awakening the vigilance of the college authorities, and frustrate the progress of the good work (as we both considered it) which was going on there so quietly. Even then, boyish as my own mind was, I could not help being struck with the manliness of the view which I saw he took of what men ought to do in such times and circumstances, namely, not to *talk* or *write* about their intentions, but to *act*. He had never before, I think, in conversation with me, alluded to the existence of the United Irish societies, in college, nor did he now, or at any subsequent time, make any proposition to me to join in them, a forbearance which I attribute a good deal to his knowledge of the watchful anxiety about me which prevailed at home. . . . He was altogether a noble fellow, and as full of imagination and tenderness of heart as of manly daring."

It is plain enough that Robert Emmet, though he was sincerely attached to Moore, felt that he was not of the stuff of which a man must be made who is to stake his future and his life on the success of a rebellion. But he had a high opinion of the young poet, and often sought his society; he was doubtless conscious of the resonance of his own ideas and dreams in the harp of Moore's soul. He used frequently to sit by him at the pianoforte whilst he played over the airs from Bunting's Irish collection; and Moore as an old man still remembered how one day, when he was playing the spirited air, "Let Erin remember the day!" Emmet exclaimed passionately: "Oh that I were at the head of twenty thousand men marching to that air!"

This was in 1797, shortly before the discovery of the great Irish conspiracy. The discovery came, with all its attendant horrors. One of its first results was a regular court of inquisition, held within the walls of the University. The roll was called, and the students were examined one by one. Most of them knew little or nothing about the plot, but there were a few, among them Robert Emmet, whose absence revealed to their comrades how much they had known of the betrayed and defeated plans. The dead silence which followed the daily calling out of their names made a profound impression on Moore. He himself proved at this trial what a high-spirited little fellow he was; he told the dreaded Lord Fitzgibbon to his face that, in taking the oath demanded of him, he reserved to himself the power of refusing to answer any question calculated to get a comrade into trouble; and he bore with manly composure the outburst of anger which followed. As he was not a member of the Society of United Irishmen, and had evidently no knowledge of their plans, he was dismissed at once.

It was during the years immediately following this incident that Moore began to appear before the public as a poet. The horrors attendant on the suppression of the rebellion did not provide him with any of his themes; they were still too near. Emmet was away, and his influence in abeyance; and, indeed, political poetry was for the moment an impossibility in Ireland. So the young poet, whose temperament naturally inclined him in the direction of light, sprightly verse, followed the course prescribed by his tastes and his age. He prepared an English version of the Odes of Anacreon, which he published before he was twenty, with a dedication to the Prince Regent, who was at that time the hope of the Liberals; and in 1801 he published, under the title of *Poetical Works of the late Thomas Little, Esq.*, a volume of poems, for the most part of an erotic, youthfully sensuous, and slightly licentious character. The Irish licentiousness reminds one of that which is not at all uncommon in Swedish erotic poetry; it has also, like the Swedish, a national stamp.

After leading a tolerably aimless existence for a year or two in London, where his talents and his Irish charm of manner made him a favourite in the best society, Moore was obliged by his poverty to go as Admiralty Registrar (a post procured for him by Lord Moira) to the Bermudas. It was, as one can easily imagine, an appointment very unsuited to his tastes, and after a short time he entrusted his duties to a deputy, made a tour in America, and returned to England. The deputy, in course of time, embezzled a considerable sum of Government money, and thus Moore, like Scott, became responsible for the payment of a heavy debt. He also, like Scott, received numerous offers of assistance ; and he discharged his liabilities, partly with the assistance of wealthy friends, partly by his own industry and strict economy for several years. His tour in America lasted from October 1803 to November 1804. He brought home with him the American Epistles, and poems which are to be found in the second volume of his works, and which contain descriptions of nature as remarkable for their correctness as for their wealth of glowing colour. With his genuine English Naturalism, he was, however, more anxious to be truthful than to be brilliant, and was very proud of the many testimonies he received both from natives and travellers as to the correct impression he conveyed of country and people. The well-known English traveller, Captain Basil Hall (who visited Scott at Abbotsford and who, when ill in Venice, was taken care of by Byron), asserts that Moore's Odes and Epistles give the most beautiful and correct description of Bermuda that is to be found ; and he draws attention to the fact that both the words and tune of the prettiest of the songs, the "Canadian Boat Song," are close imitations of what one actually hears in the boats out there, the poet having, however, rejected whatever was neither beautiful nor characteristic. Moore himself tells how exactly he kept to reality in his descriptions of landscapes and even trees. Referring to the lines :

> "'Twas thus, by the shade of a calabash-tree,
> With a few who could love and remember like me,"

he relates how, twenty-five years after writing them, he received from Bermuda a cup made from a shell of the fruit of the identical calabash tree alluded to, on the bark of which his name had been found inscribed. The unaccustomed natural surroundings of these regions had a fecundating effect on the mind of a young poet who was susceptible to luxurious, festal impressions. The democratic and republican institutions of the United States were much less to the taste of the refined writer on whom the general reaction against the eighteenth century, which was now beginning, was already producing its effect. His Epistles on the state of society in America prove that he was alive only to the defects of the Republic. He had an audience of the President; but we perceive that Jefferson's slovenly dress—slippers and blue stockings formed part of it—gave the young poet an unfavourable impression of the man who had drawn up the Declaration of Independence. What shocked him more than anything else in America was to find French philosophy, which he, the true child of his day, regarded as sinful and poisonous, so widely spread throughout the young republic.[1] He referred many years afterwards to this time as being the one period during which he had felt doubtful of the wisdom of the liberal political faith in which he might almost literally be said to have begun his life, and in which he expected to end it.

It almost seemed, for a moment, as if the impressions received by the poet in his oppressed native island during his childhood and youth were extinct, dead and buried under Anacreontic sentiments, reminiscences of travel, and the pleasures of life as lived in the most fashionable and frivolous circles of London society. But in 1807 appeared the first Number of the *Irish Melodies*, the work which is Moore's title-deed to immortality. Everything that his unfortunate country had felt and suffered during the long years of her ignominy—her agonies and sighs, her ardent struggles, her martial spirit, the smile shining through her tears—we have them all here, scattered about in songs which are written in a mood of half-gay, half-mournful levity and amorousness.

[1] "Already has the child of Gallia's school,
The foul Philosophy that sins by rule,
With all her train of reasoning, damning arts,
Begot by brilliant heads or worthless hearts—
Already has she poured her poison here
O'er every charm that makes existence dear."
—*Epistle to Lord Viscount Forbes.*

It was a wreath this, woven of grief, enthusiasm, and tenderness, a fragrant wreath, such as one binds in honour of the dead, which Moore placed on his country's brow. Not that Ireland is often mentioned ; there are as few names as possible in these poems—it was not safe to print Irish names. But now the singer would celebrate his mistress in such terms that no one could fail to recognise her as Erin, now the dearly beloved would speak with a majesty which showed her to be no mortal woman ; and, as in the old Christian allegorical hymns, the mysticism increased the poetic effect.

What had happened in the interval between the appearance of Moore's wanton, frivolous poetry and the conception of these wonderful songs ? They themselves answer the question by suppressing the answer. The fourth Melody begins :

"Oh, breathe not his name, let it sleep in the shade,
Where cold and unhonoured his relics are laid :
Sad, silent, and dark be the tears that we shed,
As the night-dew that falls on the grass o'er his head !"

There was, then, one whose name might not be named, whose body lay dishonoured in a grave where it might be wept over only in the darkness of night.

In the next song, again without any mention of a name, we read :

"When he who adores thee has left but the name
Of his fault and his sorrows behind,
Oh ! say, wilt thou weep when they darken the fame
Of a life that for thee was resigned ?
Yes, weep, and however my foes may condemn,
Thy tears shall efface their decree ;
For Heaven can witness, though guilty to them,
I have been but too faithful to thee !"

That the beloved of these lines is Ireland, we can see at the first glance ; but once more a dark veil of anonymity is cast over the man whose reputation was destroyed by his enemies, but who, though declared guilty by them, had been so faithful to the object of his worship.

Let the reader turn over a few pages, and he will come upon a poem which is closely connected with the two just quoted. It is a sweet, sad portrait of the betrothed of the anonymous dead hero.

> "She is far from the land where her young hero sleeps,
>   And lovers around her are sighing;
> But coldly she turns from their gaze, and weeps,
>   For her heart in his grave is lying.
>
> She sings the wild songs of her dear native plains,
>   Every note that he loved awaking.—
> Ah! little they think, who delight in her strains,
>   How the heart of the Minstrel is breaking!
>
> He had lived for her love, for his country he died,
>   They were all that to life had entwined him;
> Nor soon shall the tears of his country be dried,
>   Nor long will his love stay behind him.
>
> Oh! make her a grave where the sunbeams rest,
>   When they promise a glorious morrow;
> They'll shine o'er her sleep, like a smile from the West,
>   From her own loved Island of Sorrow!"

The reader has already divined that the young hero of these touching laments is no other than Moore's old college friend, Robert Emmet. It was undoubtedly this young man's tragic fate which inspired the finest of the songs of freedom contained in the *Irish Melodies*.

Robert's elder brother suffered a term of imprisonment after the revolution of 1798, and was then banished; Robert himself escaped imprisonment, and continued to employ his liberty in the service of the cause which had cost his brother so much, and was to cost his own life. In 1802 he went to Paris, and had an interview with the First Consul, who appeared to him "to care as little for Ireland as he did for the republic or for liberty," and several with Talleyrand, whom he considered no more satisfactory, for the purpose of making arrangements for the proclamation of an independent Irish Republic, supported by an alliance with the French Republic. The moment was an opportune one, for the friendly relations which had been re-established for a short time between France and England by the Peace of Amiens were on the point of giving way to renewed hostility. Bonaparte seems actually to have for a moment contemplated a landing in Ireland (he lamented at St. Helena that he had not gone to Ireland instead of to Egypt), and Robert Emmet returned in November 1802 to his native island with a distinct promise from the French authorities that the landing of their army should take place in August 1803. With untiring audacity he prepared for a new rebellion throughout the length and breadth of Ireland. He was persuaded that that of 1798 had failed because it had not had sufficient support in the capital. His great aim, therefore, was to get possession of Dublin, and more particularly of the Castle, the gates of which stood open till late in the evening. Day and night he superintended the preparations of the conspirators. In different parts of the town they rented a number of houses, where they established secret manufactories of weapons and ammunition. Emmet had a staff of fifteen men, almost all of the lower class, to assist him in the task of superintendence. Such rest as he granted himself was taken lying on a mattress on the floor of one of the powder-magazines.

Although more than a thousand persons were concerned in the conspiracy, there was not one traitor among them, and the merciless Government had not the slightest idea of what was impending. Emmet's private fortune was entirely expended on the necessary preparations, although the men who served him received no payment for their work. One of them, conversing many years afterwards with the author of *The United Irishmen*, told him that they worked, not for money, but for the cause; that they had perfect confidence in Robert Emmet, and would have given their lives for him. But in the month of July an accident occurred; one of the powder-magazines blew up, killing two men, one of whom died in Emmet's arms. The following day a Protestant newspaper informed the Government that it was sleeping on a mine.

There could now be no question of waiting for the French; half-prepared as the conspirators were, they had either to make their attempt at once or accept the certainty of annihilation without a struggle. On the morning of the 23rd of July a manly proclamation to the people of Ireland, drawn up by Emmet himself, was discovered posted up in the streets of Dublin. But when evening came, and Emmet attempted the surprise of the Castle, he proved to his sorrow how unreliable his countrymen were at a dangerous and decisive crisis. The number of his followers steadily diminished as they approached the Castle, and by the time its gates were reached it was clear that any attack which the mere handful of faithful enthusiasts left, could make on the now alert and well-armed enemy was doomed to defeat. In the first confusion the rebel leaders succeeded in escaping to the hills of Wicklow, where they were able to hold a council the following day. Most of them were certain that their cause was anything but a lost one; let them but give the signal, and the whole of Ireland would rise like one man, &c., &c. Robert Emmet alone had lost all his illusions. He succeeded in convincing his friends that to continue their endeavours at this juncture, and without other forces than the undisciplined rebels who alone were at their service, would lead to nothing but more shedding of the blood of a people who had already suffered so much. At the moment of parting, all the others entreated Emmet to take advantage of an opportunity which presented itself of escaping from the country at once in a fishing-boat belonging to one of the rebels. But, with a slight confusion of manner, he told them that he could not possibly leave Ireland for an unlimited number of years without first returning to Dublin to take leave of a lady, who was so dear to him that he must see her again if he "had to die for it a thousand times."

In Dublin the military were on his heels. His faithful housekeeper, a young, brave girl, was covered with bayonet pricks and underwent "half-hanging"; but nothing would induce her to betray her master's hiding-place. At last he was found and arrested, a pistol-shot in the shoulder preventing any attempt at escape. When the officer who arrested him was making an excuse for this shot, the prisoner said shortly: "All is fair in war."

A few days after his imprisonment, Robert Emmet wrote to the young lady for whose sake he had risked his life. This was Miss Sarah Curran, a daughter of the eminent and highly respected barrister, John Philpot Curran, who is so often named in Byron's poetry, and who had been the eloquent, undaunted defender of the political prisoners tried after the rebellion of 1798. Young Emmet had been a welcome visitor at Curran's house; but when Curran discovered the attachment between the two young people, he separated them, as he feared that Emmet's political opinions augured ill for his future; and the correspondence between them had been carried on without his knowledge. The jailer demanded a large sum from Emmet for conveying his letter to its address, and then took it straight to the Attorney-General. Fearing possible injurious consequences to the lady whom he loved, Emmet at once wrote to his judges, and, knowing that his eloquence was dreaded, offered to plead guilty and not say one word in his own defence if, in return, they would make no reference, in the hearing of the case, to his letter to Miss Curran. The offer was made in vain. The very next day, the arrival of the police to search his house informed the furious Curran of the relations between his daughter and Emmet.

Of the result of the trial no one had any doubt; the accused knew his fate. When the governor of the prison came upon him one day plaiting a lock of hair which Miss Curran had given him, he looked up and said: "I am preparing it to take with me to the scaffold." On his table was found a carefully executed pen and ink drawing—an excellent portrait of himself, the head severed from the body.

The trial began at 10 A.M. After the Attorney-General had made a speech, in which he affirmed that the only results of the conspiracy had been to elicit stronger proofs than had before existed of the attachment of Ireland to its King, Robert Emmet requested that, as his only answer, the following paragraph from the proclamation of the provisional government, as drawn up by him, might be read aloud: "From this time onward flogging and torture are forbidden in Ireland, and may not be reintroduced on any pretext whatever." Hereupon followed a speech by a hateful Irish renegade, Mr. Plunket, who had formerly belonged to the party of rebellion, but who now, as King's Counsel, overwhelmed Emmet with abuse. Then Emmet himself stood up, and, with the prospect of certain and almost immediate death before his eyes, defended himself in a speech with which every Irishman to this day is familiar. He began by saying that if he were to suffer only death after being adjudged guilty, he should bow in silence to his fate ; but the sentence which delivered his body to the executioner also consigned his character to obloquy, and therefore he must speak. The judge roughly interrupting him in the middle of his speech, he calmly said: "I have understood, my Lord, that judges sometimes think it their duty to hear with patience, and to speak with humanity," and continued his speech in such a loud voice as to be distinctly heard at the outer doors of the court-house ; and yet, though he spoke in a loud tone, there was nothing boisterous in his manner. Those who heard him declare, says Madden, that his accents and cadence of voice were exquisitely modulated. He moved about the dock as he warmed in his address, with characteristic, rapid, and not ungraceful motions. Even after the lapse of thirty years, the witnesses of the scene could not speak without emotion of the graceful majesty with which he defied his judges. A correspondent of the *Times*, who unconditionally condemned the rebellion, wrote of Emmet as follows: "But as to Robert Emmet individually, it will surely be admitted that even in the midst of error he was great ; and that the burst of eloquence with which, upon the day of his trial, with the grave already open to receive him, he shook the very court wherein he stood, and caused not only 'that viper whom his father nourished' (Mr. Plunket) to quail beneath the lash, but likewise forced that 'remnant of humanity' (Lord Norbury, who tried him), to tremble on the judgment seat, was an effort almost superhuman."

Emmet ended with these words: "My lord, you are impatient for the sacrifice. The blood which you seek is not congealed by the artificial terrors which surround your victim — it circulates warmly and unruffled through its channels, and in a little time it will cry to heaven. Be patient! I have but a few words to say—I am going to my cold and silent grave—my lamp of life is nearly extinguished —I have parted with everything that was dear to me in this life, and for my country's cause with the idol of my soul, the object of my affections. My race is run—the grave opens to receive me, and I sink into its bosom. I have but one request to ask at my departure from this world—it is *the charity of its silence.* Let no man write my epitaph; for as no man who knows my motives dare now vindicate them, let not prejudice or ignorance asperse them. Let them rest in obscurity and peace, my memory be left in oblivion, and my tomb remain uninscribed, until other times and other men can do justice to my character. When my country takes her place among the nations of the earth, then, and not till then, let my epitaph be written. I have done."

The sentence was pronounced. Robert Emmet was, on the following day, first to be hanged, and then beheaded. When the prisoner was removed from the dock it was about ten o'clock at night. As he passed the grating of a cell in which a friend was confined, he called to him: "I shall be hanged to-morrow." He was allowed no peace during his last hours. The Government became alarmed lest an attempt might be made to rescue him, and an order was sent to convey him to Kilmainham jail, two miles and a half away. Not till he reached there did a humane jailer take off the irons which had been put on so roughly that they had drawn blood. The same man gave him something to eat, no food having been provided for him since before the trial began, at ten in the morning. Emmet then slept soundly for a short time. On awaking he employed the time left him in writing letters to his brother in America, to Miss Curran's brother, and to herself. He was interrupted by a friend, who came to bid him farewell. Emmet's first inquiry was after his mother, and his friend was obliged to tell him that she had died the day before of grief. She had borne with fortitude the banishment of one of her sons for his devotion to the cause of Ireland, and she had encouraged Robert in all his proceedings; but when she knew that he, the pride of her heart, was doomed, in his twenty-third year, to such a terrible death, her heart broke. Robert received the news composedly, and said, after a silence of some moments: "It is better so." In his letter to young Curran he wrote: "I did not look to honours for myself—praise I would have asked from the lips of no man; but I would have wished to read in the glow of Sarah's countenance that her husband was respected." His writing in this letter is as firm and regular as usual.

At one o'clock, escorted by the sheriffs and followed by the executioner, he was led to the scaffold. So great was the power of his gentleness and charm over wild, rude natures, that one of the warders burst into tears at parting from him. Emmet, whose arms were bound, bent forward and kissed the man on the cheek; and the jailer, whom twenty years of service had hardened, and inured to prison scenes, fell senseless at his prisoner's feet. Before mounting the scaffold Emmet entrusted to one of his friends the letter which he had written to Miss Curran; but the friend was arrested and imprisoned, and this letter, like the other, did not reach its destination. Emmet took off his neckerchief himself, and assisted in adjusting the rope round his neck. After his head was struck from the body the executioner held it up to the crowd, proclaiming in a loud voice: "This is the head of a traitor, Robert Emmet!" Not a sound was heard in answer.

Next day the readers of the *London Chronicle*, the Government organ, were told: "He behaved without the least symptom of fear, and with all the effrontery and nonchalance which so much distinguished his conduct on his trial yesterday. He seems to scoff at the dreadful circumstances attending on him, at the same time, with all the coolness and complacency that can be possibly imagined, though utterly unlike the calmness of Christian fortitude. Even as it was, I never saw a man die like him; and God forbid I should see many with his principles. . . . The clergyman who attended him endeavoured to win him from his deistical opinions. He thanked him for his exertions, but said that his opinions on such subjects had long been settled, and that this was not the time to change them." Thus spoke the official press. Oppressed Ireland kept silence at the scaffold of her young hero, and, faithful to his wish, carved no epitaph on his tomb.

But when Moore's *Irish Melodies* appeared, it was as if the grief and wrath of a whole nation had suddenly found expression ; in these songs it rose and fell, whispered and shouted, moaned and murmured, like the waves of the sea, and with the irresistible force of a natural element. Soon there was not a peasant in Ireland, as there is not one to-day, unfamiliar with the song : "When he who adores thee." To this day Robert Emmet's last speech is read in American schools. It is the gospel of the Irish struggle for independence. But, strangely enough, Emmet's heroic death contributed less to his fame among his countrymen than did his touching love story. His betrothed, regarded by the Irish people as their hero's widow, became the object of silent veneration. Her unhappiness was increased by her being obliged to live amongst people who sided with England, and who considered, much as they pitied him, that Emmet had deserved his fate. Some years after Emmet's death Miss Curran made the acquaintance of an English officer, a Captain Sturgeon, who, touched by her forlorn position and attracted by her many charms, offered her his hand. After long hesitation she married him. As she was beginning to show symptoms of decline, he took her to Italy. Her appearance, says Admiral Napier, who saw her at Naples, was that of "a wandering statue." She died, not long after her marriage, in Sicily, "far from the land where her young hero sleeps." Washington Irving has described her in his *Sketch Book*, in the beautiful tale called "The Broken Heart." But her most worthy monument is the song : "She is far from the land." [1]

In the *Melodies*, however, the griefs of the individual are but a symbol of those of the nation, an embodiment of the

[1] Madden: *United Irishmen.—Robert Emmet:* anonymous, but known to be written by Madame d'Haussonville.

universal suffering. We come upon songs in which we seem to hear all the sons and daughters of Ireland lamenting over the fruitlessness of the great French Revolution and the disappointment of the hopes which all nations, but theirs above all others, had set upon the stability and victory of the Republic. Such a song is the touching:

> "'Tis gone, and for ever, the light we saw breaking";

with its wild lament that the first ray of liberty, welcomed with blessings by man, has disappeared, and by its disappearance deepened the darkness of the night of bondage and mourning which has again closed in over the kingdoms of the earth, and darkest of all over Erin. Truly noble and lofty is the flight of this verse:

> "For high was thy hope, when those glories were darting
> Around thee, through all the gross clouds of the world;
> When Truth, from her fetters indignantly starting,
> At once, like a sunburst, her banner unfurled.
> Oh, never shall earth see a moment so splendid!
> Then, then, had one Hymn of Deliverance blended
> The tongues of all nations; how sweet had ascended
> The first note of Liberty, Erin, from thee!"

And the poem ends with maledictions on the "light race, unworthy its good," who "like furies caressing the young hope of freedom, baptized it in blood." Other poems are of a more threatening nature, although the threat is always poetic and half-concealed. Read, for example, the song, "Lay his sword by his side."

> "Lay his sword by his side,—it hath served him too well
> Not to rest near his pillow below;
> To the last moment true, from his hand ere it fell,
> Its point was still turn'd to a flying foe.
> . . . .
> Yet pause—for, in fancy, a still voice I hear,
> . . . .
> And it cries, from the grave where the hero lies deep,
> 'Tho' the day of your Chieftain for ever hath set,
> 'Oh, leave not his sword thus inglorious to sleep,—
> 'It hath victory's life in it yet!'"

The poem which is directly aimed at the Prince Regent is the most severe and most high-toned of them all. It is the one which begins: "When first I met thee, warm and young." The Prince's name is not mentioned, but the verses can only be understood when it is known that it is to him they refer. Erin, speaking as a woman, describes her belief in him, her faith in the promises he made when "young and warm," and her continued reliance on him even when she saw him change. When she heard of his follies, she persisted in discovering, even in his faults, "some gleams of future glory." But now that the attractive qualities of youth have departed, and none of the virtues of maturity have replaced them, now that those who once loved him avoid him, and even his flatterers despise him, Erin would not give one of her "taintless tears" for all his guilty splendour. And the day will come when his last friends will forsake him, and he will call in vain on her whom he has lost for ever. She will say:

"Go—go—'tis vain to curse,
'Tis weakness to upbraid thee;
Hate cannot wish thee worse
Than guilt and shame have made thee."

Wordsworth addressed declarations of love to England when she was victorious and great; Scott sang the praises of Scotland at a time when she was beginning to take her place as a flourishing nation by the side of a sister kingdom; but Moore addressed his heartfelt, glowing strains to a country which lay humiliated and bleeding at its torturers' feet. He writes:—

"Remember thee! yes, while there's life in this heart,
It shall never forget thee, all lorn as thou art;
More dear in thy sorrow, thy gloom, and thy showers,
Than the rest of the world in their sunniest hours.

Wert thou all that I wish thee,—great, glorious, and free—
First flower of the earth, and first gem of the sea,—
I might hail thee with prouder, with happier brow,
But, oh! could I love thee more deeply than now?"

And in everything that Moore wrote, there is a remembrance of Ireland. His great Oriental poem, *Lalla Rookh,* which appeared in 1817, was prepared for by the most conscientious study. There is not an image, not a description, or name, or historical incident or reference, which has any connection with Europe. Everything, without exception, bears witness to the familiarity of the author with the life and nature of the East. Nevertheless we know that the subject did not begin to interest him until he saw a possibility of making the struggle between the Fire-worshippers and the Mohammedans a pretext for preaching tolerance in the spirit of the song, "Come, send round the wine," which he had addressed to his countrymen in the *Irish Melodies.* And the interest of the reader, too, is not really awakened until he begins to divine Ireland and the Irish under these Ghebers and their strange surroundings. Hence it is that *The Fire-Worshippers* is the only entirely successful part of the poem. The very names Iran and Erin melt into each other in the reader's ear. Moore himself says that the spirit which spoke in the *Irish Melodies* did not begin to feel at home in the East till he set it to work on the *Fire-Worshippers;* and the beautiful poem, whose hero is a noble and unfortunate rebel, and whose heroine lives amongst people who speak of her lover with detestation, might well have been inspired by the memory of Robert Emmet and Sarah Curran. Some of the incidents recall their story. Before Hafed calls the Ghebers to revolt he has been wandering, an exile, in foreign lands; Hinda, devoured by anxiety for him, hears every day of massacres of the rebels. And when, learning that her lover has been burned, she drowns herself, the poet bewails her fate in a song, entire verses of which might, if *Erin* were substituted for *Iran,* be added to "She is far from the land" without introducing a perceptibly foreign element. Take, for instance, the verse:

> "Nor shall Iran, beloved of her Hero, forget thee—
> Though tyrants watch over her tears as they start,
> Close, close by the side of that Hero she'll set thee,
> Embalmed in the innermost shrine of her heart."

And so exact is the resemblance between the spirit of the *Irish Melodies* and that which reigns in this Asiatic epic, that it was possible to employ a sentence from the latter, without the change of a single word, as motto for the collection of documents relating to the Irish Rebellion which was published in the Fifties under the title: *Rebellion Book and Black History*. The lines are as follows:—

"Rebellion! foul, dishonouring word,
Whose wrongful blight so oft has stained
The holiest cause that tongue or sword
Of mortal ever lost or gained.
How many a spirit born to bless
Hath sunk beneath that withering name,
Whom but a day's, an hour's success
Had wafted to eternal fame!"

It was Moore's polemical position as an Irishman that made it impossible for him to see European politics in the same light as they appeared to the Lake School and Scott. He directed a shower of the arrows of his wit against the Holy Alliance. In the *Fables for the Holy Alliance*, which he dedicated to Lord Byron, he jests, good-humouredly but audaciously, at the European reaction. He dreams, for example, that Czar Alexander gives a splendid ball in an ice-palace which he has erected on the frozen Neva, on the plan of that built by the Empress Anne. To it are invited all the "holy gentlemen" who, at the various Congresses, have shown such regard for the welfare of Europe.

"The thought was happy, and designed
To hint how thus the human mind
May—like the stream imprisoned there—
Be checked and chilled till it can bear
The heaviest Kings, that ode or sonnet
E'er yet be-praised, to dance upon it."

Madame de Krüdener has pledged her prophetic word that there is no danger, that the ice will never melt. But, lo! ere long an ill-omened dripping begins. The Czar goes on with his polonaise, but so glassy has the floor become that he can hardly keep his legs; and Prussia, "though to slippery ways so used, was cursedly near tumbling." But hardly has the Spanish fandango begun when a glaring light—"as 'twere a glance shot from an angry southern sun" —begins to shine in every chamber of the palace. Then there is a general "Sauve qui peut!" Instantly everything is in a flow—royal arms, Russian and Prussian birds of prey and French fleur-de-lys, floors, walls, and ceilings, kings, fiddlers, emperors, all are gone. Why, asks Moore,

"Why, why will monarchs caper so
In palaces without foundations?"

It is evident that he hoped great things from the Spanish Revolution, which had just begun.

In another fable he tells of a country where there was a ridiculous law prohibiting the importation of looking-glasses. What was the reason of this prohibition? The reason was that the royal race reigned by right of their superior beauty, and the people obeyed because *they* were declared, and believed themselves to be, ugly. To hint that the King's nose was not straight, was high treason; to suggest that one's own neighbour was as good-looking as certain persons in high position, was almost as great a crime; and the subjects, never having seen looking-glasses, did not *know themselves*. Certain wicked Radicals arranged that a ship with a cargo of looking-glasses should be driven ashore on this country's coast—and the reader guesses the rest. In a third fable the poet returns to his old symbolic characters, the Fire-worshippers. Less tolerant here than in *Lalla Rookh*, he makes the Fire-worshippers throw the whole corps of "extinguishers," who have been appointed to obstruct them in the peaceful exercise of their religious rites, into the flames which they will not allow to burn.

The work which shows Moore's humour and satire at its best, *The Fudge Family in Paris*, is full of witty sallies against the new, incapable Bourbon Government, but strikes at England in bold, dead earnest. We find such lines as:

"Everywhere gallant hearts, and spirits true,
Are served up victims to the vile and few;
While E——, everywhere—the general foe
Of truth and freedom, wheresoe'er they glow—
Is first, when tyrants strike, to aid the blow!"

And England is reminded that

> "—— maledictions ring from every side
> Upon that grasping power, that selfish pride,
> Which vaunts its own, and scorns all rights beside."

The Fourth and Seventh Letters ought to be read, with their jeers at the Prince Regent's laziness and corpulence, and their abuse of Castlereagh, of whom Moore thus writes:

> "We sent thee C——gh; as heaps of dead
> Have slain their slayers by the pest they spread,
> So hath our land breathed out—thy fame to dim,
> Thy strength to waste, and rot thee, soul and limb—
> Her worst infections all condensed in him!"

And the potentates of the Holy Alliance are called

> "That royal, ravening flock, whose vampire wings
> O'er sleeping Europe treacherously brood,
> And fan her into dreams of promised good,
> Of hope, of freedom—but to drain her blood!"

This sounds very bad and very dangerous; the distance separating such a writer from the older generation of poets strikes us as great; it seems but a step from this to Shelley and Byron. But as a matter of fact, it is a long way; for all these attacks are not quite so seriously meant as one would imagine. This champion of the cause of Ireland was no advocate of her independence; Moore did not desire the separation of his country from England; he only desired that she should be ruled better and more justly. This bold denouncer of kings was no republican, but a sincere believer in monarchy, who would have had bad kings replaced by good ones. He was no free-thinker, this man who railed so violently at the hypocrisy of the Holy Alliance, but a sincere, enlightened Catholic, who, though he brought up his children as Protestants, wrote a thick book, *Travels of an Irish Gentleman in search of a Religion*, in defence of the most important doctrines of the Catholic faith. With all his apparent unrestraint, Moore kept within the bounds prescribed by the society in which he lived. The Whig leaders had, when he came to London, received him with open arms, and Moore became and remained the Whig poet, who in a long series of playfully sarcastic letters—rhymed feuilletons one might call them—treated the public questions and Parliamentary events of the day with sparkling wit and drawing-room humour of the best style, in the spirit of the Whig party.

XIII

EROTIC LYRIC POETRY

MOORE was by nature disposed to gaiety and happiness, not to solitary conflict. He was created to occupy, in the manner of the ancient Irish bards, an honourable place at the table of the great, and while away their time with song. A sign of his being one of fortune's favourites is that he often jests even when he is most in earnest, unlike Byron, who, even when he jests, is serious, nay, gloomy. Moore plays with his theme and caresses it; Byron tears his to pieces, and turns from it in disgust. The two friends are constantly observing and reproducing nature; but under Byron's gaze the sun itself seems to be darkened, whilst Moore, with his love of rosy red and brightness and sparkle, himself creates "a morning sun which rises at noon."

Hence we get but a one-sided picture of Moore when we study him, as our plan has led us to do, chiefly as a political poet. He is also the writer of some of the best and most musical erotic lyrics in existence. The music of his verse is more exuberant than delicate; but there is magic in his handling of language. In his love poems a fascinating, glowing sensuousness and an ardent tenderness have found expression in word-melodies which are as tuneful as airs by Rossini. English admirers of Shelley, accustomed to more delicate, and, to the uninitiated, more perplexing harmonies, may, if they please, call these songs "over-sweet"; erotic verse cannot be too erotic; as the French say: "In love too much is not enough." Moore is no Mozart; but is this not almost like a Mozart air, like one of the hero's or Zerlina's in *Don Juan?*

"The young May-moon is beaming, love!
The glow-worm's lamp is gleaming, love!
How sweet to rove
Through Morna's grove,
While the drowsy world is dreaming, love!"

Songs by Rossini and Moore retain their value even though the world owned at the same time a Schubert and a Shelley. Nowhere are the distinguishing characteristics of the different English poets of this period more clearly reflected than in their love poems ; whilst at the same time the Naturalism distinguishing the period stands out in sharp contrast to the supernaturalism of the erotic poetry of the German and French reaction periods. Byron's description of his most beautiful female character as "Nature's bride and Passion's child" (*Don Juan* ii. 202), and his description of the love of Don Juan and Haidée :

> "This is in others a factitious state,
> An opium dream of too much youth and reading,
> But was in them their nature or their fate,"

might serve as characterisations of the love celebrated in the amatory poetry of the majority of his contemporaries. But only in *Don Juan* has Byron painted happy love. His erotic poems are nothing but misery and lamentation. The most marvellous of them all, "When we two parted," has a sob in its very rhythm ; and the whole pain of parting is conveyed by the manner in which the rhythm suddenly changes in the last verse. In the first lines there is still a certain calmness of passion :

> "When we two parted
> In silence and tears,
> Half broken-hearted,
> To sever for years,
> Pale grew thy cheek and cold,
> Colder thy kiss ;
> Truly that hour foretold
> Sorrow to this."

But all the misery of love is expressed in the short, abrupt cadences of the concluding stanza :

> "In secret we met—
> In silence I grieve,
> That thy heart could forget,
> Thy spirit deceive.
> If I should meet thee
> After long years,
> How should I greet thee ?—
> With silence and tears."

The peculiar domain of Byronic love-poetry is that of the tortures of love.

Thomas Campbell has not written many purely erotic poems—he prefers the shorter or longer love-story in verse to the personal outburst—but some of the few are as tender in tone as Moore's or Keats's. And, strange to say, he becomes warmer, tenderer, less restrained in expression as time passes. It is as an old man that he writes his most amatory verse. To the remonstrance of conscience, that Platonic friendship should content him at his years, he answers by a challenge to Plato himself in the skies to look into the eyes of a certain lady "and try to be Platonic."

He sings of the transient nature of love, of the suffering occasioned by the absence of the beloved; he puts into words the sufferings of the maid whose lover is "never wedding, ever wooing." But he is most characteristically himself as the erotic poet when he confesses, with a half mournful smile, that his heart is younger than his years, as in the following verses:—

"The god left my heart, at its surly reflections,
But came back on pretext of some sweet recollections,
And he made me forget what I ought to remember,
That the rose-bud of June cannot bloom in November.
Ah! Tom, 'tis all o'er with thy gay days—
Write psalms, and not songs for the ladies.

But time's been so far from my wisdom enriching,
That the longer I live, beauty seems more bewitching;
And the only new lore my experience traces,
Is to find fresh enchantment in magical faces.
How weary is wisdom, how weary!
When one sits by a smiling young dearie!"

Keats's erotic verse is, as was to be expected, burning, breathless, sensual; it revels in fragrance and sweet sounds. Read this masterly verse:—

"Lift the latch! ah gently! ah tenderly—sweet!
We are dead if that latchet gives one little clink!
Well done—now those lips, and a flowery seat—
The old man may sleep, and the planets may wink;
The shut rose shall dream of our loves, and awake
Full blown, and such warmth for the morning's take;
The stock-dove shall hatch her soft brace and shall coo,
While I kiss to the melody, aching all through."

Shelley's love-poetry is at one and the same time hyper-spiritual and meltingly sensuous. We are reminded by it of Correggio. In the productions of both these artists the expression of the most utter self-surrender is blent with the expression of the most violent sensual excitement; what Shelley describes is the erotic death-struggle. Take the concluding verse of the *The Indian Serenade*:—

> "Oh lift me from the grass!
> I die, I faint, I fail!
> Let thy love in kisses rain
> On my lips and eyelids pale.
> My cheek is cold and white, alas!
> My heart beats loud and fast;
> Oh! press it to thine own again
> Where it will break at last."

And along with it the transport with which *Epipsychidion* concludes:—

> "Our breath shall intermix, our bosoms bound,
> And our veins beat together; and our lips
> With other eloquence than words, eclipse
> The soul that burns between them, and the wells
> Which boil under our being's inmost cells,
> The fountains of our deepest life, shall be
> Confused in passion's golden purity,
> As mountain-springs under the morning Sun.
> . . . .
> One hope within two wills, one will beneath
> Two overshadowing minds, one life, one death,
> One Heaven, one Hell, one immortality,
> And one annihilation. Woe is me!
> The wingèd words on which my soul would pierce
> Into the height of love's rare universe,
> Are chains of lead around its flight of fire—
> I pant, I sink, I tremble, I expire!"

If Byron's domain is that of the tortures of the luckless or forsaken lover, Shelley's is, as we see, that of the pain of the happy lover, of self-annihilation in the rapture of love. But for the very reason that the erotic domain of both these great poets was thus definitely limited, neither of them wrote many erotic poems; to neither was this one of the most important fields of his productivity.

Moore, on the contrary, was a born erotic poet, of the type of our Christian Winther. What the majority of love-poets are possessed by is the erotic passion; Moore's distinguishing characteristic is erotic fancy. He loves everything that is beautiful, exquisite, delicate, soft, and bright, for its own sake, without requiring any background to throw it into relief. He never tells any eventful story, never sets off by any strong contrast, never undermines by deep brooding. He loves the blossoms of the tree, not its roots. The objects which fascinate him, fascinate with the first impression; they are beautiful and bright; they dazzle the senses; they enthral the eye and the ear more than the heart; they are exchanged for other objects possessing the same qualities—there is a constant gleam and flutter. But all essentially erotic poets have butterfly natures. In this matter no more striking contrast can be imagined than that between Wordsworth and Moore. The former deliberately chooses themes which in themselves are insignificant, or unattractive, or even ugly, in order to endow them with a moral or spiritual beauty; the latter detests the sordid details of human life, recoils from all its adversities, and evades every moral with a Wieland-like smile and bow. When he is forced to give the ugly a place, he cannot resist casting a soft, glittering veil over it. His style has been blamed for its overweight of gorgeous adjectives, its propensity to let every passion lose itself in a simile, and its restless glitter and gleam. It has been called artificial in comparison with Wordsworth's. "Artificial!" cries one of his Irish admirers, "when every human being can enjoy Moore's poetry, whilst a new taste has to be created to enable one to enjoy Wordsworth's!" Is it really the case, then, we are led to ask, that study and a cultivated taste are required for the enjoyment of the natural, whilst only ordinary feeling is demanded for the enjoyment of artificial beauty? Wordsworth and Coleridge were poets for a cultivated, literary public; Moore was the poet for a nation. The faults with which he may fairly be charged are the consequences of his natural limitations, of his being a musician and a colourist, but not a draughtsman; he is incapable of drawing or describing a *whole* object, what he does is to paint the separate attributes of beautiful objects. He devotes verse after verse to the praises of a blush, a smile, the melody of a voice; instead of beautiful outlines he gives us a list of beauties. Employing Voltaire's clever definition of love—"nature's cloth, which imagination has embroidered"—it must be confessed that in Moore's love-poetry the embroidery is often so gorgeous and abundant that it hardly permits the cloth to appear at all. But the cloth is there, and is nature's.

And it is only fair to add that in Moore's best and most beautiful poems the over-abundance of imagery has disappeared. Where the true Irish melancholy has taken possession of his soul, it has blown away all the tinsel and found expression in imperishable language. The style of "Take back the virgin page" and "The last rose of summer" is as simple as their metre is perfect. There is not a simile in either of them. Nor is there a single simile in the beautiful little song which, in spite of its brevity, has for Ireland all the significance of a national epic—the simple song of the lovely young girl who, though adorned with precious jewels and with a beauty still more alluring, went without fear from one end of Ireland to the other, knowing that Erin's sons, "though they love woman and golden store," love honour and virtue more. ("Rich and rare were the gems she wore.") Of the man who wrote such a song Byron might safely assert: "Moore's *Irish Melodies* will go down to posterity with their music; and both will last as long as Ireland or as music and poetry."

Moore's was a happy life. At the age of thirty-one he married a beautiful and amiable girl, Miss Bessy Dyke; and their married life was a most harmonious one. He was not always in good circumstances, but after his fame was established, his works provided him with a handsome income. Though in the *Grand Dinner of Type and Co.* he makes the rich publishers (in the manner of the legendary warriors who after death drank mead out of the skulls of their enemies) drink their wine out of the skulls of poor authors, he himself had no reason to complain of his publisher, who offered him £3000 for *Lalla Rookh* before seeing a line of it, and gave him £4200 for his excellent Life of Lord Byron. Moore was held in equal honour by the Irish and English. In 1818 he was entertained at a banquet in Dublin by all the most famous literary and public men of the country, and when he went to Paris in 1822 he was *fêted* by the British nobility there. It was not till he grew old that misfortunes came upon him. Then he lost his health and had severe trials with his children. He died in 1842.

XIV

THE BRITISH SPIRIT OF FREEDOM

THE poet Thomas Campbell, descended from an ancient Highland family, and born and brought up in Scotland, was, like Scott, an ardent Scottish patriot ; he also felt warm sympathy for Ireland, and, like Moore, sang her national memories and sorrows ; but he combined love of the two subordinate countries with an ardent and martial British patriotism.

He was, however, not only a national poet in the sense in which Wordsworth was one, but also, from his youth to his death, an enthusiastic lover of liberty. His epic poems and his ballads are not superior to corresponding productions of Wordsworth's ; but he had true lyric genius. He is the Tyrtæus or Petöfi of the Naturalistic School. To him the cause of his country and the cause of liberty are one and the same thing, and in his best verse there is a spirit, a swinging march time, and a fire, that entitle him, if only for the sake of half-a-dozen short pieces, to a place among great poets.

His poem *The Battle of the Baltic* is, naturally, little calculated to make a favourable impression on Danes. His pride in the victory Nelson won over a force so much weaker than his own, but which the poem magnifies into the same size as England's, is the very extravagance of patriotism. But, side by side with this poem, and written at the same time, we have *Ye Mariners of England*, a masterpiece, in the rhythm of which we seem to hear the gale rattling among English sails. Here the true son of the Queen of the Sea, singing of the British sailor, celebrates his mother's praises.

Notice the rushing, sweeping force and exultation compressed into the last four lines of this stanza:—

"Ye Mariners of England!
That guard our native seas;
Whose flag has braved a thousand years
The battle and the breeze!
Your glorious standard launch again
To match another foe!
And sweep through the deep,
While the stormy winds do blow;
While the battle rages loud and long,
And the stormy winds do blow.

And observe the expression of pride in England's sovereignty of the sea:—

Britannia needs no bulwarks,
No towers along the steep;
Her march is o'er the mountain-waves,
Her home is on the deep.
With thunders from her native oak,
She quells the floods below,—
As they roar on the shore,
When the stormy winds do blow;
When the battle rages loud and long,
And the stormy winds do blow.

Campbell's life was a well regulated and tranquil one. Born in Glasgow in 1777, he received an excellent education there and in Edinburgh. At the age of twenty-one he published his *Pleasures of Hope*, which, though now antiquated, created a sensation on its appearance, and with the proceeds undertook a tour in Germany, during the course of which he wrote several poems inspired by the hostilities with Denmark—among them the two above mentioned. In 1803 he married his cousin and settled in London. He wrote, lectured, and from 1820 onwards edited a newspaper. After 1830 his health was precarious and his powers were enfeebled. He lived, a shadow of himself, until 1844.

It is the same with Campbell as with all the other authors of the group to which he belonged—his poetic faculty is based upon the freshness of his receptivity to natural impressions. He has written a poem to the rainbow which, in spite of a rather prosaic and argumentative introduction, is a little masterpiece of simplicity and fancy. He begins by imagining the feelings of "the world's grey fathers" when they came forth to watch its first appearance:—

"And when its yellow lustre smiled
  O'er mountains yet untrod,
Each mother held aloft her child
  To bless the bow of God.

Methinks, thy jubilee to keep,
  The first made anthem rang
On earth delivered from the deep,
  And the first poet sang.

Nor ever shall the Muse's eye
  Unraptured greet thy beam:
Theme of primeval prophecy,
  Be still the poet's theme!

. . . . .

How glorious is thy girdle cast
  O'er mountain, tower, and town,
Or mirrored in the ocean vast,
  A thousand fathoms down!

As fresh in yon horizon dark,
  As young thy beauties seem,
As when the eagle from the ark
  First sported in thy beam."

And one of his latest poems, *The Dead Eagle*, written at Oran in Africa, bears witness to the same, unenfeebled, receptivity to all the phenomena of nature as this early one. In the later work we are conscious of a joy in natural strength and power which is characteristically English. "True," the poet writes:

"True the carr'd aëronaut can mount as high;
But what's the triumph of his volant art?
A rash intrusion on the realms of air.
His helmless vehicle, a silken toy,
A bubble bursting in the thunder-cloud;
His course has no volition, and he drifts
The passive plaything of the winds. Not such
Was this proud bird: he clove the adverse storm
And cuff'd it with his wings. He stopp'd his flight
As easily as the Arab reins his steed,

And stood at pleasure 'neath heaven's zenith, like
A lamp suspended from its azure dome,
Whilst underneath him the world's mountains lay
Like molehills, and her streams like lucid threads.
Then downward, faster than a falling star,
He near'd the earth, until his shape distinct
Was blackly shadow'd on the sunny ground;
And deeper terror hush'd the wilderness,
To hear his nearer whoop. Then, up again
He soar'd and wheel'd. There was an air of scorn
In all his movements, whether he threw round
His crested head to look behind him, or
Lay vertical and sportively display'd,
The inside whiteness of his wing declined
In gyres and undulations full of grace.
. . . .
He—reckless who was victor, and above
The hearing of their guns—saw fleets engaged
In flaming combat. It was nought to him
What carnage, Moor or Christian, strew'd their decks.
But if his intellect had match'd his wings,
Methinks he would have scorn'd man's vaunted power
To plough the deep; his pinions bore him down
To Algiers the warlike, or the coral groves
That blush beneath the green of Bona's waves;
And traversed in an hour a wider space
Than yonder gallant ship, with all her sails
Wooing the winds, can cross from morn till eve.
. . . .
. . . . . . The earthquake's self
Disturb'd not him that memorable day,
When o'er yon table-land, where Spain had built
Cathedrals, cannon'd forts, and palaces,
A palsy-stroke of Nature shook Oran,
Turning her city to a sepulchre,
And strewing into rubbish all her homes."

There is wealth of imagination in this as well as wealth of observation.

But Campbell is greatest in his poetry of freedom, in poems like *Men of England, Stanzas on the Battle of Navarino, Lines on Poland, the Power of Russia,* and such noble, profound expressions of spiritual freedom as that entitled *Hallowed Ground.* In such productions as these he plainly shows his spiritual superiority to the poets of the Lake School, who, like him, wrote glorious verse in honour of the nations who were struggling for their independence. The Lake poets honoured the struggle only when it was against the tyranny of Napoleon, England's enemy. Campbell makes no difference of this kind; in the name of freedom he often exhorts and even rebukes England, whereas to the other poets she is freedom's very hearth and home.

Note, in *Men of England,* the warmth with which he insists that the records of valour in war are as nothing compared with the glowing love of liberty in the breasts of living men, and that the glory of the martyrs of freedom is worth a hundred Agincourts.

Campbell's joy at the liberation of Greece is as genuine as his grief over the fall of Poland; but the poem on Poland is more ardent, in its indignation, its hope, its lament that "England has not heart to throw the gauntlet down." And the verses on the power of Russia display as clear an understanding of the danger to civilisation which lies in the success of Russia, and of the real significance of the defeat of Poland, as if a statesman had turned poet.

> "Were this some common strife of States embroil'd;—
> Britannia on the spoiler and the spoil'd
> Might calmly look, and, asking time to breathe,
> Still honourably wear her olive wreath.
> But this is Darkness combating with Light;
> Earth's adverse Principles for empire fight."

These are weighty words; and not less pregnant is the line:

> "The Polish eagle's fall is big with fate to man."

The poem *Hallowed Ground* is, in its bold simplicity, a plain protest against all superstition, whatever name it bears, and a manly confession of faith in the gospel of liberty as proclaimed by the eighteenth century. What is hallowed ground? asks Campbell:

> "What's hallow'd ground? Has earth a clod
> Its Maker meant not should be trod
> By man, the image of his God,
>   Erect and free,
> Unscourg'd by superstition's rod
>   To bow the knee?

That's hallow'd ground—where, mourn'd and miss'd,
The lips repose our love has kiss'd ;—
But where's their memory's mansion ? Is't
Yon churchyard's bowers ?
No ! in ourselves their souls exist,
A part of ours.

A kiss can consecrate the ground
Where mated hearts are mutual bound ;
The spot where love's first links were wound,
That ne'er were riven,
Is hallow'd down to earth's profound,
And up to heaven ! "

And, though the ashes of those who have served mankind may be scattered to the winds, they themselves, he says, live on in men's hearts as in consecrated ground ; until the high-priesthood of Peace, Independence, Truth, shall make earth at last *all hallowed ground.*

Campbell cannot be numbered among the greatest poets of the Naturalistic School ; but in his lyrics there is a simple, powerful, and melodious pathos which reminds us of the old Greek elegiac poets. Although Scotch by birth, his sympathies were with Ireland, and his spirit was British. Although, like the poets of the Lake School, ardently patriotic, he was distinctly the lover and champion of liberty, and of liberty as a divinity, not as an idol. He forms the connecting link between the national poets of Scotland and Ireland and the three great English poet-emigrants of this period.

XV

REPUBLICAN HUMANISM

DURING the period when England, as a European power, was doing the errands of the Holy Alliance, and within her own borders was oppressing the Roman Catholics and reducing the lower classes to distressful poverty by unduly favouring the landowners, there was a steady increase in the number of Englishmen who left their own country to live the life of knights-errant of freedom, and, as it were, remind the world of England's ancient fame as the protector of national independence. Such Englishmen were General Wilson, who, under Bolivar, liberated South America, and Admiral Cochrane, who won fame first in the Brazilian and then in the Greek war of liberation. And to this class also belongs *Walter Savage Landor*, the proudest and most singular figure in the literary world of his period.

Landor, born at Warwick in 1775, was the descendant of an ancient family and the heir of princely wealth. He studied at Oxford. In 1802 he resided for a time in Paris. On his return he sold the greater part of his property in Warwickshire and bought one in another county, on which he introduced every possible kind of improvement, to ensure that his numerous tenants should live under more favourable conditions than their class elsewhere in England. He spent £70,000 on these attempts at reform, which he carried out with less understanding of human nature than desire for human welfare. His benevolence was shamefully abused by its recipients, many of whom took advantage of his unselfishness and generosity to defraud him on a large scale. Enraged by the ingratitude and bad behaviour of his tenants, he determined to sell all his property, even the land which had been in the possession of his family for seven hundred years, and to live thenceforward as a free citizen of the world. This resolution he carried out in 1806.

As soon as he heard of the Spanish rebellion against the tyranny of Napoleon, Landor went to Spain, equipped a small troop at his own expense, and fought with the rebels. He received a public letter of thanks from the Spanish Junta, along with a commission as colonel in the Spanish army. This commission he returned when King Ferdinand was restored, with a letter in which he declared that, although he should always be devoted to the cause of Spain, he could have nothing to do with "a perjurer and traitor" like its King. In this one act we have the man's character—precipitate and reckless, but proud and high-minded. In this author's breast beat the heart of an independent chieftain.

In 1815 Landor settled in Italy, where he had his home for nearly thirty years. From 1835 to 1858 he lived in England (at Bath). Throughout his long life—he died in 1864, at the age of 90—he was the mortal enemy of tyranny in all its manifestations, and the ardent champion of freedom in everything. To the last he was the unwearied benefactor of political refugees and persons suffering for their opinions.

The literary activity displayed during this long, honourable life was prodigious. Landor wrote twice as much as Byron. And it is with a feeling of reverence that we open many of his books; but during the whole literary period with which we are immediately concerned, his writings were neither understood nor valued. Landor wrote without any connection with a reading public, and without receiving any encouragement from the critics, who told him nothing but that he was stiff and cold, and that his English was like a translation from a foreign language; he never enjoyed the smallest amount of popularity or any species of literary triumph. After his death he began to be admired, and about 1870 to exercise influence.

To pass from Moore to Landor is like setting foot on firm ground after rocking on the waves. Landor's distinguishing characteristic is a manly decision; he stands high as an author, but higher still as a man. He is, unfortunately, so little read that one cannot presuppose acquaintance with any of his writings, or find any point of support in the memory or fancy of one's reader on which to base criticisms; and he is not easy to describe. His decision found its most remarkable expression in an estimate of himself which is startling to many. We come upon such verdicts as this: "What I write is not written upon a slate: and no finger, not of Time himself, who dips it in the clouds of years, can efface it"; and upon such answers to the reviewers of his *Imaginary Conversations* as: "Let the sturdiest of them take the ten worst of them, and if he equals them in ten years I will give him a hot wheaten roll and a pint of brown stout for breakfast." Such pride would have made a smaller man ridiculous, but it does not harm Landor; it occasionally becomes him. It reminds us at times of the not unjustifiable, but uncontrollably arrogant feeling which Schopenhauer had of his own deserts, only that Landor's manner is always that of the refined aristocrat, whilst Schopenhauer, with his utter disregard of the laws of common politeness, is a thorough plebeian. And on rare occasions the peculiar temperament, with its grand passionateness and its even grander productivity, reminds us of a man whose name is too great to be lightly named, but who, though infinitely Landor's intellectual superior, would perhaps have acknowledged the intellectual kinship—the solitary, severe Michael Angelo.

There was something severe in Landor's nature—the severity which goes along with firmness of character and absolute truthfulness to one's self and others. In his work there is a certain salutary harshness. The poem "Hyperbion," from the *Hellenics*, may be given as a good and very characteristic example of it.

"Hyperbion was among the chosen few
Of Phœbus; and men honored him awhile,
Honoring in him the God. But others sang
As loudly; and the boys as loudly cheer'd.
Hyperbion (more than bard should be) was wroth,
And thus he spake to Phœbus: 'Hearest thou,
O Phœbus, the rude rabble from the field,

Who swear that they have known thee ever since
Thou feddest for Admetus his white bull?'
'I hear them,' said the God. 'Seize thou the first,
And haul him up above the heads of men,
And thou shalt hear them shout for thee as pleas'd.'
Headstrong and proud Hyperbion was: the crown
Of laurel on it badly cool'd his brow:
So, when he heard them singing at his gate,
While some with flints cut there the rival's name,
Rushing he seized the songster at their head:
The songster kickt and struggled hard, in vain.
Hyperbion claspt him round with arm robust,
And with the left a hempen rope uncoil'd,
Whereon already was a noose: it held
The calf until its mother's teat was drawn
At morn and eve; and both were now afield.
With all his strength he pull'd the wretch along,
And haul'd him up a pine-tree, where he died.
But one night, not long after, in his sleep
He saw the songster: then did he beseech
Apollo to enlighten him, if perchance
In what he did he had done aught amiss.
'Thou hast done well, Hyperbion!' said the God,
'As I did also to one Marsyas
Some years ere thou wert born: but better 'twere
If thou hadst understood my words aright,
For those around may harm thee, and assign
As reason that thou wentest past the law.
My meaning was that thou shouldst hold him up
In the high places of thy mind, and show
Thyself the greater by enduring him.'
Downcast Hyperbion stood: but Phœbus said:
'Be of good cheer, Hyperbion! if the rope
Is not so frayed but it may hold thy calf,
The greatest harm is, that, by hauling him,
Thou hast chafed sorely, sorely, that old pine;
And pine-tree bark will never close again.'"

Seldom has an Apollo expressed himself in a less sickly-sentimental manner on the subject of mediocrity in art. Landor's contempt for it was based on the severity of the artistic demands he made on himself. He is the severest stylist among English prose writers—not stylist in the sense of virtuoso in language, for no English is less flexible than his—but in this sense, that he represents all his characters, the most commonplace and the grandest, the ancient and the modern, in the same simple Attic style. To his marked preference for the heroic and the grand is due the majestic tranquillity which as a rule characterises his *Conversations* (the branch of literature he specially cultivated); the dialogue is Grecian in its beautiful simplicity, Anglo-Roman in its proud decision. His style is pure, correct, concise; and its antique quality specially fits it for the representation of ancient Greek and Roman characters. The public assemblies in the market-place of Athens, the Senate and Forum of Rome, these live in his *Conversations* with the life of their own day. Modern dialogue flowed much less easily and naturally from his pen; he was successful in the more modern *Conversations* only when the situation was of such a nature as to be receptive of life and warmth from his own concealed indignation.

To make acquaintance with Landor in his full vigour and brilliancy one must read his *Pericles and Aspasia,* a tale in epistolary form. It is a work of the same description as Wieland's *Aristippus,* but written in a very different spirit and style. Where Wieland is florid and coquettish, Landor is distinguished by manly grace; where Wieland is sentimental, Landor is noble and proud. This correspondence is chiselled rather than written; it represents Pericles as the republican type of noble humanity and political wisdom; and in it Aspasia is not the hetæra, but a personification of Hellenic beauty and delicacy of feeling, of pagan womanhood, and of the emancipated antique intellect and culture. There is consequently not a trace of anything resembling coquetry in the letters; everything that is small and undignified seems to lie beyond the horizon of the work and its author. But the old-fashioned epistolary form and the length of the letters make the book tedious, and the reader who has not enough patience for it will do well to turn from it to Landor's masterpiece, the Conversation between Epicurus, Leontion, and Ternissa.

This Conversation is inferior to a dialogue of Plato only in profundity of thought; it rivals Plato in grace, in revelation of character, and in naturalness. The amiable philosopher, now approaching middle-age, is walking in his beautiful garden with two young Greek girls, talking of the trivial events of the day and the serious events of life. An Attic atmosphere, a dignified sensuousness, a chaste and charming grace, distinguish the whole scene, striking us perhaps most in the little touches which describe the two girls, particularly the younger, aged sixteen, with her mixture of bashfulness and attractive straightforwardness. Landor has here created the feminine counterpart of Plato's youths; he has discovered the Greek maiden, whom Plato neglected, whom Greek tragedy represented only in solemn or majestically tragic situations, and whose outward appearance alone has been preserved for us in beautiful reliefs.

One is well repaid for one's trouble in following the windings of this Conversation. It begins with a pretty description of the surrounding scene, and with praise of the solitude which is necessary to the man who desires to think, and to write his thoughts. Behind the figure of Epicurus we here catch a glimpse of Landor, who had this same love of a retired life, at a distance from the traffic and noise of the busy world. (See Conversation between Southey and Landor.) Then Epicurus discusses playfully and charmingly with Ternissa the question whether the myth of Boreas, Zethes, and Caläis is to be accepted literally or not, whilst the elder girl teases Ternissa because of her credulousness. After this the Conversation, touching lightly for a moment on the delicious scent of the vine-leaves and on the new olive plantations, turns into an affecting, profound discussion on the fear of death. The calm, dignified attitude of Epicurus arouses the girls' admiration, and leads them violently to upbraid those who condemn and persecute him as an atheist. It comes out that Leontion has written a whole book for the purpose of refuting the charges against him made by Theophrastus. Epicurus proves to her with gentle dignity how useless replies to such attacks are, and explains to her why he will contend with no one. "I would not contend even with men able to contend with me . . . Whom should I contend with? The less? it were inglorious. The greater? it were vain." Here we perceive Landor himself again.

This was the very argument of the man who a few years before his death prefixed to his last book the motto:

> "I strove with none, for none was worth my strife:
> Nature I loved, and, next to nature, Art;
> I warmed both hands before the fire of life;
> It sinks, and I am ready to depart."

The first of these lines contains both a confession and a justification of what appeared to be his arrogance—that which small minds found it so difficult to understand or to pardon. The second tells what was the chief subject of his earnest study, and what, supplementing it, came next in order. The third line is an expression of the noble philosophy which supported and nourished his spirit under so much misunderstanding and opposition; and the last shows him prepared, with the quiet dignity which harmonised with his character, to fold his mantle round him and depart when his time came.[1]

Leontion continues the Conversation. "The old," she says, "are all against you, for the name of pleasure is an affront to them: they know no other kind of it than that which has flowered and seeded, and of which the withered stems have indeed a rueful look. What we call dry they call sound; nothing must retain any juice in it: their pleasure is in chewing what is hard, not in tasting what is savoury." Landor, who had to submit to reproaches for the licentiousness of his writings even from Byron (see preface to *A Vision of Judgment*), evidently derives his philosophy, as John Stuart Mill did his system of morality, from Epicurus, the pagan.

The Conversation passes lightly from one subject to another; now it turns on Ternissa's blushes at the remembrance of the statues of satyrs and fauns in the bath chamber, now on Leontion's feminine objections to Aristotle and Theophrastus. It concludes in a genuinely Greek, Epicurean,

[1] See *The Centenary of Landor's Birth* in *The Examiner* of 30th January 1875, an article written by the talented poet and critic, Edmund Gosse, who for us Danes possesses the special merit of being one of the most appreciative and best-informed foreign critics of Dano-Norwegian literature.

erotic manner; Epicurus and Ternissa act the scene between Peleus and Thetis, which ends with a kiss.

In this Conversation we have Landor's art and his tranquil humanism at their best. But when we turn to the modern Conversations we become acquainted with the soldier in him, the writer ever armed, ever ready for the fray, who, assuming a thousand different disguises, exposes and strikes at every form of falsehood and oppression which challenges him to the attack in his character of pagan, republican, and philanthropist. In his 125 *Imaginary Conversations* he roams, displaying an astonishing amount of information, over the whole face of the earth—from London to China, from Paris to the South Sea Islands; and throughout the whole of history—from Cicero to Bossuet, from Cromwell to Petrarch, from Tasso to Talleyrand; in every country and every age uttering a vigorous protest against tyranny, and speaking a word, sharp as a sword, in the cause of liberty. We overhear what the Empress Catharine and her favourite maid of honour say to each other while they are in the act of murdering the former's husband; and the Conversation in question is not much inferior to one of Vitet's incomparable historical scenes, which are models in this style. We hear Louis XVIII. talking politics with the supercilious, polished Talleyrand, and notice how the uncontrollable longing for plenty of pheasants and pheasants' eggs twines itself, like a scarlet thread, through the web of all His Majesty's political plans. We listen to General Kleber talking with his staff-officers in Egypt, and are conscious of the dissatisfaction with Napoleon's tyrannical measures which runs, like a subdued murmur, through all they say. We are present at the assassination of Kotzebue, and hear Sandt, in the course of his attempts to induce Kotzebue to quit the path he is treading, pronounce his own acquittal.

It was an article of Landor's political creed that the oppressor ought to fall by the sword. All his life he advocated the death of tyrants; he was not afraid openly to express his wish that Napoleon III. might be assassinated. He was a friend and spiritual kinsman of the great European revolutionists who, with Mazzini at their head, had sworn implacable enmity to the oppressors of the nations. But it is not only as a politician that Landor shoots beyond the mark; by far the greater number of his historical Conversations suffer from the too open pursuit of some aim of his own. We are always catching sight of Landor himself. Take, for example, his representation of Catharine of Russia at the terrible moment above referred to: Landor cannot resist seizing the opportunity to discourse, in the disguise of Princess Dashkoff, on the ungodliness of Voltaire's character and the immorality of his *Pucelle*, with the aim of impressing upon us what a bad influence the French spirit had upon Russia. For with all his liberal-mindedness he is sufficiently the Englishman of his day to lay the blame of everything bad on France, and never to represent a Frenchman in any but a ridiculous or contemptible light. When, for example, he writes a Conversation between Louis XVIII. and Talleyrand, he cannot refrain from making his satire so severe—Louis' foolish speeches so imbecile, Talleyrand's tone to his sovereign so ironical—that no one can believe in the historic truthfulness of the whole. Landor desires to hear the English and Wellington praised, and desires to have Louis' incapacity plainly shown, and he is rash enough to put both the eulogy of England and the mockery of Louis into the mouth of the judicious French courtier.

In the handling of the weapons of satire, Landor might have learned much from the Frenchmen whom he disliked so heartily. But he had as great a contempt for their literature as for their politics, and despised Voltaire, the author, quite as much as Voltaire, the man. In the Conversation between himself and the Abbé Delille he uses, as a critic of French tragedy, even severer language than Lessing, and shows no more appreciation than Lessing did of the great stylistic capacity inherent in the characteristically French intellect. It strikes us as comical to hear one man reproaching another with the utmost insolence for being too polished.

One hardly needs to be told that a man with this opinion of French classic poetry was a despiser of Pope, an enthusiastic admirer of Milton, and a pronounced supporter of the reform of English poetry demanded by Wordsworth. Most of the Conversations upon literary topics are written for the purpose of eulogising Wordsworth and Southey, and reproaching the reading public for its want of appreciation of such fine poetry as theirs.[1] Keats and Shelley are also warmly praised ; and Landor expresses regret that he had not made the personal acquaintance of either, and, in particular, that a false report concerning Shelley's behaviour to his first wife had kept him from calling upon that poet at Pisa. He writes of Shelley that he "united, in just degrees, the ardour of the poet with the patience and forbearance of the philosopher," and that "his generosity and charity went far beyond those of any man at present in existence." But no sooner is Byron mentioned than Landor expresses himself exactly like a poet of the Lake School. The man who believed that the two fingers which held his pen had more power than the two Houses of Parliament (see conclusion of the Conversation between Landor and Marchese Pallavicini) could never forget Byron's satire of his *Gebir.* And the remarkable friendship existing, in spite of all their political and religious differences, between him and Southey, made it equally impossible for him to forget the blows which Byron had struck at his admirer. Byron's egotism and excitable restlessness were, undoubtedly, antipathetic to Landor, but it was the treatment of Southey which influenced him most, and blinded him to many of the great poet's best qualities. The connection with Southey is, on the whole, little creditable to Landor, and Forster's long *Life of Landor* is rendered the more unreadable by the disproportionate space allotted in it to letters from and to such an uninteresting personage as Southey. In Landor's eyes Southey had the great, and certainly rare, merit of being one of the two persons who had read and bought the poem *Gebir* when it came out. De Quincey, who was the other, tells that in his youth he was hooted in the streets of Oxford as the one reader of that poem in the University. So we can understand how Southey, who not only bought and read, but praised it, and who, more-

[1] See, for example, the two Conversations between Southey and Porson, and the survey of the English poets in *Miscellaneous*, cxvi.

over, wrote a favourable review of Landor's dull *Count Julian* in the *Quarterly*, must have seemed to the self-satisfied author a man of the rarest intellectual penetration.

It is undeniable that *Gebir*, in spite of all its passionate republicanism, is a stilted, valueless composition, which bears evident traces of having been, by a characteristic whim of its author, first written in Latin verse. There was, throughout, a Latin quality in Landor's verse. Even Gosse, who admires it, feels obliged to confess that its character, like the taste of olives, is peculiar enough to acquit any person who does not like it of the charge of affectation. It is in his prose alone that his strength lies.

But a writer whose poetry is lacking in charm of expression and lyric soul, whose dramas were neither played nor read, and who found his true province in lengthy prose dialogue, spoken in all parts of the world and at all periods of history, but unconnected with any play—such a writer could not, however noble his principles and unmistakable his Radicalism, be the man to bring about a general European revulsion to liberal opinions. He repelled by his whimsicalities and crotchets, of which such instances may be given as his defence of the burning of Rome by Nero as a hygienic measure, his characterisation of Pitt as a mediocrity, and Fox as a charlatan, or, greatest absurdity of all, his advice to the Greeks, during their struggle with the Turks, to give up the use of firearms and resort to their old weapon, the bow. He was too peculiar and too much of the solitary to have admirers and imitators; he was too incomprehensible by the ordinary mind to exercise any influence upon the general public; his virtues contributed as much as his faults—his wild manliness as much as his excessive self-sufficiency—to render him unapproachable. And if he was incapable of compromising like Moore, that is to say, of ever becoming a Whig poet, he was equally incapable of ever imparting to his Radicalism a poetic form that would entrance and captivate a whole reading public. His partial understanding of the great modern movements in religion, government, and society, entitles him to be grouped with two younger and greater men, Shelley and Byron. He fought for his ideals like a brave and proud republican soldier ; but he was neither fitted to be a general nor to submit to rule ; and he had not the power of inspiring a multitude of other minds.[1]

The eldest of the three freedom-loving exiles, he outlived the other two—lived so long, indeed, that he became the contemporary of an entirely different generation of English poets. Browning was his friend ; Swinburne's cordial admiration sweetened the last years of his life ; the dedication of *Atalanta* shows the young man's feelings towards the old. Landor's great shade, extending one hand to Wordsworth, the other to Swinburne, seems to hover over the whole poetic development of England during a period of not less than eighty years.

[1] A satirical pamphlet which he published in 1836, *Letters of a Conservative, in which are shown the only means of saving what is left of the English Church*, made no impression.

XVI

RADICAL NATURALISM

If in the year 1820, any respectable, well-educated Englishman had been asked: "Who is Shelley?" he would undoubtedly, if he could answer the question at all, have replied: "He is said to be a bad poet with shocking principles and a worse than doubtful character. The *Quarterly Review*, which is not given to defamation, says that he himself is distinguished by 'low pride, cold selfishness, and unmanly cruelty,' and his poetry by 'its frequent and total want of meaning.' He has lately published a poem called *Prometheus Unbound*, the verse of which the same review calls 'drivelling prose run mad.' And the press is unanimous in this opinion. The *Literary Gazette* writes that, if it were not assured to the contrary, it would take it for granted that the author of *Prometheus Unbound* was a lunatic—as his principles are ludicrously wicked, and his poetry is a mélange of nonsense, cockneyism, poverty, and pedantry. It calls the work in question 'the stupid trash of this delirious dreamer.'"

And it is quite possible that our Englishman would have added, in an undertone: "There are very bad reports in circulation about Shelley. The *Literary Gazette*, which is always specially severe on the enemies of religion, hints at incest. It declares that 'to such a man it would be a matter of perfect indifference to rob a confiding father of his daughters, and incestuously to live with all the branches of a family whose morals were ruined by the damned sophistry of the seducer.' These expressions may be too strong, but it is hardly credible that they are entirely undeserved; for *Blackwood's Magazine*, the only periodical which has been at all favourable to Shelley, writes of his *Prometheus*: 'It seems impossible that there can exist a more pestiferous mixture of blasphemy, sedition, and sensuality.' And you may possibly have heard Theodore Hook's witty saying: '*Prometheus Unbound*—it is well named: who would bind it?'"

And if, two years later, when this harshly reviewed poet was already dead, the same curious inquirer had applied to the publisher for information as to the saleableness of the fiercely attacked works, the latter would quite certainly have complained of them as a bad business speculation, and told his questioner that, during Shelley's lifetime, not a hundred copies of any of his works, except *Queen Mab* and *The Cenci*, had been sold, and that, as far as *Adonais* and *Epipsychidion* were concerned, ten would be nearer the number.

If any one were to ask now: Who was Shelley? what a different answer would be given! But to-day there is no one in England who would ask.

It was on the 4th of August 1792 that England's greatest lyric poet was born. On the same day on which, in Paris, the leaders of the Revolution—Santerre, Camille Desmoulins, and others—were meeting in a house on the Boulevards to make the arrangements which resulted, a few days later, in the fall of monarchy in France, there came into the world at Field Place, in the English county of Sussex, a pretty little boy with deep blue eyes, whose life was to be of greater and more enduring significance in the emancipation of the human mind than all that happened in France in August 1792. Not quite thirty years later his name—Percy Bysshe Shelley—was carved upon the stone in the Protestant cemetery in Rome under which his ashes lie; and below the name are engraved the words: *Cor cordium.*

Cor cordium, heart of hearts—such was the simple inscription in which Shelley's young wife summed up his character; and they are the truest, profoundest words she could have chosen.

The Shelleys are an ancient and honourable family. The poet's father, Sir Timothy Shelley, was a wealthy landowner. He was a narrow-minded man, a supporter of the existing, for the simple reason that it existed. But revolt against rule and convention was hereditary in Shelley's family, as wildness and violence of temper were in Byron's. Percy's grandfather, a strange, restless man, eloped with two of his three wives; and two of his daughters in their turn eloped. Of these incidents we are reminded by similar occurrences in the life of the grandson—just as many an action of Byron's reminds us of the sum of untamed and reckless passionateness which was his indisputable inheritance from father and mother. Unconventionality, revolt against hard and fast rule, was, however, but an outward and comparatively unimportant part of Shelley's character and life. It was only a sign of the alert receptivity and the keen sensitiveness, the early development of which strikes every student of his biographies. At school, ill-used himself, he rebels against the ill-treatment to which, according to the prevalent English custom, the weaker and younger boys were subjected by the older boys, and in this case also by the masters. Shelley seems to have been in a very special manner the victim of this species of brutality, just as he was in later life of many other species; there was a natural antipathy between him and everything base and stupid and foul, and he never entered into a compromise with any one or any thing of this nature.

We gain a distinct idea of what his impressions were on his entrance into life, from a fragment found after his death upon a scrap of paper:—

> "Alas! this is not what I thought life was.
> I knew that there were crimes and evil men,
> Misery and hate; nor did I hope to pass,
> Untouched by suffering, through the rugged glen.
> In mine own heart I saw as in a glass
> The hearts of others."

He wrought for his soul, he tells us, "a linkèd armour of calm steadfastness." But passionate indignation had preceded this mood of quiet resistance; and the soul which he armed with steadfastness was too enthusiastic and ardent not to lay plans of attack behind its defences.

In the introduction to the *Revolt of Islam,* he recalls "the hour which burst his spirit's sleep":—

"A fresh May-dawn it was,
When I walked forth upon the glittering grass,
And wept, I knew not why: until there rose
From the near schoolroom voices that, alas!
Were but one echo from a world of woes—
The harsh and grating strife of tyrants and of foes.

And then I clasped my hands, and looked around:
But none was near to mock my streaming eyes,
Which poured their warm drops on the sunny ground.
So, without shame, I spake: 'I will be wise,
And just, and free, and mild, if in me lies
Such power; for I grow weary to behold
The selfish and the strong still tyrannise
Without reproach or check.' I then controlled
My tears, my heart grew calm, and I was meek and bold."

The generation which was born at the same time and under the same planet as the first French Republic was precocious in its criticism of all traditional beliefs and conventions. Shelley, who at school saw tyranny and feigned piety attendant on one another, and who became acquainted at a very early age with the writings of the French Encyclopædists and of Hume, Godwin, and other English freethinkers, brooded deeply, long before he was grown up, on the history, the destiny, and the errors of the human race. His thoughts were the thoughts of an immature youth, but their spirit was the spirit of liberty, as understood by the eighteenth century.

What his comrades remembered about him in later years was his defiant attitude towards authority, more particularly a habit he had of "cursing his father and the king." He went among the boys by the name of "mad Shelley," and "Shelley the atheist." Thus early was the opprobrious word applied to him which was to be coupled with his name all his life, and serve as a pretext for abuse and defamation.

It is unnecessary to dwell upon those events in Shelley's life of which every one who has heard his name has at least a superficial knowledge. We need merely recall to mind the fact that, as the undergraduate of eighteen, he had the curious habit of writing down his heresies on such subjects as God, government, and society, in the form of letters, which he sent to people personally unknown to him, with the request that they would refute his theories and provide him with the proofs against his arguments which he himself was unable to find; that, out of these letters, which consisted chiefly of extracts from the works of Hume and the French materialists, grew a little anonymous pamphlet (no longer in existence) which was entitled *The Necessity of Atheism,* and ended with a Q. E. D.; and that Shelley, in the childish hope of exercising a reforming influence on the spirit of his age, sent a copy of this pamphlet to the Bench of Bishops. What followed is equally well known. Shelley, denounced as the author, was not only expelled from the University, but from his father's house.

No one nowadays considers that any serious scientific conviction, in whatever manner it may be expressed, should bring disgrace and punishment upon its exponent; and Shelley's punishment appears to us doubly unreasonable when we discover that in his pamphlet (the substance of which he reprinted in the notes to *Queen Mab*) he is no more an atheist than, for example, our Oersted is in his well-known work, *The Spirit in Nature.* He has not yet arrived at any logical and consistent theory of life; he is only clear on the one main point, that he is not, and never can become, an adherent of any so-called revealed religion. The materialistic impressions received from the books he has read are blent in his mind with the ardent pantheism which distinguished him to the last. When Trelawny asked him in 1822, the year in which he died: Why do you call yourself an atheist? Shelley replied: "I used the name to express my abhorrence of superstition; I took up the word, as a knight took up the gauntlet, in defiance of injustice."

Shelley had grown up tall and slight, narrow-chested, his features small and not regular except the mouth, which was beautiful, clever, and fascinating; there was a feminine and almost seraphic look in the eyes, and the whole face was distinguished by an infinite play of expression. He sometimes looked the age he was—nineteen, sometimes as if he were forty. In the course of the ten remaining years of his life he became more manly in appearance, but still often struck people as boyish and feminine looking—witness Trelawny's surprise at his first meeting with Shelley: "Was it possible this mild-looking beardless boy could be the veritable monster at war with all the world, and denounced by the rival sages of our literature as the founder of a Satanic school?" His countenance assumed every expression—earnest, joyful, touchingly sorrowful, listlessly weary; but what it suggested most frequently in later years was promptitude and decision. He often expressed in his face the feeling he put into words in his poem *To Edward Williams:*

> "Of hatred I am proud,—with scorn content;
> Indifference, that once hurt me, now is grown
> Itself indifferent."

To all this we may add, employing words used by a friend of his youth, that he looked "preternaturally intelligent"; and that Mulready, a distinguished painter of the day, said it was simply impossible to paint Shelley's portrait—he was "too beautiful."

It is, then, as a youth of this nature—excitable as a poet, brave as a hero, gentle as a woman, blushing and shy as a young girl, swift and light as Shakespeare's Ariel—that we must think of Shelley going out and in among his friends. Mrs. Williams said of him: "He comes and goes like a spirit, no one knows when or where."

His health was extremely delicate all his life, and would probably have given way altogether if he had not rigidly adhered to the simplest diet. About 1812 he adopted vegetarianism, with doubtful benefit. He was of a consumptive habit and subject to nervous and spasmodic attacks, which were sometimes so violent that he rolled on the floor in agony, and had recourse to opium to dull the pain; when he had his worst attacks he would not let the opium bottle out of his hand. When he was visiting the London hospitals and studying medicine with the aim of being able to assist the poor, he himself became seriously ill, and an eminent physician prophesied that he would die of consumption. But his lungs completely righted themselves some years later. In 1817, in attending some of the poor in their cottages, he caught a bad attack of ophthalmia; and he had a relapse of the same malady at the end of the year, and another in 1821, each time severe enough to prevent his reading.

The lofty philanthropy which to him was a religion, demanded many offerings. He displayed it wherever he went. When he was living at Marlow, in anything but affluent circumstances, he made all the poor of the neighbourhood his pensioners; they came to his house every week for their allowances, and he went to them when they were kept at home by sickness. One day he appeared barefooted at the house of a neighbour; he had given away his shoes to a poor woman. Of his own accord, almost immediately after his expulsion from Oxford, he gave up, for the benefit of his sisters, his claim to the greater part of his father's estate. At the time when he was enjoying an income of about £1000 a year, he spent most of it in assisting others, especially poor men of letters, whose debts he paid, and to whom he showed generosity almost unjustifiable in a man of his means.

The story of his first marriage is as follows. Exaggerated and mistaken chivalry led him at the age of nineteen to elope with a schoolgirl of sixteen, named Harriet Westbrook, who was very much in love with him, and had complained bitterly to him of her father's ill-treatment of her (he had forbidden her to love Shelley, and tried to compel her to go to school!). Shelley, after various meetings with her, made his plans, carried her off to Scotland, and married her in Edinburgh. The censure of public opinion fell most severely on the poet for this behaviour; but W. M. Rossetti's remark is very much to the point, namely, that it would be interesting to know "what percentage of faultlessly Christian young heirs of opulent baronets would have acted like the atheist Shelley, and married a retired hotel-keeper's daughter offering herself as a mistress." The hasty union, contracted without any proper consideration, proved an unhappy one; and it was dissolved when, in 1814, Shelley made the acquaintance of Mary Wollstonecraft Godwin, then in her seventeenth year, and was inspired by her with an irresistible passion. Mary Godwin, the daughter of Mary Wollstonecraft, the first famous pleader for the emancipation of woman, and of William Godwin, the free-thinking author of the works which had had such an influence on Shelley in his earliest youth, gave him her love frankly and freely, and in so doing acted strictly according to her own code of right. The young couple's theories of marriage, which were too ideal not to be regarded as vile by the vile, were also too impracticable. Although in their eyes mutual love alone, and not any ecclesiastical or civil formality, constituted the sacred marriage tie, they nevertheless for practical reasons, and especially for the sake of their children, went through the customary marriage ceremony in 1816, after the suicide of Shelley's first wife. Before this they had been twice abroad, first on a short tour, great part of which was taken on foot, and then for a longer period of travel, during which they met Byron. Shelley's name was, accordingly, coupled with Byron's, and the English press attacked them both with the utmost fury, going so far as to put a shameful interpretation on their noble and manly friendship.

Southey found occasion for a perfect explosion of abuse in the circumstance, insignificant and harmless enough, that Shelley had written in the album kept for visitors at the Chartreuse at Montanvert in the valley of Chamounix, below a number of pious platitudes about "Nature and Nature's God," the following incorrectly spelt hexameter line:

εἰμι φιλάνθρωπος δημωκράτικός τ' ἄθεός τε.
PERCY B. SHELLEY.

The well-known outburst against Lord Byron, which has been already touched on, has this utterance as its point of departure.

Such is, given in a few words, the overture to Shelley's life and poetry.

Cor cordium was his rightful appellation—for what he understood and felt was the innermost heart of things, their soul and spirit; and the feelings to which he gave expression were those inmost feelings, for which words seem too coarse, and which find vent only in music or in such verse as his, which is musical as richly harmonised melodies.

The suppressed melancholy of Shelley's lyrics sometimes reminds us of Shakespeare. The little spinning song in *The Cenci*, for example, recalls Amiens' song in *As You Like It* or the songs of Desdemona and Ophelia.

But where Shelley is most himself he surpasses Shakespeare in delicacy; and there is no other poet with whom he can be compared; no one surpasses him. The short poems of 1821 and 1822 are, one may venture to say, the most exquisite in the English language.

Take as a specimen the little poem entitled *A Dirge*:—

> "Rough wind that moanest loud
> Grief too sad for song;
> Wild wind when sullen cloud
> Knells all the night long;
> Sad storm whose tears are vain,
> Bare woods whose branches stain,
> Deep caves and dreary main,
> Wail for the world's wrong!"

And wondrous in melody and restraint of expression is a verse like this:—

> "One word is too often profaned
> For me to profane it;
> One feeling too falsely disdained
> For thee to disdain it;
> One hope is too like despair
> For prudence to smother;
> And pity from thee more dear
> Than that from another."

The words are few, and there is nothing remarkable in the rhythm, yet there is not a line that could have come from any pen but Shelley's.

In these short poems we are clearly conscious of the poet's melancholy, a melancholy which in his longer works is veiled, or else overpowered by his belief in a bright future, his faith in the progress of the human race. The inmost recesses of his own being were penetrated by a sadness produced by the feeling of the mutability of everything, and by early experience of the manner in which feeling leads astray, love disappoints, and life deceives.

He has given imperishable expression to the feeling of mutability :—

> " The flower that smiles to-day
>   To-morrow dies :
> All that we wish to stay
>   Tempts and then flies.
> What is this world's delight?
> Lightning that mocks the night,
>   Brief even as bright.
>
> Virtue, how frail it is!
>   Friendship how rare!
> Love, how it sells poor bliss
>   For proud despair!
> But we, though soon they fall,
> Survive their joy, and all
>   Which ours we call.
>
> Whilst skies are blue and bright,
>   Whilst flowers are gay,
> Whilst eyes that change ere night
>   Make glad the day,
> Whilst yet the calm hours creep,
> Dream thou—and from thy sleep
>   Then wake to weep."

The first verse indicates the transitoriness of all earthly beauty and happiness; the second, the suffering that lies concealed in the very happiness; and the third is an exhortation to enjoy the dream of happiness as long as possible.

A mood of like nature has found expression in the incomparable poem which bears the simple title, *Lines*. This poem Shelley could not have written unless one after another of his own fond beliefs had evaporated, unless his passions for Harriet, for Mary, for Emilia Viviani, had ended in a sorrowful awakening. Yet it bears no trace of being a personal confession. It is an impassioned proclamation of the universal laws of life, first softly hummed, and then sung in a voice which has never had its equal.

> "When the lamp is shattered,
> The light in the dust lies dead;
> When the cloud is scattered,
> The rainbow's glory is shed;
> When the lute is broken,
> Sweet notes are remembered not;
> When the lips have spoken,
> Loved accents are soon forgot."

The lines on the human heart in the third verse are as condensed as a couplet of Pope's and as melodious as bars of Beethoven:—

> "O, Love, who bewailest
> The frailty of all things here,
> Why chose you the frailest
> For your cradle, your home, and your bier?"

And the poem ends with this prophecy, in which we can hear the passions that have taken possession of the heart taking their wild will with it:—

> "Its passions will rock thee,
> As the storms rock the ravens on high:
> Bright reason will mock thee,
> Like the sun from a wintry sky.
> From thy nest every rafter
> Will rot, and thine eagle home
> Leave thee naked to laughter
> When leaves fall and cold winds come."

A certain characteristic of Shelley, one which readers who know him only from anthologies will at once cite as his chief characteristic, seems to be strongly at variance with this unexampled personal intensity. I refer to the well-known fact that the most famous of his lyric poems are inspired by subjects outside of the emotional life, nay, outside of the world of man altogether; they treat of the cloud and the gale, of the life of the elements, of the marvellous freedom and stormy strength of wind and water.

They are meteorological and cosmical poems. Yet there is no real contradiction in the most intimately emotional of lyric poets being, to all appearance, the most occupied with externals. We find the reason for it given by Shelley himself in a short essay *On Love*. He describes the essence of love as an irresistible craving for sympathy: "If we reason, we would be understood; if we imagine, we would that the airy children of our brain were born anew within another's; if we feel, we would that another's nerves should vibrate to our own, that lips of motionless ice should not reply to lips quivering and burning with the heart's best blood. This is Love . . . The meeting with an understanding capable of clearly estimating our own; an imagination which should enter into and seize upon the subtle and delicate peculiarities which we have delighted to cherish and unfold in secret . . . this is the invisible and unattainable point to which Love tends. . . . Hence in solitude, or in that deserted state when we are surrounded by human beings, and yet they sympathise not with us, we love the flowers, the grass, the waters, and the sky. . . . There is eloquence in the tongueless wind, and a melody in the flowing brooks which bring tears of mysterious tenderness to the eyes, like the voice of one beloved singing to you alone."

In a note on *The Witch of Atlas*, Mrs. Shelley, too, writes that it was the certainty of neither being able to arouse the sympathy nor win the approbation of his countrymen, in combination with a shrinking from opening the wounds of his own heart by portraying human passion, which led her husband to seek forgetfulness in the airiest flights of fancy.

It was this very craving for a sympathy which his fellow-creatures refused him, that made his feeling for nature an ardent desire, and gave it its wonderful originality. Such a thing was unknown in English poetry. The stiff, artificial school of Pope had been superseded by the Lake School. Pope had perfumed the air with affectation; the Lake School had thrown open the windows and let in the fresh air of the mountains and the sea. But Wordsworth's love of nature was passionless, whatever he may say to the contrary in

Tintern Abbey. Nature was to him an invigorator and a suggester of Protestant reflections. That meanest flower which gave him thoughts that often lay too deep for tears, he put into his buttonhole as an ornament, and looked at sometimes in a calmly dignified manner, revolving a simile. Shelley flees to nature for refuge when men shut their doors upon him. He does not, like others, feel it to be something entirely outside of himself—cold, or indifferent, or cruel. Its stony calm where man's woe and weal are concerned, its divine impassibility as regards our life and death, our short triumphs and long sufferings, are to him benevolence in comparison with man's stupidity and brutality. In *Peter Bell the Third* he jeers at Wordsworth because in the latter's love of nature it was "his drift to be a kind of moral eunuch"; he himself loves her like an ardent lover; he has pursued her most secret steps like her shadow; his pulse beats in mysterious sympathy with hers. He himself, like his Alastor, resembles "the Spirit of Wind, with lightning eyes and eager breath, and feet disturbing not the drifted snow."

He calls animals and plants his beloved brothers and sisters, and compares himself, with his keen susceptibility and his trembling sensitiveness, to the chameleon and the sensitive plant. In one of his poems he writes of the chameleons, which live on light and air, as the poet does on love and fame, and which change their hue with the light twenty times a day; and compares the life led by the poet on this cold earth with that which chameleons might lead if they were hidden from their birth in a cave beneath the sea. And in one of the most famous of all he tells how

"A Sensitive Plant in a garden grew;
And the young winds fed it with silver dew;
And it opened its fan-like leaves to the light,
And closed them beneath the kisses of night.

. . . .

(And) each (flower) was interpenetrated
With the light and the odour its neighbour shed,
Like young lovers whom youth and love make dear,
Wrapped and filled by their mutual atmosphere.

But the Sensitive Plant, which could give small fruit
Of the love which it felt from the leaf to the root,
Received more than all; it loved more than ever,
Where none wanted but it, could belong to the giver:—

For the Sensitive Plant has no bright flower;
Radiance and odour are not its dower;
It loves even like Love,—its deep heart is full;
It desires what it has not, the beautiful."

Even more characteristically, even more personally, does Shelley's inmost feeling, his heart's heart, such as it became after hard fate had set its stamp upon it, express itself in the beautiful elegy on Keats, which was written in a frame of burning indignation produced by the base and rancorous attack in the *Quarterly Review*. He is describing how all the poets of the day come to weep over their brother's bier:—

"'Midst others of less note came one frail form,
A phantom among men, companionless
As the last cloud of an expiring storm
Whose thunder is its knell. He, as I guess,
Had gazed on Nature's naked loveliness
Actæon-like; and now he fled astray
With feeble steps o'er the world's wilderness,
And his own thoughts along that rugged way
Pursued like raging hounds their father and their prey.

A pard-like Spirit beautiful and swift—
A love in desolation masked—a power
Girt round with weakness; it can scarce uplift
The weight of the superincumbent hour.
It is a dying lamp, a falling shower,
A breaking billow;—even whilst we speak
Is it not broken? On the withering flower
The killing sun smiles brightly: on a cheek
The life can burn in blood even while the heart may break.

His head was bound with pansies overblown,
And faded violets, white and pied and blue;
And a light spear topped with a cypress cone,
Round whose rude shaft dark ivy-tresses grew
Yet dripping with the forest's noonday dew,
Vibrated, as the ever-beating heart
Shook the weak hand that grasped it. Of that crew
He came the last, neglected and apart;
A herd-abandoned deer struck by the hunter's dart.

All stood aloof, and at his partial moan
Smiled through their tears. Well knew that gentle band
Who in another's fate now wept his own.
As in the accents of an unknown land
He sang new sorrow, sad Urania scanned
The Stranger's mien, and murmured, 'Who art thou?'
He answered not, but with a sudden hand
Made bare his branded and ensanguined brow,
Which was like Cain's or Christ's—Oh! that it should be so."

Shelley here compares himself to Actæon, whom the sight of Nature's naked loveliness drove distracted. It is plain that the strength of his strong will was required to keep this man with the fragile, delicate body from positive destruction by the visions and apparitions of his imagination. He often felt as if they were more than his brain could bear; and when he then, an exile in a foreign land, sought alleviation in solitude, he experienced such impressions of nature as that which is preserved in the entrancing *Stanzas Written in Dejection near Naples,* stanzas which contain the very essence of Shelley's poetry. He does not describe the landscape. He never does describe. It is not the outward forms and colours of things which he shows us, but that to which he is extraordinarily alive, what we have called their spirit and soul.

One or two touches, and the Bay is before us:—

"The sun is warm, the sky is clear,
The waves are dancing fast and bright;
Blue isles and snowy mountains wear
The purple noon's transparent might."

The waves break upon the shore "like light dissolved, in star-showers thrown." The lightning of the noontide ocean is flashing, and a tone arises from its measured motion. "How sweet," cries the poet, "did any heart now share in my emotion!"

"Alas! I have nor hope nor health,
Nor peace within nor calm around;
Nor that content, surpassing wealth,
The sage in meditation found,
And walked with inward glory crowned;

Nor fame nor power nor love, nor leisure.
Others I see whom these surround—
Smiling they live, and call life pleasure ;—
To me that cup has been dealt in another measure.

Yet now despair itself is mild,
Even as the winds and waters are ;
I could lie down like a tired child,
And weep away the life of care
Which I have borne and yet must bear,—
Till death like sleep might steal on me ;
And I might feel in the warm air
My cheek grow cold, and hear the sea
Breathe o'er my dying brain its last monotony.

Some might lament that I were cold,
As I when this sweet day is gone,
Which my lost heart, too soon grown old,
Insults with this untimely moan.
They might lament—for I am one
Whom men love not, and yet regret ;
Unlike this day, which, when the sun
Shall on its stainless glory set,
Will linger, though enjoyed, like joy in memory yet."

The man over whose dying brain cruel waves were so soon to close, feels, with a gentle mournfulness, his being dissolve into the beneficent elements of nature, and compares his last breath to that of the beautiful southern summer day. He did not, like Byron, love nature only in its agitated, wild moments ; simple of heart himself, he loved its simplicity, its holy calm.

But this is not his most characteristic feature. Himself of the race of Titans and giants, he loves the Titanic and gigantic beauty of nature—his manner of doing so again differing entirely from Byron's. It is not the tangible, easily accessible poetry of nature, that of the flowers of the field or the trees of the forest, which inspires him at his highest. No! the finest inspirations of his great spirit are received from the grand and the distant, from the forceful motions of the sea and the air and the dance of the spheres in the firmament of heaven. In this familiarity with the great phenomena and the great vicissitudes of nature Shelley resembles

Byron, but he resembles him as a fair genius resembles a dark, as Ariel resembles Lucifer the Son of the Morning.

The poetry of the sea was to Byron the poetry of shipwreck, of the raging hurricane, of the insatiable cry of the waves for prey; to him the poetry of the sky lay in the howling of the storm, the roaring of the thunder, the crackle of the lightning. It is nature as the annihilator that he lives with and glories in. The famous passage in the Fourth Canto of *Childe Harold,* beginning: "Roll on, thou deep and dark blue Ocean, roll!" is a jubilant record of the sea's exploits in sweeping argosies from its surface and sinking empires into its depths. It boasts that nothing longer-lived than a bubble tells where man has gone down. The passage is like a prelude to the magnificent Deluge scene which is entitled *Heaven and Earth,* and which is a glorification of the lust of annihilation.[1]

After such verse read Shelley's famous poem, *The Cloud.* In it we hear all the elementary forces of nature playing and jesting, with the gaiety of giants, benevolent giants, who joy in pouring bounteous gifts upon the earth. What freshness in the lines:

> "I bring fresh showers for the thirsty flowers
> From the seas and the streams;
> I bear light shade for the leaves when laid
> In their noonday dreams."

How wanton is the cloud when it sings:

> "I wield the flail of the lashing hail
> And whiten the green plains under;
> And then again I dissolve it in rain,
> And laugh as I pass in thunder.
> I sift the snow on the mountains below,
> And their great pines groan aghast;
> And all the night 'tis my pillow white,
> While I sleep in the arms of the Blast."

And

> "The volcanoes are dim, and the stars reel and swim,
> When the Whirlwinds my banner unfurl."

---

[1] Swinburne, who in his masterly little essay on Byron points out that Byron and Shelley were engrossed by the same natural phenomena, does not note the difference which existed along with the similarity.

How proud when it shouts:

"The sanguine Sunrise, with his meteor eyes,
And his burning plumes outspread,
Leaps on the back of my sailing rack,
When the morning star shines dead."

What calm is in this:

"And, when Sunset may breathe, from the lit sea beneath,
Its ardours of rest and of love,
And the crimson pall of eve may fall
From the depth of heaven above,
With wings folded I rest on mine airy nest,
As still as a brooding dove."

What consciousness of power in:

"From cape to cape, with a bridge-like shape,
Over a torrent sea,
Sunbeam-proof, I hang like a roof;
The mountains its columns be.
The triumphal arch through which I march
With hurricane, fire, and snow,
When the Powers of the air are chained to my chair,
Is the million-coloured bow."

Yet the real spirit of the Cloud is playfulness, the playfulness of a child. Even when the sun has swept it from the sky, it only laughs:—

"I silently laugh at my own cenotaph,—
And out of the caverns of rain,
Like a child from the womb, like a ghost from the tomb,
I arise, and unbuild it again."

It is not only the unlikeness to Byron's gloomy passion which strikes us in the sublime childlikeness and bounty and all-embracing love of this Cloud; there is another characteristic in this poetry, which we shall merely mention here, and devote more attention to later, namely, its antique, its absolutely primitive, spirit. We are reminded of the most ancient Aryan poetry of nature, of the Vedas, of Homer.

In comparison with this, Byron is altogether modern. When the Cloud sings:

"That orbèd maiden with white fire laden
Whom mortals call the Moon,
Glides glimmering o'er my fleece-like floor
By the midnight breezes strewn!
And wherever the beat of her unseen feet
Which only the angels hear,
May have broken the woof of my tent's thin roof,
The Stars peep behind her and peer;"

and when it speaks of "the sanguine Sunrise, with his meteor eyes," the poet transports us, by the primitive freshness of his imagination, back to the time when the phenomena of nature in all their newness were transformed into myths.

To Shelley these phenomena were ever new. He lived among them in a way which no poet had done before or has done since. By far the greater part of his short life of thrity years was spent under the open sky. The sea was his passion; he was constantly sailing; his most beautiful poems were written while he lay in his boat with the sun beating on him, browning his soulful face and delicate hands. It was a passion that was the pleasure of his life and the cause of his death. Everything that had to do with boats and sailing had an attraction for him. He had a childlike hobby for floating paper boats; it is said that on one occasion, having no other paper at hand, he launched a £50 bank-note on the pond in Kensington Gardens.

He never learned to swim. At the time when he was constantly, by day and by night, sailing on the Lake of Geneva with Lord Byron, their boat was once very nearly upset. Shelley refused all help, and calmly prepared himself to go down. "I felt in this near prospect of death," he afterwards wrote, "a mixture of sensations, among which terror entered, though but subordinately. My feelings would have been less painful had I been alone, but I knew that my companion would have attempted to save me, and I was overcome with humiliation when I thought that his life might have been risked to preserve mine." A few years later he had no painful feelings at all in contemplating such an end. When, some months before his death, Trelawny rescued him from drowning, all he said was: "It's a great temptation; if old women's tales are true, in another minute I might have been in another planet."

In Italy he lived in the open air; now he would be riding with Byron in the country near Venice, Ravenna, or Pisa; now spending whole days in a rowing-boat on the Arno or the Serchio; now out at sea in his yacht. It is interesting to observe how frequently a boat serves him as a simile. He wrote often out at sea, very seldom under the shelter of a roof. *Prometheus* he wrote in Rome, upon the mountainous ruins of the Baths of Caracalla; wandering among the thickets of odoriferous trees on the immense platforms and dizzy arches, he was inspired by the bright blue sky of Rome and the vigorous, almost intoxicating, awakening of spring in that glorious climate. *The Triumph of Life* he wrote partly on the roof of his house at Lerici, partly lying out in a boat during the most overpowering heat and drought. Shelley belonged to the salamander species; broiling sunshine was what suited him best.

It was while lying in a grove on the banks of the Arno, near Florence, that he wrote the most magnificent of his poems, the *Ode to the West Wind.*

In its first stanza the wind is the breath of autumn, driving the dead leaves, "yellow, and black, and pale, and hectic red, pestilence-stricken multitudes"; and of spring, filling "with living hues and odours plain and hill"—we hear it blowing, and we hear its echo in the appealing refrain: "Hear, oh hear!"

In the second stanza we are again reminded of the old mythologies, when the poet sings of the loose clouds on the Wind's stream, "shook from the tangled boughs of heaven and ocean," and of "the locks of the storm" spread on the blue surface of the airy surge "like the bright hair uplifted from the head of some fierce Mænad."

But along with the breath of the West Wind we have Shelley's whole soul in the final outburst:

> "Oh! lift me as a wave, a leaf, a cloud!
> I fall upon the thorns of life! I bleed!
> A heavy weight of hours has chained and bowed
> One too like thee—tameless, and swift, and proud.
>
> Make me thy lyre, even as the forest is:
> What if my leaves are falling like its own?
> The tumult of thy mighty harmonies
> Will take from both a deep autumnal tone,
> Sweet though in sadness. Be thou, Spirit fierce,
> My spirit! be thou me, impetuous one!
> Drive my dead thoughts over the universe,
> Like withered leaves to quicken a new birth;
> And, by the incantation of this verse,
> Scatter as from an unextinguished hearth
> Ashes and sparks, my words among mankind!
> Be through my lips to unawakened earth
> The trumpet of a prophecy! O Wind,
> If Winter comes, can Spring be far behind?"

Compare this Ode with the beautiful passage in the Third Canto of *Childe Harold*, in which Byron cries:

> "Could I embody and unbosom now
> That which is most within me,—could I wreak
> My thoughts upon expression, and thus throw
> Soul, heart, mind, passions, feelings, strong or weak,
> All that I would have sought, and all I seek,
> Bear, know, feel, and yet breathe—into *one* word,
> And that one word were Lightning, I would speak;
> But as it is, I live and die unheard,
> With a most voiceless thought, sheathing it as a sword."

Or with his apostrophe to night, during the wild storm on the Lake of Geneva:—

> "Most glorious night!
> Thou wert not sent for slumber! let me be
> A sharer in thy fierce and far delight,—
> *A portion of the tempest and of thee!*"

There could not be a better example of the difference between the attitude towards nature of an all-embracing and an all-defying poetic intellect. Shelley does not, like Byron, desire to possess himself of her thunderbolts. He loves her, not as his weapon, but as his lyre; loves her, unappalled by her gigantic proportions, familiar with her prodigious forces, feeling that the universe is his home. His imagination delights in occupying itself with the heavenly bodies; he is fascinated by their beauty and life as others are by the beauty of the forget-me-not and the rose.

What powerful, all-compelling imagination in the poem which he writes on hearing of the death of Napoleon!

"What! alive and so bold, O Earth?
Art thou not over-bold?
What! leapest thou forth as of old
In the light of thy morning mirth,
The last of the flock of the starry fold?
Ha! leapest thou forth as of old?
Are not the limbs still when the ghost is fled,
And canst thou move, Napoleon being dead?

How! is not thy quick heart cold?
What spark is alive on thy hearth?
How! is not *his* death-knell knolled,
And livest *thou* still, Mother Earth?
Thou wert warming thy fingers old
O'er the embers covered and cold
Of that most fiery spirit, when it fled—
What, Mother, dost thou laugh now he is dead?

. . . .

'Still alive and still bold,' shouted Earth,
'I grow bolder and still more bold.
The dead fill me ten thousandfold
Fuller of speed and splendour and mirth.
I was cloudy and sullen and cold,
Like a frozen chaos uprolled,
Till by the spirit of the mighty dead
My heart grew warm: I feed on whom I fed.'"

With the eyes of his soul Shelley beheld the soulèd spheres circling in space, glowing within, sparkling without, lighting up the night; his gaze sounded the unfathomable abysses where verdant worlds and comets with glittering hair, and pale, ice-cold moons, glide past each other. He compares them to the drops of dew which fill the flower chalices in the morning; he sees them whirl, world after world, from their genesis to their annihilation, like bubbles on a stream, glittering, bursting, and yet immortal, ever generating new beings, new laws, new gods, bright or sombre—garments wherewith to hide the nakedness of death. He sees them as Raphael painted them in Rome in the church of Santa Maria del Popolo, each governed and guided by its angel; and, wielding the absolute poetic power of his imagination, he assigns to the unfortunate Keats, lately dead, the throne of a yet kingless sphere.

His Witch of Atlas has her home in the ether. Like Arion on the dolphin, she rides on a cloud, "singing through the shoreless air," and "laughs to hear the fire-balls near behind." In this poem Shelley plays with the heavenly bodies like a juggler with his balls; in *Prometheus Unbound* he opens them as the botanist opens a flower. In the Fourth Act of *Prometheus* the earth is represented transparent as crystal; the secrets of its deep heart are laid bare; we see its wells of unfathomed fire, its "water-springs, whence the great sea even as a child is fed," its mines, its buried trophies and ruins and cities. Shelley's genius hovers over its surface, inhaling the fragrant exhalations of the forests, watching the emerald light reflected from the leaves, and listening to the music of the spheres. But to him the earth is not a solid, composite sphere; it is a living spirit, in whose unknown depths there slumbers an unheard voice, the silence of which is broken when Prometheus is unbound.

When Jupiter has fallen, has sunk into the abyss, the Earth and the Moon join in an exulting antiphon, a hymn of praise that has not its equal. The Earth exults over its deliverance from the tyranny of the Deity; the Moon sings its burning, rapturous love-song to the Earth—tells how mute and still it becomes, how full of love, when it is covered by the shadow of the Earth. Its barrenness is at an end:—

"Green stalks burst forth, and bright flowers grow,
And living shapes upon my bosom move:
Music is in the sea and air,
Wingèd clouds soar here and there,
Dark with the rain new buds are dreaming of:
'Tis Love, all Love!"

Shelley's imagination resolves nature into its elements, and rejoices over each of them with the naïveté of a child. The Witch of Atlas delights in fire:—

> "Men scarcely know how beautiful fire is;
> Each flame of it is as a precious stone
> Dissolved in ever-moving light, and *this*
> Belongs to each and all who gaze thereon."

And she loves the beauty of sleep:—

> "A pleasure sweet doubtless it was to see
> Mortals subdued in all the shapes of sleep.
> Here lay two sister-twins in infancy;
> There a lone youth who in his dreams did weep;
> Within, two lovers linkèd innocently
> In their loose locks which over both did creep
> Like ivy from one stem; and there lay calm
> Old age with snow-bright hair and folded palm."

Shelley feels with the streams, which are loved by the sea and disappear in his depths; he sings by the death-bed and bier of nature in autumn and winter; he remembers the flowers that were strewn over Adonis; he describes the goddess of the summer and of beauty, who (like a female Balder) tends the flowers of the gardens; and he paints the progress of the Spirits of the Hours through the heavens (*Arethusa, Hymn of Apollo, Hymn of Pan, Autumn, The Sensitive Plant,* the Hours in *Prometheus Unbound*).

For everything in life and nature he has found the fitting poetic word—for the waste and solitary places,

> "Where we taste
> The pleasure of believing what we see
> Is boundless, as we wish our souls to be";

for time,

> "Unfathomable sea, whose waves are years!
> Ocean of time, whose waters of deep woe
> Are brackish with the salt of human tears!"

for snow, "and all the forms of the radiant frost."

The whole poem in which these last words occur ought to be read. Into it, in a sad mood, he has compressed all his love of nature. It is called simply *Song,* and is addressed to the Spirit of Delight. This Spirit, the poet complains, has deserted him ; it forgets all but those who need it not ; and such an one as he, can never win it back again, for it is dismayed with sorrow, and reproach it will not hear. Yet, he goes on to say,

> "I love all that thou lovest,
> Spirit of Delight !
> The fresh earth in new leaves dressed,
> And the starry night,
> Autumn evening, and the morn
> When the golden mists are born.
>
> I love snow, and all the forms
> Of the radiant frost ;
> I love waves and winds and storms,—
> Everything almost
> Which is Nature's, and may be
> Untainted by man's misery.
>
> I love tranquil solitude,
> And such society
> As is quiet, wise, and good.
> Between thee and me
> What difference ? But thou dost possess
> The things I seek, not love them less."

But Shelley's spirit rises on the wings of his sublime enthusiasm for liberty high into the clear air above all these mournful moods. His ode *To a Skylark,* the poem which indicates the transition to the poetry of liberty, is written in a perfect intoxication of joy and freedom from care. It is almost safe to assert that there had been nothing in the older English literature finer in its way than the best of Wordsworth's songs to the lark, which are so typical of the spirit and art of the Lake School.

> "Leave to the nightingale her shady wood ;
> A privacy of glorious light is thine,"

writes Wordsworth ; and, as the true conservative poet, he goes on to apostrophise the lark as

> "Type of the wise, who soar, but never roam—
> True to the kindred points of Heaven and Home."

Turn from this to Shelley's lark:—

> "Like a cloud of fire
> The blue deep thou wingest,
> And singing still dost soar, and soaring ever singest."

We seem to hear all the winds ringing with its "shrill delight," and seem to glide into and be engulfed by a sea of eternally fresh melody. This is the youngest, freshest, gladdest pæan of the pure spirit of freedom. It forms the transition to the long series of poems of freedom, the great group of works in which Shelley's genius is the loud herald of the approaching revolutions. His poetry of freedom is one long war-cry, garbed in ever-changing melodies. Whether it takes the shape of odes to liberty and its champions (poems as beautiful and grand as the Marseillaise), of political satires levelled at customs or persons, of Aristophanic comedy ridiculing the abuses and follies of the day in England, or of mythical or historical tragedy, it is in its essence always the same mighty wail over injustice and hypocrisy, the same powerful appeal to all of his contemporaries who were still capable of feeling anything whatsoever a degradation.

Immediately after his first marriage Shelley began to play the part of a political agitator. He went to Dublin to further the cause of Catholic emancipation, wrote a very juvenile address to the Irish people, in which he besought them to refrain from the violent deeds with which the French Revolution had been stained, and was childish enough to throw down copies of it from the balcony of his hotel, in front of any of the passers-by who looked as if they might be responsive. We gain some idea of the childish spirit in which both he and his young wife regarded the matter, from reading that, one day when they were walking together, he could not resist amusing himself by popping the address into the hood of a lady's cloak, a performance which made his wife, as she herself writes, "almost die of laughing." Shelley attended several political meetings, and on one occasion spoke for more than an hour in the presence of

O'Connell and other celebrities. The accounts of his eloquence given by contemporaries are so enthusiastic that they might almost lead us to believe him to have been even greater as an orator than as a poet.

The next time Shelley came into collision with the party in power, the collision was of a much more violent and tragic nature. Harriet was dead, and her father had filed a petition in Chancery to determine which was the fit and proper person to educate her children—he, their grandfather, the retired hotel-keeper, or their father, Shelley, the author of *Queen Mab* and *Alastor*, who was accused of atheism, and would in all probability bring up his children as atheists.

Lord Eldon's judgment was to the effect that, seeing that Shelley's conduct had hitherto been highly immoral, and that, far from being ashamed of this, he was proud of his immoral principles and tried to impress them upon others, the law was in its right in depriving him entirely of the custody of his children, and at the same time decreeing that he should be deprived of a fifth of his income for their maintenance. The children were placed in charge of a clergyman of the Church of England. Shelley felt this blow so terribly that even his most intimate friends never dared speak of the children to him.

In his poem *To the Lord Chancellor*, he cries:

"I curse thee by a parent's outraged love;
By hopes long cherished and too lately lost;
By gentle feelings thou could'st never prove;
By griefs which thy stern nature never crossed.

. . . .

By the false cant which on their innocent lips
Must hang like poison on an opening bloom;
By the dark creeds which cover with eclipse
Their pathway from the cradle to the tomb.

. . . .

(By) the despair which bids a father groan,
And cry, 'My children are no longer mine;
The blood within those veins may be my own,
But, tyrant, their polluted souls are thine.'"

And in the poem to William Shelley, his little son by Mary, he writes:

"They have taken thy brother and sister dear,
  They have made them unfit for thee;
They have withered the smile and dried the tear
  Which should have been sacred to me.
To a blighting faith and a cause of crime
They have bound them slaves in youthly time;
And they will curse my name and thee
Because we are fearless and free.

. . . .

Fear not the tyrants will rule for ever,
  Or the priests of the evil faith;
They stand on the brink of that raging river
  Whose waves they have tainted with death.
It is fed from the depths of a thousand dells,
Around them it foams and rages and swells;
And their swords and their sceptres I floating see
Like wrecks, on the surge of eternity."

Fearing that this son of his second marriage might also be taken from him, Shelley left his native country, never to return. At the time when the Lord Chancellor was branding him as less fit for the most rudimentary duties of social life than any other man in England, he was preparing to prove that he was one of the few men then in existence who were predestined to immortality. He left England, stamped as a criminal, and most of the Englishmen whom he met abroad feared and hated him as capable of any crime. He appears to have been actually once or twice subjected to personal molestation.

As already mentioned, Shelley in 1817 published a pamphlet on the subject of Parliamentary Reform. As a proof of the moderation and practicability of the views elaborated in its pages, it need only be mentioned that the Tories in 1867 passed almost the very scheme of Reform which the "atheist and republican" had planned fifty years before. He "disavowed any wish to establish universal suffrage at once, or to do away with monarchy and aristocracy." And on many other occasions he declared himself to be against precipitate changes. His Radicalism consisted simply in his being fifty years ahead of his day.

Attacked and persecuted by the narrow-minded society of the period, Shelley now hurled his poems of liberty at England. His political poems are written with his blood. The employment of such similes for Castlereagh and Sidmouth as "two bloodless wolves whose dry throats rattle" and "two vipers tangled into one," was allowable in his case. It must not be forgotten that to him Castlereagh, Sidmouth, and Eldon, were not men, but personifications of a principle—of the great, fateful principle of reaction to which his career and his happiness had been sacrificed. He writes in *The Masque of Anarchy*:

"I met Murder on the way—
He had a mask like Castlereagh.
Very smooth he looked, yet grim;
Seven bloodhounds followed him.

. . . .

Clothed with the bible as with light,
And the shadows of the night,
Like Sidmouth next, Hypocrisy
On a crocodile came by.

. . . .

One fled past, a maniac maid,
And her name was Hope, she said,
But she looked more like Despair;
And she cried out in the air:

'My father Time is weak and grey
With waiting for a better day;
See how idiot-like he stands,
Fumbling with his palsied hands!

'He has had child after child,
And the dust of death is piled
Over every one but me—
Misery! oh Misery!'"

It was not, however, only in bellicose lyrics that Shelley incorporated his political and social ideas and passions at this period. In the year 1818 he wrote two very characteristic narrative poems, *Julian and Maddalo* and *Rosalind and Helen*. The first-mentioned gives a vivid description of the poet's life in Venice with Byron, and affords one of the many proofs of his noble and ardent admiration for Byron's poetry. It contains an account of a visit paid by the two friends to a lunatic asylum in the neighbourhood of Venice, and describes the impression produced upon Shelley. The man "whose heart a stranger's tear might wear as water-drops the sandy fountain-stone," and who "could moan for woes which others hear not," could not but be deeply moved by compassion for the unfortunates who at that time were still kept in fetters and punished by flogging.

We gain the best idea of the utter want of understanding of mental disease in those days, and the barbarity displayed in its treatment, from reading of the manner in which an insane patient of such rank as King George the Third was treated in 1798. The King's mental alienation displayed itself chiefly in excessive talkativeness; there was no inclination to any kind of violence. Nevertheless from the very beginning, and throughout the whole duration of the attack, he was kept in a strait-waistcoat, was closely confined, deprived of the use of knife and fork, and subjected to the whims of his pages, who knocked him about, struck him, and used abusive language to him. All this is known because the King retained a distinct remembrance after his recovery of what had happened during his illness.

Shelley's gentleness and love of his fellow-men are evident in the plea which he, ignorant of the humaner treatment of the insane inaugurated in France during the Revolution, utters for these afflicted ones:

> "Methinks there were
> A cure of these with patience and kind care,
> If music thus can move."

The second poem, *Rosalind and Helen*, which gives a powerful general impression of the misery which prejudice and intolerance have brought upon the human race, has not hitherto been properly understood or valued according to its deserts. It attempts to give a comprehensive representation of all that truly good and liberal-minded human beings have to suffer from antiquated ideas and principles in combination with human malignity. We have the description of a father who was a coward to the strong, a tyrant to the weak; hard, selfish, false, rapacious ; the torturer of his wife and terror of his children, who became pale and silent if they heard, or thought they heard, his footstep on the stair. He dies, and Rosalind, the mother, is distressed because her children involuntarily rejoice at their father's death, and because she herself cannot but feel it to be a relief. The dead man had been strictly orthodox. He has, as it appears when his will is read, decreed that the children shall inherit nothing if they continue to live with their mother, because she secretly holds the Christian creed to be false, and he must save his children from eternal fire. The mother feels that she must leave her children. "Thou know'st," she says—

> "Thou know'st what a thing is poverty
> Among the fallen on evil days.
> 'Tis crime, and fear, and infamy,
> And houseless want in frozen ways
> Wandering ungarmented, and pain,
> And, worse than all, that inward stain,
> Foul self-contempt, which drowns in sneers
> Youth's starlight smile, and makes its tears
> First hot like gall, then dry for ever.
> And well thou know'st a mother never
> Could doom her children to this ill,—
> And well he knew the same."

Rosalind's fate serves, above all else, to show the misery of an unhappy marriage, more particularly the wife's condition of dependence on a bad and tyrannical husband. Shelley's own grief over the loss of his children is also distinctly perceptible in the poem ; and Helen's fate recalls the persecution to which the author in his character of philosopher was subjected. The whole representation of Lionel's life and ideas is self-representation. Could there be a better description of Shelley's own love of his fellow-man than this :—

> "For love and life in him were twins,
> Born at one birth. In every other,
> First life, then love, its course begins,
> Though they be children of one mother."

Young, rich, well-born, Lionel at the time of the Revolution enthusiastically takes his place in the ranks of the reformers whose aim it is to emancipate humanity from the tyranny of creeds.

"Men wondered, and some sneered to see
One sow what he could never reap:
'For he is rich,' they said, 'and young,
And might drink from the depths of luxury.
If he seeks Fame, Fame never crowned
The champion of a trampled creed:
If he seeks Power, Power is enthroned
'Mid ancient rights and wrongs, to feed
Which hungry wolves with praise and spoil
Those who would sit near Power must toil.'"

The reaction comes:

"None now hoped more. Grey Power was seated
Safely on her ancestral throne;
And Faith, the python, undefeated,
Even to its blood-stained steps dragged on
Her foul and wounded train; and men
Were trampled and deceived again."

Lionel's enemies succeed in imprisoning him because he has blasphemed their gods. He passes a long time in solitary confinement, separated from the woman he loves. Then he meets her again, and they celebrate their nuptials under the starry sky.

Rosalind and Helen is a poem which bears traces of having been written in a mood of profound despair; in no other work does Shelley go to such extremes in his war upon all traditional law and convention. We have, in a previous volume of this work, touched upon the fact that many writers at the beginning of this century occupied themselves with the theory that the horror of incest has its source in prejudice. Both in *Rosalind and Helen* and in *The Revolt of Islam*, the hero and heroine of which would, but for the earnest entreaties of the publisher, have been brother and sister, Shelley wasted much eloquence on this sinister paradox—which also greatly occupied Byron's mind, and was to give occasion to a foolish and revolting attack upon his memory.

The year 1820 was the year of the scandalous royal divorce case. On the 8th of April 1798, the Prince Regent, compelled by his position to marry, had wedded Princess Caroline of Brunswick. So little regard did he show from the very beginning for even the decencies of the situation, that at their first meeting in St. James's Palace, when the Princess was kneeling before him, he called to Lord Malmesbury: "Get me a glass of brandy! I don't feel well." Lord Malmesbury asked if a glass of water would not be preferable, upon which the Prince rushed out of the room, swearing, without a word to his fiancée. He was drunk at the wedding, and hiccupped incessantly during the ceremony. Ere long he was not content with displaying the utmost indifference to his wife and slighting her by his liaisons with numbers of other women, but actually treated her with great brutality—kept her in confinement, surrounded her with spies, and, on the ground of a false accusation, took her daughter from her, a proceeding which gave occasion to constant scenes at court. The Princess's conduct does not seem to have been long irreproachable. She was at first only incautious, but in course of time sought consolation in behaviour which was neither blameless nor dignified. At the age of fifty she was travelling all over Europe in the company of her courier and chamberlain Bergami—a man who had formerly been her footman—an Italian Ruy Blas, on whom she conferred one honour and order after another, and whom she loved devotedly.

When, at the time of her husband's accession to the throne, she returned to England, expecting to be crowned Queen, the miserable, contemptible sovereign determined to employ, in procuring a divorce, all the evidence against her which he had obtained by means of paid spies. She was accused before the House of Lords of unfaithfulness. Whole shiploads of foreign hotel waiters and chambermaids were landed in England amidst the angry demonstrations of the populace, to give witness against the Queen. Anything more indecent than this trial it would be difficult to find. Investigations into the positions of bedrooms and beds, descriptions of the clothing or absence of clothing of a Queen and her chamberlain, filled the English newspapers day after day until—the accusation was withdrawn; partly on account of the supposed insufficiency of the proofs, partly on account of the pitch which public contempt for the King, as the author of the scandal, had reached.

It was this divorce case which gave occasion to Shelley's excellent satire, *Œdipus Tyrannus,* or *Swellfoot the Tyrant,* an essay in political comedy. The action of the play passes in Bœotia. A people, who call themselves *Bulls* (*i.e.* John Bulls), nevertheless make their appearance as pigs ; consequently, the nature and power and spirit of the English are comprehensively expressed by the word *piggishness* :—

> "The taxes, that true source of piggishness
> (How can I find a more appropriate term
> To include religion, morals, peace, and plenty,
> And all that fit Bœotia as a nation
> To teach the other nations how to live ?)
> Increase with piggishness itself."

The hypocrisy of the royal husband, the Queen's impudent asseverations of her own chastity, the hypocritical attitude of Castlereagh and Sidmouth—all this is caricatured with the pen of a master.

But Shelley's genius was not of a nature to spend much of its force in satirising the distortions of the age. Untrammelled and ethereal, it was supremely fitted to present to the intellects of the day a glorious conception of the century's ideal of liberty.

And from his boyhood this had been the aim of all Shelley's endeavours. His first works were long, melodious, but, unfortunately, formless poems, which are in their essence protests against kings and priests, against the religions which "people the earth with fiends, hell with men, and heaven with slaves," against the injustice of governments and the servility of the administrators of the law, against compulsory marriages, against the exclusion of women from free competition in bread-winning occupations, against cruelty in the slaughtering of animals. They are protests, in short, against every form of oppression and intolerance, written with no less ambitious an aim than the reformation of humanity, which is to be brought about by showing it how it may remove the causes of its misfortunes and attain to a state which, in comparison with the existing, would be a true golden age.

Shelley had, as he himself laughingly acknowledges, "a passion for reforming the world." In spite of his aversion for didactic poetry, it was (as he puts it in the preface to *The Revolt of Islam*) his object to excite in his reader a generous impulse, an ardent thirst for excellence.

"The panic," he writes, "which, like an epidemic transport, seized upon all classes of men during the excesses consequent upon the French Revolution, is gradually giving place to sanity. It has ceased to be believed that whole generations of mankind ought to consign themselves to a hopeless inheritance of ignorance and misery, because a nation of men who had been dupes and slaves for centuries were incapable of conducting themselves with the wisdom and tranquillity of freemen so soon as some of their fetters were partially loosened. . . . If the Revolution had been in every respect prosperous, then misrule and superstition would lose half their claims to our abhorrence, as fetters which the captive can unlock with the slightest motion of his fingers, and which do not eat with poisonous rust into the soul."

Shelley's purpose was to set forth the principles of the Revolution in a transfigured form. Hence his poetry became a sermon; his imagination embodied, not his observations, but his wishes.

He was firmly persuaded that imagination is the true reformatory power. The man whom crass ignorance has reviled as a materialist had, in the school of Hume and Berkeley, saturated himself with the extremest idealism. To him everything was thought—things were layers of thoughts; the universe itself was but a gigantic coagulation of old thoughts, images, ideas. Hence it is that the poet, whose calling it is to create new imagery of the kind which makes the strongest impression, is always agitating, disturbing, remodelling the world. "Imagination," says Shelley, "is the faculty of human nature on which every gradation of its progress—nay, every, the minutest, change—

depends." Either by gently inducing the congealed ideas to flow again, or by forcibly breaking through the crust of outworn opinions, the poet shows himself to be the true reformer.

In his youth devoted to philosophy, but indifferent to history, Shelley, during the one completed period of his life—that preceding the writing of *The Cenci*—sought no foundation in time or space for his visions of reformation; being merely desires, they had no historic reality. And this deficiency entails the absence of various essential qualities in his personages, which only historical and local relations can confer. The qualities they do possess are mainly the deepest seated, original qualities of human nature. In constructing his characters, he goes back to the earliest records of the race. They are half mystical personages—gigantic, vaguely outlined, spiritualised figures; no ordinary human sympathies can lay hold of them, for the reason that "history"—what the ordinary mind regards as the interesting element in a poem—is despised and ignored by Shelley. Hence his unsuitability for the multitude. An author like Sir Walter Scott will never cease to find a public among all who can read; Shelley will always be the author only of the few elect.

When, however, Shelley chooses a theme suited to his peculiar turn of mind he produces poetry of the very highest rank. His productive gift, from the point of view from which we are now considering it, was of the Greek type; and the same may be said of his religious feeling and of the whole development of his imaginative and reasoning powers. "We are all Greeks," he says somewhere. It was true of himself.

It was, however, only the earliest Greek poetry which treated of such natural phenomena, such gods, and such heroes as we find in Shelley's; therefore it is only with it that his is to be compared. Shelley's lyrics remind us of the Homeric hymns; his political comedy recalls Aristophanes both by its reckless satire and the lyric vigour of its songs, and is worthy of comparison with Aristophanes; it remains to be told that in serious drama he was a worthy rival of

Æschylus. His *Prometheus Unbound* is the modern counterpart of the Greek tragedian's *Prometheus Bound;* his *Hellas*, a prophecy of the triumph of Greece, the modern counterpart of *The Persians*.

Let us linger for a moment over *Prometheus*, the magnificent poem in which his poetry of freedom culminates. In Prometheus, Shelley at last found, and succeeded in representing, the typical figure of his poetry and his period. Many types had passed through his mind, amongst others Job and Tasso, who at this time were also engrossing the imagination of Byron and Goethe. He chose Prometheus. High above the lakes and hills of contemporaneous English poetry, Byron's Alps with his Manfred, and Shelley's Caucasus with his Prometheus, soar into the sky.

Ever since the emancipation of the human mind had begun in real earnest, this typical figure had given occupation to all the great poets. It suggests itself about the beginning of our century to Goethe, Byron, and Shelley. Goethe's beautiful poem represents the labours, the artistic productivity, of the human spirit which has freed itself from faith in gods—the man, proud of his hut, which no god built for him, occupied in forming figures in his own image. Goethe's Prometheus is the creative and free. Byron's hard, short, fiery lines describe the martyr who suffers with clenched teeth, silently; from whom no torture can extract confession, and whose ambition it is that no one shall divine his sufferings; this is a Titan who would never, in the manner of the Prometheus of the ancients, have accepted consolation from the daughters of Oceanus or told his woes to them. Byron's is the defiant and bound Prometheus.

Shelley's resembles neither of these. His is the beneficent human spirit which, warring with the principle of evil, is for an immeasurable length of time held in subjugation and tortured by it—and not by it alone, but by all other beings, even the good, who are fooled into accepting evil as necessary and right. He is the spirit who can only for a time be imprisoned and fettered; long as that time may be, the day comes when, to the joy of all, he is released—he is Prometheus unbound, Prometheus triumphant, greeted by the acclamations of all the elements and all the heavenly spheres.

Even during his sufferings he is perfectly calm; for he knows that Jupiter's reign is but a passing period in the life of the universe. He would not exchange his place of torture for all the voluptuous joys of Jupiter's court. When the Furies "laugh into his lidless eyes," and threaten him, he only says:

> "I weigh not what ye do, but what ye suffer,
> Being evil."

How differently a Byronic Prometheus would have answered! This Titan is full of love—love for his enemies and for the whole human race. Nor have his sufferings closed his heart to the more earthly love passion. In the midst of his agony he remembers his bride—

> "Asia, who, when my being overflowed,
> Wert like a golden chalice to bright wine."

Asia is nature herself, who loves the Titan. She is the child of light, the life of life, whose

> "lips enkindle
> With their love the breath between them,
> And whose smiles, before they dwindle,
> Make the cold air fire."

When the age of suffering and injustice has passed, Jupiter sinks into the abyss of eternity, with cowardly wails and supplications to Prometheus to have mercy on him. The Promethean age begins; the air becomes a sea of sweet, eternally new love melodies; the mighty, deep-toned jubilation of the Earth is heard in alternation with the Moon's enchanting song of bliss; and then the whole universe chimes in in a chorus of rejoicing unsurpassed even by that with which Beethoven's Ninth Symphony ends.

We cannot do much more than allude to the fact that

Shelley, after competing with Æschylus, began to produce on Shakespeare's lines. Taking a sudden excursion into the realms of history, he gave England what even Byron pronounced to be the best tragedy written by any of her sons since the days of Shakespeare. *The Cenci* reminds the reader slightly of such a play as *Measure for Measure,* although Shakespeare was not possessed by the ardent hatred of tyranny which inspired Shelley's play.

To the Romans the name of Beatrice Cenci is to this day the great symbol of liberty. The young girl who defended her honour against her atrocious father (whose deed of violence was indirectly sanctioned by the corruption of the rulers of the country from the Pope downwards) is still regarded by the Roman as a heroine and martyr. Whenever, during the long oppression of the Papacy, there has been a little clearing of the air, a little brightening of the horizon, her name has been heard, her picture has circulated, in Rome. Shelley, forgetting all theories, is here entirely absorbed by history. But what evidently impressed him in this tragic collision of duties, was the violent break with all traditional morality which the father's crime necessitated; and he was also attracted by the opportunity the situation offered for throwing a glaring search-light on the accepted theological doctrine of the paternal benevolence displayed in the regulation of the universe. Beatrice says:

> "Thou great God,
> Whose image upon earth a father is,
> Dost thou indeed abandon me?"

And when she is asked:

> "Art thou not guilty of thy father's death?"

She answers:

> "Or wilt thou rather tax high-judging God
> That he permitted such an act as that
> Which I have suffered, and which he beheld;
> Made it unutterable, and took from it
> All refuge, all revenge, all consequence,
> But that which thou hast called my father's death?"

In the torture chamber she says:

"My pangs are of the mind and of the heart
And of the soul: ay, of the inmost soul,
Which weeps within tears as of burning gall
To see, in this ill world where none are true,
My kindred false to their deserted selves;
And with considering all the wretched life
Which I have lived, and its now wretched end;
And the small justice shown by Heaven and Earth
To me or mine; and what a tyrant thou art,
And what slaves these; and what a world we make,
The oppressor and the oppressed."

It is plain that what specially attracted Shelley in Beatrice's character was its combination of energy and gentleness.

When the hour of death has come, a horror seizes her at the thought that after death she may meet her father again. She cries:

"If there should be
No God, no heaven, no earth, in the void world,
The wide, grey, lampless, deep, unpeopled world!
If all things then should be my father's spirit,
His eye, his voice, his touch, surrounding me,
The atmosphere and breath of my dead life!
If sometimes, as a shape more like himself,
Even the form which tortured me on earth,
Masked in grey hairs and wrinkles, he should come,
And wind me in his hellish arms, and fix
His eyes on mine, and drag me down, down, down!
For was he not alone *omnipotent*
On earth, and ever present? Even though dead
Does not his spirit live in all that breathe,
And work for me and mine still the same ruin,
Scorn, pain, despair? Who ever yet returned
To teach the laws of Death's untrodden realm?
Unjust perhaps as those which drive us now,
Oh whither, whither?"

It was of this, the most mature and best planned of Shelley's works, that the *Literary Gazette* wrote: "*The Cenci* is the most abominable work of the time, and seems to be the production of some fiend." The reviewer hopes never again to see a book "so stamped with pollution, impiousness, and infamy."

The hostility evinced depressed Shelley, who thought that this time he had done his best. He was not intimidated by it, but his desire to produce became less strong. During the last two years of his life no long works came from his pen. In November 1820 he writes: "The reception the public have given me might go far to damp any man's enthusiasm."

His last letters are full of remarks on the criticism meted out to him.

April 1819:—"As to the Reviews, I suppose there is nothing but abuse; and this is not hearty enough or sincere enough to amuse me."

March 1820:—"If any of the Reviews abuse me, cut them out and send them; if they praise, you need not trouble yourself. I feel ashamed if I could believe that I should deserve the latter: the former, I flatter myself, is no more than a just tribute."

In 1821 he writes the poem on Keats with the terrible outburst against the reviewer who is supposed to have been the cause of the young poet's death:

> "Hot shame shall burn upon thy secret brow,
> And like a beaten hound tremble thou shalt—as now."

June 1821:—"I hear that the abuse against me exceeds all bounds. Pray, if you see any one article particularly outrageous, send it me. As yet, I have laughed; but woe to these scoundrels if they should once make me lose my temper. I have discovered that my calumniator in the *Quarterly Review* was the Reverend Mr. Milman. Priests have their privilege."

August 1821:—"I write nothing, and probably shall write no more."

Byron, when his enemies irritated him, stopped his work for a moment and showed them the lion's claw. Shelley was of a different nature. The satire of the reviewers contained in his *Peter Bell the Third* is sportiveness in comparison with Byron's sanguinary attacks on Southey and the others. Whenever Shelley made his appearance the creeping things of literature began to swarm and stir beneath his feet. They stung his heel; he could not bruise their heads, for such creatures have, as Swinburne has observed, too little head to be perceived and bruised. Byron's poetry had, moreover, made for him friends and admirers by the thousand; he shared Parnassus with Goethe; he had begun to set the stamp of his spirit on the continent of Europe. Shelley was too far in advance of his age. The crowd will follow a leader who marches twenty steps in advance; but if he is a thousand steps in front of them, they do not see and do not follow him, and any literary freebooter who chooses may shoot him with impunity.

Moore was a man of great talent, and exercised influence as such. What Shelley had was not talent, either great or small, but genius. He was the very genius of poetry; and he had all the power which genius gives; where he fell short was in his grip of reality. He has influenced the succeeding generations of English poets throughout this whole century, but he had not the twentieth part of the merely talented Moore's influence upon his own contemporaries. Byron was, as none had ever been before, the poet of personality, and as such was excessively egotistic; prejudice and vanity could not in his case be entirely eradicated without nobler qualities suffering from the process. Shelley, perfectly free from vanity and egotism, was absorbed in his ideals; he expanded his Ego until it embraced the universe. But what was ideal virtue in him as a man entailed a fatal defect in his poetry, at any rate in the works produced during the first part of his too short life. This poet, so devoid of all thought of self, was long entirely deficient in self-restraint. A sense of form as regarded a great composition in its entirety was for many years denied him. In making his first appearance as a poet he stumbled over the threshold, and it takes more than genius to make the reading public forget such an entrance. *The Revolt of Islam*, with all the beauty of its detail, is vague and formless; it hovers transcendentally in the air. With its shadowy, bloodless characters, it is distended to such proportions that it is a task to read it to the end; and it was a task which few accomplished. Until Shelley wrote *The Cenci* he seems to have had no idea of the infinite attractiveness and infinite value of the characteristics of the individual. Even Prometheus and Asia in their quality of types are destitute of any peculiarly distinguishing feature; their names are merely headings to the most beautiful lyric verse which England has ever produced. *The Cenci* shows how capable Shelley was of acquiring what he was naturally deficient in; but, alas! he was carried off before he could fulfil the rich promise of his youth, and before his contemporaries had had their eyes opened to what they possessed in him. Although his shorter lyrics surpass in depth and freshness, naturalness and charm, everything else in the shape of lyric poetry that the century has produced, they could not influence his own generation, as most of them were not even printed during his lifetime.

Thus Shelley was no more capable than Moore or Landor of bringing about the spiritual revolution of which Europe stood in need and expectancy. It required a poet who was as personal as Shelley was universal, as passionate as Shelley was idealistic, as savagely satirical as Shelley was harmonious and graceful, to perform the Herculean task of clearing the political and religious atmosphere of Europe, awaking the slumberers, and plunging the mighty into the abyss of ridicule. A man was required who could win the sympathies of his age alike by his vices and his virtues, his excellences and his faults. Shelley's instrument was an exquisite violin; a trumpet was what was needed to pierce the air and give the signal for battle.

Little remains to be told of Shelley's life—only the story of his last sail from Leghorn to Lerici, of the sudden gale in which he perished, of the long days spent by his despairing wife in searching the coast, and of the discovery of the almost unrecognisable corpse. The Tuscan law required any object thus cast ashore to be burned. Shelley's body was committed to the flames by Byron and Trelawny with Grecian and pagan observances that were in harmony with his character. Frankincense, wine, salt, and oil, were poured on the fuel. The day was beautiful and the surroundings were glorious—the calm sea in front, the Apennines behind. A curlew wheeled round the pyre, and would not be driven away. The flame arose golden and towering. The body was consumed, but, to the surprise of all, the heart remained entire. Trelawny snatched it from the glowing furnace, severely burning his hand. The ashes were deposited near the Pyramid of Cestius in Rome, which Shelley had spoken of as an ideal resting-place.

The first-mentioned of the men who consigned his body to the flames was his spiritual heir. This man's name is to be read on every page of the history of his day. We see his way prepared by Wordsworth, Coleridge, and Scott; he is hated by Southey, misunderstood by Landor, loved by Moore, admired, influenced, and sung by Shelley. He occupies a place in every one's life. It is he who sets the final and decisive stamp on the poetical literature of the age.

XVII

BYRON: THE PASSIONATE PERSONALITY

ENTERING the Thorvaldsen Museum in Copenhagen, and turning to the right, the first work that meets one's eye is the marble bust of a noble-looking young man, with beautiful features and curly hair—the bust of Lord Byron. In room No. 12 we find the same work in plaster, and in No. 13 stands the statue executed (after Byron's death) from the bust. Let us examine the plaster bust, which is without doubt the most speaking likeness. Beauty and distinction are the first qualities that strike us in this head and face; but the next moment we are attracted by an expression of energy, which comes chiefly from a restless quiver of the brow—indicating that clouds might gather on it and lightning flash from the clouds—and from something imperiously compelling in the glance. This brow betokens irresistibility.

When one remembers the dissimilarity of Thorvaldsen's and Byron's natures, remembers that in all probability Thorvaldsen never read a line of Byron's poetry, and also that the poet did not show his best side to the sculptor, the result of the meeting of the two great men must be regarded as extraordinarily satisfactory. The bust gives what is necessarily a feeble and incomplete, but nevertheless a true and beautiful representation of a main aspect of Byron's character which one would hardly have expected Thorvaldsen to grasp. The idyll is that sculptor's real province. When he sets himself to represent Alexander's triumphal entry into Babylon, he is much more successful with the shepherds, the sheep, the fishermen, the women, the children, the procession in general, than with the hero himself; the heroic is not to the same extent his affair; how much less, then, the combatant nature in the complicated, modern form of it which has been dubbed the dæmonic. And yet he understood Byron. In the bust (not in the statue) he has given the world a monument of him, which, although it satisfied neither the Countess Guiccioli nor Thomas Moore, is worthy both of the poet and of the artist. If Thorvaldsen had really known Byron, the work would probably have been still better ; the face would have had a touch of the frankness and attractiveness which impressed all who knew him well. This is absent. But the Danish sculptor has succeeded in penetrating into what lay beneath the gloomy expression which he considered an assumed one, and showing us the suffering, the restlessness, the genius, the noble and terrible power.

It was, undoubtedly, with the Byron of the Museum that the next generation to his in Denmark grew up. But the image presented to them there was invariably connected in their minds with the story of the poet's visit to Thorvaldsen's studio, and with the latter's observation: "It was his fancy to be unhappy;"[1] and they wondered why such a great man should not have been perfectly natural. And so the first attitude of the Danes to Byron was a wrong, or at any rate an uncertain one. And an uncertain one it still remains. He is little fitted to be the hero of the present age. The very things which were much more effectual than his greatness as a poet in arousing the admiration of our grandfathers and grandmothers, are the things that repel the present generation—all those mythical traditions (which really obscure his history to us) of Byron the stage hero, with the tie which every one imitated ; Byron, the hero of romance, whose pistols were his constant companions, and whose amorous adventures were as famous as his verse ; Byron, the aristocrat, with the title which he valued so highly, but which makes little impression on a generation that recognises no aristocracy but that of the intellect. And our practical age has, moreover, a distinct contempt for what Byron sometimes imagined his honour required him to be, and sometimes really was—the dilettante.

[1] Thiele: *Thorvaldsen i Rom.* i. 342.

It was a matter of honour with him to practise his art in a non-professional manner. His position and his pursuits (so he writes in the preface to his first volume of poetry) make it highly improbable that he will ever take up the pen again. In 1814, at the very summit of the celebrity won for him by his first narrative poems, he determines to write no more poetry, and to suppress all that he has written. A month afterwards he writes *Lara*. Jeffrey criticised the character of the hero as too elaborate. Byron asks (in a letter of 1822): "What do they mean by '*elaborate?*' I wrote *Lara* while undressing after coming home from balls and masquerades, in the year of revelry 1814." We feel that he lays stress on the careless manner of production and the planlessness consequent thereon, from a desire to show that he is not a professional poet, but, in the first instance, a man of the world, in the second, that which his gifts forbade his being, namely, a poetical dilettante.

Though he was incapable of being a dilettante in the calling in which he was determined to play that part (a determination which nowadays detracts from our respect for him), he was indisputably one in another field of activity, where it was by no means his intention, namely, in politics. Practical though he always showed himself to be when it came to political action, his politics were in reality—whether he took part in the conspiracies of the Carbonari at Ravenna or led the Suliotes at Missolonghi—the politics of the emotionalist and the adventurer. His first proceeding after he had resolved to go to Greece was to order for himself and his friends gilded helmets with his crest and motto engraved on them. The great politician of our days is the man who lays plans, adheres to them and develops them year after year, and, obstinate and regardless of side issues, carries them out in the end, without the heroic apparatus, but with the hero's determination.

It must not be forgotten that a whole succession of Byron's admirers and imitators have forced themselves in between him and us, obscuring the figure, and confusing our impression, of the great departed. Their qualities have been imputed to him, and he has been blamed for their faults.

When the literary reaction set in against those who had understood him half and wrongly—against the brokenhearted, the *blasés*, the enigmatical, writers—his great name suffered along with theirs; it was swept aside along with the lesser ones. It had deserved better of fate.

George Gordon Byron, born on the 22nd of January 1788, was the son of a passionate and unhappy mother, who a short time before his birth left her dissipated, brutal husband. This man, Captain Byron, who had served for a time in America as an officer in the Guards, was known in his youth as "mad Jack Byron." He eloped to the Continent with the wife of the Marquis of Carmarthen, married her when her husband obtained a divorce from her, spent all her money, and treated her so badly that she died of grief a few years after her marriage. Captain Byron returned to England with his little daughter, Augusta, and, solely with the view of improving his circumstances, married a wealthy Scottish heiress, Miss Catherine Gordon of Gight, who became the mother of the man who still enjoys a world-wide fame. Immediately after the wedding Captain Byron began to make away with the fortune of his second wife. In the course of a year he had reduced it from £24,000 to £3000. She left him in France and, coming to London, gave birth there to her only child. By an accident, said to have occurred at the time of his birth, one of the child's feet was malformed.

Two years later the mother went with her boy to Scotland, and took up her residence at Aberdeen. Captain Byron, during a pause in his dissipations, followed them there, in the hope of extracting more money from his wife. She generously gave him the shelter of her roof for a time, and afterwards they still continued to visit each other, until Captain Byron, to evade his creditors, was obliged to return to France, where he died in 1791. When the news of his death reached his wife, who had never ceased to love him, her grief bordered on distraction, and her shrieks were so loud as to be heard in the street.

Uncontrollable passionateness, differing only in its manifestations and its force, was thus a characteristic of both Byron's parents. And farther back in the families of both, we find the same temperament, revealing itself in the mother's family in attempts at suicide and poisoning, and in the father's, now in heroic daring, now in reckless excess. Byron's paternal grandfather, Admiral John Byron, generally known as "hardy Byron," took part in the naval warfare against Spain and France, made voyages of discovery in the South Sea, circumnavigated the globe, and went through perils and adventures without number; the peculiarity that he could never take a voyage without encountering terrible storms gained him the nickname among the sailors of "foul-weather Jack." Byron compares his own fate with his grandfather's. The family temperament shows itself in its worst form in the poet's grand-uncle, William, Lord Byron, a dissolute brawler, who achieved notoriety by killing his neighbour, Mr. Chaworth (after a quarrel), in a duel fought without seconds. It was only in his quality of peer of England that he escaped sentence for murder; ever after his trial he lived on his estate of Newstead, shunned like a leper. He was hated by all around him; his wife procured a separation from him; among the superstitious country people extravagantly horrible stories of his doings circulated and were believed.

Thus the poet had wild blood in his veins. But it was also very aristocratic blood. On the mother's side he claimed descent from the Stuarts, from King James the First of Scotland; on his father's he was the descendant (though with a bar-sinister in the arms, a circumstance Byron himself never alludes to) of the Norman noble Ralph de Burun, who accompanied William the Conqueror into England. And when the grand-uncle just named lost, first his only son, and then, in 1794, his only grandson, it became probable that "the little lame boy who lives at Aberdeen," as his uncle called him, would inherit both Newstead and the family title.

It was with this prospect before him that the lame boy grew up. He was proud and uncontrollable by nature. When he was still in petticoats, his nurse reprimanding him angrily one day for having soiled a new frock, he got into one of his "silent rages" (as he himself called them), turned as pale as a sheet, seized his frock with both hands, and tore it from top to bottom. His mother's treatment of him was little calculated to correct these tendencies. She alternately overwhelmed him with reproaches and with passionate caresses; when she was in a rage she vented on him the anger which his father's treatment of her aroused; she sometimes even reproached him with his lameness. The fault lies partly with her that this physical infirmity cast such a dark shadow over little George's mind; he heard his own mother call him "a lame brat." Bandaging and various kinds of surgical treatment only increased the evil; the foot gave him much pain, and the proud little boy exercised all the strength of his will in concealing his suffering, and, as much as possible, his limp. Sometimes he was unable to bear any allusion to his deformity; at other times he would speak with a mocking bitterness of his "club-foot."

Though Byron was not diligent at school, he developed a passion, the moment he could read, for history and books of travel; the seeds of his longing for the East were sown in his earliest youth. He himself tells that before he was ten he had read six long works on Turkey, besides other books of travel and adventure, and Arabian tales. As a little boy his favourite story was *Zeluco,* by John Moore, the hero of which is a youth whose mother's bad education of him after his father's death has led to his giving way to all his own caprices; he becomes "as inflammable as gunpowder." In this hero of romance, who reminds us of William Lovell, the boy saw himself reflected. One of the qualities which were to play a decisive part in the poet's life revealed itself very early, namely, his passionate attraction towards the other sex. At the age of five he was so deeply in love with a little girl, Mary Duff, that when, eleven years afterwards, he heard of her marriage, his feelings nearly threw him into convulsions.

With pride, passionateness, melancholy, and a fantastic longing for travel, there was combined, as the determining quality of his character, an ardent love of truth. Naïve sincerity distinguished the child who was destined as a man to be the great antagonist of the hypocrisies of European society. His defiant spirit was only one of the forms of his truthfulness. His nurse took him one night to the theatre to see *The Taming of the Shrew.* In the scene between Catherine and Petruchio, where Petruchio insists that what Catherine knows to be the moon is the sun, little Geordie (as they called the child) started from his seat and cried out boldly: "But I say it is the moon, sir."

When George was ten, his grand-uncle, Lord Byron, died. One of the child's first actions after being told what had happened, was to run to his mother and ask if she noticed any difference in him since he had become a lord. On the morning when his name was first called out in school with the title of "Dominus" prefixed to it, he was so much agitated that he was unable to give utterance to the usual answer, "Adsum"; after standing silent for a moment he burst into tears. Byron's intensest pleasures were at first, and for long, those of gratified vanity. But to understand his agitation properly in this case, one must remember what the title of "lord" implied, and still implies, in England. The nobility proper of that country consists of not more than about four hundred titled persons—about the number of princes in Germany. On their own estates these noblemen exercise an almost unlimited political and social influence; their position is not much inferior to that of reigning princes, and, as a rule, their wealth corresponds to their rank. Such, however, was not the case in this instance; Byron had no private fortune, and the property of Newstead Abbey was in a neglected condition, and heavily mortgaged.

In the autumn of 1798 Mrs. Byron took her little son to Newstead. When they came to Newstead toll-bar, affecting to be ignorant of the neighbourhood, she asked the woman of the toll-house, to whom the park and mansion they saw before them belonged. She was told that the owner of it had been some months dead. "And who is the next heir?" asked the proud and happy mother. "They say," answered the woman, "it is a little boy who lives in Aberdeen." "And this is he, bless him!" exclaimed the nurse, no longer able to contain herself, and turning to kiss with delight the young lord, who was seated on her lap.

In 1801 the boy was sent to Harrow, one of the great English public schools which is much in favour with the aristocracy. The system of instruction (strictly classical) was uninteresting and pedantic, and did not produce much effect on Byron, whose relations with his masters were as strained as his friendships with his comrades were enthusiastic. "My school friendships," he writes in his diary in 1821, "were with *me passions* (for I was always violent)." As a friend he was generous, and loved to play the part of protector. When Peel, the future Prime Minister, was one day being unmercifully thrashed by the elder boy whose fag he was, Byron interrupted, and, knowing he was not strong enough to fight the tyrant, humbly begged to be allowed to take half the stripes the latter meant to inflict. When little Lord Gart, after having had his hand burned with a piece of red-hot iron by one of the monitors, as a punishment for making bad toast, refused, when the matter was investigated into, to tell the name of the culprit, Byron offered to take him as his fag, promising that he should not be ill-used. "I became his fag," said Lord Gart (see Countess Guiccioli's *Reminiscences*), "and was perfectly delighted when I found what a good, kind master I had, one who was always giving me cakes and sweets, and was most lenient with my faults." To his favourite fag, the Duke of Dorset, Byron, in his *Hours of Idleness*, addressed some charming lines in memory of their school days.

When the boy was at home in the holidays, his mother's behaviour towards him was as erratic, her temper as uncontrollable, as ever; but now, instead of being afraid of her, he could not resist laughing at the fat little woman's outbreaks. Not content with smashing cups and plates, she sometimes employed poker and tongs as missiles.[1]

[1] The relation between mother and son has been so accurately and vividly described by Disraeli in his novel *Venetia*, that I append a scene from the book in question,—merely condensing it, and substituting the real names for the fictitious (Cadurcis, Plantagenet, Morpeth, &c.). The scene takes place one morning

Let us imagine, after such a scene as that described in the footnote, a smiling, golden-haired girl entering the room and softening the defiant boy's mood with a look, and we have a situation such as cannot have been at all uncommon at Annesley, the residence of the Chaworth family (relations of the man whom Byron's grand-uncle

at Annesley, a country house in the neighbourhood of Newstead. A post-chaise drives up to the hall, and from it issues a short, stout woman with a rubicund countenance, dressed in a style which remarkably blends the shabby with the tawdry. She is accompanied by a boy between eleven and twelve years of age, whose appearance is in strong contrast with his mother's, for he is pale and slender, with long curling black hair and black eyes, which occasionally, by their transient flashes, agreeably relieve a face, the general expression of which might be esteemed somewhat shy and sullen. It is a first visit. The visitors enter tired and hot.

"'A terrible journey,' exclaimed Mrs. Byron, fanning herself as she took her seat, 'and so very hot! George, my love, make your bow! Have not I always told you to make a bow when you enter the room, especially where there are strangers? Make your bow to Mrs. Chaworth.'

The boy gave a sort of sulky nod, but Mrs. Chaworth received it so graciously and expressed herself so kindly to him that his features relaxed a little, though he was quite silent and sat on the edge of his chair, the picture of dogged indifference.

'Charming country, Mrs. Chaworth,' said Mrs. Byron. . . . 'Annesley is a delightful place, very unlike the Abbey. Dreadfully lonesome, I assure you, I find it there. Great change for us from a little town and all our kind neighbours. Very different from Dulwich; is it not, George?'

'I hate Dulwich,' said the boy.

'Hate Dulwich!' exclaimed Mrs. Byron; 'well, I am sure, that is very ungrateful, with so many kind friends as we always found. Besides, George, have I not always told you that you are to hate nothing? It is very wicked.—The trouble it costs me, Mrs. Chaworth, to educate this dear child!' continued Mrs. Byron turning to her hostess. 'But when he likes, he can be as good as any one. Can't you, George?'

Lord Byron gave a grim smile, seated himself at the very back of the deep chair and swung his feet, which no longer reached the ground, to and fro.

'I am sure that Lord Byron always behaves well,' said Mrs. Chaworth.

'There, George,' continued Mrs. Byron, 'only listen to that. Hear what Mrs. Chaworth says. Now mind, never give her cause to change her opinion.

George curled his lip, and half turned his back on his companions. . . .

'George, my dear, speak. Have not I always told you, when you pay a visit, that you should open your mouth now and then. I don't like chattering children, but I like them to answer when they are spoken to.'

'Nobody has spoken to me,' said Lord Byron in a sullen tone.

'George, my love,' said his mother in a solemn voice, 'you know you promised me to be good.'

'Well! what have I done?'

'Lord Byron,' said Mrs. Chaworth, interfering, 'do you like to look at pictures?'

killed in the notorious duel), when Mrs. Byron and her son were visiting there. The golden-haired girl, Mary Anne Chaworth, was seventeen when Byron was fifteen. He loved her passionately and jealously. At balls, where she was in great request as a partner, and his lameness prevented his dancing, it occasioned him agonies to see her

'Thank you,' replied the little lord in a more courteous tone; 'I like to be left alone.'

'Did you ever know such an odd child!' said Mrs. Byron; 'and yet, I assure you, Mrs. Chaworth, he can behave, when he likes, as pretty as possible.'

'Pretty!' muttered the little lord between his teeth.

'If you had only seen him at Dulwich sometimes at a little tea-party,' said Mrs. Byron, 'he really was quite the ornament of the company.'

'No, I wasn't,' said Lord Byron.

'George!' said his mother again in a solemn tone, 'have I not always told you that you are never to contradict any one?'

The little lord indulged in a suppressed growl.

'There was a little play last Christmas,' continued Mrs. Byron, 'and he acted quite delightfully. Now you would not think that, from the way he sits upon that chair. George, my dear, I do insist upon your behaving yourself. Sit like a man.'

'I am not a man,' said Lord Byron, very quietly; 'I wish I were.'

'George!' said the mother, 'have I not always told you that you are never to answer me? It is not proper for children to answer. . . . Do you hear me?' she cried, with a face reddening to scarlet, and almost menacing a move from her seat.

'Yes, everybody hears you, Mrs. Byron,' said the little lord.

'Don't call me Mrs. Byron; that is not the way to speak to your mother; I will not be called Mrs. Byron by you. . . . I have half a mind to get up and give you a good shake, that I have. O Mrs. Chaworth,' sighed Mrs. Byron, while a tear trickled down her cheek, 'if you only knew the life I lead, and what trouble it costs me to educate that child!'

'My dear madam,' said Mrs. Chaworth, 'I am sure that Lord Byron has no other wish but to please you. Indeed you have misunderstood him.'

'Yes! she always misunderstands me,' said Lord Byron in a softer tone, but with pouting lips and suffused eyes.

'Now he is going on,' said his mother, beginning herself to cry dreadfully . . . and, irritated by the remembrance of all his naughtiness, she rushed forward to give him what she had threatened, and what she in general ultimately had recourse to, a good shake.

Her agile son, experienced in these storms, escaped in time, and pushed his chair before his infuriated mother; Mrs. Byron, however, rallied, and chased him round the room; in her despair she took up a book and threw it at his head; he laughed a fiendish laugh, as, ducking his head, the book flew on and dashed through a pane of glass. Mrs. Byron made a desperate charge, and her son, a little frightened at her almost maniacal passion, saved himself by suddenly seizing Mrs. Chaworth's work-table and whisking it before her. She fell over the leg of the table, and went into hysterics, while Lord Byron, pale and dogged, stood in a corner."

in the arms of other men. The climax was put to his sufferings when he overheard her one evening saying to her maid: "Do you think I could care anything for that lame boy?" He darted out of the house, late though it was, and, scarcely knowing where he was running, never stopped till he came to Newstead. Thirteen years later, in the Villa Deodati, by the Lake of Geneva, he wrote, with the tears streaming from his eyes, a poem, *The Dream*, which treats of this attachment, and shows the deep impression made by the early disappointment.[1]

The cleverer Byron became in preserving a sarcastically calm attitude during his mother's fits of rage, the more unnatural became the relations between mother and son. The scenes were sometimes terrible. It is told as a curious example of their idea of each other's violence, that, after parting one evening, each went privately later in the night to the apothecary's to inquire whether the other had been to purchase poison, and to caution the man not to attend to such an application, if made. In his letters young Byron writes with melancholy humour of the manner in which he is every now and then driven to take flight, to escape from scenes at home. He gives not the slightest hint to any one of the intended excursions, for fear, he says, of rousing "the accustomed maternal war whoop."

In 1805 Byron went to Cambridge, where he spent his time less in study than in the practice of all the varieties of athletic exercise to which from his childhood he had eagerly devoted himself, in the hope of atoning by his proficiency in them for his bodily infirmity. Riding, swimming, driving, shooting, boxing, cricket-playing, and drinking, were accom-

[1] Very characteristic of Mrs. Byron is the manner in which she communicated to her son (two years after he had been obliged to give up all hope) the news of Mary Chaworth's marriage. A visitor who was present tells the story:—" 'Byron,' she said, 'I have some news for you.' 'Well, what is it?' 'Take out your handkerchief first, for you will want it.' He did so, to humour her. 'Miss Chaworth is married.' An expression very peculiar, impossible to describe, passed over his pale face, and he hurried his handkerchief into his pocket, saying, with an affected air of coldness and nonchalance, 'Is that all?' 'Why, I expected you would have been plunged in grief!' He made no reply, and soon began to talk about something else." The less he could confide in his mother, the more impelled he felt to express his feelings and sorrows on paper.

plishments in which he was determined to excel. He began to develop the signs of a dandy; and it satisfied his youthful love of bravado to take excursions in company with a pretty young girl, who went about with him in male attire, and played the part of his valet, or sometimes of his younger brother—in which character he was impertinent enough to introduce her to a lady at Brighton who was unacquainted with his family.

Newstead Abbey had been let for a term of years. As soon as it was vacant, Byron went to live there. It is a real old Gothic abbey, with refectory and cells, the earliest parts of it dating from 1170. The house and gardens are surrounded by a battlemented wall. In the courtyard is a Gothic well. In front is a park, with a large lake. At Newstead, Byron and his friends, in their youthful, defiant antipathy to all rules, led a life of dissipation which showed traces of the mania for originality to which, as history shows, men of genius have not unfrequently been subject before becoming conscious of their proper tasks and aims. These young men got up at 2 P.M. and fenced, played shuttlecock, or practised with pistols in the hall; after dinner, to the scandal of the pious inhabitants of the neighbourhood, a human skull filled with Burgundy went round. It was the skull of some old monk, which the gardener had unearthed when digging; Byron, in a capricious mood, had had it mounted in silver as a drinking-cup, and he and his companions took a childish pleasure in using it as such, themselves dressed up as monks, with all the proper apparatus of crosses, beads, tonsures, &c.[1] It is a mistake, however, to regard the action simply as an evidence of that want of feeling which so often—among medical students, for instance—accompanies joviality; to a man like Byron the sight of this *memento mori* in the midst of his carousals probably acted as a kind of bitter stimulant. In the lines which he addressed to it he writes that, to the dead man, the touch of human lips must be preferable to the bite of the worm.

Byron's excesses did not proceed from too high spirits.

[1] The present owner of Newstead has, from religious reasons, had it buried.

He was oppressed, not only by the melancholy which attacks most youths of remarkable ability when they find themselves, with their untried powers, face to face with nothing but questions, but, in addition to this, by the melancholy which was a result of his passionate character and his upbringing. Two stories, which to most of his biographers seem very pathetic, are told of him at this period of his life. The first is in connection with his dog, Boatswain. In 1808, he composed an excessively misanthropic inscription for this favourite's grave, in which he lauds him at the expense of the whole human race; and at the same time he made a will (afterwards cancelled), in which he desired that he should be buried beside his dog, his only friend. The other proof of his forlorn mood is the manner in which he spent his twenty-first birthday, the day of his coming of age, an occasion which is celebrated among the English nobility with all manner of festivities—illuminations, fireworks, a ball, and the entertainment of all the tenants. Byron was so poor that he was obliged to have recourse to the money-lenders for the wherewithal to give his tenants a ball and roast the customary ox for them. But no long train of carriages bringing visitors of high degree drew up at the doors of Newstead Abbey on the 22nd of January 1809; neither mother, sister, guardians, nor relations, near or distant, were there. Byron himself spent the day at a hotel in London. In a letter of the year 1822 he writes: "Did I ever tell you that the day I came of age I dined on eggs and bacon and a bottle of ale? For once in a way they are my favourite dish and drinkable; but as neither of them agree with me, I never use them but on great jubilees—once in four or five years or so."

It is, naturally, pleasanter to be rich than to be poor, and more flattering to one's self-esteem to receive the congratulations of relatives and friends than to feel one's self homeless and solitary; but in comparison with the difficulties and privations and humiliations which every young modern plebeian has to encounter at the outset of his career, the adversities of this young patrician dwindle into nothing. What gave them their importance was that they early drove Byron, who, as a young aristocrat, might otherwise have been absorbed by the pursuits and ideas of his class and kin, exclusively to those resources which he possessed as the single, isolated individual.

It was not one of the great political events of the day, no transport of joy or anger occasioned by the great political revolutions in which the period was so fertile, that tore Byron away from the disorderly, aimless life at Newstead. Such events as the death of Fox, or that proceeding which redounded so little to the honour of England—the bombardment of Copenhagen, made no impression whatever on the youth who, as a man, was to be so strongly affected by every historical occurrence, every political deed or misdeed. It was a private literary contrariety which made the first turning-point in his life. Whilst living (from the summer of 1806 till the summer of 1807) in the little town of Southwell, Byron had produced his first attempts at poetry, which had met with much appreciation from the younger members of a family named Pigot, who were his intimates at the time. In March 1807 a collection of these poems was published under the title, *Hours of Idleness*. The volume contained nothing very remarkable; the poems which really testify to strength of feeling are swamped by quantities of school-boy verses, some of them translations and imitations of the school classics and Ossian, the rest, sentimental poems of love and friendship, immature in conception and style. In one or two, we readers of the present day, wise after the event, can plainly detect Byron's future personality and style. In the poem *To a Lady*, which is addressed to Mary Chaworth, occur two genuinely Byronic verses:—

"If thou wert mine, had all been hush'd:—
This cheek now pale from early riot,
With passion's hectic ne'er had flush'd,
But bloomed in calm domestic quiet.

. . . .

But now I seek for other joys:
To think would drive my soul to madness;
In thoughtless throngs and empty noise,
I conquer half my bosom's sadness."

The poems were really of little value, and the ample provision of childish, foolish notes, the pretentious preface, and the appendage of the words "A Minor" to the author's name on the title-page, lent themselves to ridicule.

In January 1808, the *Edinburgh Review*, at that time the highest literary court of appeal, contained an extremely sarcastic review of the volume, probably written by Lord Brougham. "The noble author," writes the reviewer, "is peculiarly forward in pleading minority; we have it in the title-page, and on the very back of the volume. . . . If any suit could be brought against Lord Byron, for the purpose of compelling him to put into court a certain quantity of poetry, and if judgment were given against him, it is highly probable that an exception would be taken, were he to deliver *for poetry* the contents of this volume. To this he might plead *minority;* but, &c. &c. . . . Perhaps however, in reality all that he tells us about his youth is rather with a view to increase our wonder than to soften our censures. He possibly means to say, 'See how a minor can write! This poem was actually composed by a young man of eighteen, and this by one of only sixteen!' . . . So far from hearing, with any degree of surprise, that very poor verses were written by a youth from his leaving school to his leaving college, inclusive, we really believe that it happens in the life of nine men in ten who are educated in England, and that the tenth man writes better verse than Lord Byron. . . . We must beg leave seriously to assure him that the mere rhyming of the final syllable, even when accompanied by the presence of a certain number of feet —nay, although (which does not always happen) those feet should scan regularly, and have been all counted accurately upon the fingers—is not the whole art of poetry. A certain portion of liveliness, somewhat of fancy, is necessary to constitute a poem . . . &c. &c."

The reviewer's advice to Byron is to give up poetry and employ his gifts and his leisure hours better. As an exhortation addressed to the epoch-making English poet of the age by one whose profession it was to assay and value the works of literary aspirants, the article, in spite of its partial justification, was undeniably a gross blunder. But as far as Byron himself was concerned, nothing better could have happened to him. It affected him like a challenge; it was a terrible blow to his vanity, and roused that which was to survive him—his pride. A friend who saw him in the first moments of excitement after reading the article, has described the fierce defiance of his looks, and added that it would be difficult for sculptor or painter to imagine a subject of more fearful beauty than the young poet in his wrath.

Byron concealed his feelings from every one. In a letter written about this time he expresses regret that his mother has taken the affair so much to heart, and assures his correspondent that his own repose and appetite have not been discomposed—that these "paper bullets of the brain" have only taught him to stand fire. But a dozen years afterwards he writes: "I well recollect the effect which the critique of the Edinburgh Reviewers on my first poem had upon me—it was rage and resistance, and redress; but not despondency nor despair. A savage review is hemlock to a sucking author, and the one on me knocked me down—but I got up again . . . bent on falsifying their raven predictions, and determined to show them, croak as they would, that it was not the last time they should hear from me." Thus came the stimulus from the outside world which for the first time drove all the young man's passionate, scattered emotions into one channel, and made of them one feeling, one aim. With obstinate determination he set to work; he slept during the day, rising after sunset in order to be less disturbed, and for several months worked every night and all night long at his first famous satire.

XVIII

BYRON: THE PASSIONATE PERSONALITY—(*Continued*)

FAMOUS it is, and famous it deserved to become, though not because of its wit and humour, for it has neither the one nor the other—nor yet because of its effectiveness, for it is satire which for the most part hacks and hews blindly, here, there, and everywhere—but because of the power, the self-consciousness, the unexampled audacity, which underlie and which found expression in the whole. The attacks of the reviewers had produced in Byron for the first time the feeling which was soon to become constant and dominant in his breast, the feeling which first made him completely conscious of himself, and which may be expressed in the words: "Alone against you all!" To him, as to the other great combative characters of history, this feeling was the elixir of life. "Jeer at *me* with impunity! Crush *me*, who am stronger than all of them together!" was the refrain that rang in his ears whilst he wrote. The Edinburgh Reviewers were accustomed, when they crushed a trumpery little poet and flung him on the ground like a fly, or by mischance shot a poor little song-bird, to no resistance on the part of the victim. He either rebelled against the verdict in silence, or humbly laid the blame on his own want of ability. In either case what followed was profound silence. But now they had lighted upon the man whose prodigious strength and weakness lay exactly in the peculiarity that he never blamed himself for a misfortune, but furiously turned upon others as its authors. In this case, too, a silence of a year and a half followed upon the review. But then happened what we read of in Victor Hugo's poem (*Les Châtiments*. "La Caravane"):

> "Tout à coup, au milieu de ce silence morne
> Qui monte et qui s'accroît de moment en moment,
> S'élève un formidable et long rugissement !
> C'est le lion."

And the image is the correct one. For this satire, with its deficiency in beauty, grace, and wit, is more a roar than a song. The poet who has the throat of the nightingale, rejoices when he for the first time hears that his own voice is melodious; the ugly duckling becomes happily conscious of its swan-nature when it is cast into its own element; but the roar which tells him that now he is grown up, that now he is a lion, startles the young lion himself. It is in vain, therefore, to look in *English Bards and Scotch Reviewers* for sword-thrusts, given with a steady hand and sure aim; these wounds are not the work of a hand; they are torn with a claw—but the claw is the claw of a lion. It is in vain to search for criticism, moderation, reason; does the wounded beast of prey display discernment and tact when a bullet, intended to kill it, has only slightly wounded it? No; its own blood, which it sees flowing, dims its eyes, and it desires nothing but to shed blood in revenge. It does not even seek the firer of the shot alone; if one of the troop has wounded the young lion, then woe to the troop! All the literary celebrities of England, even the greatest and most popular—all who were in favour with the *Edinburgh Review* and all who wrote in it—are in this satire treated like schoolboys by a youth of twenty, scarcely more than a schoolboy himself. They run the gauntlet one after the other, English poets and Scotch reviewers. There is many a hard hit that does not miss its mark. The empty fantasticalness of Southey's *Thalaba*, and its author's abnormal productivity; the proofs afforded by Wordsworth's own poems of the truth of his doctrine that verse is the same as prose; Coleridge's childish naïveté; Moore's licentiousness—all these receive their due share of attention. An attack is made on Scott's *Marmion* which reminds us of the jeers of Aristophanes at the heroes of Euripides. But by far the greater proportion of the attacks made, are so rash and graceless that they became the occasion of much more annoyance to their author than to the persons attacked. Byron's guardian, Lord Carlisle, to whom he had but lately dedicated *Hours of Idleness*, but who had declined to introduce him to the House of Lords; and men like Scott, Moore, and Lord Holland, who at a later period were among the poet's best friends, were here abused on perfectly incorrect premises, and with a want of judgment which is paralleled only by the astonishing alacrity with which Byron, as soon as he was convinced that he had been in the wrong, apologised and strove to efface the impression of his errors. Some years later he tried in vain to put an end to the existence of the satire by destroying the whole fifth edition.

In the meantime it created a great sensation, and produced the desired effect, the rehabilitation of its author.

In the beginning of 1809 Byron had gone to live in London, partly to superintend the publication of his satire, partly for the purpose of taking his seat in the House of Lords. As he had no friend among the peers to introduce him, he was obliged, contrary to custom, to present himself alone. His friend, Mr. Dallas, has described the scene. When Byron entered the House he was even paler than usual, and his countenance betrayed mortification and indignation. The Chancellor, Lord Eldon, put out his hand warmly to welcome him, and paid him some compliment. But this was thrown away upon Lord Byron, who made a stiff bow, and put the tips of his fingers into the Chancellor's hands. The Chancellor did not press a welcome so received, but resumed his seat. Byron carelessly seated himself on one of the empty Opposition benches, remained there for a few minutes to indicate to which party he belonged, and then left. "I have taken my seat," he said to Dallas, "and now I will go abroad."

He left England in June 1809. He had, as he wrote to his mother in 1808, long felt, that "if we see no nation but our own, we do not give mankind a fair chance—it is from *experience,* not books, we ought to judge of them. There is nothing like inspection, and trusting to our own senses." He now went first to Lisbon (see the poem *Huzza! Hodgson!*) The description of Cintra in the First Canto of *Childe Harold* is a recollection of the impressions received during his short stay in Portugal. From Lisbon he and his friend Hobhouse travelled on horseback to Seville and Cadiz, and thence to Gibraltar by sea.

None of the magnificent historical monuments of Seville made any impression on Byron, but both there and at Cadiz he was deeply interested in the women. The advances made by various beautiful Spanish ladies flattered the young man, who took with him as a remembrance from Seville a lock of hair about three feet in length. Gibraltar, being an English town, is, of course, a "cursed place."

But, though little impressed by the historical memories of the countries he is visiting, he is already beginning to interest himself in their political relations. Those of Spain with England occupy him first. The first two cantos of *Childe Harold* show that he felt nothing but contempt for the foreign policy of England. He jeers at what the English called their victory of Talavera, where they lost 5000 men without doing the French much harm ; and he is audacious enough to call Napoleon his hero.

From Spain Byron went to Malta. Its memories of the days of yore, which so delighted old Sir Walter Scott, made no more impression on the young nobleman than those of Seville had done. He was as entirely devoid of the romantic historical sense as of romantic national feeling. What he thought of, and longed for, were not the green pastures of England, or the misty hills of Scotland, but the Lake of Geneva in all its glory of colour, and the bright Ægean Sea. His mind did not dwell on the historical exploits of his countrymen, on wars like the War of the Roses ; it was occupied with the politics of the day ; and in the past nothing interested him but the great struggles for liberty. To him the old statues were only stone ; the living women were more beautiful in his eyes than the ancient goddesses (" than all the nonsense of their stone ideal," as he puts it in *Don Juan*) ; but on the field of Marathon he fell into a deep reverie, and he celebrates its memories in both his long narrative poems. When, during the last year of his life, he visited Ithaca, he rejected all offers to show him the remains of antiquity on the island, remarking to Trelawny : " I detest antiquarian twaddle. Do people think I have no lucid intervals, that I came to Greece to scribble more nonsense ?" The poetic enthusiasm for liberty was in the end swallowed up by the practical. With Byron Romantic sentimentality comes to an end; with him the modern spirit in poetry originates; therefore it was that he influenced not only his own country but Europe.

At Malta he was greatly captivated by a beautiful young lady, a Mrs. Spencer Smith, who for political reasons was subjected to persecution by Napoleon. An enthusiastic friendship sprang up between the two, which is commemorated in several of Byron's poems. (*Childe Harold*, ii. 30. *To Florence. Lines Written in an Album. Stanzas composed during a Thunderstorm. Stanzas Written in Passing the Ambracian Gulf.*) From Malta the travellers went by way of Western Greece to Albania, the "rugged nurse of savage men," as Byron in *Childe Harold* calls the country,

> "(Where) roams the wolf, the eagle whets his beak,
> Birds, beasts of prey, and wilder men appear."

It is characteristic of him, that in his first travels he visited regions which lay practically without the pale of civilisation, countries where the personality of the inhabitant was almost entirely untrammelled by convention. Natural affinity attracted him to these scenes and these beings. Like the young man in Wordsworth's *Ruth*,

> "Whatever in those climes he found
> Irregular in sight or sound
> Did to his mind impart
> A kindred impulse, seem'd allied
> To his own powers, and justified
> The workings of his heart."

A direct descendant of Rousseau, he had a strong sympathy for all the races still living in "the state of nature."[1] The

[1] Byron has described Rousseau in a stanza which might have been written about himself:—

> "Here the self-torturing sophist, wild Rousseau,
> The apostle of affliction, he who threw
> Enchantment over passion, and from woe
> Wrung overwhelming eloquence, first drew
> The breath which made him wretched; yet he knew
> How to make madness beautiful, and cast
> O'er erring deeds and thoughts a heavenly hue
> Of words, like sunbeams, dazzling as they pass'd
> The eyes which o'er them shed tears feelingly and fast."
>
> *Childe Harold*, iii. 77.

Albanians were at that time almost as savage as their Pelasgian ancestors. Their law was the law of the sword, the vendetta their idea of justice. The people of the country, as Byron first beheld them assembled, the setting sun illuminating their magnificent dresses and the rich trappings of their horses, whilst drums beat and the muezzins called the hour from the minaret of the mosque, presented such a spectacle as we read of in the *Thousand and One Nights*.

Janina proved to be a more important town than Athens. It was on their journey to or from Janina that the travellers were deserted by their guide. In their perilous condition among these wild mountains, with the prospect before them of dying of hunger, Byron was the member of the party who kept up the spirits of all the others by that dauntlessness which distinguished him in all dangerous situations.

The day after their arrival in the capital, Byron was introduced to Ali Pacha, "the Turkish Bonaparte," whom he had always admired in spite of his savage cruelty. Ali received his visitor standing, was extremely friendly, desired his respects to Byron's mother, and flattered Byron himself very agreeably by telling him that he knew him at once to be a man of noble birth by his small ears, curling hair, and little white hands. The visit to Ali provided matter for some of the principal scenes in the Fourth Canto of *Don Juan*. Lambro and several other Byronic figures are drawn from him. (He is also described by Victor Hugo in *Les Orientales*.) Ali treated Byron like a spoiled child, sending him almonds and sugared sherbet, fruit and sweetmeats, twenty times a day.

Protected by a guard of fifty men given him by Ali from the numerous troops of brigands which infested the country, Byron now travelled all through Albania. His wild followers became so attached to him that, when he had an attack of fever, they threatened to kill the doctor if the patient were not cured. The doctor ran away—and the patient recovered. It was in the course of this tour, before retiring to rest for the night in a cave by the shore of the Gulf of Arta, that Byron saw the scene (the Pyrrhic war-dance to the accompaniment of song) which he afterwards described in *Childe Harold*, ii. 71, 72, and which inspired the beautiful song, "Tambourgi, Tambourgi!"

During his stay in Athens, the indignation he felt at the plundering of the Parthenon by England, in the person of Lord Elgin, inspired him with the poem, *The Curse of Minerva;* and a transient attachment to one of the daughters of the English consul produced the song, *Maid of Athens*, the heroine of which, even after she had become a little pale old lady, continued to be tormented with visits from English tourists. On the 3rd of May, Byron performed his famous feat of swimming across the Dardanelles, from Sestos to Abydos, in an hour and ten minutes; he writes of it in *Don Juan*, and was proud of it all his life.

All that he saw and did on this tour was, a few years later, to provide him with poetic material. In Constantinople he one day saw the street dogs devouring the flesh of a corpse; on this real scene are based the descriptions of horrors in *The Siege of Corinth* and in the Eighth Canto of *Don Juan* (assault of Ismail). After his return to Athens from a tour in the Morea, he would seem himself to have been concerned in the love affair on which *The Giaour* is based. (See the Marquis of Sligo's letter to Byron.) What we know for certain is, that one day, as he was returning from bathing at the Piræus, he met a detachment of Turkish soldiers carrying, sewn up in a sack, a young girl, who was to be thrown into the sea because she had accepted a Christian as her lover. Pistol in hand, Byron compelled the savage troop to turn back, and partly by bribery, partly by threats, procured the girl's release.

This life of travel and adventure did not produce the mental equilibrium which Byron lacked. His last letters from abroad reveal settled melancholy. The disgust with life which is the result of aimlessness seems to weigh him to the earth. And he feels that he is coming home deep in debt, "with a body shaken by one or two smart fevers," and to a country where he has no friends. He expects to be met only by creditors. What did meet him was the news of his mother's dangerous illness. He hastened to Newstead to see her once more, but she had died the day before he arrived. Her maid found him in the evening sitting beside the corpse. She had heard his sobs through the closed door. On her begging him to try to control his grief, he burst into tears, and exclaimed: "Oh, Mrs. By, I had but one friend in the world, and she is gone!" Nevertheless, his excessive dislike to his grief being witnessed by others, was sufficient to prevent his following his mother's remains to the grave. He stood at the Abbey door till the funeral procession had moved off; then, turning to his attendant, young Rushton, desired him to fetch the sparring-gloves, and proceeded to his usual exercise with the boy. At last, the struggle to keep up seeming too much for him, he flung away the gloves and retired to his room. During the protracted fit of melancholy into which he sank, he made a will, in which he again ordered that he should be buried beside his dog.

Byron had hardly landed before his friend Dallas asked him if he had brought any poetry back with him from his travels. The young poet, who was tolerably destitute of the critical sense, produced, not without pride, *Hints from Horace*, a new satire in Pope's style. With this work Mr. Dallas was very justifiably disappointed. On returning it next morning he asked if his friend had written nothing else, on which Byron handed him some short poems, and what he called "a number of stanzas in Spenser's measure," chiefly descriptive of the countries he had visited. These last were the first two cantos of *Childe Harold;* and at the urgent request of Dallas they were at once given to the printer.

In the mind of the reader of to-day, the impression produced by these two cantos is apt to be mixed up with that produced by the last two (written six or seven years later); but whoever desires to understand Byron's development must be careful to keep the two impressions perfectly distinct from each other. The gap between the first and the second half of *Childe Harold* is as wide as the gap between this same second half and *Don Juan*.

The stanzas which Byron showed Dallas are melodious, sincere in feeling, and occasionally grand; they were the first of the full, harmonious strains which were henceforward to issue from the lips of this poet as long as he breathed the breath of life. But they only faintly forecast what the man was to be, with whose fame, ten years later, the continent of Europe rang. As yet, powerful descriptions of nature form the main ingredient in his poetry; the lyric outbursts are few and far between; to the casual reader these stanzas would seem simply to convey a world-weary young English aristocrat's impressions of travel, ennobled by the stateliness of the style—for the tone of *Childe Harold* is as idealistic and serious as that of *Don Juan* is realistic and humorous.

The mood is one of monotonous melancholy. Byron is not yet the poet who bounds from one feeling to another, by preference its exact opposite, in order to make each as strong as possible, and then hacks and hews at them—the harder, the extremer the tension he has produced. But though we as yet only catch the outline of this poet's countenance, though we perceive nothing of its keenly satirical expression or of its now impudent, now merry smile, we nevertheless divine from the fervent youthful pathos that we are in the presence of the strongest personality in the literature of the day. There is an Ego in this poem which dominates every detail, an Ego which does not lose itself in any feeling, does not forget itself in any cause.

The other literary personalities of the day could metamorphose—could etherealise, liquefy, crystallise—themselves; they could become invisible behind another personality, or transform themselves into cosmic beings, or merge themselves entirely in sensations received from without; but here we have an Ego which, whatever happens, is always conscious of itself, and always comes back to itself; and it is an agitated, passionate Ego, of whose emotions the movement of even the most unimportant lines reminds us, as the whisper of the shell reminds us of the roar of the ocean.

Childe Harold (in the first draft Childe Burun) leaves his country after an ill-spent youth, in a mood of splenetic melancholy, leaving behind no friends and no loved one. His is the youthful weariness of life induced by a constitution and state of health inclining to melancholy, and by an all too early satiety of pleasure. There is not a trace in him of the confident gaiety of youth or of its desire for amusement and fame; he believes, little as he has seen of life, that he has done with everything; and the poet is so completely one with his hero that not for one moment does he ever soar above him on the wings of irony.

All this, which made such a powerful impression on the public of Byron's day, is tolerably unattractive to a critical modern reader; the aim at effect is plainly discernible, and the time when vague world-weariness was interesting is past. But no one with a practised eye can fail to see that in this case the mask—for mask it is—covers an earnest and a suffering countenance. The mask is that of a hermit; pluck it off, and there still remains a man of a solitary nature! The mask is grandiose melancholy; throw it away; beneath it there is real sadness! Harold's shell-bedecked pilgrim's cloak may be nothing but a kind of ball domino; but it covers a youth of ardent feelings, with a keen understanding, gloomy impressions of life, and an unusually strong love of freedom. In Childe Harold's better Ego there is no insincerity; Byron himself will be answerable for all his hero thinks and feels. And to those who remember what Byron's own conduct, immediately after he wrote *Childe Harold*, was, and who see a direct contradiction between the fictitious personage's elderly melancholy and the real personage's youthfully ardent pursuit of sensual pleasures, we reply, that the reason of the apparent contradiction is simply this—that Byron, who in his poetry was still an idealist, was unable to reveal his *whole* nature in the earlier cantos of *Childe Harold*. All that is there is certainly Byron, but there was in him, along with this, another and perfectly different man; and it was not until he wrote *Don Juan* that he succeeded in introducing this other Byron, as he lived and thought and spoke, into his poetry. The incompleteness of the self-description must not be mistaken for simulation or affectation.

In February 1812 Byron made his maiden speech in Parliament. He spoke in behalf of the poor weavers of Nottingham, whom it was proposed to punish most severely for having destroyed the machinery that was depriving them of their bread. It is a youthful and rather elaborate speech, but full of life and warmth. Byron was quite in his element in pleading the cause of the starving and desperate crowd. He very sensibly pointed out to his countrymen that a tenth part of the sum which they had willingly voted to enable the Portuguese to carry on war, would be sufficient to relieve the misery which it was proposed to reduce to silence by imprisonment and the gallows. Byron's vigorous and obstinate hatred of war is one of the grains of sound common-sense which are to be found in solution in his poetry; it lends animation to the earlier cantos of *Childe Harold*.

His second Parliamentary speech was on the subject of Catholic Emancipation. Though it did not please, it is an excellent one; in it Byron acknowledges, and with correct logic disposes of, one of the arguments against giving religious liberty to the Catholics, namely, that it might equally well be given to the Jews. In reference to this same emancipation question, we find the following youthfully facetious entry in his notebook: "On one of the debates on the Catholic question, when we were either equal or within one (I forget which), I had been sent for in great haste to a ball, which I quitted, I confess, somewhat reluctantly, to emancipate five millions of people." Playful utterances of this kind (as another example of which take his saying: "After all we must end in marriage; and I can conceive nothing more delightful than such a state in the country, reading the county newspaper, &c., and kissing one's wife's maid") have, because they are so little in keeping with Childe Harold's melancholy, amply proved to stupid people that nothing was sacred to him. The truth was that, being very young and somewhat of a coxcomb, he considered it derogatory to his dignity to express himself with any feeling; he unconsciously adopted as his motto the saying of St. Bernard: *Plus labora celare virtutes quam vitia!*

The maiden speech was a great success, and helped to draw the attention of the public to the first two cantos of *Childe Harold*, which came out only two days after the speech had been made. The impression produced by *Childe Harold* was astounding; Byron instantaneously became a celebrity—London's new lion, the lawful sovereign of society for the year 1812. The metropolis, as represented by its most beautiful, most distinguished, most brilliant, and most cultivated inhabitants, prostrated itself at the feet of this youth of twenty-three. If these earlier cantos of *Childe Harold* had been distinguished by the qualities of the later, namely, profound originality and vigorous honesty, they would not have made the noise in the world they did. Great honesty and great originality never find favour at once with the general public. It was the veiledness, the vague weariness of the world and its pleasures, which impressed the crowd; the power of which they caught a glimpse, produced all the more effect by revealing itself in a somewhat theatrical manner.

This was the heyday of dandyism. The upper class of London society, with Beau Brummell as its master of ceremonies, gave itself up to a luxuriousness and licentiousness which had not had their parallel since the days of Charles II. Dinner-parties and balls, the play-house, the gaming-table, pecuniary entanglements, amorous intrigues, seductions and the duels consequent thereon, occupied the days and nights of the aristocracy. And Byron was the hero of the day—nay, of the year. Could there have been a more suitable object for the admiration and worship of a society which was bored and burdened by its own inanity? So young, so handsome, and so wicked! For no one doubted but that he was as dangerous a roué as his hero. Byron had not Scott's coldbloodedness and mental equilibrium to oppose to temptations and flattery. He allowed himself to glide with the stream which supported him on its surface. The artist in him craved for an experience of every mood, and rejected none. He maintained his fame as a poet with ease; there followed on one another with short intervals his narrative poems, *The Giaour* (May 1813), *The Bride of Abydos* (December of the same year), and *The Corsair* (completed on New Year's Day 1814). Of this last work 13,000 copies were sold in one day. The bitter *Ode to Napoleon*, on the occasion of his abdication, showed that Byron, in his pursuit of poetry, was not entirely oblivious of the political events of the day. In 1815 he wrote *Parisina* and *The Siege of Corinth.* The novelty, the foreignness, and the passion of these works, entranced the blasé aristocratic society of London. Their author was the prodigy on whom all eyes were turned. In the drawing-rooms young ladies trembled with the delightful hope that he might take them in to dinner, and at the dinner-table hardly dared to partake of what was set before them, because it was known that he did not like to see women eating. Owners of albums in which he had deigned to write a few lines were objects of envy. A specimen of his handwriting was in itself a treasure. People talked of all the Greek and Turkish women to whom his love must have meant death, and wondered how many husbands he had killed. His brow and his glancing eye suggested wickedness. He wore his hair unpowdered, and it was as wild as his passions. Different in everything from ordinary mortals, he was as abstemious as his Corsair; the other day at Lord ——'s had he not let eleven courses go by untasted and asked for biscuits and soda-water? What an uncomfortable position for the lady of the house, who was so proud of her cook! And what an extraordinary piece of eccentricity in a country where a hearty appetite is one of the national virtues!

We see Childe Harold transformed into Don Juan. The solitary pilgrim becomes the drawing-room lion. On the ladies, Byron's rank, youth, and remarkable beauty naturally made almost more impression than his poetry. In the Life of Sir Walter Scott we find the following opinion given by him on the subject of his fellow-author's personal appearance: "As for poets, I have seen, I believe, all the best of our own time and country—and, though Burns had the most glorious eyes imaginable, I never thought any of them would come up to an artist's notion of the character except Byron. . . . And the prints give one no impression of him—the lustre is there, but it is not lighted up. Byron's countenance is a thing to dream of." One of the beauties of the day said to herself the first time she saw him: "That pale face is my fate."

Women had, undoubtedly, always occupied a large share of Byron's time and thoughts; but expressions in *Childe Harold* gave rise to the report that he had maintained a regular harem at Newstead—the harem appearing as a matter of fact to have consisted of one odalisque. Absurdly exaggerated stories were in circulation of the amorous adventures in which he had played the part of hero during his travels. The consequence of all this was that he was positively besieged by women; his table was covered every day with letters from ladies, known and unknown to him. One came to his house (probably in imitation of Kaled in *Lara*) disguised as a page; many came undisguised. He told Medwin that one day very soon after his wedding he found three married ladies in his wife's drawing-room, whom he at once recognised as "all birds of the same feather."

This life, crowded with empty pleasures and with triumphs for his vanity, at any rate suited Byron better than quiet; for, as he says in *Childe Harold*, "quiet to quick bosoms is a hell." But, in all this whirl of excitement, did his heart ever really come into play? It would seem not. The love-affair which engrossed him much at this time and also influenced his future, was, as we know from his own letters, only a whirlpool within the whirlpool, and as such attracted him; but it left his heart quite cold.

Lady Caroline Lamb, a young lady of good family, and wife of the statesman afterwards known as Lord Melbourne, had long cherished an ardent desire to make the acquaintance of the author of *Childe Harold*. Hers was a wild, fantastic, restless nature, which rebelled against every kind of control and promptly followed the inspiration of the moment; therefore she was in so far a kindred spirit of the poet. She was three years older than Byron, fair-haired, with a slender, beautiful figure, and a soft voice; her manner, though affected, was exceedingly attractive. She played in Byron's life the part which Frau von Kalb played in Schiller's.[1]

[1] In Lady Morgan's *Memoirs* we find the following lively account by Lady Caroline Lamb herself of the beginning of her acquaintance with Byron:—"Lady Westmoreland knew him in Italy. She took on her to present him. The women suffocated him. I heard nothing of him, till one day Rogers (for he, Moore, and

Her connection with him made the lady so much talked of, that her mother did everything in her power to break it off. Lady Caroline was at last persuaded to go to Ireland on a visit. Byron wrote a farewell letter to her, of which she allowed Lady Morgan to make a copy—a letter which is typical of his style in his immature years, and in which no one with any knowledge of the human heart will find the language of love. It reminds us of Hamlet's ambiguous letter to Ophelia.

"If tears which you saw, and know I am not apt to shed,—if the agitation in which I parted from you,—agitation which you must have perceived through the whole of this most nervous affair, did not commence until the moment of leaving you approached,—if all I have said and done, and am still but too ready to say and do, have not sufficiently proved what my real feelings are, and must ever be towards you, my love, I have no other proof to offer. . . . Is there anything in earth or heaven that would have made me so happy as to have made you mine long ago? You know I would with pleasure give up all here and beyond the grave for you, and in refraining from this, must my motives be misunderstood? I care not who knows this, what use is made of it,—it is to you and to *you* only that they are,

Spencer, were all my lovers)—Rogers said, 'You should know the new poet,' and he offered me the MS. of *Childe Harold* to read. I read it, and that was enough. Rogers said, 'He has a club-foot, and bites his nails.' I said, 'If he was as ugly as Æsop I must know him.' I was one night at Lady Westmoreland's; the women were all throwing their heads at him. Lady Westmoreland led me up to him. I looked earnestly at him, and turned on my heel. My opinion in my journal was, 'mad—bad—and dangerous to know.' A day or two passed; I was sitting with Lord and Lady Holland, when he was announced. Lady Holland said, 'I must present Lord Byron to you.' Lord Byron said, 'That offer was made to you before; may I ask why you rejected it?' He begged permission to come and see me. He did so the next day. Rogers and Moore were standing by me: I was on the sofa. I had just come in from riding. I was filthy and heated. When Lord Byron was announced, I flew out of the room to wash myself. When I returned, Rogers said, 'Lord Byron, you are a happy man. Lady Caroline has been sitting here in all her dirt with us, but when you were announced, she flew to beautify herself. . . . From that moment, for more than nine months, he almost lived at Melbourne House. It was then the centre of all gaiety, at least, in appearance. . . . All the *bon ton* of London assembled here every day. There was nothing so fashionable, Byron contrived to sweep them all away." These utterances, reported with stenographic exactness, give an excellent idea of the fashionable life of the day in London.

yourself. I was and am yours freely and entirely to obey, to honour, love, and fly with you when, where, and how yourself *might* and *may* determine."

It will surprise no one to learn that a few months later Byron himself put an end to the *liaison;* his love had never been anything but the kind of reflected love which imitates in a mirror all the motions of the flame, without fire of its own. Meeting Byron at a ball soon afterwards, Lady Caroline, maddened by his indifference, seized the first sharp thing that she could lay hold of—some say a pair of scissors, others a broken glass—and tried to cut her throat with it. After the ineffectual attempt at suicide, she (according to Countess Guiccioli) made "the most incredible promises" to a young nobleman on condition that he would challenge and kill the faithless one; nevertheless she herself soon called at her quondam lover's apartments, "by no means with the intention of cutting either her own throat or his." He was not at home. The words which she wrote on a title-page of a book she found on his table, inspired the epigram: "Remember thee!" which is to be found amongst Byron's poems.

Pining for revenge, Lady Caroline now seized her pen and wrote the novel, *Glenarvon*, which came out at the most unfortunate moment possible for Byron, namely, just after his wife had left him, and was one of the most active ingredients in the ferment of public disapproval. The book, which has as its motto two lines from *The Corsair:*—

> "He left a name to all succeeding times,
> Link'd with one virtue and a thousand crimes,"

pictures Byron as a perfect demon of dissimulation and wickedness, endowed with all his hero's worst characteristics. But, possibly by way of excuse for her own conduct, the authoress has not been able to resist giving him some admirable and attractive qualities. One passage runs: "Had he betrayed in his manner that freedom, that familiarity so offensive in men, but yet so frequent amongst them, she would have shuddered; but from what was she to fly? Not from the gross adulation, or the easy, flippant protestations to which all women are, soon or late, accustomed; but from a respect at once refined and flattering, an attention devoted even to her least wishes, yet without appearing subservient—a gentleness and sweetness as rare as they were fascinating; and these combined with all the powers of imagination, vigour of intellect, and brilliancy of wit which none ever before possessed in so eminent a degree."

In 1817, when Byron was living in Venice, an Italian translation of *Glenarvon* was sent to press there. The censor refused to sanction its publication until he had ascertained if Lord Byron had any objections. Byron assured him that he had none. Only once again in the biography of Lord Byron is mention made of Lady Caroline Lamb. As the funeral procession following his corpse (which had been brought home from Greece) was slowly making its way from London to Newstead, it was met by a lady and gentleman on horseback. The lady inquired who it was that was to be buried. When she heard, she fell fainting from her horse. She was the authoress of *Glenarvon.*

Byron's giddy, wild London career was arrested by the most fateful event of his life—his marriage. Life, as he had lived it, had not inspired him with much respect for woman; but the kind of woman he loved was the devoted, self-sacrificing creature whom he delighted in portraying in his poems. The woman whom chance made his wife had a strong, obstinate English character. Miss Anne Isabella Milbanke was the only child of a rich baronet. Byron was attracted by her simplicity and modesty, and tempted by the prospect of restoring Newstead with the help of her fortune. She annoyed him by refusing his hand when he first offered it to her, but fascinated him again by soon afterwards beginning a friendly correspondence with him of her own accord. In course of time she returned a favourable answer to a letter of proposal which he had written in an unwarrantably frivolous mood, and sent because a friend who read it thought it a pity that such "a pretty letter" should not go.

From motives which were, one and all, bad—motives of vanity, motives of vulgar aggrandisement—Byron rushed into a marriage which did not end worse than might have been expected. His mood during his engagement was a comparatively cheerful one. "Of course I am very much in love," he writes to a lady friend, "and as silly as all single gentlemen must be in that sentimental situation." And to another friend he writes: "I am now the happiest of mortals, for I became engaged a week ago. Yesterday I met young F., also the happiest of mortals, for he too is engaged." So childish are all the letters written at this time that, if we believe them, we must suppose Byron's only serious trouble to have been the necessity of being married in a blue coat. However, as the wedding-day approached, he became ever more ill at ease; the relations between his parents had early inoculated him with a dread of marriage. His feelings during the wedding ceremony he has described in *The Dream*. He told Medwin that he trembled and gave wrong answers.

"The treacle-moon," as Byron calls it, did not run its course unshadowed by clouds. Two months after his marriage he writes to Moore from the country, where he and his wife were staying with her parents: "I am in a state of sameness and stagnation, totally occupied in consuming the fruits, and sauntering, and playing dull games at cards, and yawning, and trying to read old Annual Registers and the daily papers, and gathering shells on the shore, and watching the growth of stunted gooseberry bushes in the garden." A few days later he writes: "I have been very comfortable here—listening to that d—d monologue which elderly gentlemen call conversation, and in which my pious father-in-law repeats himself every evening—save one, when he played upon the fiddle. However, they have been very kind and hospitable. . . . Bell is in health and unvaried good-humour and behaviour."

Pegasus was beginning to feel the yoke gall. However, the young couple presently went to London, where they lived in great style, keeping carriages and horses, and entertaining sumptuously, until Byron's creditors began to push their claims. Lady Byron's dowry of £10,000 disappeared like dew in sunshine, quickly followed by £8000, to which

Byron had lately fallen heir. Things became so bad that he had to sell his library. In order to prevent this sale, Murray, his publisher, offered him £1500 as remuneration for his writings; but Byron's false pride led him to return the draft torn in pieces. Eight executions followed on each other in as many months; the very beds were seized at last.

Such was the position of affairs when, in December 1815, Lady Byron gave birth to her daughter Ada.

The spoiled young heiress had, of course, never dreamt that such experiences awaited her. The married life of the couple was at first by no means unhappy. They drove out together, and the young wife waited patiently in the carriage while her husband paid calls. She wrote letters for him and copied out poems, among others *The Bride of Corinth.* But there had very soon been small misunderstandings. Lady Byron seems to have been in the habit of constantly interrupting her husband with questions and remarks when he was writing, thereby giving occasion to outbursts of temper which she considered most unseemly. She had had no experience of such passionate violence and eccentric behaviour as she was soon to witness. On one occasion she saw Byron, when in a passion, throw his watch into the fire and break it to pieces with the poker; on another, in fun or by accident, he fired off a pistol in her room. Ere long, too, she was suffering the pangs of jealousy. She knew of his notoriety as the hero of many amours, and knew more particularly about his connection with Lady Caroline Lamb, who was her own near relative. Byron had, unfortunately for his domestic peace, become a member of the Committee of Management of Drury Lane Theatre, and his correct lady was much perturbed by the business relations with actresses, singers, and ballet-dancers which this entailed. A person in her service (described by Lord Byron in *A Sketch*) began to act the spy, ransacking Byron's drawers and reading his letters. And there is yet another disagreeable matter, which we shall notice later.

With her husband's consent, the young wife, about a month after the child's birth, left the unsettled and unhappy home, and went on a visit to her parents. But hardly had she arrived before her father intimated to Byron that she would not return to him. While on the journey she had written a letter to him (now in print) which begins: "Dear Duck," and ends quite as affectionately. Byron's surprise may be imagined. He replied to his father-in-law that in this matter he could not acknowledge paternal authority, and must hear from his wife herself. Her communication was to the same effect. In 1830 Lady Byron publicly affirmed that she had written to her husband as affectionately as she did, in the belief that he was insane; and that if this idea of hers had proved to be the correct one, she would have borne everything as his faithful wife, but that in no other case could she have continued to live with him.

In a fragment of a novel, written by Byron in 1817, we have a corroboration of this assertion:—"A few days after, she set out for Aragon, with my son, on a visit to her father and mother. I did not accompany her immediately, having been in Aragon before. . . . During her journey I received a very affectionate letter from Donna Josepha, apprising me of the welfare of herself and my son. On her arrival at the château, I received another, still more affectionate, pressing me, in very fond and rather foolish terms, to join her immediately. As I was preparing to set out from Seville, I received a third—this was from her father, Don José di Cardozo, who requested me, in the politest manner, to dissolve our marriage. I answered him, with equal politeness, that I would do no such thing. A fourth letter arrived—it was from Donna Josepha, in which she informed me that her father's letter was written by her particular desire. I requested the reason by return of post: she replied, by express, that as reason had nothing to do with the matter, it was unnecessary to give any—but that she was an injured and excellent woman. I then inquired why she had written to me the two preceding affectionate letters, requesting me to come to Aragon. She answered, that was because she believed me out of my senses—that, being unfit to take care of myself, I had only to set out on this journey alone, and, making my way without difficulty to Don José di Cardozo's,

I should there have found the tenderest of wives and—a strait-waistcoat."

When it became known that Byron's wife had left him, a sudden and complete change in the attitude of the public towards him took place. He had awakened one morning after the publication of *Childe Harold* to find himself famous; now came a morning when he awoke to find himself infamous, regarded by society as an outlaw.

Chief among the causes of this revulsion was envy—not that envy in the hearts of the gods which the ancients regarded as the cause of the downfall of the great—but foul, base envy in the breasts of his fellow-men. He stood so high; he was so great; with all his faults he had never sunk to the level of vulgar, mechanical respectability; confident in his powers and the favour of fortune, he had never deigned to seek friends who could protect him, or heeded how many enemies he made. These latter had long been innumerable. Chief among the envious were his literary rivals; and amongst all the many species of envy, the envy of authors is one of the most venomous. He had derided them, had called them the writers of a decadent period, had taken from some the name they had won, and made it impossible for others to win a name—why should he be admired and idolised whilst they were in vain arranging their locks for the reception of a wreath which never came? What joy to be able to tear him from the golden throne of fame and besmirch him with the mud in which they themselves stood!

He had long been suspected and secretly hated by the orthodox in religion and politics. The couple of stanzas in *Childe Harold* which venture in the most cautious terms to express a doubt that we shall meet our friends again after death, had been greeted with a cry of—heresy! and a whole book, *Anti-Byron*, had been written against them. The two verses to the Princess Charlotte, which, under the title, *Lines to a Lady Weeping*, were appended to the first edition of *The Corsair*, and in which the poet condoles with the daughter on the occasion of her father, the Prince Regent's, desertion of the Liberal side in politics, had set the whole Tory party violently against him. But hitherto he had been protected by his magic influence over men's minds as by an invisible coat of mail. This unfortunate episode in his private life offered a weak point, against which his enemies diverted the full force of public opinion.

The life led by Lady Byron and her family was the life on which English public opinion has set the seal of its peculiar approbation; and it was easy to convince the public that the man whom such a wife felt obliged to leave must indeed be a monster. Rumours began to spread; the slanders once conceived and brought forth, developed feet to walk on, wings to fly with, and swelled as they flew. Their voices rose from a whisper to a cry, from a cry to a deafening roar. Who does not know that concerted piece in the production of which baseness and stupidity collaborate, and during the performance of which ignorance sings in chorus with conscious villainy, whilst spite heightens the effect by the contribution of its most piercing trills!

Envy in this case entered the service of hypocrisy, and took its wages. Refined hypocrisy was, far on into the nineteenth century—as long, namely, as the period of religious reaction lasted—a social power, the authority of which differed from that of the Inquisitional tribunals of the sixteenth century only in the means it employed, not in the reach and efficacy of these means. It wrought through public opinion, and public opinion had become what Byron calls it in *Childe Harold*,

"an omnipotence,—whose veil
Mantles the earth with darkness, until right
And wrong are accidents, and men grow pale
Lest their own judgments should become too bright,
And their free thoughts be crimes, and earth have too much light."

As for hypocrisy, he felt incapable of doing justice to it unaided. "Oh for a forty-parson power!" he cries in *Don Juan*:—

"Oh for a *forty-parson power* to chant
Thy praise, Hypocrisy! Oh for a hymn
Loud as the virtues thou dost loudly vaunt,
Not practise! Oh for trump of cherubim!"

Such a state of matters was inevitable at a period which has so much in common with the age when the ancient religions and theories of life were in process of dissolution; a period when an old theological theory of the universe and of life, everywhere undermined and riddled by science, and unable to support itself by its own inherent truth, was obliged to cling to the conventional morality of the upper classes, which it made as rigid as possible in order to have a support in it; a period when ecclesiastical authority and narrow-minded social conservatism, both in a tottering condition, were endeavouring to uphold each other. Taking a bird's-eye view of the psychological history of Europe during the first two decades of the century, it actually seems to us as if the whole edifice of hypocrisy, the foundations of which were laid in the writings of the French *émigrés*, which rose steadily in those of the German Romanticists, and towered to a giddy height during the French Reaction, now suddenly fell on the head of one man.

Macaulay, in his essay on Moore's *Life of Byron*, writing on this subject, says:—"We know no spectacle so ridiculous as the British public in one of its periodical fits of morality. In general, elopements, divorces, and family quarrels, pass with little notice. We read the scandal, talk about it for a day, and forget it. But once in six or seven years our virtue becomes outrageous. We cannot suffer the laws of religion and decency to be violated. We must make a stand against vice. We must teach libertines that the English people appreciate the importance of domestic ties. Accordingly some unfortunate man, in no respect more depraved than hundreds whose offences have been treated with lenity, is singled out as an expiatory sacrifice. If he has children, they are to be taken from him. If he has a profession, he is to be driven from it. He is cut by the higher orders, and hissed by the lower. He is, in truth, a sort of whipping-boy, by whose vicarious agonies all the other transgressors of the same class are, it is supposed, sufficiently chastised. We reflect very complacently on our own severity, and compare with great pride the high standard of morals established in England with the

Parisian laxity. At length our anger is satiated. Our victim is ruined and heart-broken. And our virtue goes quietly to sleep for seven years more."

If the causes of Byron's downfall were of a complex nature, the means were simple enough. It was compassed by the Press, the only effective instrument in such cases. Several of the papers and magazines had taken the opportunity to spread slanders about him when criticising his verses to the Princess Charlotte; and more than one of them periodically calumniated him. Now they were all at liberty to discuss and attack his private life freely, thanks to the anonymity which, in spite of the want of naturalness and the corruption it entails, still prevails in the English Press. What anonymity really means is simply this, that the paltriest scribbler, who is hardly fit to hold the pen with which he writes his lies, is enabled to put the trumpet of moral public opinion to his lips, and let the voice of injured virtue resound in thousands of homes. Nor is it enough that the one anonymous writer should be able to constitute himself the voice of the public in the thousands of copies of one newspaper; he can assume hundreds of forms, can write with all kinds of fanciful signatures, and in a dozen different newspapers and magazines. A single scribbler would have sufficed to provide the whole Press with base attacks on a man outlawed by public opinion; it is easy, then, to imagine the number that were made on Byron, whose enemies were legion. Among the names given him by the Press he himself remembered Nero, Apicius, Caligula, Heliogabalus, and Henry VIII.—that is to say, he was accused of inhuman cruelty, of insane brutality, of animal and unnatural lust; he was painted with all the colours which vileness smears on its palette. The most terrible of all the accusations was that which even then went the round of the newspapers, and which sullied the fair name of the being dearest to him—the accusation of incest. And to all this he could not answer a word! He could not fight with the mire that bespattered him.

Slanders sped from mouth to mouth. When Mrs. Mardyn, the Drury Lane actress, made her first appearance after the divorce, she was hissed off the stage, because of the perfectly groundless report of a *liaison* between her and Byron, to whom, as a matter of fact, she had only spoken twice. He himself could not appear on the streets without danger. On his way to the House of Lords, where his presence was ignored, he was insulted by a respectable crowd.

Defence or retort being impossible, no course was left him, proud as he was, but to bow his head and go. "I felt," he writes, "that, if what was whispered, and muttered, and murmured, was true, I was unfit for England; if false, England was unfit for me." On the 25th of April, 1816, he set sail, never to return alive.

It is from this moment that Byron's true greatness dates. The blow struck by the *Edinburgh Review* had roused him, for the first time, to intellectual activity. This new blow made of him a knight. There is no comparison possible between what Byron wrote before, and what he wrote after, the event which he himself regarded as his greatest misfortune. It was a misfortune sent him by the genius of History, to snatch him from the unmanning influence of idolisation, to sever the enfeebling connection between him and that society and social spirit against which it was his historic mission to arouse, with more fortune and more power than any other individual, the hostility which was its undoing.

XIX

BYRON: HIS SELF-ABSORPTION

WHEN he had become for the second time a homeless and solitary pilgrim, Byron began to occupy himself again with the poem of travel in which his youthful sentiments had found expression. He added the Third and Fourth Cantos to *Childe Harold*. He turned back and felt the youthful feelings once again. But what breadth and depth they had gained in the interval! The chord struck in the First and Second Cantos was composed of three notes—the note of solitariness, the note of melancholy, and the note of freedom. Each one of these had become far clearer and more resonant.

Throughout the first half of the work it is the feeling of solitariness which produces the love of nature. "To sit on rocks, to muse o'er flood and fell," to climb the trackless mountain and lean over the foaming waterfall, alone, was not solitariness, but communion with nature; true solitariness was to wander amidst "the crowd, the hum, the shock of men," unloving and unloved. (*Childe Harold*, ii. 25, 26, 27.) The outbursts in the stanzas referred to are evoked by remembrances of the poet's childhood, spent in the beautiful mountain districts of Scotland, or of his visit to the hermit's home on "lonely Athos." This was still a love of the solitude of nature which resembled Wordsworth's, and which was based upon fear of an unknown, strange world of men and women. The difference between Wordsworth's and Byron's feeling was no more than this—that Wordsworth dwelt silently on the natural impression, in the manner of the countryman and the landscape painter, while Byron seized it with the longing, nervous ardour of the townsman; and, moreover, that Wordsworth loved nature best in her quiet moods, Byron in her wrath. (*Childe Harold*, ii. 37.)

In the second half of the work the character of the poet's solitariness has changed. There is a marked difference between the desire for solitary communion with nature which Harold felt as an inexperienced youth, and that which he felt as a man, at the end of his first circumnavigation of the world of men and things. It was now no longer fear of human beings, but disgust with them, which drove him to take refuge with nature. Society, the best society of a great metropolis, which to the untrained eye seemed so humane, so right-thinking, so refined and chivalrous, had turned its wrong side towards him—and the wrong side is interesting, but not beautiful. He had learned how much friendship the ruined man may reckon on, had learned that the only force which he who is making plans for his future can exactly calculate is the self-love of his fellow-men, with its consequences. So he withdrew into himself again; and the poetry he wrote at this time is not for men of a sociable nature. But the man who has had even a short experience of what it is to turn his back on his fellow-men—who in his desire to escape from them has left his home, his country, in search of a new earth and new skies—who in the solitudes of his choice has felt the sight of an approaching human being equivalent to a foul spot on his pure, free horizon—in the souls of this man and his like, Byron's lyric outbursts will find an echo.

Childe Harold is a solitary. He has learned that he is "the most unfit of men to herd with man," because he is unable "to submit his thoughts to others . . . to yield dominion of his mind to spirits against whom his own rebelled." But,

> "Where rose the mountains, there to him were friends;
> Where roll'd the ocean, thereon was his home.
> . . . .
> The desert, forest, cavern, breaker's foam,
> Were unto him companionship; they spake
> A mutual language, clearer than the tome
> Of his land's tongue, which he would oft forsake
> For Nature's pages glass'd by sunbeams on the lake."

Amongst men he droops like a wild-born falcon with clipt wing. But in his case, to fly from, is not to hate, mankind.

It is not discontent or defiance which keeps his "mind deep in its fountain," but fear lest it should "overboil in the hot throng," where in a moment

> "We may plunge our years
> In fatal penitence, and in the blight
> Of our own soul, turn all our blood to tears."

He feels that it is better to be alone, and thus to become a portion of what surrounds him. High mountains are "a feeling" to him, but the hum of human cities is a torture. The mountain, the sky, and the sea are a part of him, and he is a part of them, and to love them is his purest happiness. In solitude he is least alone; then his soul is conscious of infinity, a truth which purifies it from self. Harold has not loved the world, nor has it loved him. He is proud of not having "flattered its rank breath," nor bowed the knee to its idols, nor smiled hypocritically, nor echoed the cries of the crowd. He was *among* them, but not *of* them. But he desires that the world and he should part fair foes. "I do believe," he says,

> "Though I have found them not, that there may be
> Words which are things,—hopes which will not deceive,
> And virtues which are merciful . . .
> That two, or one, are almost what they seem."[1]

The feeling of solitariness gradually becomes the feeling of *melancholy*. This note, too, had been struck in the first two cantos; but their melancholy was nothing but the discontent of youth. With a wasted youth behind him, he had stood, like a phlegmatically mournful Hamlet, at the grave of Achilles, declaiming, with a skull in his hand, on the worthlessness of life and fame—this young poet who had not yet tasted the sweetness of celebrity, and who in reality hungered for nothing so much as for that very fame which, with so much argumentative philosophy, he feigned to condemn and despise. Now he has tasted it, and learned how little nourishment is to be derived from such food.

[1] *Childe Harold*, iii. 114.

His heart is

> "Even as a broken mirror, which the glass
> In every fragment multiplies; and makes
> A thousand images of one that was,
> The same and still the more, the more it breaks."

In the depth of his dejection he turns to the element in nature which, by its contrast with his present mood, solaces his sufferings—the sea, the free, open sea, upon whose mane he had laid his hand as a boy, and which knows him as the horse knows his rider. He loves the sea because it is unconquerable, because time cannot even write a wrinkle on its brow, and it rolls now as it rolled at the dawn of creation. But everything in nature reminds him of suffering and warfare. The peal of distant thunder is to him an alarm-bell, "the knoll of what in me is sleepless—if I rest." Even the beautiful, calm lake of Nemi does not remind him of anything peaceful and sweet; he calls it "calm as cherished hate." (iv. 173.)

His melancholy becomes actually choleric. Could he breathe all his passion "into *one* word, and that one word were Lightning," he would speak. "Anything but rest!" is his watchword. "Quiet to quick bosoms is a hell." There is a fire in the soul which, once kindled, is quenchless, and the flames of which rise ever higher and wilder; there is a fever which is fatal to all whom it attacks.

> "This makes the madmen who have made men mad
> By their contagion; Conquerors and Kings,
> Founders of sects and systems, to whom add
> Sophists, Bards, Statesmen, all unquiet things
> Which stir too strongly the soul's secret springs,
> And are themselves the fools to those they fool;
> Envied, yet how unenviable! what stings
> Are theirs! One breast laid open were a school
> Which would unteach mankind the lust to shine or rule.
>
> Their breath is agitation, and their life
> A storm whereon they ride, to sink at last,
> And yet so nursed and bigoted to strife,
> That should their days, surviving perils past,
> Melt to calm twilight, they feel overcast

With sorrow and supineness, and so die ;
Even as a flame unfed, which runs to waste
With its own flickering, or a sword laid by,
Which eats into itself, and rusts ingloriously."

And in a still more despairing mood Harold cries:

"We wither from our youth, we gasp away—
Sick—sick; unfound the boon—unslaked the thirst,
Though to the last, in verge of our decay,
Some phantom lures, such as we sought at first—
But all too late,—so are we doubly curst.
Love, fame, ambition, avarice—'tis the same,
Each idle—and all ill—and none the worst—
For all are meteors with a different name,
And Death the sable smoke where vanishes the flame.

. . . .

Our life is a false nature—'tis not in
The harmony of things,—this hard decree,
This uneradicable taint of sin,
This boundless upas, this all-blasting tree,
Whose root is earth, whose leaves and branches be
The skies which rain their plagues on men like dew—
Disease, death, bondage—all the woes we see,
And worse, the woes we see not." . . .

In the First Canto of *Childe Harold* we already find the *love of freedom* (the third note in the chord struck by the poem) exalted as the one force capable of emancipating from the despair with which the universal misery (the *Weltschmerz*, as the Germans call it) has overwhelmed the soul. It has this power because it provides a practical task. During his first visit to Portugal, Childe Harold exclaimed: "Oh, that such hills upheld a free-born race!" And to the Spaniards he cried:

"Awake, ye sons of Spain! awake! advance!
Lo, Chivalry, your ancient goddess, cries."

And it was in the course of his first tour, too, that he thus apostrophised the subjugated Greeks, who went on hoping for help from other nations:—

"Hereditary bondsmen! know ye not
Who would be free themselves must strike the blow?
By their right arms the conquest must be wrought?
Will Gaul or Muscovite redress ye? no!

True, they may lay your proud despoilers low,
But not for you will Freedom's altars flame.
. . . .
When riseth Lacedemon's hardihood,
When Thebes Epaminondas rears again,
When Athens' children are with hearts endued,
When Grecian mothers shall give birth to men,
Then may'st thou be restored ; but not till then."

But his love of liberty at that time was of a purely political nature ; it was the free-born Englishman's indignation at seeing other nations unable to shake off a foreign yoke to which his own nation would never have dreamt of submitting.

Now he has learned what liberty in the wide, full, universal meaning of the word is. Now he feels that free *thought* is the first essential requisite of all spiritual life.

" Yet let us ponder boldly—'tis a base
Abandonment of reason to resign
Our right of thought—our last and only place
Of refuge ; this, at least, shall still be mine :
Though from our birth the faculty divine
Is chain'd and tortured—cabin'd, cribb'd, confined,
And bred in darkness, lest the truth should shine
Too brightly on the unprepared mind,
The beam pours in, for time and skill will couch the blind."

And it is his intention not merely to ponder, but to act. Invoking Time, the great avenger, whom he reminds that he has borne the hatred of the world with calm pride—and he has experienced all its varieties of hatred,

" From mighty wrongs to petty perfidy,
. . . .
From the loud roar of foaming calumny
To the small whisper of the as paltry few,
And subtler venom of the reptile crew "—

he concludes with the prayer : " Let me not have worn this iron in my soul in vain ! "

Now, his personal woes shrink into nothing when he beholds the gigantic ruins of Rome ; and, like the Sulpicius with whose feelings Chateaubriand endowed the hero of *Les Martyrs*, he feels the insignificance of his fate compared with that which has swept away the cities of Greece. He writes :—

> " Oh Rome ! my country ! city of the soul !
> The orphans of the heart must turn to thee,
> Lone mother of dead empires ! and control
> In their shut breasts their petty misery.
> . . . .
> Wandering in youth, I traced the path of him,
> The Roman friend of Rome's least mortal mind,
> The friend of Tully."

And when, not satisfied with liberty of thought alone, he turns his attention to practical matters and occupies himself with the great political struggles of the day, he does not content himself with repeating the old invocations to the departed, or with crying to Venice that she has drowned the glory and honour of centuries in the mire of slavery, and that it would be better for her to be whelm'd beneath the waves. No, he boldly attacks the mighty, the victors of Waterloo, whom he scornfully calls " the apes of him who humbled once the proud " ; and then passes from the outward, political aspect of the great European conflicts, to their inner, social significance.

To all appearance, he says, France has uprooted old prejudices, and laid in ruins " things which grew, breathed from the birth of time," only to see dungeons and thrones rebuilt upon the same foundation. " *But this will not endure.*" Mankind have at last felt their strength. And even though France " got drunk with blood to vomit crime,"

> " Yet, Freedom ! yet thy banner, torn, but flying,
> Streams like the thunderstorm *against* the wind ;
> Thy trumpet voice, though broken now and dying,
> The loudest still the tempest leaves behind ;
> Thy tree hath lost its blossoms, and the rind,
> Chopp'd by the axe, looks rough and little worth,
> But the sap lasts—and still the seed we find
> Sown deep, even in the bosom of the North ;
> So shall a better spring less bitter fruit bring forth."

And of himself the poet writes:—

> "But I have lived, and have not lived in vain:
> My mind may lose its force, my blood its fire,
> And my frame perish even in conquering pain;
> But there is that within me which shall tire
> Torture and Time, and breathe when I expire,
> Something unearthly, which they deem not of,
> Like the remember'd tone of a mute lyre."

Thus do the three chief feelings expressed in this beautiful poem—solitariness, melancholy, and love of freedom—gradually become one greater feeling; the mind of the poet widens and deepens with each canto. Wordsworth had identified his Ego with England; Scott and Moore had given the feelings of Scotland and Ireland expression in their poetry; but Byron's Ego represents universal humanity; its sorrows and hopes are those of all mankind. After this Ego has, in manly, energetic style, withdrawn into itself and lived for a time absorbed in its solitary grief, that grief widens into compassion for all the sufferings and sorrows of humanity; the hard, selfish crust of the Ego is broken, and there issues forth the ardent love of liberty, to encompass and to elevate the poet's whole generation. Now his mind is attuned to worship, and he cries:—

> "Not vainly did the early Persian make
> His altar the high places and the peak
> Of earth-o'ergazing mountains. . . .
> . . . . . . Come and compare
> Columns and idol-dwellings, Goth or Greek,
> With Nature's realms of worship, earth and air,
> Nor fix on fond abodes to circumscribe thy prayer."

XX

BYRON: THE REVOLUTIONARY SPIRIT

AFTER visiting the battle-field of Waterloo, Byron went, by way of the Rhine, to Switzerland, where he spent several months, residing most of the time in the neighbourhood of Geneva. In a boarding-house there, he for the first time met Shelley. Shelley, who was Byron's junior by four years, had sent him, at the time of its publication, a copy of *Queen Mab;* but the letter accompanying the book had miscarried, and no further communication had passed between them. Shelley had arrived at Geneva a fortnight before Byron, accompanied by Mary Godwin and her step-sister, Miss Jane Clairmont, who had always passionately admired Byron. His illegitimate daughter Allegra was the fruit of the brief connection between him and this young lady.

Intercourse with Shelley produced on Byron's mind some of the strongest, deepest impressions which it was capable of receiving. The first great impression was that made by Shelley's personality and view of life. In him Byron for the first time came into contact with a man of a perfectly modern and perfectly emancipated mind. In spite of his genius for assimilating everything that harmonised with his own nature, it was but a half education, in philosophy as in literature, which Byron had received; and he had hitherto been led by sympathies rather than convictions. Now Shelley, glowing with the enthusiasm of an apostle, his doubts long since disposed of, a true priest of humanism, came across his path. The dissipated life of London society, and the pressing burden of his private misfortunes, had allowed Byron neither tranquillity of mind nor leisure to reflect on the problems of existence or on the reformation of humanity; he had been too much occupied with himself.

Now, at the moment in his literary career when his Ego was beginning to expand, he was brought into contact with a spirit which baptized with fire. He gladly welcomed the new influence; and in much of what he now wrote it is plainly perceptible. The numerous pantheistic outbursts in the Third Canto of *Childe Harold* are undoubtedly, one and all, the fruit of conversations with Shelley; worthy of special attention is the beautiful passage (iii. 100) in which everything in Nature is assumed to be a manifestation of "undying Love"—an expression of Shelley's theory of love and beauty being the mysterious powers which uphold the world. In one of the notes in his journal, Byron at this time goes so far in his Shelley-derived pantheism as to write: "The feeling with which all around Clarens and the opposite rocks of Meillerie is invested, is of a still higher and more comprehensive order than the mere sympathy with individual passion; it is a sense of the existence of love in its most extended and sublime capacity, and of our own participation of its good and of its glory: it is the great principle of the universe, which is there more condensed, but not less manifested; and of which, though knowing ourselves a part, we lose our individuality, and mingle in the beauty of the whole."

Shelley's influence is also traceable in the spirit scenes in *Manfred*, and very specially in the third act of the drama, which was re-written by his advice. And as to *Cain*, even if Shelley, as he affirms, had no actual share in the writing of the work, it certainly would not have been what it is if Byron had never known him.

The two poets saw Chillon and all its beautiful surroundings in company; and Byron received the second great impression which was to bear fruit in his poetry—the impression of the Alps. Coming from the confinement and close atmosphere of the London drawing-rooms, it was a relief to him to let his eye rest on the eternal snow, and the giant peaks that tower sky-high above the haunts of men. His poetic forerunner, Chateaubriand, hated the Alps; their grandeur had an oppressive effect on his vanity; Byron felt at home among them.

Manfred, which derives its truest claim to admiration from its matchlessness as an Alpine landscape, was a direct result of the impressions of nature received at this time. Taine let himself be tempted to use the strong expression, that Byron's Alpine Spirits in *Manfred* are only stage gods; but Taine, when he wrote this, did not himself know Switzerland.

Nowhere else do circumstances in the same degree incline the mind to the personification of nature. Even the ordinary traveller feels the temptation. I remember standing one evening on the summit of the Righi, looking down on the beautiful lakes at the foot of the mountain, and the vapoury clouds which were driving across them, quite close to their surface. Suddenly, far away on the horizon, a little solid white cloud appeared. By the time it had reached Pilatus, a minute later, it was an enormous vapoury mass. With frightful speed it rushed onwards, covering the whole sky with the league-wide flaps of its mantle. Sinking down towards the lakes, it enveloped the mountain peaks, rode along the ridges, filled the hollows; then, spreading itself out still wider, it mounted in circles like smoke towards the sky, and sank like lead over the towns and villages, effacing every colour, and turning the whole into one monotonous expanse of grey. The white of the snow, the green of the trees, the thousand gleams and colours of the sunlit clouds were deluged and gone in one moment. The eye, which had but a second before been wandering at will over the immeasurable expanse now, irresistibly attracted, gazed steadfastly at the shapeless mass, which, tearing through the sky with the force of a sphere in its earliest stage, rapidly approached the beholder. It was like the hosts of heaven, like hundreds of thousands of ethereal riders, sweeping onwards in closed ranks upon winged, silent horses, and, more irresistible than any earthly army, tracklessly effacing everything behind them, like the hordes of Asia or Attila's Huns. A Scandinavian could not but think of the ride of the Valkyries. The moment the cloud reached the Righi, the watchers there began to lose sight of each other; first one, then another, disappeared from the view of his companions; the mist slung itself in a clammy, tight embrace round each one, closing his mouth and weighing on his breast.

Natural phenomena of this description suggested the apparitions which appear to Manfred. Passage after passage from Byron's journal is incorporated in his poem. Not unfrequently the entries in their original, careless form are fully as effective as when transcribed in verse. "Arrived at the Grindelwald; dined; mounted again, and rode to the higher glacier—like *a frozen hurricane.* (In *Manfred,* for the sake of the verse—"a tumbling tempest's foam, frozen in a moment.") Starlight, beautiful, but a devil of a path! . . . A little lightning; but the whole of the day as fine in point of weather as the day on which Paradise was made. Passed *whole woods of withered pines, all withered;* trunks stripped and barkless, branches lifeless; done by a single winter,—their appearance reminded me of me and my family." All these expressions occur, with slight alterations, in the poem.

But the time Shelley and Byron spent together, profitable and enjoyable as it was, would have been happier but for the behaviour of some of their fellow-countrymen, whose curiosity led them to dog the footsteps and spy the actions of the two poets. English tourists had the incredible impertinence to force their way into Byron's house. When a stop was put to this, they stood with telescopes on the shore or on the road; they looked over the garden-wall; and hotel waiters were bribed, as the Venetian gondoliers afterwards were, to communicate all that went on. The first report set in circulation was, that Byron and Shelley lived in "promiscuous intercourse" with two sisters; and, gossip by degrees making the two poets out to be incarnate devils, the reports gained steadily in repulsiveness. It consequently hardly surprises us to read that, one day at Madame de Staël's, when Byron was announced, a pious old English lady, Mrs. Hervey, the novel-writer, fainted when she heard the name, as if, says Byron, it had been "his Satanic majesty" himself who was appearing.

Our attempt to understand this actual fear of Byron's person, which to us appears so absurd, leads us to the consideration of the last great impression received by him during his stay by the Lake of Geneva, namely, that produced by his clear apprehension of the exact nature of a certain calumny which had been for some time in circulation in England, and also of the wide-spread belief in it. This was the same story which Mrs. Beecher Stowe in the sixties published to the world, as having been confidentially communicated to herself by Lady Byron, "whilst a heavenly brightness shone from that lady's ethereal countenance"—the story of the criminal relations between Lord Byron and his step-sister, Augusta Leigh. The assurance that such relations had existed became in course of time so firmly rooted in Lady Byron's mind that (as is proved by a work entitled *Medora Leigh*, published in 1869) she did not even shrink from telling Augusta's daughter, Medora, who applied to her for assistance when in difficulties, that she was not a daughter of Colonel Leigh, but of Lord Byron. Lady Byron at the same time promised Medora that she would always provide for her maintenance—a promise she did not keep.

At the time he left England, Byron had evidently known nothing, or as good as nothing, of this report. He had probably not read all the hostile newspaper articles. He himself writes that it was not till some time afterwards that he heard of all his enemies had done and said; and he blames his friends for having concealed various things from him. It was while he was in Switzerland that he learned everything. Knowing this, we understand the full meaning of the poetry addressed at that time to Augusta. In the Third Canto of *Childe Harold* we find the following stanza:—

"And there was one soft breast, as hath been said,
Which unto his was bound by stronger ties
Than the Church links withal; and, though unwed,
That love was pure, and, far above disguise,
Had stood the test of mortal enmities
Still undivided, and cemented more
By peril, dreaded most in female eyes;
But this was firm, and from a foreign shore
Well to that heart might his these absent greetings pour!"

The *Stanzas to Augusta* express similar sentiments; and the line, "Though slander'd, thou never couldst shake" (in the second of the poems to her), shows that she, too, knew of the shameful rumours.

And now we also have the explanation of the sudden revulsion which occurred in Switzerland in Byron's feeling towards Lady Byron. In the days immediately following the separation he had written: "I do not believe that there ever was a better, or even a brighter, a kinder, or a more amiable and agreeable being than Lady B.," and had laid the blame of everything on his own violence and inconsiderateness; but now he sees only the blemishes in her character; and it is while under the overpowering impression made by the accusation just alluded to, that he begins the ugly war upon a woman, which, if we did not know the circumstances, would seem utterly inexcusable, and draws the unflattering portrait of his wife as Donna Inez in the First Canto of *Don Juan*.

Decisive, and positively crushing, evidence against Lady Byron was produced in 1869, in the *Quarterly Review*. Seven letters and notes were printed, written after the separation by her to Mrs. Leigh, all brimming over with tenderness and assurances of affection. It is her "great comfort" that Mrs. Leigh is with Lord Byron. "Shall I still be your sister? I must resign my rights to be so considered; but I don't think that will make any difference in the kindness I have so uniformly experienced from you." "In this at least I *am* 'truth itself' when I say that whatsoever the situation may be, there is no one whose society is dearer to me, or can contribute more to my happiness. These feelings will not change under any circumstances. . . . Should you hereafter condemn me, I shall not love you the less." Thus did Lady Byron write to the woman whom, after the lapse of many years, she accused as the guilty person who had driven her from her husband's house. This friendly correspondence between Lady Byron and Mrs. Leigh actually continues till Byron's death. His last unfinished letter begins with the words: "My dearest Augusta, I received a few days ago your and Lady Byron's report of Ada's health." And yet we are asked to believe that Lady Byron the whole time regarded Augusta, who continued to be the reconciling intermediary between the spouses, as the unnatural criminal who was one of the authors of the misfortune of her life. What a chaos of lies and insanity!

Insanity is the right word, for, as the *Quarterly Review* has remarked, "Lady Byron could at first account for her gifted husband's conduct on no hypothesis but insanity; and now, by a sort of Nemesis, there is no other hypothesis on which the charitable moralist can account for hers. But there is this marked difference in their maladies: he morbidly exaggerated his vices, and she her virtues; his monomania lay in being an impossible sinner, and hers in being an impossible saint. . . . He in his mad moods did his best to blacken his own reputation, whilst her self-delusions invariably tended to damage the characters of all that were nearest and should have been dearest to her. Which was the more dangerous or less amiable delusion of the two?"[1]

The last impression received by Byron in Switzerland was, then, the crushing one of this slander. His thoughts revolved round the story, and the artist in him was ever more fascinated by it. George Sand, in a letter to Sainte-Beuve, has, with a few rapid touches, described her nature, and the nature of the poet generally. She is writing about Jouffroy the philosopher, who has expressed a desire to be introduced to her, but of whom, as an extremely rigorous and unimaginative moralist, she is a little afraid. She remarks: "I have once or twice said to myself: Might it not be permissible to eat human flesh? You have said to yourself: People doubtless exist who think that it might be permissible to eat human flesh! Jouffroy has said to himself: Such an idea never occurred to any one, &c."—a clever definition of the nature of the poet as compared with that of the observer and the moralist.

Byron was one of those who permit their imaginative and their reflective powers every possible experiment; he had a strong inclination to brood over, and let his fancy

[1] *Quarterly Review*, October 1869. Compare with Karl Elze's admirable work: *Lord Byron*, p. 179.

play with, what people in general fear and avoid. The well-known anecdote (which aroused such horror) of his exclaiming, with a knife in his hand: "I wish I knew what it feels like to have committed a murder," means this and nothing more. There was the same fascination for him in thinking and working himself into the feeling of guilt which accompanies a criminal attachment, as there was in imagining the feelings which accompany a murder. His earliest heroes, such as the Giaour and Lara, have committed a mysterious murder; and, as is well known, Byron was promptly credited with the crime of his heroes. Even the aged Goethe allowed himself to be so far led astray by the gossip that reached his ears as to characterise (in his review of *Manfred*) as "extremely probable" the foolish tale of Byron's doings in Florence—where, as a matter of fact, he spent one afternoon. The story reported him to have had an intrigue there with a young married woman, who was, in consequence, killed by her husband—the husband in his turn being killed by Byron. Just as the public of that day saw evidence of Byron's murderous deeds in Lara's tragic mien, the public of our day have seen evidence of his incest in Manfred's despair and Cain's marriage with his sister. It is not surprising that Byron and Moore should have meditated writing an imaginary biography of Lord Byron, in which he was to seduce so many members of the one sex and murder so many of the other, that the scandal-mongers would be outbid and possibly silenced. The project was only relinquished from fear that the public might take the jest as sober earnest.

It is probable that the subject of love between brother and sister was one often discussed by Shelley and Byron in the course of their conversations, all the more probable from the circumstance that the younger poet's mind was also exercised by the unprofitable question. What incensed Byron more than anything else was the pious horror displayed by the orthodox Bible Christians, one article of whose faith it is that the human race, as descended from one man and woman, multiplied by means of marriage between brother and sister. Hence he lays emphasis in *Cain* on the circumstance that Cain and Adah are brother and sister, and makes Lucifer explain to Adah that *her* love for her brother is not a sin, though the same passion in her descendants will be ; to which Adah very logically replies :

> "What is the sin which is not
> Sin in itself? Can circumstance make sin
> Or virtue?"

Manfred and *Cain* were the products of all the psychological elements which have now been indicated. *Manfred* is the less important of the two works. It does not bear the comparison with Goethe's *Faust* which it invites and which has been so often instituted. Goethe himself said that an interesting lecture might be given on the subject. They have since been given in abundance ; there is more originality and talent in Taine's than in any other known to me.

At only one point does *Manfred* rise superior to *Faust*. To the critic there is no surer criterion of the value of the different parts of a work than the circumstance that, after a certain length of time, he remembers this or that part and has forgotten the rest. I know with certainty that, a year after I had read *Manfred*, all that I remembered of it was the scene in which, in the hour of his death, the hero, who has judged himself so severely, first repulses the Abbot and such comfort as he would fain give, and then with proud contempt dismisses from his presence the evil spirits with whom he has nothing in common, and to whom he has never given the slightest power over him. The difference between this man and Faust, who sells himself to Mephistopheles and falls on his knees before the Earth Spirit, is very striking. The English poet has had before his eyes a higher ideal of independent manhood than has the German; Byron's hero is a typical man, Goethe's a typical human being. Alone in death as in life, Manfred has no more communion with hell than he has with heaven. He is his own accuser and his own judge. This is Byron's manly ethical standpoint. Not till he reaches the lonely heights above the snow-line, where human weakness and pliability do not thrive, does his soul breathe freely. And the Alpine landscape is the natural, inevitable background for his hero, whose stern wildness is akin to such scenes.

But in *Manfred* only the egoistic side of Byron's nature reveals itself. His wide human sympathies find full expression for the first time in *Cain*. *Cain* is Byron's confession of faith—that is to say, the confession of all his doubts and all his criticism. When we remember that he had neither, like Shelley and the great poets of Germany, attained by dint of thought to an emancipated, humanistic view of the world and life, nor, like the authors of our own days, had the advantage of being able to base his ideas and imaginings on the subject of the beliefs of the past and the present upon a groundwork of facts established by natural science and scientific Biblical criticism, we cannot but marvel at the intellectual power and earnestness which he in this work brings to bear on the most vital problems of life.

As a private personage Byron was, undoubtedly, as much of the dilettante in his free-thought as in his politics. His admirable reasoning power revolted against belief in what was contrary to reason; but, like most of the great men at the beginning of the century—that is to say, before the remarkable development of religion and science which has taken place during its progress—he was sceptical and superstitious at one and the same time. As a child, religion had been made a weariness to him; his mother dragged him regularly to church, and he revenged himself when he was bored beyond all measure by pricking her with a pin. As a youth, he was roused to revolt by the rigid literal beliefs of the Church of England, as contained in its Thirty-nine Articles; he wrote in his memorandum-book: "It is useless to tell me *not* to *reason*, but to *believe*. You might as well tell a man not to wake, but *sleep*." The belief in eternal hell-fire was a subject of eternal merriment with him. He writes to Moore in 1822: "Do you remember Frederick the Great's answer to the remonstrance of the villagers whose curate preached against the eternity of hell's torments? It was thus:—'If my faithful subjects of Schrausenhaussen prefer being eternally damned, let them.'" And he horrified his fellow-countrymen by writing in *Don Juan:*

> "There's nought, no doubt, so much the spirit calms
> As rum and true religion." [1]

He disliked the clergy. Trelawny reports him to have said: "When did parsons patronise genius? If one of their black band dares to think for himself, he is drummed out or cast aside, like Sterne and Swift"; and Moore gives as one of his ejaculations: "These rascals of priests have done more harm to religion than all the unbelievers." But, in spite of all his jests and jeers, his feeling was one of uncertainty. He dared not endorse the conclusions to which Shelley was led by his reflections; and he sent his little daughter to be educated in a convent, to withdraw her from the influence of the sceptical talk of Shelley and his wife. A beautiful and very characteristic letter from Shelley gives decisive evidence on the subject of Byron's uncertainty. "Lord Byron," he writes, "has read me one or two letters of Moore to him, in which Moore speaks with great kindness of me; and of course I cannot but feel flattered by the approbation of a man, my inferiority to whom I am proud to acknowledge (!) Amongst other things, however, Moore seems to deprecate my influence on Lord Byron's mind on the subject of religion, and to attribute the tone assumed in *Cain* to my suggestion. . . . I think you know Moore. Pray assure him that I have not the smallest influence over Lord Byron in this particular; if I had, I certainly should employ it to eradicate from his great mind the delusions of Christianity, which, in spite of his reason, seem perpetually to recur, and

[1] What Byron refers to in his anecdote of Frederick the Great must be a story I find told in D'Alembert's *Éloge de Milord Maréchal:* Les pasteurs de Neufchâtel, attachés encore à l'ancienne doctrine, ou voulant seulement le paraître, osèrent déclarer au roi de Prusse, suivant le style ordinaire, que *leur conscience ne leur permettait pas* de souffrir l'hérétique Petit-Pierre au milieu d'eux, malgré la protection dont ce grand prince l'honorait. Le roi répondit *que puisqu'ils avaient si fort à cœur d'être damnés éternellement, il y donnait volontiers les mains, et trouvait très-bon que le diable ne s'en fît faute.*"

See *Gespräche Friedrichs des Grossen mit H. de Catt und dem Marchese Lucchesini*, herausgegeben von Dr. Fritz Bischoff; Leipzig, 1885.

to lie in ambush for the hours of sickness and distress. *Cain* was *conceived* many years ago, and begun before I saw him last year at Ravenna. How happy should I not be to attribute to myself, however indirectly, any participation in that immortal work!"

Thus we see that Byron, the private individual, had by no means arrived at any definite conclusions on the great subjects which engage the mind of man. And we are consequently all the more impressed by the manner in which, in his poetry, his genius takes possession of him, and makes him great and victorious in his argument, directing his aim with absolute certainty to the vital points. In European literature, which in 1821 lay stifling in the clutches of orthodoxy, there was a perfect revolution when *Cain* appeared, like a herald of revolt; the only comparison possible is with the impression produced in the scientific world fourteen years later by Strauss's *Life of Jesus*. The great German poets had, in their liberal Hellenism, left the orthodox belief untouched. This less emancipated poet was confined in the cage of dogma, but was uneasily pacing round and round in it like an imprisoned wild animal, shaking at its bars.

Cain is not written with the haste of inspiration—is not a work that storms and thunders. In it Byron has succeeded in accomplishing what for passionate natures is the most difficult of all tasks—the accomplishment of which is, indeed, the supreme triumph of morality—he has *canalised* his passion, that is to say, caused its wild currents to fertilise. The play is a product of reflection—of the thought that burrows and mines, the acuteness that splits, the reasoning power that shivers. Here more than anywhere else is what Goethe makes Byron say of himself (as Euphorion in the Second Part of *Faust*) applicable—namely, that he has a distaste for what is easily won, and delights only in what he takes by force. But the whole hammering, crushing, intellectual machinery, which to all appearance works under such complete control, is set in movement by an enkindled, glowing imagination; and at the very centre of everything there is a panting, sobbing heart. Byron's faith helped him as much as did his scepticism. With perfect simplicity he takes the

Old Testament story as he finds it. He treats its characters, not as symbolic figures, but as realities; and he does it in all sincerity—his scepticism attacks traditions; it accepts tradition. Besides, was he not himself, both in his intellect and his emotions, a man of the Old Testament type? In his soul resounded lamentations like those of Job when he was comforted and reproved by his friends, and cries for vengeance like those in the Psalms. The *Hebrew Melodies* prove how naturally the Jewish garment accommodated itself to the forms of his feeling.

In all sincerity, then, Byron for the time being acknowledges the claims of tradition and bows the neck of his reason to its yoke; but in *Cain* we see human reason writhing under this yoke, rebelling against it—tortured by its pricks and kicking against them. And what lends special attraction to the spectacle is, that the human reason in this case is a young, newborn one. On the true poet the rising of the sun makes as powerful an impression as if he were beholding it rise on the first day of creation; to Byron, all doubts and questions were so fresh that they could be put into the mouth of the first questioner and doubter. The formation of the doubts and complaints had demanded nothing less than the whole long succession of the human generations who had sighed and groaned over the cruelty of life and the irrationality of tradition. But although they are the accumulated woes of many thousand years—the ever increasing sufferings of thousands of generations of free human spirits in the torture-chambers of orthodoxy—which are here voiced by the first rebel, he expresses it all with as much originality and simplicity as if the thought-task of millions had at once been accomplished by the first thinking brain. This is the first of those contradictions in the poem which are so effective.

The part of the drama in which all the discrepancies in the Jewish-Christian tradition are laid bare, and its incompatibility as a whole with reason is proved—the veiled attack on orthodoxy, in short—possesses tolerably little interest for us nowadays; the human race has progressed so far since 1821 that all the subtlety displayed in refuting the theology of the Book of Genesis affects us much in the same manner as a disputation on the belief in werewolves. Nor are these attacks intended to be taken literally; Byron had, of course, no intention of writing blasphemously, of scoffing at a being whom he himself regarded as the supreme, the all-embracing being. What Cain combats is in reality only the belief that the order of nature is a moral order and that goodness, instead of being one of the aims of human life, is its postulate. It must be remembered that the language of human beings is full of words which were formed in ages past, and which we are obliged to use because the language owns no others, but the interpretation of which has changed many times in the course of centuries. Such words are, for example, soul and body, eternity, salvation, Paradise, the first temptation, the first curse. Byron has retained in his poem all the expressions of the Book of Genesis. The second suggestive contradiction in the drama is, therefore, the constant inward disagreement between the spirit of the poem and its letter. This second contradiction thoroughly arouses the readers who have been startled by the first.[1]

Side by side in this drama with the exposure of the hollowness of the general orthodox belief in God, we have a passionate representation of the infinite misery of human existence. To what underlies this, the empty, unmeaning name of *pessimism* has been given; the true definition is, a profound compassion for the undeniable sufferings of humanity. Far deeper down in Byron's soul than wrath with the power which creates only to destroy, lies the feeling of the obligatory sympathy of all with all—sympathy with

[1] Renan writes on this subject: "Supposez même que, pour nous philosophes, un autre mot fût préférable, outre que les mots abstraits n'expriment pas assez clairement la réelle existence, il y aurait un immense inconvénient à nous couper ainsi toutes les sources poétiques du passé, et à nous séparer par notre langage des simples qui adorent si bien de leur manière; Le mot *Dieu* étant en possession des respects de l'humanité, ce mot ayant pour lui une longue prescription et ayant été employé dans les belles poésies, ce serait renverser toutes les habitudes du langage que de l'abandonner. Dites aux simples de vivre d'aspiration à la vérité, à la beauté, à la bonté morale, ces mots n'auront pour eux aucun sens. Dites-leur d'aimer Dieu, de ne pas offenser Dieu, ils vous comprendront à merveille. Dieu, Providence, immortalité, autant de bons vieux mots, un peu lourds peut-être, que la philosophie interprétera dans les sens de plus en plus raffinés, mais qu'elle ne remplacera jamais avec avantage.—*Études d'Histoire religieuse*, p. 418.

all the suffering which it is impossible to relieve, but equally impossible not to be conscious of. *Cain* is a tragedy dealing with the source of all tragedy—the fact that man is born, suffers, sins, and dies.

Byron revolves in his mind the Bible legend: Adam has been tamed; Eve has been cowed; Abel is a gentle, submissive boy; Cain is young humanity—pondering, questioning, desiring, demanding. He is to take part in the general thanksgiving. Praise and give thanks for what? For life? Am I not to die? For life? Did I ask to live? Am I still in the garden of Eden? Why should I suffer? For Adam's transgression?

> "What had *I* done in this?—I was unborn:
> I sought not to be born; nor love the state
> To which that birth has brought me. Why did he
> Yield to the serpent and the woman? or,
> Yielding, why suffer? What was there in this?
> The tree was planted, and why not for him?
> If not, why place him near it, where it grew,
> The fairest in the centre? They have but
> One answer to all questions: ''Twas *his* will,
> And *he* is good.' How know I that? Because
> He is all-powerful, must all-good, too, follow?"

Goodness would not create evil, and what hath He created but evil? And even supposing evil leads to good?—why not create good at once? He has "multiplied himself in misery," and yet He is happy. Who could be happy alone, happy in being the only happy one? And that is what He is—the "indefinite, indissoluble tyrant."

We are nothing in His sight. "Well," says Cain, "if I am nothing, for nothing shall I be an hypocrite, and seem well-pleased with pain?" War of all with all, and death for all, and disease for nearly all, and suffering, and bitterness; these were the fruits of the forbidden tree. Is not man's lot a miserable one? One good gift the fatal apple has given—reason. But who could be proud of a mind which is chained to an enslaving body, "to the most gross and petty paltry wants, all foul and fulsome, the very best of its enjoyments a sweet degradation, a most enervating and filthy cheat!" Not Paradise, but death, is our inheritance on this wretched little earth, the abode of beings "whose enjoyment was to be in blindness—a Paradise of Ignorance, from which knowledge was barred as poison." And oh! the thought that all this misery is to be propagated and inherited!—to see the first tears shed and shudderingly anticipate the oceans that will flow! Would it not be better to snatch the infant in his sleep and dash him against the rocks, and thus choke the spring of misery at its source? Were it not infinitely better that the child had never been born? How dare any one bring children into such a world? And this is the existence for which I am to offer thanks and praise!

Such is Cain's mood at the moment when he is compelled to offer sacrifice; and it is largely due to the suggestions of Lucifer. For Lucifer prefers torment to "the smooth agonies of adulation, in hymns and harpings, and self-seeking prayers." This Lucifer is no devil. He says himself:

> "*Who* covets evil
> For its own bitter sake?—*None*—nothing! 'tis
> The leaven of all life, and lifelessness."

Nor is he a Mephistopheles. Except for one faint jest, he is severely earnest. No! this Lucifer is really the bringer of light, the genius of science, the proud and defiant spirit of criticism, the best friend of man, overthrown because he would not cringe or lie, but inflexible, because, like his enemy, he is eternal. He is the spirit of freedom. But it is significant that what he represents is not the frank, open, struggle for liberty, but the feeling which inspires gloomy conspirators, who seek their aim by forbidden ways—the feeling which prevailed among the despairing young friends of liberty in Europe in the year 1821.

In his work, *Justice in the Revolution and the Church*, Proudhon, addressing the Archbishop of Besançon, exclaims: "Liberty is your Antichrist. Come, then, O Satan! thou maligned of priests and kings, let me embrace thee, let me clasp thee to my heart! Thy works, thou blessed one, are not always fair and good, but they alone give meaning to the universe. What would justice be without thee? An instinct. Reason? A habit. Man? An animal." Satan, thus understood, is simply the spirit of free criticism; and if Byron's poetry had been named "Satanic" after him, it might have borne the name without shame.

With the assistance of Lucifer, part of the action of *Cain* takes place in the region of the supernatural; for that spirit conveys his pupil through the abyss of space, shows him all the worlds with their inhabitants, the realms of death, and, through the mist of the future, the generations yet unborn. He demands from Cain neither blind faith nor blind submission. He does not say: "Believe—and sink not! doubt—and perish!" He does not make belief in him the condition of Cain's salvation; he requires neither homage nor gratitude; he opens Cain's eyes.

Cain returns to earth; and the first rebel leaves the first murderer alone, a prey to his consuming doubt. Sacrifices are to be offered, and he has to choose an altar. What are altars to him? So much turf and stone. Abhorring suffering, he will not slaughter innocent animals in honour of a bloodthirsty God; on his altar he lays the fruits of the earth.[1] Abel prays in correctly pious fashion. Cain, too, must pray. What shall he say?

> "If thou must be induced with altars
> And softened with a sacrifice, receive them!
> . . . .
> If thou lov'st blood, the shepherd's shrine, which smokes
> On my right hand, hath shed it for thy service;
> . . . . . . If a shrine without victim,
> An altar without gore, may win thy favour,
> Look on it! and for him who dresseth it,
> He is—such as thou mad'st him; and seeks nothing
> Which must be won by kneeling."

Fire comes down from heaven and consumes Abel's sacrifice, the flames greedily licking up the blood on the altar. But a whirlwind throws down Cain's altar and scatters the fruits upon the earth. Did God, then, rejoice in the pain of the bleating mothers when their lambs were

[1] Here the influence of Shelley is apparent.

taken from them to be slaughtered? and in "the pangs of the sad ignorant victims under the pious knife"? Cain's blood boils; he begins to demolish the offending altar. Abel opposes him. "Beware!" cries Cain; "thy God loves blood!" And, driven by his wrath, his misery, his fate, into the snare spread for him by the Lord, he commits the first murder, without knowing what it means to kill, and thus himself brings death to his kind—death, the very name of which, when the future of humanity was revealed to him, had filled him with horror. The deed is repented of before it is done; for Cain, who loves all men, is tenderly attached to Abel. There follow, nevertheless, the curse, the sentence, the banishment, and the mark of Cain.

This mark of Cain is the mark of humanity—the sign of suffering and immortality. Byron's drama represents the struggle between suffering, searching, striving humanity and that God of hosts, of lightnings, and of storms, whose weakened arms are forced to let go a world which is writhing itself free from his embrace. To exterminate this world which denies him, he causes rivers of blood to flow, and hundreds of martyr fires to be kindled by his priests; but Cain rises unscathed from the ashes of the fire, and flagellates the priests with undying scorn. Cain is thinking humanity, which with its thought cleaves the old "firmament of heaven," and beholds millions of spheres rolling in freedom, high above Jehovah's rattling thunder-chariot. Cain is working humanity, which is striving in the sweat of its brow to produce a new and better Eden—not the Eden of ignorance, but an Eden of knowledge and harmony; a humanity which, long after Jehovah has been sewn into His shroud, will be alive, pressing to its breast Abel, who has been restored from the dead.[1]

Cain was dedicated to Sir Walter Scott, who gave it as his opinion that Byron's Muse had never before taken so lofty a flight, and who answered in advance the attacks that were likely to be made on the author. But this did not prevent the appearance of the work being regarded and lamented as a positive national calamity. Before it went to

[1] Compare Leconte de Lisle: *Poèmes barbares. Kaïn.*

press, Murray was anxious that Byron should make some alterations. But Byron wrote: "The two passages cannot be altered without making Lucifer talk like the Bishop of Lincoln, which would not be in the character of the former." Immediately after publication the play was pirated, and Murray applied to Lord Eldon for an injunction to protect his property in the work. The Lord Chancellor refused it in terms which may be epitomised thus: "This court, like the other courts of justice in this country, acknowledges Christianity as part of the law of the land. Its jurisdiction in protecting literary property is founded on this. The publication in question being intended to bring into discredit that portion of Scripture history to which it relates, no damages can be recovered in respect of a piracy of it." Thus *Cain*—like Southey's *Wat Tyler*—was regarded as such a criminal work that the law refused even to vindicate the right of property in it.

Meanwhile, Moore was writing to Byron: "*Cain* is wonderful, terrible, never to be forgotten. If I am not mistaken, it will sink deep into the world's heart." History has endorsed this verdict.

XXI

COMIC AND TRAGIC REALISM

WHEN, in the autumn of 1816, Switzerland began to be overrun by crowds of English tourists, residence there became intolerable to Lord Byron, and he betook himself with Mr. Hobhouse, the travelling companion of his youth, to Italy. At Milan he met Beyle, one of the most acute of observers; and it is a strong proof of the extraordinary impression produced by the poet's personality, that he captivated even this man, who was always on his guard against being led into hasty enthusiasms, and who quickly detected what was assumed in Byron's manner. Beyle writes: "Ce fut pendant l'automne de 1816, que je le rencontrai au théâtre de la *Scala*, à Milan, dans la loge de M. Louis de Brême. Je fus frappé des yeux de Lord Byron au moment où il écoutait un sestetto d'un opéra de Mayer intitulé *Elena*. Je n'ai vu de ma vie rien de plus beau ni de plus expressif. Encore aujourd'hui, si je viens à penser à l'expression qu'un grand peintre devrait donner au génie, cette tête sublime reparaît tout-à-coup devant moi. J'eus un instant d'enthousiasme. . . . Je n'oublierai jamais l'expression divine de ses traits; c'était l'air serein de la puissance et du génie."

From Milan Byron proceeded to Venice, the city which he preferred to all others, and which he has celebrated in the Fourth Canto of *Childe Harold*, in *Marino Faliero*, in *The Two Foscari*, in the *Ode to Venice*, and in *Beppo*, which last work was written in Venice. Never had he been overcome by such deep depression as now; never had forgetfulness been so desirable. The enchanting climate and air of Italy acted on him like a charm. He was twenty-nine. With its beautiful women, its loose morals, and all its southern manners and customs, Venice invited to a wild revel of the senses. An ardent longing for happiness and enjoyment was part of Byron's nature; and it is also to be remembered that his defiant temper had been thoroughly roused. He had been stigmatised as capable of every enormity; he might just as well, for once, give his countrymen abroad something real to write home about, and the old women at home real cause to swoon; they wrote and they swooned whatever his behaviour was.

His first proceedings in Venice were to engage a gondola and gondolier, a box at the theatre, and a mistress. The last was easily found. He had taken apartments in the house of a merchant, whose wife, Marianna Segati, then aged twenty-two, he describes as having large, black, Oriental eyes and being in "appearance altogether like an antelope." She and Byron became so enamoured of each other, that Byron allowed Hobhouse to go on alone to Rome. "I should have gone too," he writes, "but I fell in love, and must stay that over." The young beauty compelled him to join, in her company, in all the distractions of the Carnival. He devoted his nights, like the born Venetian, to pleasure; but in his fear of becoming stout, he adhered to his usual extremely sparing diet, ate only vegetables and fruit, and was obliged to drink large quantities of his favourite beverage, rum and water, to keep up his strength. For he was completing *Manfred* at this time. We receive a sad impression of the aimlessness of his life when we read that, to counterbalance all the distractions, to give his days a centre of gravity, he spent several hours of each at the Armenian monastery of San Lazaro, learning Armenian from the monks. The mornings were devoted to this, the afternoons to physical exercise, chiefly riding. He had his horses brought to Venice, and with Shelley and other friends used to cross over to the Lido and ride there.

We have a reminiscence of the talk during these rides in Shelley's *Julian and Maddalo.* At sunset he and Byron see on one of the islands a dreary, windowless pile, rising in dark relief against the flaming sky behind it. They hear, clanging from the open tower on the top of the house, the iron tongue of a bell. Said Byron :—

> "What we behold
> Shall be the madhouse and its belfry tower,
> . . . . . . and ever at this hour
> Those who may cross the water, hear that bell
> Which calls the maniacs, each one from his cell
> To vespers. . . . .
> And like that black and dreary bell, the soul
> Hung in a heaven-illumined tower, must toll
> Our thoughts and our desires to meet below
> Round the rent heart and pray—as madmen do
> For what—they know not."

No better image of Byron's own life at this period could be desired. Most assuredly at this time his longings and desires were like maniacs, all gathered together only once a day by the bell of the madhouse.

It was with difficulty, after being ill with a sharp fever, contracted in the unhealthy air of Venice, that he tore himself away from Marianna Segati long enough to pay a short visit to Ferrara and Rome. After his return, however, his violent passion for her subsided, as he began to discover that she sold the jewellery he gave her, and made as much profit generally as she could, out of her position as his mistress. During the first part of his stay in Venice, Byron had mixed much in the refined society which had its chief meeting-place at the house of the cultivated, literary Countess Albrizzi; now he withdrew himself entirely from its restraining influence. He rented for himself and his menagerie a magnificent palace on the Grand Canal. This palace soon became a harem, in which the favourite sultana was a beautiful young woman of the lower orders, Margarita Cogni, who, from the circumstance of her husband being a baker, was called Byron's Fornarina. Her face was of "the fine Venetian cast of the old time"; her figure, though she was perhaps rather tall, was also fine, and exactly suited the national dress. She had all the naïveté and droll humour of the Venetian lower classes, and, as she could neither read nor write, she could not plague Byron with letters. She was jealous; she snatched off the masks of ladies whom she found in Byron's company, and she sought his presence whenever it suited her, with no great regard to time, place, or persons. He writes: "When I first knew her, I was in 'relazione' with la Signora ——, who was silly enough one evening at Dolo, accompanied by some of her female friends, to threaten her. . . . Margarita threw back her veil (fazziolo), and replied in very explicit Venetian, '*You* are *not* his *wife*. *I* am *not* his *wife*: you are his Donna, and *I* am his *Donna*: your husband is a *becco*, and mine is another. For the rest, what *right* have you to reproach me? If he prefers me to you, is it my fault?' Having delivered this pretty piece of eloquence, she went on her way, leaving a numerous audience with Madame —— to ponder at her leisure on the dialogue between them." In time Margarita established herself as housekeeper in Byron's house, reduced the expenses of the establishment to less than half, marched about in a gown with a train, and wore a hat with feathers (articles of dress which had been the height of her ambition), beat the maids, opened Byron's letters, and actually studied her alphabet in order to be able to detect which of them were from ladies. In her wild way she loved him; her joy at seeing him return safe from a sail in which his boat had been caught in a storm, was that of a tigress over her returned cubs. Her ungovernableness increased to such an extent that Byron was obliged to tell her that she must return home. After trying to attack him with a knife, she threw herself in her anger and despair into the canal. She was rescued and sent home, and Byron wrote her story at full length to Murray; he knew that his letters to his publisher were passed from hand to hand like public documents; and half the pleasure of his excesses consisted in the certainty of their creating a scandal in England.

From the letter just quoted it is easy to see that the dissolute Venetian life did not absorb him heart and soul; he quite saw the comic side of it all. And it was actually of service in furthering his development as a thinker and a poet. His friends at home were in despair at the way in which he was compromising his dignity and his reputation; but this wild, jovial, Carnival life, lived amongst the women of the people under the bright Italian skies, was producing a new, realistic style in his poetry. In the works of his youth he had, sadly, and with a heart wrung with anguish, described the ebb-tide of life; in *Beppo* the spring-tide suddenly began to rise. *Beppo* was real life, in a setting of laughter and jest. In Byron's youthful pathos there had been a certain monotony, along with a good deal of artificiality. In this work his genius, as it were, sloughed its skin; the monotony was broken by a constant change of theme and key, the artificiality was dispelled by hearty laughter. In his youthful satire there had been a good deal of snappishness and a decided lack of grace and humour. Now that his own life had for a short time assumed the character of a Carnival play, the Graces, of their own accord, came tripping and twining through his verses, keeping time to the tinkling of the bells of humour.

Beppo is the "Carnival of Venice" itself—that old theme which Byron, like another Paganini, found upon his way, lifted on the point of his divine bow, and proceeded to adorn with a multitude of daring and ingenious variations, with a luxurious embroidery of pearls and golden arabesques. There had come into his hands an English comic poem on the subject of King Arthur and the Knights of the Round Table, in which the Honourable John Hookham Frere had imitated the first poem written in the *ottava rima* (Berni's paraphrase of *Orlando Furioso*). The reading of Frere's work aroused in Byron the desire to attempt something in the same style, and the result was *Beppo*, the complete originality of which effaced every recollection of a model. Now he had found the form which suited his purpose, the weapon which he could wield with the most effect—the *ottava rima*, with its sextett of alternate rhymes, to the solid mass of which the concluding rhymed couplet adds now a jest, now a key, now a stylistic antic, now a stinging wit-dart.

And what is the poem about? About just as little as Alfred de Musset's *Namouna*, or Paludan-Müller's *Danserinden*, which were written in much the same style sixteen years later (1833). The story in itself is nothing: A Venetian goes to sea, and stays so long away that his wife makes sure he is dead. She has long been as good as married to another man, when he suddenly turns up again. He has been sold as a Turkish slave, and, on his return, dressed as a Turk, he finds his wife at a masked ball, on the arm of the Count who has now for several years filled his place. When the couple, returning from the ball, step out of their gondola, they find the husband standing at the door of his own house. As soon as all three have recovered a little from the first surprise, they call for three cups of coffee, and conversation begins in the following style, Laura speaking:

> "Beppo! what's your pagan name?
> Bless me! your beard is of amazing growth!
> And how came you to keep away so long?
> Are you not sensible 'twas very wrong?
>
> "And are you *really*, *truly*, now a Turk?
> With any other women did you wive?
> Is't true they use their fingers for a fork?
> Well, that's the prettiest shawl!—as I'm alive!
> You'll give it me! They say you eat no pork," &c. &c.

This is all the explanation the husband receives, or asks. As he cannot go about dressed as a Turk, he borrows a pair of trousers from Laura's *cavaliere servente*, the Count, and the story ends in perfect amicability on all sides. In itself it is of little importance, but it was Byron's study for his masterpiece, *Don Juan*—the only one of his works which, as it were, contains the whole wide ocean of life, with its storms and its sunshine, its ebb and its flood.

Byron's friends tried every means in their power to induce him to return to England, in the hope of thereby reclaiming him from the life he was leading. But instead of returning he sold Newstead Abbey, which in his youth he had vowed he would never part with (receiving £94,000 for it). Indeed, so strong was his antipathy to the thought of return, that he could not even bear the idea of being taken back as a corpse. "I trust," he writes, "they won't think of 'pickling, and bringing me home to Clod or Blunderbuss Hall.' I am sure my bones would not rest in an English grave, or my clay mix with the earth of that country. I believe the thought would drive me mad on my deathbed, could I suppose that any of my friends would be base enough to convey my carcass back to your soil. I would not even feed your worms, if I could help it."

But now occurred an event which in an unforeseen manner put an end to the polygamy in which Byron was living in Venice—an event that constituted a turning-point in his life. In April 1819, he was presented to Countess Teresa Guiccioli, daughter of Count Gamba of Ravenna, a lady who was at this time only sixteen, and had just been married to Count Guiccioli, a man of sixty, who had been twice left a widower. The introduction took place against the inclination of both; the young Countess was tired that evening and longed to go home, and Byron was unwilling to make new acquaintances; both assented only from the desire to oblige their hostess. But no sooner had they entered into conversation than a spark, which was never extinguished, passed from soul to soul. The Countess afterwards wrote:—"His noble and exquisitely beautiful countenance, the tone of his voice, his manners, the thousand enchantments that surrounded him, rendered him so different and so superior a being to any whom I had hitherto seen, that it was impossible he should not have left the most profound impression upon me. From that evening, during the whole of my subsequent stay at Venice, we met every day."

A few weeks later, Teresa was obliged to return with her husband to Ravenna. The parting with Byron agitated her so terribly that during the course of the first day's journey she fainted several times; and she became so ill that she arrived at Ravenna half dead. She was also much distressed at this time by the loss of her mother. The Count owned several houses on the road from Venice to Ravenna, and it was his habit to stop at these mansions, one after the other, on his journeys between the two cities. From each the enamoured young Countess now wrote to Byron, expressing in the most passionate and pathetic terms her despair at leaving him, and entreating him to come to Ravenna. Very touching is the description which she gives, after her arrival, of the complete change in all her feelings. She, who formerly had thought of nothing but balls and fêtes, has, she says, been so entirely changed by her love that solitude has become dear and welcome to her. She will, according to Byron's wish, "avoid all general society, and devote herself to reading, music, domestic occupations, riding"—everything, in short, that she knew he would most like. Longing and grief brought on a dangerous fever, and symptoms of consumption showed themselves. Then Byron set out for Ravenna. He found the Countess in bed, apparently in a very serious condition. He writes: "I greatly fear that she is going into a consumption. . . . Thus it is with every thing and every body for whom I feel anything like a real attachment. . . . If anything happens to my present Amica, I have done with the passion for ever—it is my last love. As to libertinism, I have sickened myself of that, as was natural in the way I went on, and I have at least derived that advantage from vice, to *love* in the better sense of the word." The attitude assumed towards the young foreigner by the Count astonished every one; he showed him all manner of polite attentions; used to come for him every day with a "coach and six," and drive about the country with him, like "Whittington with his cat," Byron declared.

It was a happy time for Byron. This, his one perfect and fully returned attachment, brought back all the emotions of his youth. The beautiful *Stanzas to the Po*, which reveal deep, chivalrous feeling, and end with the prayer, "Let me perish young!" were the first-fruits of the new passion. He loved truly and with his whole heart, and loved like a youth, without at any point taking up a position outside of his feeling or attempting to rise superior to it. When, in August, the Countess was obliged to accompany her husband on his visits to his other estate, Byron went daily to her house, and, causing her apartments to be opened, sat turning over her books and writing in them. On the last page of a copy of *Corinne* he wrote the following note:—

MY DEAREST TERESA—I have read this book in your garden;—my love, you were absent, or else I could not have read it. It is a favourite book of yours, and the writer was a friend of mine. You will not understand these English words, and *others* will not understand them—which is the reason I have not scrawled them in Italian. But you will recognise the handwriting of him who so passionately loved you, and you will divine that, over a book which was yours, he could only think of love. In that word, beautiful in all languages, but most so in yours—*Amor mio*—is comprised my existence here and hereafter. . . . Think of me, sometimes, when the Alps and the ocean divide us,—but they never will, unless you *wish* it. BYRON.

BOLOGNA, *August* 25, 1819.

It is needless to compare the expressions in this note with those of the farewell letter to Lady Caroline Lamb; one feels at once that this is the language of a truer love.

When, in September, Count Guiccioli was called away by business to Ravenna, he left the young Countess and her lover to the free enjoyment of each other's society at Bologna; and he was quite agreeable, when the physicians ordered her to Venice, that Lord Byron should be the companion of her journey. Byron had a villa at La Mira, near Venice; he placed it at her disposal, and resided there with her. Of the journey and the ensuing period she wrote to Moore after Byron's death: "But I cannot linger over these recollections of happiness;—the contrast with the present is too dreadful. If a blessed spirit, while in the full enjoyment of heavenly happiness, were sent down to this earth to suffer all its miseries, the contrast could not be more dreadful between the past and the present, than what I have endured from the moment when that terrible word reached my ears, and I for ever lost the hope of again beholding him, one look from whom I valued beyond all earth's happiness."

The woman to whom the world owes a debt of gratitude for having saved Byron from ruining himself by degrading dissipation, lost her standing in the eyes of Italian society from the moment when she took up her residence in her lover's house. The Italian moral code of that day—of which De Stendhal's Italian tales give an excellent idea—permitted a young married woman to have a friend (*Amico*); and, indeed, regarded him practically as her husband, but only on the condition that those outward conventions were respected, which Countess Guiccioli was now disregarding.

It was not light-mindedness that led her to expose herself to the censure of public opinion. She saw her own relation to Lord Byron in a poetic light; she regarded it as her mission to free a noble and gifted poet from the fetters of ignoble connections, and to restore his faith in pure and self-sacrificing love. She hoped to act on him as a Muse. She was very young, and very beautiful—fair, with dark eyes; small, but beautifully proportioned. West, the American painter, to whom Byron sat for his portrait at the Villa Rossa, near Pisa, gives the following description of her:—"Whilst I was painting, the window from which I received my light became suddenly darkened, and I heard a voice exclaim: '*E troppo bello!*' I turned, and discovered a beautiful female stooping down to look in, the ground on the outside being on a level with the bottom of the window. Her long golden hair hung down about her face and shoulders, her complexion was exquisite, and her smile completed one of the most romantic-looking heads, set off as it was by the bright sun behind it, which I had ever beheld." The more important it became to the Countess not to be regarded simply as one of Byron's many mistresses, the more did she endeavour to raise his poetry into a higher and purer atmosphere than that in which it moved at this time.

One evening when he was sitting turning over the leaves of the manuscript of *Don Juan*, two cantos of which had been completed before his acquaintance with the Countess began, she leant over his shoulder, pointed to a verse on the page he was just turning, and asked him what it meant. "She had stumbled," writes Byron, "by mere chance on the 137th stanza of the First Canto. I told her 'Nothing; but your husband is coming.' As I said this in Italian with some emphasis, she started up in a fright, and said, 'Oh, my God, is he coming?' thinking it was her own." But this accident aroused her curiosity regarding *Don Juan*; she read the two cantos in a French translation; her delicacy was shocked by the indecency of much of the contents, and she implored Byron not to go on with the poem. He at once promised what his *Dictatrice* demanded. This was Countess Guiccioli's first direct influence upon Byron's work—and it was certainly not a beneficial one; but she soon withdrew her prohibition, on the condition, however, that there should be no obscenity in the part as yet unwritten. A whole series of fine works which now proceeded from Byron's pen are the beautiful and enduring mementos of his life with her. The manner in which in *Don Juan* he tore the veil from all illusions, and mercilessly mocked at sentimentality, wounded the Countess's womanly feelings; for woman is ever unwilling that the illusions which, as long as they last, beautify life, should be rudely dispelled.

Countess Guiccioli, thus, did her utmost to prevent Byron writing works calculated to destroy belief in human nature and the value of life. The themes which she, the romantic lover of the grand, and the ardent Italian patriot, led him to choose, were themes calculated to elevate her countrymen's minds and quicken their desire for the emancipation of their country from a foreign yoke. It was to gratify her that he wrote *The Prophecy of Dante*, and translated from the *Inferno* the famous episode of *Francesca of Rimini*; and it was under her influence that he wrote the Venetian dramas, *Marino Faliero* and *The Two Foscari*, plays which, though they are written in English, really belong, from their style and subject, rather to Romance than to English literature—just as they belong, as a matter of fact, to the Italian, not the English, stage. They are plays with a passionate political purpose, written in careless, and occasionally ill-sounding iambics. Their aim was, by the employment of the strongest means possible, to excite the lethargic Italian patriots to unanimous revolt against the oppressors. They are scenically effective. Whilst under the first impression of his attachment to the Countess, Byron also wrote *Mazeppa*, the heroine of which bears her name; and her personality was directly transferred to the two best and most beautiful female characters which he created at this period—Adah in *Cain*, and Myrrha in *Sardanapalus*.

In Countess Guiccioli Byron found the realisation of the

ideal of femininity which had always been before his eyes, but which in his earlier narrative poems he had not succeeded in portraying naturally. He himself naïvely confessed to Lady Blessington the difficulty in which he found himself, and the manner in which he personified his ideals. "I detest thin women," he said; "and unfortunately all, or nearly all plump women have clumsy hands and feet, so that I am obliged to have recourse to imagination for my beauties, and there I always find them. I flatter myself that my Leila, Zuleika, Gulnare, Medora, and Haidée will always vouch for my taste in beauty; these are the bright creations of my fancy, with rounded forms, and delicacy of limbs, nearly so incompatible as to be rarely, if ever, united. . . . You must have observed that I give my heroines extreme refinement, joined to great simplicity and want of education. Now, refinement and want of education are incompatible, at least, I have ever found them so: so here again, you see, I am forced to have recourse to imagination." The concoctions were as impossible as they were beautiful; these fair ones produced next to no impression of reality, herein resembling the heroes whom they worshipped.

From *The Giaour* to *The Siege of Corinth*, Byron's narrative poems are of the Romantic type, but bear the imprint of a strong individuality. Passion is idolised in both sexes. The heroes are, to borrow an expression from *The Giaour*, "wracks, by passion left behind"; but "wracks" which choose rather to continue being tossed by its tempests than to live in drowsy tranquillity. They do not love with the cold love begotten of a cold climate; theirs "is like a lava flood." The most characteristic of these now extremely antiquated Byronic heroes is the noble Corsair—who is proud, capricious, scornful, revengeful to the point of cruelty, a prey to remorse, and so nobly magnanimous that he will rather submit to the most barbarous tortures than kill a sleeping enemy. This interesting bandit, with his mysterious countenance, his theatrical deportment, and his boundless chivalry towards woman, is the Byronic counterpart of Schiller's Karl Moor. The sovereign of a law-abiding people, hampered by the conventions of a court, could not be Byron's ideal man ; there was no possibility in such a life of romantic exploits, of perils by land or by water. So he took a pirate chieftain, and, to the qualities induced by such a man's manner of life, superadded the finest qualities of his own soul. The Corsair, who is accustomed to wade in blood, turns with a shudder from the young Sultana who loves him, when he sees the little spot of blood on her forehead—not because it is imaginable that a Conrad would have shuddered at so little, but because Byron himself would have shrunk from such a sight. It has been cleverly said that the real reason of the marvellous attraction of all the heroes and heroines of these poems of Byron's youth for the general public was, that they all moved where they had no joints. The public were not more enraptured by the passion of the lyric portions and by the poetical gems inserted here and there (almost always during the process of proof-reading), than by the deeds which were really impossible to human nature. It was admiration of the same kind as is displayed for the daring acrobat, who does breakneck feats by unnatural contortions of his body.

But in these same characters some of the finer, deeper-lying qualities of Byron's ideal also revealed themselves. Conrad's inflexibility under suffering foreshadows Manfred's ; and he will no more bow the knee than will Cain to Lucifer, or Don Juan to Gulbeyaz. Compassion for those less fortunately situated than himself, a feeling which never disappeared from Byron's soul, exists, though chiefly in the shape of hatred of despots, in Lara ; and in both *The Giaour* and *The Siege of Corinth* we have the longing for the emancipation of Greece. It was a strange ordering of destiny that the poet himself should end his life as a commander of just such wild men as those he had described. The Viking blood in his veins gave him no rest until he himself became a Viking leader, like the Normans from whom he was descended. And even if all these desperadoes (Alp, the renegade, who leads the Turks against his countrymen, no less than Lara, who makes war on his peers) are simply the imaginary creatures of the poet's brain, there is in the characters of all, one realistic trait, a trait which also develops in those who attach themselves to them—the proud endurance of terrible fates. The humour of *Beppo* is the form in which naturalness overcomes the staginess and artificiality of Byron's earlier works. The sympathy with human suffering, which in his serious poetry gradually swallows up all other sympathies, is the form in which the feeling of the reality of life prevails over his Romanticism and supersedes it.

This feeling gained in intensity after his breach with England. *The Prisoner of Chillon* had described the suffering of the noble Bonnivard, who for six long years was chained to a pillar in an underground dungeon by a chain too short to allow of his lying down, and compelled to witness the agonies and death of his brothers, who were fettered in the same manner, without being able to put out his hand to help them. On it followed *Mazeppa*—the youth bound to the back of the wild horse, which gallops with dripping mane and steaming flanks through the forests and across the steppes, whilst he, torn from the arms of his beloved, whose fate is unknown to him, and looking forward to a horrible fate himself, suffers agonies of thirst, pain, and shame. So far Byron has by preference dwelt upon the things that are most terrible to flesh and blood; even when, as in the case of Bonnivard, there was a spiritual element in the suffering, and the theme presented an opportunity for the description of a heroic personality, he dwelt most on the purely physical torture. But now that his sympathies were aroused for the great martyrs of Italy, his conception of the tragic was ennobled.

In *The Prophecy of Dante* he thus describes the lot of the poet:—

"Many are poets, but without the name,
For what is poesy but to create
From overfeeling good or ill; and aim
At an external life beyond our fate,
And be the new Prometheus of new men,
Bestowing fire from heaven, and then, too late,
Finding the pleasure given repaid with pain,
And vultures to the heart of the bestower,
Who, having lavish'd his high gift in vain,
Lies chain'd to his lone rock by the sea-shore."

And he makes the great poet, who was, like himself, unjustly exiled, exclaim :

> 'Tis the doom
> Of spirits of my order to be rack'd
> In life, to wear their hearts out, and consume
> Their days in endless strife, and die alone."

Of Tasso Byron had already written. Even a superficial comparison of Goethe's *Tasso* with Byron's *Lament of Tasso* is sufficient to show us what a resistless attraction hopeless suffering had for Byron's imagination. Goethe takes Tasso the youth, the lover, the poet, and places him in the society of the beautiful women of the court of Ferrara, where, happy and unhappy, he is admired and humiliated. Byron takes Tasso alone, ruined, shut out from society, shut into the cell of a madhouse though he is quite sane, a prey to the cruelty of his former protectors:—

> "I loved all solitude—but little thought
> To spend I know not what of life, remote
> From all communion with existence, save
> The maniac and his tyrant ;—had I been
> Their fellow, many years ere this had seen
> My mind like theirs corrupted to its grave.
> But who hath seen me writhe, or heard me rave?
> Perchance in such a cell we suffer more
> Than the wreck'd sailor on his desert shore ;
> The world is all before him—*mine* is *here*,
> Scarce twice the space they must accord my bier.
> What though *he* perish, he may lift his eye,
> And with a dying glance upbraid the sky ;
> I will not raise my own in such reproof,
> Although 'tis clouded by my dungeon roof."

Of the court of Ferrara, a court where Lucrezia Borgia has her residence, a court where the passions and the cruelty of the Renaissance period flourish, Goethe makes a little German Weimar, where everything is ruled by the most refined humanitarianism of the eighteenth century ; Byron is magnetically attracted by what he considers the revolting barbarity of the Duke of Ferrara, and his poem turns into a declamation against the injustice and tyranny of princes.

We have another description of tragic suffering, along with still more violent accusation—both, however, decidedly overdone—in *The Two Foscari*, a tragedy in which a father is compelled to sentence the son he loves to the agonies of the torture-chamber, and in which the son, who is the hero of the tragedy, is stretched on the rack during almost the whole duration of the play, and only rises from it to die of grief because he is banished. In *The Two Foscari*, as in his other tragedies, Byron, as if in defiance, follows the French fashion of strict adherence to the Aristotelian rules. In his conviction that this is the one right style, he risks the comical paradox, that England has hitherto possessed no drama.

It has created much surprise that Byron, who, like all the other English poets of the day, was a pronounced Naturalist—which means that he preferred the forest to the garden, the unsophisticated to the civilised human being, the original to the acquired language of passion—that this same Byron should have been such an enthusiastic admirer of Pope and of the small group of poets (including Samuel Rogers and Crabbe) who still paid homage to classical tradition, even to the extent of imitating the antique dramatic style.

The first reason for the admiration of Pope is to be sought in Byron's spirit of contradiction. The fact that the poets of that Lake School which he despised were continually reviling Pope, was in itself a sufficient reason for his exalting him to the skies, calling him the greatest of all English poets, and declaring that he would willingly himself defray the expense of erecting a monument to him in the Poet's Corner of Westminster Abbey, from which, as a Catholic, he was excluded. Secondly, we have to remember that the traditions of Harrow never lost their influence over Byron; and at Harrow Pope had always been held up as the model poet. A third thing to be remembered is Byron's own great deficiency in critical acumen, as an instance of which we may take his remark to Lady Blessington that Shakespeare owed half his fame to his low birth. There still remain the predisposing circumstances—that Pope was deformed, and in spite of his deformity had a beautiful head; that he did not belong to the Established Church; that he was the poet of good society; and that his deformity begot in him a certain satirical gloom—all things in which Byron sympathised with him. And, lastly, we have Byron's personal bias (possibly attributable to his Norman descent) towards rhetoric of the style peculiar to the Latin races.

The circumstance that Byron championed the art theories of a past age, whilst he in everything else belonged to the party of progress, produces a certain likeness between him and Armand Carrel, who also remained faithful to antiquated classicism in literature, though he held the most emancipated views in politics and religion. As both of them adopted the standpoint of eighteenth century France in most matters intellectual and spiritual, it was not unnatural that they should also conform to it in the only domain in which it was a conventional standpoint, namely, that of *belles-lettres*. Certain it is that his theoretical caprices had a baneful influence on Byron's Italian dramas. These consist of monologues and declamation. Byron's genius and Countess Guiccioli's patriotism combined did not suffice to communicate to them more than a very meagre quantum of poetic inspiration.

But during the production of *Cain* and *Sardanapalus* the young Countess was what it was her desire to be, Byron's Muse.

The best thing in *Cain* is the character of Adah. It has been often remarked that Byron's male characters all resemble one another; what his critics have been less apt to observe is, how dissimilar his women are. Adah is not a female Cain, though she is the one imaginable wife for him. Cain's female counterpart is the proud, defiant Aholibamah of *Heaven and Earth*. Cain sees annihilation everywhere; Adah sees growth, love, germinating power, happiness. To Cain, the cypress which spreads its branches above little Enoch's head is a tree of mourning; all Adah sees is that it gives shade to the child. After Cain has despairingly made it plain to himself and Adah that all the world's evils and misfortunes are to be transmitted through Enoch, Adah says:

> "Oh, Cain, look on him; see how full of life,
> Of strength, of bloom, of beauty, and of joy,
> How like to me—how like to thee, when gentle!"

Out of so little is Adah made, that all her speeches put together would not occupy one octavo page. When Cain has to make his choice between love and knowledge, she says: "Oh, Cain! choose love." When Cain, having killed Abel, stands alone, cursed and avoided as a murderer, she answers his ejaculation of: "Leave me!" with the words: "Why, all have left thee." And this character Byron created almost without departing from the letter of the Bible, simply by sometimes putting what is really said by one into the mouth of another. In Genesis, Cain, when he has been cursed by the Lord, says: "My punishment is greater than I can bear," &c. In Byron's play, Cain, when the terrible curse of the angel has fallen, stands mute; but Adah lifts up her voice and says:

> "This punishment is more than he can bear.
> Behold, thou driv'st him from the face of earth,
> And from the face of God shall he be hid.
> A fugitive and vagabond on earth,
> 'Twill come to pass that whoso findeth him
> Shall slay him"—

the exact words which the Bible puts into the mouth of Cain. Byron, with the eye of genius, saw in this one utterance, this Old Testament lump of clay, the outlines of a whole human figure; and with nothing but the pressure of his hand moulded it into a statuette of the first loving woman.

The other character in which we feel, and feel still more strongly, the influence of the young Countess, is Myrrha, the Greek female slave in *Sardanapalus*. *Sardanapalus* is the best of Byron's historical tragedies.—With careless contempt for his fellow-men and the world in general, the proud Sardanapalus has given himself up to voluptuous pleasures. Martial fame he despises; he cares not to win a great name by shedding the blood of thousands of unoffending human beings; and as little does he desire to be worshipped, like his fathers, as a god. His careless magnanimity amounts to imprudence. He returns to the rebel priest the sword which has been snatched from him, with the words:

> "Receive your sword, and know
> That I prefer your service militant
> Unto your ministry—not loving either."

His manly vigour appears to be ebbing away in a life of voluptuous enjoyment, when Myrrha, the Ionian, his favourite slave, determines to rescue him. She implores him to rouse himself, and prepare to defend himself against his enemies. It is almost as great a grief to her that she loves him as that she is a slave.

> "Why do I love this man? My country's daughters
> Love none but heroes. But I have no country!
> The slave has lost all save her bonds. I love him;
> And that's the heaviest link of the long chain—
> To love whom we esteem not. . . . .
> And yet methinks I love him more, perceiving
> That he is hated of his own barbarians."

But when the enemies attack the palace, and Sardanapalus, after rejecting the clumsy sword as hurting his hand, and the heavy helmet as "a mountain on his temples," plunges bareheaded and lightly armed into the midst of the fray and fights like a hero, Myrrha triumphs as if a burden of shame were lifted from her heart:—

> "'Tis no dishonour—no—
> 'Tis no dishonour to have loved this man.
> . . . .
> . . . . If Alcides
> Were shamed in wearing Lydian Omphale's
> She-garb, and wielding her vile distaff, surely
> He, who springs up a Hercules at once,
> Nursed in effeminate arts from youth to manhood,
> And rushes from the banquet to the battle,
> As though it were a bed of love, deserves
> That a Greek girl should be his paramour,
> And a Greek bard his minstrel, a Greek tomb
> His monument."

It is as if Byron were prophesying his own fate. And was it not true of the poet, as of his hero, that he had known a thousand women, but never a true woman's heart till now?

"MYRRHA. Then thou wouldst know what thou canst never know.
SARDANAPALUS. And that is——
MYRRHA. The true value of a heart;
At least, a woman's.
SARDANAPALUS. I have proved a thousand—
A thousand, and a thousand.
MYRRHA. Hearts?
SARDANAPALUS. I think so.
MYRRHA. Not one! The time may come thou may'st."

Like Myrrha, the young Italian Countess set before her lover more manly aims than voluptuous enjoyment; like Myrrha, she rescued him from a life which was unworthy of his great and noble mind.

We left the lovers at the country house of La Mira, near Venice, where Byron wrote, amongst other things, the Memoirs which he presented to Thomas Moore, to be left as a legacy to the latter's little son, but which were burned at the instigation of Byron's family, and for reasons which have never been satisfactorily explained. The peaceful life at La Mira was not of long duration. Count Guiccioli suddenly determined that he would put an end to the existing state of matters. The Countess would not give up Byron, and a separation from her husband was the result. With the consent of her family, she relinquished fortune and position in society; a small yearly allowance was to be paid her; but the conditions of the separation only held good as long as she continued to reside in her father's house. Here Byron regularly spent his evenings with her; he loved to hear her play, or sing airs by Mozart or Rossini. His diary of January and February 1821 chiefly consists of the following regularly repeated entries: "Rode—fired pistols—dined—wrote—visited—heard music—talked nonsense—went home—read."

As long as Count Guiccioli was still playing the rôle of possible avenger, the situation had contained the element of danger and excitement which to Byron was the spice of life. He believed that he owed his safety from assassination in the course of his rides to the fact of his being known to carry pistols and to have an unerring aim, and from assassination at home to the avaricious Count's disinclination to pay the twenty scudi which were the hire of a first-class bravo. This excitement was now at an end, but there was substituted for it a new and nobler one.

The whole Italian peninsula was in a state of silent but violent ferment. After the overthrow of Napoleon's rule, the old rulers "by the grace of God" had at once begun to conduct themselves with overweening arrogance. Every trace of French influence in the shape of beneficent reform was to be effaced, and the old abuses were to be re-introduced. The unbearable oppression during the general European reaction which followed the formation of the Holy Alliance, drove the Italians to form a wide-spread conspiracy; great secret leagues of the Carbonari, imitated from those of the Freemasons, were soon in existence in all parts of the country.

The Countess introduced Byron into the circle of the conspirators. The whole Gamba family belonged to the secret society. The Countess's brother, Pietro, a warm-hearted youth of twenty, who was an enthusiastic admirer of Byron and eventually accompanied him to Greece, was one of its most ardent and best-informed leaders. Carbonarism seemed to Byron the poetry of politics. The wooden Parliamentary politics of his native country had repelled him, but this appealed strongly to his imagination. He was advanced to a high rank in the society, and was made chief of a division called the Americani. He provided the conspirators with supplies of weapons, and offered the "constitutional" government at Naples one thousand Louis-d'ors as his contribution to the expenses of carrying on the war against the Holy Alliance. His letters display positive fury with the Austrian tyrants. Wherever he resided, he was an eyesore to the Austrian authorities; his letters were opened; the Italian translation of *Childe Harold* was prohibited in the Austrian provinces of Italy; and the police, as he well knew, were incited to assassinate him. Nevertheless, he calmly took his usual ride every day. On this, as on other occasions, his conduct and language were distinguished by a mixture of stoic heroism and boyish bravado. There is something attractively boyish in his writing to Murray: "I wonder if they can read my letters when they have opened them; if so, they may see, in my MOST LEGIBLE HAND, THAT I THINK THEM DAMNED SCOUNDRELS AND BARBARIANS, and THEIR EMPEROR A FOOL." When proclamation was made that extremely severe penalties would be incurred by all in whose houses weapons were found, he stored the weapons of all the conspirators of the Romagna in his villa, which became a regular arsenal. The cupboards and drawers were crammed with the revolutionary proclamations and oath-formulas. He thought, and thought rightly, that the authorities would hardly dare to search the house of a member of the English House of Peers.

It was easier for them to drive him away than to imprison him; it was done simply by ordering the Counts Gamba to leave the country within twenty-four hours. It being one of the agreements of the separation that the young Countess was to be obliged, if she left her father's house, to enter a convent, the authorities felt sure that the step they were taking was a sure means of getting rid of Byron. Teresa's letter to her lover on hearing of this order ends thus: "Byron! I am in despair!—If I must leave you here without knowing when I shall see you again, if it is your will that I should suffer so cruelly, I am resolved to remain. They may put me in a convent; I shall die—but—but then you cannot aid me, and I cannot reproach you. I know not what they tell me, for my agitation overwhelms me; and why? Not because I fear my present danger, but solely, I call Heaven to witness, solely because I must leave you."[1]

[1] The long work, *Lord Byron Jugé par les Témoins de sa Vie*, which Countess Guiccioli published in 1868, though it does not really help us to understand either Byron's character or his art, bears touching evidence to the strength and depth of the Countess's love. The solution of the problem which the world calls Byron, is, for her, contained in one word: He was an *angel*—beautiful as an angel; good as an angel; an angel in everything. The 1100 pages of the book are divided into chapters bearing the titles of his different virtues; one is consecrated to his philanthropy, another to his modesty, &c., &c. The chapter upon his faults proves in the most

The fortune into possession of which Byron came through his marriage, and which, strange to say, he had no scruples in keeping; another fortune, produced by the sale of Newstead; and the £20,000 which he had in course of time received from Murray in payment of his poems, had placed him in a position to exercise benevolence on a grand scale. When it was reported that he intended to leave Ravenna, the poor of the neighbourhood sent a petition to the Cardinal Legate that he might be allowed to remain. But it was this very devotion of the people to him that made him dangerous to the Government. He removed from Ravenna to Pisa. The Tuscan Government being quite as much afraid of Byron and the Gambas as was the Government of the Papal States, there was soon another expulsion, and the party proceeded to Genoa, Byron's last place of residence in Italy.

satisfactory manner that he had none. The description given of his person corresponds to that of his character. We have separate disquisitions on the beauty of his voice, of his nose, of his lips. It is incomprehensible how such a shameful aspersion can have been spread abroad as that Lord Byron was lame or had a club-foot. His limp was so slight that it was impossible to detect which foot caused it; and his lordship's shoemaker, who still owns the last on which his boots were made when he lived at Newstead, bears witness (his attestation being appended) to the slightness of the defect. It is equally incomprehensible how the foolish report can have found credence, that Lord Byron's hair had begun in his later years to recede from his forehead; certainly that part of his head was rather bare, but simply for the reason that he chose to have it shaved. Another unaccountable and foolish falsehood is the assertion that his legs grew very thin. Certainly they were thinner in the last years of his life than they had been when he was younger; but was that at all remarkable in a man who spent most of his leisure hours on horseback?—When we remember that this book was published forty-four years after Byron's death we cannot but acknowledge that the love which inspired it was strong and lasting.

XXII

CULMINATION OF NATURALISM

IN the period between 1818 and 1823 Byron wrote *Don Juan*. Immediately after the first part of the manuscript reached England, he was inundated by communications from friends and critics who had been allowed to see it—expressions of consternation, entreaties to omit this or that, deprecations of the immorality of the poem. Immorality!—that was the cry Byron had to hear at each step of his life, and which pursued him after death; their immorality was made the pretext for burning his memoirs, and his immorality the pretext for refusing his statue a place in Westminster Abbey. Byron replies in a letter to Murray: "If they had told me the poetry was bad, I would have acquiesced; but they say the contrary, and then talk to me about morality—the first time I ever heard the word from anybody who was not a rascal that used it for a purpose. I maintain that it is the most moral of poems; but if people won't discover the moral, that is their fault, not mine . . . I will have none of your damned cutting and slashing. If you please you may publish *anonymously;* it will perhaps be better; but I will battle my way against them all, like a porcupine."

This poem, which, with its savage dedication to Southey, had to be published, not only anonymously, but actually without any publisher's name on the title-page, and which, as Byron said, had more difficulty in making its way into an English drawing-room than a camel in passing through the eye of a needle, is the one poem of the nineteenth century which can be compared with Goethe's *Faust;* for it, and not the comparatively insignificant *Manfred*, is Byron's poem of universal humanity. Its defiant motto is the famous speech in *Twelfth Night:* "Dost thou think, because thou art virtuous, there shall be no more cakes and ale?—Yes, by Saint Anne, and ginger shall be hot i' the mouth, too!" —a motto which promises nothing but offence and satiric pleasantry. Nevertheless it was with justifiable and prophetic pride that Byron said to Medwin: "If you must have an epic, there's *Don Juan* for you; it is an epic as much in the spirit of our day as the *Iliad* was in that of Homer." It was Byron who produced what Chateaubriand imagined he had produced in *Les Martyrs*, namely, the modern epic poem —which it was not possible to construct, as Chateaubriand had attempted to do, on a Christian-Romantic basis, or as Scott had thought it might be done, on the foundation of national history and manners. Byron succeeded because he took as his foundation nothing less than the most advanced civilisation of the century.

Juan is no Romantic hero; neither his mind nor his character raises him much above the average; but he is a favourite of fortune, an exceptionally handsome, proud, bold, lucky man, who is led more by his destiny than by intention or plan—the proper hero for a poem which is to embrace the whole of human life. It would never have done for him to have any special province; for, from the very beginning, there was no limit set to the scope and reach of the work.

The poem rises and falls like a ship borne upon sunlit and storm-tossed billows; it passes from one extreme to another. On the ardent love-scenes between Juan and Julia follows the shipwreck, with its horrors of starvation and its death agonies; on the shipwreck follows the splendid and melting harmony of youthful love—that highest, freest, sweetest happiness of life. Juan and Haidée are a study of the nude, as beautiful as an animate Amor and Pysche; above them the moonlit sky of Greece; in front of them the wine-coloured sea—the melodious lapping of its waves, the accompaniment of their words of love; around them the enchanting atmosphere of Greece; at their feet all the splendour of the East—scarlet and gold, crystal and marble. All this had followed upon peril and suffering; and now, upon the festival in Haidée's palace, follows such agony for Haidée that her heart breaks, and, as Juan's lot, a sabre gash on the forehead, crushing fetters, and sale as a slave. But it is to a seraglio he is sold, and presently we have the droll episode of his introduction, disguised as a girl, to the favourite sultana, and the mischievous night scene, with all its fire and fragrance, all its merry and voluptuous fun. Straight from this we are taken to the assault of Ismail—to human slaughter on the hugest scale, and to all the cruelty of a reckless war, carried on by a brutal soldiery—the whole described with more power and at greater length than any similar episode had been before in the poetry of any country. We next find Juan at the court of Catherine of Russia, among the "polished boors" of Eastern Europe, who are ruled by a gifted Messalina; and thence we follow him to England, the promised land of highway robbery, of morality, of the power of birth and wealth, of marriage, of virtue, and of hypocrisy.

This rough outline merely suffices to convey an idea of the capacious proportions of the poem. Not only does it contain, in extraordinary variety, representations of the strange contradictions in human life, but each of these contradictions is followed out to its extremest development. In each case the sounding-lead of the poet's imagination has been let down to the bottom, both in the psychological and in the external, tangible situation. Goethe's antique temperament inclined him, wherever it was possible, to moderation; even in *Faust*, where, in terrible earnest, he lifts the veil from human life, he lifts it with a careful hand. But the result of this moderation is often a deficiency in the highest potency of life. In Goethe's works the geniuses of life and death are seldom allowed unlimited space in which to spread their giant wings. Byron has never the desire to tranquillise his reader, never thinks of sparing him. He himself is not calm until he has said everything there is to say; he is a mortal enemy of the idealism which beautifies by selecting this, rejecting that; his art consists in pointing to reality and nature, and crying to the reader: Know these!

Take any one of his characters—take Julia, for instance.

She is twenty-three; she is charming; almost without being aware of it, she is a little in love with Juan; she is contented with her husband of fifty, but also, almost unconsciously, has a faint wish that he could be divided into two of five-and-twenty. After a hard struggle to remain virtuous she gives way; but for a time there is nothing base or comical in the relations of the lovers. Then Byron shows her to us in a difficult position; the pair are surprised by the husband; and all at once we discover a new stratum of her nature—she lies, she deceives, she acts a part with astounding facility. She was not, then, good and amiable, as she at first appeared to be? We were mistaken? Not at all. Byron shows us yet another deeper-lying stratum of her soul, in the famous farewell letter she writes to Juan, an effusion of sincere womanly feeling, one of the gems of the poem. Mental agony does not incapacitate for devotion; love does not preclude deceit; nor deceit extreme delicacy and beauty of feeling at given moments. And the letter—what becomes of it? Juan reads it, sighing and weeping, on board ship; in the middle of its affecting comparison of the manner in which men love with that in which women love, he is interrupted—by sea-sickness. Poor letter, poor Julia, poor Juan, poor humanity!—for is not this human life? Once again, poor letter! After the shipwreck, when the crew of the boat have devoured their last ration and have long gazed hungrily at each other's famished figures, they agree to determine by lot which one of them shall be killed and eaten by the others. Search is made for paper, but not a scrap is to be found in the boat except Julia's poetical and loving letter; it is snatched from Juan and cut into squares, which are numbered. One of these numbered squares brings death to Pedrillo. Is there, then, really a sphere in the firmament of heaven where idealistic love and cannibal instincts are to be found side by side, nay, meet upon one square inch of paper? Byron answers that he knows one—the Earth.

From the shipwreck scene we are transported straight to Haidée. Compared with her, all the Greek maidens of Byron's earlier poems are immature attempts. Nowhere in the whole range of modern poetry had the love of a child of nature been so beautifully described. Goethe's best girl figures, Gretchen and Clärchen, charming as they are, are little *bourgeoises;* we feel that their creator was a Frankfort citizen, to whom nature revealed herself in his position as a member of the middle class, and culture displayed itself at a small German court. In Byron's most beautiful female characters there is nothing bourgeois—no middle-class manners and customs have modified their free naturalness. We feel, when we read of Juan and Haidée, that Byron is a descendant of Rousseau ; but we also feel that his high and independent social position, in combination with the character of the fortunes that had befallen him, had given him a much more emancipated view of human nature than Rousseau ever attained to.

"And thus they wander'd forth, and hand in hand,
  Over the shining pebbles and the shells,
Glided along the smooth and harden'd sand,
  And in the worn and wild receptacles
Work'd by the storms, yet work'd as it were plann'd,
  In hollow halls, with sparry roofs and cells,
They turn'd to rest ; and, each clasp'd by an arm,
Yielded to the deep twilight's purple charm.

They look'd up to the sky, whose floating glow
  Spread like a rosy ocean, vast and bright ;
They gazed upon the glittering sea below,
  Whence the broad moon rose circling into sight;
They heard the waves' splash, and the wind so low,
  And saw each other's dark eyes darting light
Into each other—and, beholding this,
Their lips drew near, and clung into a kiss ;

A long, long kiss, a kiss of youth, and love,
  And beauty, all concentrating like rays
Into one focus, kindled from above ;
  Such kisses as belong to early days,
Where heart, and soul, and sense, in concert move,
  And the blood's lava, and the pulse a blaze,
Each kiss a heart-quake. . . .

. . . .

Haidée spoke not of scruples, ask'd no vows,
  Nor offer'd any ; she had never heard
Of plight and promises to be a spouse,
  Or perils by a loving maid incurr'd."

What reader (especially if he comes straight from the erotic hypocrisy of the literature of the French reactionary period) but feels carried away by this strong current of warm youthful passion, by the poet's ardent enthusiasm for natural beauty, and by his profound scorn for the prudishness of conventional morality! Is there, then, a world, a world of law in which 2 and 2 make 4, an animal world in which all the lowest and most disgusting instincts may come to the surface at any moment, and yet in which such revelations of beauty in human life—revelations lasting for a moment, or a day, or a month, or a year, or an eternity of years—occur? Yes, answers Byron, there is such a world, and it is the world in which we all live. And now, away from these scenes to the slave market, to the seraglio, to the battlefield, to systematic murder and rape and the bayoneting of little children!

The poem is made up of such contrasts and contradictions. But it is not a sensuous, playfully satiric epic of the nature of Ariosto's; it is a passionate work, instinct with political purpose, full of wrath, scorn, threats, and appeals, with from time to time a loud, long blast on the revolutionary war trumpet.[1] Byron does not merely describe horrors; he interprets them. After quoting "the butcher" Suwarrow's rhymed despatch to Catherine announcing the capture of Ismail, he adds:

> "He wrote this Polar melody, and set it,
> Duly accompanied by shrieks and groans,
> Which few will sing, I trust, but none forget it—
> For I will teach, if possible, the stones
> To rise against earth's tyrants. Never let it
> Be said that we still truckle unto thrones;—
> But ye, our children's children! think how we
> Show'd *what things were* before the world was free!"

If, considering both from this point of view, we compare *Don Juan* with *Faust*, the great poem of the beginning of the century, we feel that the strong, practical, historical

[1] "I have prated
Just now enough; but by and by I'll prattle
Like Roland's horn in Roncesvalles' battle."

spirit of *Don Juan* carries, as it were, more weight with it than the philosophical spirit which inspires *Faust.* And if we place it for a moment in imagination beside its Russian offspring, Pushkin's *Jevgeni Onjægin,* and its Danish offspring, Paludan-Müller's *Adam Homo,* the fresh sea breeze of nature and fact in the English poem seems to us all the stronger in contrast with the polish and the political feebleness of the Russian, and the narrow morality of the clever Danish, poem. In *Don Juan* we have nature and fact; in *Faust,* nature and profound reflection. *Don Juan* gives us in full, broad detail the human life which *Faust* condenses into a personification; and the whole work is the production of an indignation which has written where it can be read by the mighty of all ages its "*Mene, Mene, Tekel, Upharsin.*"

Not until he wrote this work was Byron completely himself. The thorough experience he had now had of life had cured him of all youthful credulity. He knew now exactly what went to the composition of the average man, and what regulated that man's life. He has been called misanthrope because of his savage satire of such lives. He himself gives the proper answer to the impeachment (ix. 21):—

> "Why do they call me misanthrope? *Because*
> *They hate me, not I them.*"

There is no doubt that he is occasionally cynical, but it is where nature herself is shameless.

Is he very far wrong when he says (v. 48, 49):

> "Some talk of an appeal unto some passion,
> Some to men's feeling, others to their reason;
> . . . .
> no
> Method's more sure at moments to take hold
> Of the best feelings of mankind, which grow
> More tender, as we every day behold,
> Than that all-softening, overpowering knell,
> The tocsin of the soul—the dinner-bell."

Is he wrong when (ix. 73) he affirms love to be vain and selfish? Or does he let his satirical temper carry him too far when he says, in describing the happiness of family life (iii. 60):

"Yet a fine family is a fine thing
(Provided they don't come in after dinner);
'Tis beautiful to see a matron bring
Her children up (if nursing them don't thin her)."

Alas! as long as there is a wrong side to the most beautiful things, it is in vain to forbid the poet to show it to us, let the moralist groan as he will. These passages are among the most cynical in the poem. And it is to be remarked that the bitter, Rousseau-like attacks on civilisation (as the joys of which the poet enumerates "war, pestilence, the despot's desolation, the kingly scourge") are always accompanied by ardent declarations of love for nature (see especially viii. 61–68).

Byron exclaims (iii. 104):

"Some kinder casuists are pleased to say,
In nameless print—that I have no devotion;
. . . .
My altars are the mountain and the ocean,
Earth, air, stars, all that springs from the great Whole,
Who hath produced, and will receive the soul."

But, unfortunately, natural religion of this kind was not in accordance with theological ritual. Like a refrain from *Childe Harold* recurs the glorification of liberty of thought (xi. 90):—

"I may stand alone,
But would not change my free thoughts for a throne."

There are savage attacks on the theory of the origin of sin advanced by theology, and satire of orthodoxy and its doctrine that sickness and misfortune make us good. Of sin we read (ix. 19):—

"'But heaven,' as Cassio says, 'is above all—
No more of this, then, let us pray!' We have
Souls to save, since Eve's slip and Adam's fall,
Which tumbled all mankind into the grave,
Besides fish, beasts, and birds. 'The sparrow's fall
Is special providence,' though how it gave
Offence, we know not; probably it perch'd
Upon the tree which Eve so fondly search'd."

We observe how much freer and bolder the tone has become since the days when *Cain* was written. On the subject of sick-bed orthodoxy Byron writes :—

> " I don't know what the reason is—the air
> Perhaps ; but as I suffer from the shocks
> Of illness, I grow much more orthodox.
>
> The first attack at once proved the Divinity
>   (But *that* I never doubted, nor the Devil) ;
> The next, the Virgin's mystical virginity ;
>   The third, the usual origin ef evil ;
> The fourth at once established the whole Trinity
>   On so uncontrovertible a level,
> That I devoutly wish'd the three were four
> On purpose to believe so much the more."

Byron had now reached the stage in his literary career when he had difficulty in getting his works published. Murray was apprehensive, and drew back. Not even a bookseller was to be found who would sell the earlier cantos of *Don Juan* at the author's risk. Byron says, when comparing his own fate with Napoleon's (*Don Juan*, xi. 56) :—

> " But Juan was my Moscow, and Faliero
>   My Leipsic, and my Mont Saint Jean seems Cain :
> ' La Belle Alliance ' of dunces down at zero,
>   Now that the Lion's fall'n, may rise again."

We have already noted what Southey dared to say in the preface to his servile poem, *The Vision of Judgment*. Adopting the rôle of informer, he called upon the Government to prevent the sale of Byron's works—for that his attack was upon Byron he plainly avowed in his rejoinder to Byron's answer, triumphantly boasting: "Of the work which I *have* done, it becomes me not here to speak, save only as relates to the Satanic School, and its Coryphæus, the author of *Don Juan*. I have held up that school to public detestation, as enemies to the religion, the institutions, and the domestic morals of the country. I have given them a designation *to which their founder and leader answers*. I have sent a stone from my sling which has smitten their Goliath in the forehead. I have fastened his name upon the gibbet, for reproach and ignominy, as long as it shall endure.—Take it down who can!"

Thus wrote the retained and salaried scribbler, who, as Byron says, had lied himself into the post of Poet-laureate. Byron replied in his admirable satire, HIS *Vision of Judgment.* In it, as in Southey's vision, George the Third arrives at the gates of heaven and requests to be admitted. But Saint Peter is not at all willing to open for him. The locks and keys are rusty; there has been so little doing; since 1789 every one has been going to hell. Cherubs arrive to insist on the old man's being admitted—for all the angels are Tories. But Satan makes his appearance as accuser, and he and Saint Michael dispute possession of the dead man. Both produce witnesses, and amongst others Southey is called. Southey begins to read his own works aloud, and goes on so long that all, angels and devils, take flight, and in the general confusion the old King slips into heaven. Saint Peter upraises his keys and knocks the poet down with them:—

"Who fell, like Phaëthon, but more at ease,
Into his lake, for there he did not drown;

. . . .

He first sank to the bottom—like his works,
But soon rose to the surface—like himself;
For all corrupted things are buoy'd like corks."

The little masterpiece is composed on exactly the same lines as the poem of Southey's which it parodies.[1] The difficulty was to get it printed. Murray would not accept it, nor would any other London publisher.

It was while he was in this dilemma that Byron was guilty of the literary imprudence which injured him more than any other in the estimation of the English reading public. A talented, but not much respected man, the Radical author, Leigh Hunt, whom Byron as a young man, to show his politics, had (in company with Moore) visited when he was in prison for libelling the Prince Regent, and who was now on terms of intimacy with Shelley, conceived the idea of starting a Radical periodical in collaboration

[1] For other attacks on Southey, see *Don Juan*, i. 205; iii. 80, 93; ix. 35; x. 13.

with Shelley and Byron. Shelley, out of modesty, held back himself, but no sooner had he intimated to Hunt that there was a possibility of his obtaining Byron's assistance, than Hunt gave up all his occupations and chances of earning a living in England, and landed, penniless and helpless, with wife and family, in Italy, where Byron generously gave them shelter under his roof. But it soon became evident that no real community was possible between two men of such different natures and different calibre; Byron could not stand Hunt's indiscreet familiarity; Hunt was offended by Byron's haughtiness. But the worst misfortune was, that Byron sank incredibly in the estimation of his countrymen by this alliance with such an inferior man.

In vain did Thomas Moore, when refusing to contribute to the proposed journal, write: "I deprecate such a plan with all my might. . . . You are, single-handed, a match for the world—which is saying a good deal, the world being, like Briareus, a very many-handed gentleman,—but, to be so, *you must stand alone.* Recollect that the scurvy buildings about St. Peter's almost seem to overtop itself." Byron had promised to help Hunt, and would not be induced to take back his word. He little thought that, after his death, Leigh Hunt's first action would be to write three volumes with the purpose of sullying his fame.[1] He gave him *The Vision of Judgment* and *Heaven and Earth,* the grand poem on the destruction of the world by the Flood, to which we Danes trace a likeness in Paludan-Müller's *Ahasuerus.* But the periodical, which it was originally proposed to call *The Carbonari,* but which, from political reasons, came out under the

[1] Thomas Moore aptly compares Hunt to the dog which was allowed by the lion to live in his cage, but which, after the lion's death, had nothing but evil to say of him:—

"Though he roar'd pretty well—this the puppy allows—
It was all, he says, borrow'd—all second-hand roar;
And he vastly prefers his own little bow-wows
To the loftiest war-note the lion could pour.
. . . .
Nay, fed as he was (and this makes it a dark case)
With sops every day from the lion's own pan,
He lifts up his leg at the noble beast's carcase,
And—does all a dog, so diminutive, can."

feeble name of *The Liberal*, was received with such complete disapprobation that it was given up after only four numbers had appeared. The arena of literature was thus almost closed for Byron, and the only field that really remained open to him was that of action, of war, in the literal sense of the word, for his ideas.

But before embarking on this new venture he gave his revolutionary feelings vent in *Don Juan* and *The Age of Bronze.* Shelley considered that Byron was qualified by his ambition and his powers to be "the redeemer of his degraded country." But he was mistaken; Byron was little suited to take part in the obstinate, slow struggle of the English Opposition for liberty. Besides, it was not the political predicament of England alone that aroused his sympathies and occupied his thoughts; in his revolt against all oppression and hatred of all hypocrisy he made himself the spokesman of the whole suffering world. His blood boiled when he thought of the slaves in America, of the ill-treatment of the Irish lower classes, of the martyrdom of the Italian patriots.

Of the French Revolution Byron had always approved. He admired Napoleon in the first stages of his career; but when the hero of the age passed

> "The Rubicon of man's awaken'd rights,
> To herd with vulgar kings and parasites,"

and finally, at Fontainebleau, preferred abdication to suicide, he overwhelmed his quondam ideal leader with the fiercest satire. There is much resemblance between Byron's attitude towards Napoleon and Heine's. Both pour ridicule on the so-called wars of liberation waged against him by their respective countries. The great difference is, that the Englishman's inflexible pride and his devotion to liberty made it impossible for him to lose himself in the almost feminine admiration and enthusiasm by which the German was possessed. Napoleon's military fame made no impression on the man who has beautifully said (*Don Juan*, viii. 3) that

> "The drying up a single tear has more
> Of honest fame, than shedding seas of gore";

and who admired no warriors but those who, like Leonidas and Washington, fought for freedom.

Byron had long flourished his lash above the Prince Regent's head, and many a telling stroke had fallen upon that royal personage's fat body:—"Though Ireland starve, great George weighs twenty stone." "Charles to his people, Henry to his wife," &c. Now he took the country itself to task. His lash falls upon everything false and objectionable, from the legend of the Virgin Queen, "our own half-chaste Elizabeth," as he calls her in *Don Juan* (ix. 81), down to the latest requirements of public opinion (*Don Juan*, vii. 22):

"Then there were Frenchmen, gallant, young, and gay;
  But I'm too great a patriot to record
Their Gallic names upon a glorious day;
  I'd rather tell ten lies than say a word
Of truth;—such truths are treason."

He is daring enough to attribute great part of the honour of Waterloo to the Prussians; to call (in imitation of Béranger) Wellington "Villainton," and to tell him that he has obtained great pensions and much praise for doing nothing but "repairing Legitimacy's crutch." And with a feeling and fervour far surpassing that displayed by Moore in his satirical letters, he tells England of the hatred of herself which she has aroused in other nations by her Tory politics. "I've no great cause," he writes (*Don Juan*, x. 66):

"I've no great cause to love that spot of earth,
  Which holds what *might have been* the noblest nation;
But though I owe it little but my birth,
  I feel a mix'd regret and veneration
For its decaying fame and former worth.

. . . .

Alas! could she but fully, truly know
  How her great name is now throughout abhorr'd;
How eager all the earth is for the blow
  Which shall lay bare her bosom to the sword;
How all the nations deem her their worst foe,
  That worse than *worst of foes*, the once adored
False friend, who held out freedom to mankind,
And now would chain them, to the very mind;—

Would she be proud, or boast herself the free,
  Who is but first of slaves? The nations are
In prison,—but the gaoler, what is he?
  No less a victim to the bolt and bar.
Is the poor privilege to turn the key
  Upon the captive, freedom? He's as far
From the enjoyment of the earth and air
Who watches o'er the chain, as they who wear."

Byron had now reached the altitude at which all ordinary conventions lost their hold upon him. He pursued the "Ministry of Mediocrities," as he called it, with his satire even after the death of its members. He would not let Castlereagh rest quietly in his grave, because, as he says in one of the prefaces to *Don Juan*, the system of oppression and hypocrisy with which that statesman's name is synonymous, endured long after his death. The watchword of the day, sovereignty "by the grace of God," was obnoxious to him, as was also the perpetual recurrence of the phrases: Britannia's rule of the waves, the glorious British constitution, the noble Emperors, and the pious Russian people. On the coins of gold appear once more, he writes after the fall of Napoleon, faces with the old "sterling, stupid stamp." The universal idolisation of the most uncivilised nation of Europe disgusted him. One could not go anywhere at that time without hearing the sentimental Cossack's song of farewell to his sweetheart, the first words of which, "Schöne Minka," are not yet forgotten.

Thus it was Byron who, towards the middle of the twenties, inaugurated the Radical campaign against political Romanticism and that Holy Alliance which was nothing but a systematisation of the political hypocrisy of Europe. Byron called it:

"An earthly trinity! which wears the shape
Of heaven's, as man is mimick'd by the ape.
A pious unity! in purpose one—
To melt three fools to a Napoleon."

He jeered at "the coxcomb Czar, the autocrat of waltzes and of war." He ridiculed the "twenty fools" at Laybach, who imagined that their hypocritical proceedings could determine the destiny of the human race. He cried:

> "O Wilberforce! thou man of black renown,
> Whose merit none enough can sing or say,
> Thou hast struck one immense Colossus down,
> Thou moral Washington of Africa!
> But there's another little thing, I own,
> Which you should perpetrate some summer's day,
> And set the other half of earth to rights;
> You have freed the *blacks*—now pray shut up the whites.
>
> Shut up the bald-coot bully Alexander!
> Ship off the Holy Three to Senegal;
> Teach them that 'sauce for goose is sauce for gander,'
> And ask them how *they* like to be in thrall?"

What language! What tones breaking the death-like silence of oppressed Europe! The political air rang with the shrill notes; for no word uttered by Lord Byron fell unheard to the ground. The legions of the fugitives, the banished, the oppressed, the conspirators, of every nation, kept their eyes fixed upon the one man who, amidst the universal debasement of intelligences and characters to a low standard, stood upright, beautiful as an Apollo, brave as an Achilles, prouder than all the kings of Europe together. Free, in his quality of English peer, from molestation everywhere, he made himself the mouthpiece of the dumb revolutionary indignation which was seething in the breasts of the best friends and lovers of liberty in Europe.

He himself had defined poetry as passion;[1] and inspired passion was what his own became. Listen to some of the thunders that pealed over Europe:

> "You hardly will believe such things were true
> As now occur, I thought that I would pen you 'em;
> . . . .
> And when you hear historians talk of thrones
> And those that sate upon them, let it be
> As we now gaze upon the mammoth's bones,
> And wonder what old world such things could see."
> (*Don Juan*, viii. 136, 137).

---

[1] "Poetry, which is but passion." *Don Juan*, iv. 106.

"Think if then George the Fourth should be dug up!
How the new worldlings of the then new East
Will wonder where such animals could sup!"
(*Don Juan*, ix. 39).

"But never mind;—'God save the king!' and kings!
For if *he* don't, I doubt if *men* will longer—
I think I hear a little bird, who sings
The people by and by will be the stronger:
The veriest jade will wince whose harness wrings
So much into the raw as quite to wrong her
Beyond the rules of posting,—and the mob
At last fall sick of imitating Job.

At first it grumbles, then it swears, and then,
Like David, flings smooth pebbles 'gainst a giant;
At last it takes to weapons such as men
Snatch when despair makes human hearts less pliant.
Then comes 'the tug of war;'—'twill come again,
I rather doubt; and I would fain say 'fie on't,'
If I had not perceived that revolution
Alone can save the earth from hell's pollution."
(*Don Juan*, viii. 50, 51).

"And I will war, at least in words (and—should
My chance so happen—deeds), with all who war
With Thought;—and of Thought's foes by far most rude,
Tyrants and sycophants have been and are.
I know not who may conquer: if I could
Have such a prescience, it should be no bar
To this my plain, sworn, downright detestation
Of every despotism in every nation."
(*Don Juan*, ix. 24).

XXIII

BYRON'S DEATH

HE had prophesied revolution ; he had sorrowfully witnessed the failure of the plans laid by the Carbonari ; but now at last the expected revolution had begun.

> "On Andes' and on Athos' peaks unfurl'd,
> The self-same standard streams o'er either world."

He had been expelled from the ranks of literature in England. He had been driven from town to town in Italy. It had long been a saying with him that a man ought to do more for his fellow-men than write poetry, and over and over again had he talked of art with the contempt of a Hotspur. Now everything conspired to urge him to action. Consideration for the Countess Guiccioli alone restrained him. He had thoughts of taking part in the Creoles' struggle for liberty ; he made careful inquiries into the condition of matters in South America. His *Ode on Venice* ends with the words :

> "Better be
> Where the extinguish'd Spartans still are free,
> In their proud charnel of Thermopylæ,
> Than stagnate in our marsh,—or o'er the deep
> Fly, and one current to the ocean add,
> One spirit to the souls our fathers had,
> One freeman more, America, to thee !"

The attraction to the country which had first inspired him to song proved the strongest. He tore himself away from the Countess Guiccioli, who was anxious to accompany him, but whom he dared not expose to the dangers and hardships of a campaign. The Committee of the English friends of Greece had elected him their representative, and supplied him amply with funds. On the day of his departure from

Leghorn he received his first and last greeting from Goethe, in the shape of the old master's famous sonnet to him.

For five months he continued to reside on the island of Cephalonia, occupied in carefully investigating into the real state of matters in Greece, and besieged by the different Greek leaders, who were at enmity with each other, and each of whom was eager to enlist Byron on his side. The distribution of money, ammunition, and other materials of war necessitated an immense amount of correspondence, to which Byron attended with dogged industry. He at last made his choice among the Greek leaders, determining to join Prince Mavrocordato at Missolonghi. During his stay in Cephalonia proposals had been made to him which must have been most flattering to his ambition. The Greeks had a strong bias towards monarchical government, and Trelawny, who was in a position to know, was convinced that, if Byron had been alive at the time of the Congress of Salona, the crown of Greece would have been offered to him.

When Byron landed at Missolonghi he was received like a prince. The fortress fired a salute, bands played, the whole population crowded to the shore to welcome him. At the house prepared for his reception, Mavrocordato awaited him at the head of a staff of officers, both Greek and foreign. Five thousand armed men were quartered in the town. Byron took five hundred Suliotes (natives of Albania), who had been left leaderless by the death of Marco Bozzari, into his own pay. He selected for himself, as if death were what he desired, the most dangerous of the commands, that of the troops which were to proceed to Lepanto, hoping to compensate by energy and courage for his want of military experience; his staff were to be responsible for the strategical direction of the force. He had occasion, while holding this command, to be astonished by the powerful impression which personal accomplishments and personal intrepidity make upon half-savage natures; nothing produced such respect for him in the minds of his Suliotes, who themselves were bad marksmen, as his unerring aim and his indifference to danger. But he had undeniably become a nobler man. Though not free from attacks of his old melancholy, he saw the path of glory clear before him. Evidence of his feeling at this time is borne by the beautiful poem, one of the finest he ever wrote, which he composed on his thirty-sixth birthday. If we compare it with the despairing lines which bear the date of his thirty-third birthday, the difference is clearly perceptible. Along with premonition of his approaching death we have manly resolve:—

"'Tis time this heart should be unmoved,
Since others it hath ceased to move:
Yet, though I cannot be beloved,
Still let me love!

My days are in the yellow leaf;
The flowers and fruits of love are gone;
The worm, the canker, and the grief
Are mine alone!

. . . .

But 'tis not *thus*—and 'tis not *here*—
Such thoughts should shake my soul, nor *now*,
Where glory decks the hero's bier,
Or binds his brow.

The sword, the banner, and the field,
Glory and Greece, around me see!
The Spartan, borne upon his shield,
Was not more free.

. . . .

Seek out—less often sought than found—
A soldier's grave, for thee the best;
Then look around, and choose thy ground,
And take thy rest."

Byron's very first endeavour was, as might have been expected of him, to modify, as far as possible, the barbarity of the method in which the war was being carried on. He released several Turkish officers, and sent them to Yussuf Pacha with a dignified and beautiful letter, in which he begs him in return to treat such Greeks as may henceforth fall into his hands with humanity, since the horrors of war are sufficiently great without being aggravated by wanton cruelties on either side. Then he turned all his attention to the task he had set himself, and displayed a clear-sighted practicality which stood out in marked contrast to the poetical visionariness of those with whom he was associated.

The other Englishmen of the Committee, in their unworldly idealism, hoped to civilise Greece by means of a free press, newspaper articles, &c., &c.; but in Byron, the Carbonaro had made way for the practical politician. He built everywhere, energetically and firmly, upon the actually existing conditions—first and foremost upon the hatred of Turkey which existed in the breast of every Greek. He considered it much safer to reckon upon this than upon their devotion to freedom and republicanism. Stanhope wished to open schools. Byron demanded and distributed cannon. Stanhope endeavoured, through the agency of missionaries, to introduce Protestant Christianity. Byron, who saw that this foolishness would alienate the whole Greek priesthood, would have nothing introduced but weapons and money. And he left off making attacks upon the different European Governments. He had witnessed the collapse of Carbonarism when brought into contact with organised authority; hence his desire was to obtain for Greece recognition by the Great Powers.

Unfortunately his health was not equal to the carrying out of his great plans. At Missolonghi he rode out as usual every day, and, to impress the inhabitants, was always attended by a bodyguard of fifty Suliotes on foot. These men were such splendid runners that, though they carried their carbines, they were able to keep up with the horses galloping at full speed. On one of these rides Byron was drenched by a heavy shower. Count Gamba tried to persuade him to return home at once, but he refused, saying: "I should make a pretty soldier, indeed, if I were to care for such a trifle." The following day he was seized with violent convulsions—three men were hardly able to hold him—and the pain was so excessive that he said: "I do not care for death, but these agonies I cannot bear." While he was lying in an almost fainting condition after this attack, a band of rebellious Suliotes made their way into his room, brandishing their sabres, and demanding reparation for some supposed slight. Byron raised himself up in bed, and with a powerful exercise of will, ever calmer the more they raged and screamed, mastered them with his look and manner, and dismissed them.

He had written to Moore some months previously: "If anything in the way of fever, fatigue, famine, or otherwise, should cut short the middle age of a brother warbler, I pray you to remember me in 'your smiles and wine.' I have hopes that the cause will triumph; but whether it does or no, still 'honour must be minded as strictly as milk diet.' I trust to observe both." On the 12th of April he had again to take to bed, and from this date the fever never abated. The 18th was Easter Day, a holiday which the Greeks were accustomed to celebrate by firing off muskets and salvos of artillery; but out of consideration for their benefactor, the townspeople kept perfectly quiet. The 19th was the last day of Byron's life. During part of it he was delirious; he imagined himself to be commanding troops, and shouted: "Forwards—forwards—courage!" When he came to himself again, he began to give his last orders to his servant, Fletcher. "Go to my sister," he said; "tell her —go to Lady Byron—you will see her, and say——." Here his voice became indistinct, and only names could be made out—"Augusta—Ada—Hobhouse." He then said: "Now, I have told you all." "My lord," replied Fletcher, "I have not understood a word your lordship has been saying." "Not understood me?" exclaimed Lord Byron, with a look of the utmost distress. "What a pity! Then it is too late; all is over." He still continued to utter a few disconnected words: "Poor Greece!—poor town!—my poor servants!" Then his thoughts must have turned to Countess Guiccioli, for he murmured: "Io lascio qualche cosa di caro nel mondo." Towards evening he said: "Now I shall go to sleep," and, turning round, fell into that slumber from which he never awoke.

The announcement of Byron's death fell like a thunderbolt upon Greece. It affected the nation in the manner of a terrible natural catastrophe, the consequences of which were incalculable. On the day he died the following proclamation was issued:—

PROVISIONAL GOVERNMENT OF WESTERN GREECE.

The present day of festivity and rejoicing has become one of sorrow and of mourning. The Lord Noel Byron departed this life at six o'clock in the afternoon, after an illness of ten days . . . I hereby decree:—

1st, To-morrow morning at daylight, thirty-seven minute guns will be fired from the grand battery, being the number which corresponds with the age of the illustrious deceased.

2nd, All the public offices, even the tribunals, are to remain closed for three successive days.

3d, All the shops, except those in which provisions or medicines are sold, will also be shut; and it is strictly enjoined that every species of public amusement, and other demonstrations of festivity at Easter, shall be suspended.

4th, A general mourning will be observed for twenty-one days.

5th, Prayers and a funeral service are to be offered up in all the churches.

A. Mavrocordato.

Given at Missolonghi
this 19th day of April 1824.

No other evidence is required of the impression which the news of Byron's death made upon all who were intimately connected with him. At Missolonghi people ran through the streets crying: "He is dead! The great man is gone!" The corpse was conveyed to England. The clergy refused it a place in the Poet's Corner in Westminster Abbey. But, dependent neither on the blame of England nor the praise of Greece, his renown established itself throughout the earth.

In the intellectual life of Russia and Poland, of Spain and Italy, of France and Germany, the seeds which he had strewn broadcast with such a lavish hand fructified—from the dragon's teeth sprang armed men. The Slavonic nations, who were groaning under tyrannical rule, who were by nature inclined to be melancholy, and in whom their history had developed rebellious instincts, seized on his poetry with avidity; and Pushkin's *Onjægin*, Lermontoff's *A Hero of Our Own Days*, Malczewski's *Marja*, Mickiewicz's *Conrad* and *Wallenrod*, Slowacki's *Lambro* and *Beniowski* witness to the powerful impression made upon their authors. The Romance races, whose fair sinners his verses had celebrated, and who were now in the act of revolt, eagerly translated and studied his works. The Spanish and Italian exile-poets took up his war-cry; in Spain the "Myrtle" Society was formed; in Italy his influence was most plainly manifest in the writings of Giovanni Berchet, but hardly less so in those of Leopardi and Giusti. His death made an extraordinary impression in France. A week or two after it happened, Chateaubriand went over to the Opposition, and his first action after his fall was to become a member of the Greek Committee. Hugo's *Les Orientales* was not a flight straight to the East, like the Oriental poetry of Germany; his way lay through Greece, and he had much to say of the heroes of the war of liberation. Delavigne devoted a beautiful poem to Byron; Lamartine added a last canto to *Childe Harold;* Mérimée allowed himself to be influenced by Byron's occasional spirit of savagery; Alfred de Musset attempted to take up the mantle which had fallen from the shoulders of the great poet; and even Lamennais began to employ a style in which many of the words and expressions recalled the language of Byron's sallies. Germany was still politically too far behind the other nations to have exiles and emigrants among its poets; but its philologists had, with quiet rejoicing, beheld in the rising of Greece the resurrection of ancient Hellas; poets like Wilhelm Müller and Alfred Meissner wrote beautiful verse in honour of Byron; and there were other writers who were still more deeply moved by Byron's poetry—men of Jewish extraction, whose feelings were those of the exiled and excommunicated—chief among them Börne and Heine. Heine's best poetry (notably *Deutschland, ein Wintermärchen*) is a continuation of Byron's work. French Romanticism and German Liberalism are both direct descendants of Byron's Naturalism.

XXIV

CONCLUSION

NATURALISM as an intellectual tendency in England, makes its appearance in Wordsworth in the form of love of all the external phenomena of nature, a habit of storing up natural impressions, and piety towards animals, children, country people, and the "poor in spirit." With him as its representative, it strays for a moment into a blind alley, that of uninspired imitation of nature. In Coleridge, and even more in Southey, it approaches the German Romanticism of the day, follows it into the world of legend and superstition, but avoids its worst excesses by treating Romantic themes in a Naturalistic manner and keeping an open eye on land and sea and all the elements of reality. In Scott, Naturalism occupies itself with the character and history of a whole nation, and in vivid colours paints man as the son of a race and a period; in Keats, it takes possession of the whole world of the senses, and reposes for a moment on the neutral ground between tranquil contemplation of nature and the proclamation of a gospel of nature and of natural rights. In Moore it becomes erotic, and espouses Liberalism in politics; the sight of the sufferings of his native island drives this poet into the ranks of the lovers of liberty, intellectual and political. In Campbell, it becomes eulogy of England as Queen of the Sea and expression of English liberal views. In Landor, it takes the shape of pagan Humanism, of too repellent and proud a character to win the suffrage of Europe. It is transformed in Shelley into a soulful love of nature and a poetic Radicalism, which have at their command poetic gifts of the very highest order; but the incorporeal universality of Shelley's Naturalism, in combination with the circumstance that he is much too far ahead of his age, and with his early death, causes his song to die away unheard, Europe never learning what a poet she possesses and loses.

Then, like Achilles arising in his wrath after he has burned the body of Patroclus, Byron, after Shelley's death, arises and lifts up his mighty voice. European poetry was flowing on like a sluggish, smooth river ; those who walked along its banks found little for the eye to rest on. All at once, as a continuation of the stream, appeared this poetry, under which the ground so often gave way that it precipitated itself in cataracts from one level to another—and the eyes of all inevitably turn to that part of a river where its stream becomes a waterfall. In Byron's poetry the river boiled and foamed, and the roar of its waters made music that mounted up to heaven. In its seething fury it formed whirlpools, tore itself and whatever came in its way, and in the end undermined the very rocks. But, "in the midst of the infernal surge," sat such an Iris as the poet himself has described in *Childe Harold*—a glorious rainbow, the emblem of freedom and peace—invisible to many, but clearly seen by all who, with the sun above them in the sky, place themselves in the right position.

It presaged better days for Europe.

THE END

Printed by BALLANTYNE, HANSON & Co.
Edinburgh & London

Printed in Great Britain
by Amazon

44577617R10215